The Church Our Story

The Church Our Story

Catholic Tradition, Mission, and Practice

Patricia Morrison Driedger

ave maria press   notre dame, indiana

The Subcommittee on the Catechism, United States Conference of Catholic Bishops, has found that this catechetical high school text, copyright 2013, is in conformity with the *Catechism of the Catholic Church* and that it fulfills the requirements of Course IV of the *Doctrinal Elements of a Curriculum Framework for the Development of Catechetical Materials for Young People of High School Age*.

Nihil Obstat: Reverend Michael Heintz
                Censor Liborum

Imprimatur: Most Reverend John M. D'Arcy
                Bishop of Fort Wayne-South Bend
                Given at Fort Wayne, Indiana on 10 April 2005.

The *Imprimatur* is an official declaration that a book or pamphlet is free of doctrinal or moral error. No implication is contained therein that those who have granted the *Imprimatur* agree with its contents, opinions, or statements expressed.

Cardinal Avery Dulles, S.J. (1918–2008), author of the Foreword, was the Laurence J. McGinley Professor at Fordham University. He is the author of *Models of the Church* (New York: Doubleday, 1974, 1987, 2002).

Patricia Morrison Driedger, author of the Student Text, has worked in youth ministry and campus ministry. She is the primary author of *Believe in Me, Stand by Me*, and *Be with Me*, the textbooks for grades seven, eight, and nine of the *We Are Strong Series* published by the Canadian Conference of Catholic Bishops. She is also the author of *Our Sacramental Life* (Ave Maria Press, 2003).

Scripture passages are taken from *The New American Bible with Revised New Testament*, copyright © 1988 by the Confraternity of Christian Doctrine, Washington, D.C. All rights reserved.

English translation of the *Catechism of the Catholic Church* for the United States of America copyright © 1994, United States Catholic Conference, Inc.— Libreria Editrice Vaticana. Used with permission.

Code of Canon Law: Latin-English Edition. 1983. Washington: Canon Law Society of America—Libreria Editrice Vaticana.

The Liturgy Documents. Simcoe, Mary Ann, editor. 1985 Chicago: Liturgy Training Publications.

The Rites of the Catholic Church: Study Edition. International Commission on English in the Liturgy, translator. 1969. New York: Pueblo Publishing Company.

Vatican Council II: The Conciliar and Post Conciliar Documents. Austin Flannery, O.P., editor. 1975. Northport, New York: Costello Publishing Company.

Other references cited on pages 341–342.

Founded in 1865, Ave Maria Press is a ministry of the United States Province of Holy Cross.

www.avemariapress.com

ISBN-10 1-59471-057-0   ISBN-13 978-1-59471-057-5

Project Editor: Michael Amodei

Cover and text design by Brian C. Conley

Printed and bound in the United States of America.

CONTENTS

FOREWORD 6

UNIT 1: WHAT IS CHURCH? 8

    1.1 A HOUSE ON A ROCK 11

UNIT 2: THE CHURCH IS MYSTERY 34

    2.1 ENDURING AND DEVELOPING 37

    2.2 PERMANENT AND UNCHANGING 59

UNIT 3: THE CHURCH IS THE PEOPLE OF GOD 88

    3.1 TOGETHER AS ONE 91

    3.2 WHO IS CATHOLIC? .107

UNIT 4: THE CHURCH IS TEACHER 124

    4.1 CREEDS, LAWS, DOGMAS, AND DOCTRINES 127

    4.2 THE GOOD NEWS PROCLAIMED 151

UNIT 5: THE CHURCH IS SACRAMENT 174

    5.1 A SIGN AND SOURCE OF GOD'S GRACE 177

    5.2 SACRAMENTS FOR GOD'S FAITHFUL 195

UNIT 6: THE CHURCH IS SERVANT 214

    6.1 THE SOCIAL DOCTRINE OF THE CHURCH 217

    6.2 RESPONDING TO THOSE IN NEED 237

UNIT 7: THE CHURCH IS A COMMUNION OF SAINTS 256

    7.1 WHO ARE THE SAINTS? 259

    7.2 MARY: MODEL AND MOTHER OF THE CHURCH 277

UNIT 8: THE CHURCH IS 290

    8.1 REVIEW AND PREVIEW 293

APPENDIX 313

GLOSSARY 337

REFERENCES CITED 341

INDEX 343

Somewhat like the twenty-five young people whose reception into the Church is described in the first pages of this book, I became a Catholic as a graduate student in 1940. The decision to take that step was the most important of my life; every major decision I have subsequently taken has rested upon it. To this day I remain at heart a convert, passionately attached to the Church. For me, however, the Church has never been an end in herself, but only a means of union with Jesus, the Lord of the Church, and with the triune God. The Church is the place where God is preeminently to be found.

In Unit 1 this books begins, as we all should, with the Church as a mystery—that is to say, a reality imbued with the hidden presence of God. Because the Church is a mystery, we can never describe her exhaustively; she remains ever open to new and deeper exploration. Different aspects of the Church are illuminated by the various biblical metaphors presented in Unit 2 of this volume. While taking on different forms in different ages and cultures, the Church remains ever herself, one and catholic, as stated in Unit 3. In Unit 4, the book treats the creeds and dogmas that bind the Church unconditionally to the truth of Christ, her divine Teacher. As a herald, the Church is commissioned to preach the truth of Christ to all nations of the world. The sacraments of the Church, treated in Unit 5, are privileged points of encounter with the living Lord. Although her sacraments are reserved for her own members, the Church labors for all. Just as Christ came not to be served but to serve, she strives to bind up the wounds of a broken humanity (Unit 6). Her goal is to overcome alienation and establish a universal communion of faith and love in which the barriers of selfishness and greed are overcome. Unit 7 describes the Church as a communion of saints striving to reach this goal.

All of these aspects of the Church are luminously set forth in this very comprehensive text. I hope and pray that it will lead many students to a richer understanding and deeper love of the Church. By entering more fully into that mystery they will progressively put on the mind and heart of Christ.

—*Cardinal Avery Dulles, S.J.*

F O R E W O R D

U N I T O N E

W H A T I S C H U R C H ?

WHAT IS CHURCH?

The word "Church" may elicit many definitions and images, from the most elementary of your early religious education formation, to those laced with positions the Church takes on contemporary issues, to the descriptions offered by Church documents, especially the *Catechism of the Catholic Church*.

But consider how St. Joan of Arc once described the Church: "About Jesus Christ and the Church I simply know they're just one thing, and we shouldn't complicate the matter."

Our faith in the Catholic Church depends entirely on our faith in Jesus Christ. According to one of the favorite images from the Church Fathers, the Church is like the moon, all of its light reflected from the sun.

When the Church proclaims the Gospel to all people, it also shines light on itself. Jesus Christ *is* the light of the Church.

The Church is also a place where, in the words of St. Hippolytus, "the Spirit flourishes."

Our Catholic creeds describe our belief that the Church is holy and catholic, and also one and apostolic, and that it is inseparable from belief in God in three persons—Father, Son, and Holy Spirit. But as we learn more about the Church, it is important to attribute all the gifts of the Church—including the four marks of the Church described in detail in chapter 1—as from God.

And remember the words of St. Joan of Arc: Jesus Christ and the Church are just one thing.

When you have completed Unit 1, you will be able to

- explain the relationship between faith in Christ and membership in the Church;

- define faith and explain how the Church fosters and supports faith;

- summarize the role of the Church in the world;

- evaluate your own willingness to answer God's call to "come out of the world and into the community of faith";

- name and define the four marks of the Church and explain why these marks are essential;

- propose ways and take steps to improve or strengthen your relationship with the Church.

EVERYONE THEN WHO LISTENS TO THESE WORDS OF MINE AND ACTS ON THEM WILL BE LIKE A WISE MAN WHO BUILT HIS HOUSE ON ROCK. THE RAIN FELL, THE FLOODS CAME, AND THE WINDS BLEW AND BUFFETED THE HOUSE. BUT IT DID NOT COLLAPSE; IT HAD BEEN SET SOLIDLY ON ROCK.

—*Matthew 7:24–25*

I BELIEVE AND PROFESS . . .

Outside, the prairie winds rattled the doors and whistled through the gutters, while the sleet pelted the stained glass windows. Inside, the flame on the eight foot candle spat and sputtered as it burned through the last remaining drops of snow and rain surrounding its wick. This was not the way anyone had imagined Easter would

be, and yet, inside St. Thomas Aquinas Church in central Iowa no one doubted that it really was Easter. Somehow, in that dark, cold, slightly smoky church, the joy of the Resurrection seemed almost tangible. Perhaps that was because of the six newly baptized adults in long, damp robes who were standing in the church sanctuary and grinning from ear to ear, in spite of their wet

hair. Or perhaps it was the confident joy of nineteen others who stood with them, mostly university students, who also called out for all to hear, "I believe and profess all that the Holy Catholic Church believes, teaches, and proclaims to be revealed by God."

"I believe and profess all that the Holy Catholic Church believes, teaches, and proclaims to be revealed by God." As those words echoed back through the church, I couldn't help wondering how many of us who have been Catholic all our lives would have the courage to stand before a congregation and proclaim the same thing. Moreover, how many would do it with the joy and enthusiasm of those twenty-five? I asked myself how they could be so sure of what they were saying. Were they just naive? Were they unaware of all of the imperfections of the Catholic Church and of all the tensions among her members? For a moment I was able to comfort myself with the thought that these twenty-five people gathered in the church sanctuary could do what I would find difficult because they did not know what I know. But then I looked at their sponsors.

I knew most of those sponsors well. They were people of faith, but also people with doubts. They were people who sometimes struggled with the Catholic Church, and I knew that they had not hidden those struggles from the ones they were sponsoring. Yet all of their struggles and all of their doubts had not changed the desire of these twenty-five to embrace the Catholic Church and to commit their lives to her. I had to ask "Why?" What is it that we as a Church have that these people wanted? In a world that encourages us constantly to try new things and keep our options open, in a world that encourages us to let go of the past and look to the future, in a world that places entertainment and comfort above almost everything else, what attracted twenty-five very different young adults to a Church that expects commitment, is slow to change, is guided by the past, finds value in suffering, and makes no significant effort to keep people entertained?

Yes, I knew these people were attracted by the fact that we have Jesus, we have the Holy Spirit, and we have the love of God the Father. But that isn't what made them Catholics, only what made them

Christians—and nineteen of those young adults were already Christians in other denominations. So why were they coming to the Catholic Church? What new understanding of living out their faith had they found? More importantly, what did they have to teach and to remind me?

JOURNAL ASSIGNMENT

- WHAT ATTRACTS YOU TO THE CATHOLIC CHURCH?
- WHAT DO YOU FIND DIFFICULT ABOUT BEING CATHOLIC?
- WHAT MAKES YOU CATHOLIC?

FAITH AND THE CHURCH ARE CONNECTED

Those new Catholics remind us of the connection between faith and the Church. Faith and the Church should not be treated as two independent things. Many people do seem to believe that Christian faith and participating in the Church can be separated. It is not uncommon to hear people say,

- "I believe in God, but I have no use for Church."
- Or, "As long as you accept Jesus, the question of whether you belong to a church is irrelevant."
- Or even, "Don't commit yourself to any church. Churches get in the way of real faith."

From a Catholic perspective, however, Christian faith cannot be separated from a relationship with the Church because where the Church is, God is.

The Catholic faith is rooted in faith in God who became incarnate in history in the

person of Jesus of Nazareth. In Jesus, people were able to touch, listen to, and speak to God directly. In Jesus, people came to know God's healing and forgiveness in an immediate way. In Jesus, God's offer of Salvation and fullness of life became a tangible reality. Following Jesus' Passion, Death, Resurrection, and Ascension, Salvation and fullness of life became accessible to all people through the Church. Jesus breathed his Spirit into the Church so that the Church could become his Body on earth. Because of the gift of the Holy Spirit, the Church is able to be God's continuing physical presence in the world.

If the Church is indeed the visible presence of God, then it is obvious that we cannot separate our response to God's call from our relationship to the Church. The very word "Church" reveals the connection between answering God's call and being part of a community. The Greek word for "Church," used in the New Testament, is *ekklésia*, meaning "to call out of." Ekklésia was commonly used to refer to any legislative assembly; when it was used in Scripture, it referred to the community called out of the world by God to live and act in a way that was different from others. But God's call does not invite us as isolated individuals. The meeting place is not a private dinner with God. Rather, God's call resounds through all creation, summoning those who hear to gather in an assembly and to act together on behalf of and in the name of God. God's call is a call to be united with Christ, to be part of his Body. In other words, God's call to faith is a call to be Church.

STUDY QUESTIONS

- WHAT DOES THE WORD "CHURCH" MEAN?
- WHY CAN FAITH AND CHURCH MEMBERSHIP NOT BE SEPARATED?

JOURNAL ASSIGNMENT

- HOW WOULD YOU ANSWER SOMEONE'S CLAIM THAT "CHURCHES GET IN THE WAY OF REAL FAITH"?

FAITH IS A HUMAN ACT

In order to accept and live out our role as the Body of Christ on earth, in order to be Church, we need **faith**. Pope John Paul in his encyclical letter *Redemptoris Mater* says that faith is "contact with the mystery of God."[1] Faith is a free gift from God, and without God's help we could not believe. But faith is also an authentically human act. It is our response to God's gift, a surrendering of ourselves to God. When we believe in, or surrender ourselves to the mystery of God which has been revealed to us, our faith is deepened. Before we can act as members of the Body of Christ, God must touch us with the gift of faith and we must respond. Then, and only then, will we experience the fullness of faith which is unity with Christ, the head of the Body.

Each individual member of the Body of Christ needs to believe in Christ if he or she is going to act on behalf of Christ in the world. To believe in Christ means "to abandon ourselves to Christ,"[2] that is, to allow ourselves to be shaped by Christ and to let go of those things which keep us from listening to and following him. No one can act as part of the Body of Christ who does not have a faith which connects him or her to Christ.

faith—Contact with the mystery of God. Faith begins as a freely given gift from God.

How the Gift of Faith Begins

The gift of faith can begin in many ways. It may begin with a single life-changing event or it may begin with the commitment of parents to raise their children in a way that is shaped by Jesus. Faith may come in a moment or it may be part of a longer process in which the person gradually takes ownership of all that has been taught to him or her. In either case, believing is not something that happens once and for all time. Since God never takes away our freedom, we are always free to stop allowing Christ to shape our lives. We can separate ourselves from the Body of Christ either through a deliberate decision, or by gradually developing habits that move us further and further from Christ. For this reason, we must nourish our faith if we are to remain committed to what we believe. Faith needs to be sustained by prayer, study, reflection, and the regular reception of the Sacraments. And, faith needs to be exercised in loving action.

The Need for Community

No one acting alone can be the Body of Christ. Each one of us is only a single member of that Body. A true disciple of Christ must join with others. Our faith must be communal as well as personal. We must believe in Christ not only as individuals but also as groups—families, groups of friends, parishes, and communities. In other words, we cannot really answer God's call unless the groups that we form and the way those groups function are shaped by Christ.

It is not easy to surrender our lives to Christ as individuals; it is even more difficult to do so as members of communities in which the many different individuals have different concepts of what it means to surrender. Nonetheless, the Church believes that we can be united in faith. As Jesus said, "Where two or three are gathered in my name, there I am in the midst of them" (Matthew 18:20). As Christians we trust that as we are blessed in our personal relationship with God, so we will be even more deeply blessed in our communal relationships with God. It is only in the context of a community that we can really come to know and understand the God who "is love."

Christians in general, and Catholics in particular, believe in a

CONVERSION

The Church is comprised of remarkable stories of those who have converted to the Catholic faith and been baptized—from St. Jerome and St. Augustine to Dorothy Day and Thomas Merton.

Research information about a famous Catholic who was a convert. Explain whether their *epiphany* to the faith was gradual or came about all at once. Also, interview a Catholic convert who you know. Ask the person to explain why he or she chose to be Catholic. Report on all of your findings.

God who acts through (or is mediated by) the created world. Our belief is rooted in the ancient Israelites' belief that anyone who looked upon the face of God would die. God is so much beyond human comprehension that we cannot cope with a direct encounter with the divine. Even in moments of deepest prayer and personal communion, we are only able to see God indistinctly as if in a dull mirror (1 Corinthians 13:12). In order that we might know, understand, and experience God better without being overwhelmed, God has chosen to be mediated to us through that which is familiar and understandable. God

has chosen to make his love and fidelity known to us through one another when we gather in his name.[3]

Our faith is deepened and fortified by the community's faith. Our community's faith also makes it possible for us to do what God calls us to do: to know and love God more fully and to live, not as isolated individuals, but as members of the one Body of Christ. The faith of the community exists wherever two or more people gather to share their faith, to pray, or to support and encourage one another out of love rooted in love for God.

STUDY QUESTIONS

- DEFINE FAITH.
- WHAT IS NEEDED TO SUSTAIN FAITH?
- WHY MUST FAITH BE COMMUNAL AS WELL AS PERSONAL?

FAITH IS SUPPORTED BY FORMAL STRUCTURES

Because the community of faith—that is, the Church—is made up of sinful individuals, the Church can easily fall into sin. Just as individual Christians can be blinded to and caught up in the secular culture of their day, so too the Church. Christian communities often accept and adopt the methods of operation and patterns of group interaction of the culture around them. Some of those patterns and standards may be so common that Christians do not notice that they are contrary to the Gospel.

For this reason the Church needs to develop formal structures that help preserve essential truths. These formal structures take the form of creeds, doctrines, and rituals. The formal aspects of Catholicism have ensured that the faith given by Jesus Christ has survived even when the Church herself has sinned.

The formal structures help both individuals and communities establish, express, and maintain their identities as believers. The formal structures make our communal relationship with God visible and tangible. The task of defining and interpreting these formal structures of faith is held by the Church's Magisterium. The Magisterium refers to the bishops in communion with the pope who is the successor of St. Peter. Unless we commit ourselves to the formal structures of faith, we may find that we are picking and choosing our faith in such a way that it no longer shapes and challenges us. If we reject the formal structures of faith we will probably end up selecting those which demand the least of us and which are most in keeping with the secular culture in which we live.

There are those who, in the name of **ecumenism**, will try to ignore the formal structures of faith which separate one church from another. They seem to think that the truth of Christian community can be found in its lowest common denominator. In fact true ecumenism—the reconciliation of all Christians in the unity of the Church—involves the efforts of all. More importantly we must remember that achieving this unity trancends human powers and gifts and is in the hands of God.

ecumenism—The movement and activities which seek to promote religious unity within the Christian Church and among all the people of the world.

STUDY QUESTIONS

- HOW DO THE FORMAL STRUCTURES OF THE CHURCH SUPPORT FAITH?
- DEFINE ECUMENISM. WHO IS RESPONSIBLE FOR THE RECONCILIATION OF ALL CHRISTIANS IN THE UNITY OF THE CHURCH?

JOURNAL ASSIGNMENT

- HOW HAS GOD REVEALED HIS PRESENCE TO YOU THROUGH ANOTHER PERSON?
- TELL SEVERAL WAYS THAT THE GROUPS YOU BELONG TO—FAMILY, SCHOOL, FRIENDSHIP, AND CHURCH—ARE SHAPED BY CHRIST.

THE MARKS OF THE CHURCH

"I believe and profess all that the Holy Catholic Church believes, teaches, and proclaims to be revealed by God." On that Easter vigil night in March, twenty-five young adults, nineteen of whom were already baptized Christians, committed their lives not only to God but also to the Catholic Church. They committed themselves to a church because they knew that they could not answer God's call to be the Body of Christ without making such a commitment. They committed themselves to the Catholic Church because in the formal structures of Catholicism as it exists today they found the most complete expression of what it means to be the Body of Christ.

The notion that the Church must have certain specific characteristics dates back to early Christianity:

- St. Paul wrote of the importance of unity among members of the Church because of their membership in the Body of Christ.
- A few years later St. Ignatius of Antioch (d. AD 107) wrote that there could only be one Church and that that Church was known by its unbroken connection with the Apostles whom Christ appointed.

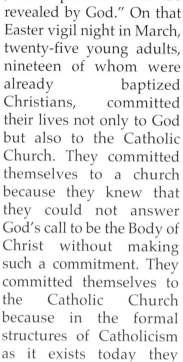

- St. Irenaeus of Lyon (b. AD 130) wrote that the role of the Church is to unite people with Christ.

The teachings of Paul, Ignatius, Irenaeus and many others were formalized in the **Nicene Creed**. This creed is shared by most Christian churches; it (along with the Apostles' Creed) is understood to contain the most essential truths of Christianity.

In 381 at the first council of Constantinople the words "[I believe] in one, holy, catholic and apostolic church," were officially added to the creed. Those who were gathered at this second ecumenical (all Church) council—the council of Nicaea was the first—pointed out that one could not separate faith in the Trinity from a belief that the Church is "one, holy, catholic, and apostolic."[4] The nature of the Church is not something that can be changed to suit the wishes of different people in different times and places. The nature of the Church is an expression of Christ. Through the Holy Spirit, Christ makes the Church one, holy, catholic, and apostolic. These characteristics are known as the four **marks of the Church**. The Church does not posses them of itself, but from Christ who is their source. The Church will manifest these qualities in different ways at different times according to the culture in which it exists. And because those who belong to the Church are imperfect, sometimes these qualities will be imperfectly expressed.

As Catholics, we believe that the Church is the first sacrament of

Nicene Creed—A statement of the Church's beliefs issued at the first ecumenical council at Nicaea in 325 and later confirmed at the Council of Constantinople in 381. It taught that Jesus is of the same substance as God and thus divine.

marks of the Church— One, holy, catholic, and apostolic.

THE HOPIS AND IQ

There is a story told of the Native American Hopi people that can help us understand what it means to truly live as one. Years ago, when the concept of an intelligence quotient (IQ) test to measure potential was first developed, a variety of preliminary test groups were selected from different regions. One of these groups was selected from the Hopi nation. On the day of the test the examiner explained the instructions and then handed out the test questions. He was shocked when people immediately started to discuss the questions with one another; he quickly explained that it was essential that each person answer all of the questions on his or her own, otherwise the test results would be useless. The Hopi test group was outraged and refused to continue with the test. They had no interest in measuring themselves against one another. Since no two people were the same or should be the same, there was little to be gained by comparing them. What was important was not what each person knew and could do on his or her own, but what all of them knew and could do together. No one could do everything well alone, but if they pooled their strengths, they could do great things together. The Hopi saw no point in a test that could only make them appear less than they were. They were not isolated individuals who needed to prove that they could each make it alone; they were a people who would move forward together. The weakness of one was the responsibility of all, and the strength of one was the gift of all.

Christ.[5] In other words, the Church is a symbol and instrument of God's presence on earth and movement through time. The Church makes Christ visible to people and provides a means by which they can come in contact with the Holy One. Therefore, the Church must be constantly shaped by Christ through the Holy Spirit and individual Catholics must cooperate with God's grace. The four marks of the Church, described in the sections that follow, help us to understand how the Church is the Sacrament of Christ.

The Church is One

The Church is one because of the unity in the Trinity of one God, the Father, the Son, and the Holy Spirit.[6] The Church is one because of its founder, Jesus Christ, who came to restore unity among all people and between all people and the Father. Christ is the principle of the Church's unity. The Church is one because of the Holy Spirit who brings about the communion of the faithful and joins them in Christ.[7] The "true Church of Christ," that is, the Church which Christ entrusted to Saint Peter and the other apostles, "subsists in the Catholic Church" which is governed by the pope and the bishops in communion with him.[8]

FOUNDATIONS OF DOCTRINE AND CREEDS

Choose and complete one of the following projects:

- Research and report on the words of St. Paul, St. Ignatius of Antioch, and St. Irenaeus of Lyon on the importance of unity in the Church.
- Report on the issues addressed at the First Council of Constantinople. See www.newadvent.org/cathen/04308a.htm.
- Present background information about the culture and needs that led to the development of at least two creeds in the Church. For example, the Apostles' Creed; the Athanasian Creed; or the professions of faith at certain Councils such as Toledo, Lateran, Lyons, or Trent.

Unity and true peace are essential characteristics of Christ's kingdom. Unless our life as a Church is characterized by our solidarity with one another, we have distanced ourselves from Christ and his mission. Without a commitment to unity we cannot act effectively as the Body of Christ on earth.

Living in unity with one another is not the same thing as agreeing about everything, or doing everything in the same way.

Throughout its history, the Church has been marked by a great diversity stemming from both the variety of God's gifts and the diversity of those who receive them.[9] The diversity of the Church is not opposed to its unity, though sin and its consequences have threatened the gift of unity. As Saint Paul reminded Christians to "maintain the unity of the Spirit in the bond of peace" (Ephesians 4:3), the unity of the Church is also maintained by certain structures which support unity.

Unity Is Not Uniformity

The formal structures of the Catholic Church underscore the importance of unity and help us to make our unity visible in our daily lives. As Catholics we are united by a profession of one faith received from the Apostles, common celebration of divine worship, especially the sacraments, and apostolic succession through the Sacrament of Holy Orders.[10] Catholics from every culture, every race, and every nation profess the same faith, can understand and participate in one another's worship (even if they do not speak the same language), and are guided by pastors who can all trace their ministry in an unbroken line back to the apostles.

Our unity as Catholics does not, however, result in a uniformity in the way we live out our faith. Within the unity of the Church, a multiplicity of people and cultures is gathred together. There are twenty-one Eastern Catholic Churches and one Western Church, all in union with the Pope. Certain local churches and religious orders also have their own rites which have been recognized by the Catholic Church. Within each of these rites the essence of the sacraments is the same as it is in the Roman rite, but the form used in celebrating the sacraments is not the same.

The very nature of the Catholic Church helps us to understand that the call to be "one" is not a call to lose our individual identities; rather, it is a call to develop our individuality while still maintaining our commitment to the unity shared with us from Christ through the Apostles. As Saint Paul reminds us, diversity is as necessary to the body of Christ as unity is. A body cannot function without unity among its members, but it also cannot function without diversity. "If [all the parts of the body] were one part, where would the body be? But as it is, there are many parts, yet one body" (1 Corinthians 12:19–20). The unfathomable mystery of Christ can never be exhausted by a single liturgical rite or a single spirituality, nor can it be limited to the concepts and modes of expression of a single culture or a single philosophy.[11]

From the Saint Thomas Aquinas Parish during the celebration of the Easter vigil, it was easy to see how one could be drawn to the Catholic Church because of its unity in the midst of diversity. In the pews were three students from Indonesia, one from Panama, and one from Cuba. There was a woman from India dressed in a sari, a professor from Italy, and a family from France. Mixed together throughout the church there were people who prayed the Rosary every day, others who belonged to charismatic prayer groups, and still others who were most comfortable with the Thursday night teen liturgies where homilies were often combined with dialogue and everyone sat on the floor. There were scientists, engineers, farmers, business executives, and artists. There were Republicans and Democrats and even a few Socialists. There were peace activists and those who served in the military. There were two men who lived on the streets and a family that owned the nicest home in town. There were people who thought that the Church was changing too fast and others who thought it was changing far too slowly. But all of these people were Catholic. All of them belonged to the one body of Christ and recognized the others as members of that same body.

Despite their differences, none of these people had chosen to leave the Catholic Church to join another denomination of more like-minded people. God's call to be one in our diversity is fundamental to Catholicism. As Catholics we believe that we must remain together, challenging and submitting to one another out of love. In many other denominations it is a common and accepted practice to form new congregations, or even new denominations, when the differences among members become uncomfortable. This is not an option for Catholics.

STUDY QUESTIONS

- WHY IS THE CHURCH ONE?
- WHICH OF THE CHURCH'S STRUCTURES SUPPORT UNITY WITHIN THE CHURCH? HOW IS THIS SO?

JOURNAL ASSIGNMENT

- RELATED TO BEING A CATHOLIC, WHAT IS THE DIFFERENCE BETWEEN UNIFORMITY AMONG MEMBERS AND UNITY AMONG MEMBERS?

The Church Is Holy

The Church is holy because it is the body of Christ—the Holy One of God. The Church is also holy because the Holy Spirit dwells within it. Holiness means "to be set apart." All holiness has its root in God who alone is truly holy. God alone is totally other. God alone is completely set apart from all of creation because God alone is uncreated. The Church is holy or set apart from the rest of creation because of its intimate connection to God. All human beings are called to live in holiness.

In the Old Testament God was called the "holy One of Israel." Holiness was understood as God's innermost essence. Holiness expressed the perfection of God and referred to God's majesty, power, and transcendence. But God's holiness was not something that distanced people from God; in fact, it was something that was only revealed to those who drew near to God. God showed his holiness only to those who came close enough to be made holy themselves.

When people were made holy, or sanctified, they were set apart by God for a special purpose. They were given the task of expressing the essence of divine holiness through their lives. The people of Israel understood that they had been made holy by God. They had become "a people set apart," a people whom God had claimed for his own. They had become a people who were committed to living in such a way that others would realize and confess that the God of Israel was indeed the true God. They were a people committed to doing God's will and bearing witness to God's abiding presence, even when that meant being different from everyone around them.

From its earliest days the Church has understood itself to be the heir of the people of Israel. It too has been set apart by God for a special purpose. The members of the Church, like the people of Israel, have been given the task of living in a way that is different from those around them. We have been chosen by God to make his presence and his holiness visible to the world through the actions of our lives.

ANSWERING A CALL TO HOLINESS

On August 8, 1948, Sister Teresa left the convent of her Loretto, Frrance sisters. She was to continue in the religious life, but it was to be under the Archbishop of Calcutta (India).

To symbolize her new lifestyle and mission, Sister Teresa had laid aside her religious habit and clothed herself in a white Indian sari with a blue border. She wanted to serve the poor purely for the love of God, and she was soon to find out that God was going to bless her in ways she had never dreamed.

In 1949, one of her former pupils, Shubashini Das, a Begali, came to her and said that she wanted to become a religious and work with Sister Teresa as a nun. One by one Indian girls came to surrender themselves to God and to serve the poorest of the poor— "to give their all to God" as Sister (now Mother) Teresa described.

Thus Mother Teresa and her little group, which would eventually become the worldwide religious community of men and women called the Missionaries of Charity, came to live in the slums of Calcutta amid all the dirt and disease and dying.

Later in her life, Mother Teresa described her work as "love that seeks to serve." She said:

Love cannot remain by itself—it has no meaning. Love has to be put into action and that action is service.
I never look at the masses as my responsibility.
I look at the individual. I can love only one person at a time. I can feed only one person at a time.
Just one, one, one.
You get closer to Christ by coming closer to each other. As Jesus said, "Whatever you do to the least of my brethren, you do to me."
So you begin . . . I begin.
I picked up one person—maybe if I didn't pick up that one person I wouldn't have picked up 42,000.
The whole work is only a drop in the ocean. But if I didn't put the drop in, the ocean would be one drop less. Same thing for you, same thing in your family, same thing in the Church where you go.
Just begin . . . one, one, one.

Mother Teresa died on September 5, 1997. She is a candidate for sainthood.

The Church is holy. The Church is not perfect. The Church is the assembly established by Christ to be God's presence in the world and to continue Christ's own work. The Church is the bride of Christ, his partner in bringing to birth the Kingdom of God. It is the very essence of the Church to be holy—to be set apart as the community united with Christ. As the people of Israel were set apart to reveal the One true God, the Catholic Church is set apart to reveal that this One God has become incarnate in Jesus and is present in the Spirit. If the Church is not holy, she is not the Church.

This does not, however, mean that if the Church is not perfect she is not the Church. The Church is holy because it has been set apart to reveal God. And the God whom the Church reveals is love.[12] Therefore we say that the soul of our holiness is love, and where there is love there is holiness.[13] As long as the Holy Spirit is within the Church, love will be present and the Church will be holy. Nonetheless, even though love is present, it may be poorly expressed. The love of the Church can only be expressed through the members of the Church, and these members are all sinners. The weeds of sin are intertwined with the wheat of the gospel in each person in the Church.[14] Each one of us will at some point obscure the holiness of the Church by failing to live in love; yet, as long as some in the Church continue to live in love, the Church will be holy.

There have been times in history when the Church has done some atrocious and unloving things. However, at no point in history has the Church been without people who showed tremendous love precisely because they were members of the Church. Even though her holiness has sometimes been clouded, the Church has always been holy. Unfortunately, some have mistakenly believed that if the Church is holy then everything that is done in the name of the Church is also holy. Those who have believed in this way have fallen into the sin of **idolatry**, substituting the Church for God. They have wrongly equated life in the Church with life in the kingdom of God.

But the Church can never be the Kingdom of God. In fact, when the Kingdom of God comes into its fullness, the Church as we know it will pass away.[15] The Church has been chosen by Christ to be his spouse. The Church is Christ's partner in giving birth to the Kingdom. The Church is the sign and reality of the kingdom of God, even as a pregnant woman is the sign and reality of a new life. But the Church is not the same as the Kingdom, any more than the pregnant woman is the same as the new baby.

Three Ways the Church Supports Holiness

Three aspects of Catholic faith and practice are particularly important in giving form to holiness. These are: the moral teachings of the Church; the **evangelical counsels** and the witness of those who live by them; and the sacraments. Each of these will be dealt with in greater detail in later chapters, so we will address them only briefly at this point.

idolatry—The practice of honoring or revering a creature instead of God, whether it be gods or demons (for example, satanism), power, pleasure, race, ancestors, the state, money, etc. (see *CCC*, 2113.)

evangelical counsels—Poverty, chastity, and obedience. The aim of the evangelical counsels is to help a person remove everything from his or her life which might hinder the ability to love as Christ loved. They are vows taken by sisters, brothers, and religious priests, but they are also recommended for all the faithful.

The Catholic Church has a body of moral teachings which helps clarify many of the practical aspects of living as a "community set apart." Certain attitudes and behaviors which are common in the world are unacceptable for Catholics because they have been judged to be fundamentally opposed to the truth which God has revealed in Jesus. Catholic moral teaching challenges us to do what is right and helps us to stand apart from sin.

The evangelical counsels also call Catholics to stand apart from temptation and to give witness to the love and justice of the Kingdom of God. There are three evangelical counsels: poverty, chastity, and obedience. Each of the counsels stands in opposition to something which can draw us away from God and into the world which has separated from God. A commitment to poverty frees one from the temptation to sin for the sake of material wealth. A commitment to chastity frees one from the temptation to sin for the sake of physical pleasure. A commitment to obedience frees one from the temptation to sin for the sake of power. While the evangelical counsels are lived in a specific way by men and women who are members of a religious order, they are held up as ideals for all Catholics.

The greatest witness to and support for holiness comes in dioceses and parishes in the celebration of the sacraments. The sacraments all point to the essence of a life lived in holiness: cleansing from sin, life in the Spirit, unity with Christ, unity with others, healing and wholeness, and fidelity and service. The sacraments also give us the grace which we need to give holiness concrete form in our lives. One of the things that distinguishes Catholic theology is our understanding of the power of the sacraments to change people and make them more holy.

Why did twenty-five young adults join the Catholic Church in Saint Thomas Aquinas Parish? Why did thousands more join the Catholic Church that same evening in other parishes all around the world? Because in the Catholic Church they heard God's call to holiness, and in the Catholic Church they found the support which they needed to answer that call. They found the sacraments. They found the witness of many who had vowed to live according to the evangelical counsels. And they found a consistent and solid ethic rooted in the teachings of Jesus and his apostles. They joined the Catholic Church because they believed that being a Catholic is significant. Anyone who chooses to become Catholic likely does so because he or she believes Catholics are a people set apart, a people who live differently because of their faith, a people whose communal structures help them to bear witness to God.

STUDY QUESTIONS

- WHY IS THE CHURCH HOLY?
- DEFINE HOLINESS.
- WHAT IS THE RELATIONSHIP BETWEEN THE CHURCH AND THE KINGDOM OF GOD?
- WHICH OF THE CHURCH'S STRUCTURES SUPPORT US IN OUR EFFORTS TO BE HOLY?

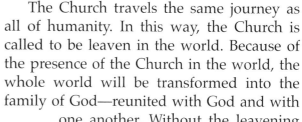

The Church Is Catholic

Catholic means "universal." Catholic also means "in totality" or "in keeping with the whole." To say that the Church is "catholic" is to say that it is whole; it is complete. The totality of the body of Christ is present in the Church. There is nothing that is good, no virtue, no spiritual gift, no wisdom, no cure for sin that exists outside of the Church but not inside her. There is nothing of God that is lacking in Christ, therefore there is nothing that is lacking in Christ's Body, the Church.

To say that the Church is "catholic" is also to say that she is for all people. Christ came to bring Salvation to all people, and Christ established the Church that she might be "the universal sacrament of salvation."[16] Jesus said, "Go . . . and make disciples of all nations, baptizing them in the name of the Father, and of the Son, and of the holy Spirit, teaching them to observe all that I have commanded you" (Matthew 28:19–20).

It is from God's love for humanity and God's desire that all are saved and come to knowledge of the truth that the Church gets her missionary motivation. Salvation is found in the truth. Those who obey the truth through the promptings of the Holy Spirit are on the path of Salvation. It is the Church's missionary mandate to go out and meet those on the way to truth, and to bring them to the truth. It is also important to remember that it is the Holy Spirit who leads the Church on her missionary path. As Pope John Paul II put it, the Holy Spirit is "the principal agent of the whole of the Church's mission."[17]

The Church travels the same journey as all of humanity. In this way, the Church is called to be leaven in the world. Because of the presence of the Church in the world, the whole world will be transformed into the family of God—reunited with God and with one another. Without the leavening of the Church this transformation would not occur. For this reason we say that the Church is necessary for Salvation. Furthermore, all who recognize and understand the necessity of the Church for Salvation are obligated to be part of that Church. Any who reject the Church with full knowledge of the role which God has given the Church are rejecting God.

Because the Church is "catholic," she has a role everywhere and in every situation. There is no region or culture in which the Church cannot belong. In fact the presence of the Church can help the spiritual qualities of every age, nation, and culture to blossom more fully.[18] Furthermore, there is no walk of life from which the Church is excluded. The faith of committed members of the Church can make a positive difference in every profession from farming, to science, to medicine, to literature, to music. Likewise the faith of the Church can challenge and bring out the best in every political, social, and economic system.

Church Teaching Is Based on the Whole of Revelation

Finally, to say that the Church is "catholic" is to say that what the Church teaches is based upon the whole of Revelation: all of Scripture, the teachings of all of the Apostles, and the understanding and witness of Christians from all times and all places. The early Church first started describing itself as "catholic" to highlight the differences between it and many of the heretical sects that were springing up, in particular those involving **Gnosticism**. Each of the gnostic groups claimed special, privileged knowledge of God and of God's will. This knowledge supposedly originated from the secret teachings of one of the Twelve Apostles. The "catholic" Church, on the other hand, claimed a broad-based foundation for her teachings, saying that they were based on the testimony of all of Jesus' Apostles. As time went on this broad base of authority for Church teachings came to refer not only to the common witness of all of the Apostles, but also to the common witness through history of all of the successors to the Apostles.

It is this final understanding of the term catholic that particularly distinguishes the Catholic Church from other denominations today. The Catholic Church—the Church in union with the pope, the bishop of Rome—bases its teachings on the understanding of Revelation which has developed through history. Her claim to authority is based on the consistent witness of every generation of the faithful. Many of the Christian denominations which have their roots in the Protestant reformation base their teachings on the witness of the early Church, on the reformer's interpretation of the witness of the early Church, and on modern theology. They feel no particular obligation to maintain a connection with the understanding of Revelation in other periods of history. These Protestant Christians are free to disregard the things which Christians of other generations have professed to be true if those truths no longer make sense to them. Catholics, on the other hand, are never free to disregard those things which have been declared truths of faith by the Church in earlier generations. The Catholic Church places a strong emphasis on the presence of the Holy Spirit guiding the Church in all generations. The Catholic Church does not ignore the faith of any of the generations of the Church because all of the generations are a part of the whole.

When people join the Catholic Church they are committing themselves to a community which can never disregard past or future generations. They are also committing themselves to a community which can never disregard anything or anyone within the present generation. Those who join the Catholic Church are joining a community that has a universal vocation and mission. They are joining a community that knows that it is called to change the whole world, and they are accepting personal responsibility for facilitating that change. They are saying that as members of this Church they are willing to act as leaven. Through their words and their actions they will do their best to bring the Gospel to every person they meet and into every situation in which they find themselves.

Before the Sacraments of Initiation were celebrated at the Easter vigil on that stormy night in Iowa, the whole congregation joined in a spirited litany of the saints. They called upon holy men and women from every generation to join with them in celebration:

> *Holy Mary, Mother of God, pray for us.*
> *Saint Peter and Saint Paul, pray for us.*
> *Saint Mary Magdelane, pray for us.*
> *Saint Perpetua and Saint Felicity, pray for us.*
> *Saint Joan of Arc, pray for us.*
> *Saint Francis, Saint Claire and Saint Dominic, pray for us.*
> *Saint Thomas Aquinas, pray for us.*
> *Saint Jean Vianney, pray for us.*
> *Saint Martin de Porres, pray for us.*
> *Saint Olga and Saint Vladimir, pray for us.*
> *Saint Kizito, pray for us.*
> *Saint Elizabeth Seton, pray for us.*
> *Saint Paul Chong Hasang, pray for us.*
> *Blessed Kateri Tekakwitha, pray for us.*
> *All holy men and women, pray for us.*

As their prayer rose to a crescendo, they acknowledged the fact that we are a universal Church, a Church for all times and all places. We are a Church that is apostolic, governed by the successor of Peter and the bishops in communion with him who have received from Christ the power to act in his person. The pope and bishops have received from Christ, who founded the Church, the power to act in his person and to guide the Church in every age. We are a universal Church, a Church of all people and a Church for all people.

Gnosticism—One of the earliest Christian heresies. It stressed the importance of secret knowledge passed on to a select few. It denied the goodness of creation and the material world.

STUDY QUESTIONS

- WHAT DOES THE TERM "CATHOLIC" MEAN?
- NAME THREE THINGS THAT WE ARE SAYING ABOUT THE CHURCH WHEN WE DESCRIBE HER AS "CATHOLIC."
- WHAT DOES IT MEAN TO COMMIT TO A CHURCH THAT IS "CATHOLIC"?

JOURNAL ASSIGNMENT

- WRITE A PLAN FOR YOUR DAY EXPLAINING HOW YOU WILL BRING THE GOSPEL IN WORDS AND ACTIONS TO EVERY PERSON YOU MEET AND IN EVERY SITUATION.

The Church Is Apostolic

Jesus was sent by the Father. He in turn sent the Apostles, giving them a mission to continue his work on earth and transform the world. The word apostolic means "having been sent." The Church is apostolic because it has been sent into the world by Christ; unless it remains apostolic, she cannot remain the Church. The Church has an identity and a reason to exist only because she has been sent by Christ with a purpose. If the Church were to forget the One who sends her or the reason for which she was sent, she would become nothing more than another assembly within the world. It is the apostolic nature of the Church which keeps the Church from being swallowed up by the secular world.

The Church remains faithful to her apostolic nature in three ways:

- First, the Church remains faithful by recognizing that she is built upon the foundation of the Apostles who were appointed by Jesus. We reveal our apostolic nature when we point to Jesus as both the source and the focal point of all we do.
- Second, the Church remains faithful to her apostolic nature by following the guidance of the Holy Spirit; adhering to the foundation laid by the Apostles and written down in Scripture; and faithfully interpreting, living, and teaching what the Apostles taught. Every member of the Church bears

All Catholics are called to witness daily to the gospel by their words and actions. Prepare a personal testimony (about a ten minute talk) explaining why you believe in Jesus. Include in your talk some or all of the following points:

· the occasion of the reception of the sacraments;

· your family's history as Catholics;

· a special occasion when you became aware of Christ's presence in your life;

· how you plan to share the Lord with others in the future.

Share your witness talk with classmates, younger students, a youth ministry group, or family members.

syncretism—The practice of blending all religions and faith traditions into one.

witness to the apostolic nature of the Church by teaching and modeling the faith of the Apostles in situations where no one else can.

- Third, the Church remains faithfully apostolic by accepting the continued guidance of the Apostles through their successors and, in particular, by accepting the guidance of Peter's successor—the pope. We point to the apostolic nature of the Church when we allow the teachings of the pope and the bishops to challenge us despite our personal beliefs or preferences.

For many from other Christian denominations who join the Catholic Church, this final way of remaining faithfully apostolic is the most difficult to understand and to accept. Some ask why it should matter that each priest and each bishop can trace his ordination back to the Apostles. Why must each bishop be ordained by others who are already bishops and who in turn were ordained by others who were already bishops? Others accept this notion of apostolic succession, but wonder why it is necessary that one of the apostolic successors be given a role that is greater than that of any of the others. Some answers to these questions follow.

Apostolic Succession in History

The emphasis on apostolic succession has its roots in the history of the early Church. In the years after the Resurrection of Jesus, Christianity spread rapidly, drawing converts from very diverse places and backgrounds. Because of this the Church was enriched, but it was also challenged. Each person and group that joined the Church brought elements of their old beliefs and world views into Christianity. Some of these world views were compatible with Christianity, others were not. Those with incompatible views threatened the very foundations of Christian faith.

These difficulties were exacerbated by the tendency of the time toward **syncretism**. The Greco-Roman culture of the Church's first centuries, much like modern American culture, encouraged the choosing and combining of bits and pieces from a variety of religious and philosophical traditions rather than the whole-hearted adherence to any one system. As a result, many different groups were claiming Christ and yet drastically changing his message. One of the most significant examples of this was found in the teachings of the gnostics.

The gnostics claimed to have a secret mystical knowledge which was necessary for Salvation but which had been given to only a select group of people with superior understanding. The gnostics claimed they had been made aware of the "fact" that the physical world was an evil illusion which trapped the good spirit. In contrast to Jewish tradition, the gnostics claimed that the world was not created by God, but rather by one of the spiritual creatures of God who had tried to turn away from God. According to the gnostics, the physical universe was thus the result of sin and had no lasting reality or value.

In response to the gnostics the Church began to formalize many of her structures. Over time a universally accepted canon, or list of approved Scripture, was developed. Furthermore, around the year A.D. 150 the Church compiled the basic outline of the Apostles' Creed as a summary of the beliefs which any person seeking Baptism must affirm. But a canon and creed were not enough to respond to the gnostics. The real issue was not who had a canon and who had a creed, but whose canon and creed were right? The Church and the gnostics each claimed to be the true interpreters of Jesus, but they could not both be right. The question was: Who really spoke with the authority of Jesus?

It is at this point that the notion of apostolic succession began to take on fundamental importance. The Church argued that if Christ really had a secret knowledge which he wished to pass on, he would have given that knowledge to the same Apostles to whom he gave the Church. These Apostles in turn would have passed that knowledge on to their successors—the bishops. Since all the direct successors to the Apostles rejected the notion of any sort of secret knowledge or plan, such a knowledge and plan must not exist.

It then became important for the bishops of the early Church to prove that they were indeed in direct line from the Apostles. This was not too difficult. Most local churches already had records connecting their current bishops to one of the Apostles. If a church did not have such a record it was considered apostolic as long as it was in agreement with a church that did have a bishop proven to be a direct descendant of an Apostle. What was crucial to apostolic succession was that a local church be able to demonstrate that its bishop had not broken with the fundamental teachings of the Apostles.

In principle, apostolic succession requires that no bishop teach anything that is contrary to what has been handed down to him by his predecessors. Apostolic succession protects the Church against the influx of ideas that are antithetical to Christianity. It ensures that no one group of people will claim to have been given some secret revelation or means to salvation that has not been given to everyone else by Christ. Apostolic succession protects the true teachings of the Church.

Apostolic Succession Today

The notion of apostolic succession protects and preserves Christianity as much today as it did in the early Church. Once again we live in a world in which people are inclined to pick and choose different aspects of different religious traditions and create whole new systems of belief. The name of Christ is often linked to beliefs and practices which are contrary to all that Christ said and did.

To protect against this some Christians insist on a literal reading of and adherence to Scripture. They believe that a dependency on Scripture alone will protect them from anything that is contrary to Christ. Unfortunately, Scripture was written by human beings in another language, in another culture, and in another age. Scripture cannot be directly applied to our language, culture, and age without interpretation. In trying to interpret Scripture for our own situation, even those with the best intentions can be swayed too much by the forces of the culture in which we live if we do not have something on which to anchor our interpretation, something like the unbroken apostolic witness.

As Christ gives the Apostles a share in his own mission, the successors of the Apostles, the bishops in union with the pope, are able to guarantee that the teachings of the Church will never be detached from the teachings of Christ, and that the teachings of the Church will never threaten the true Revelation of God made known in Christ.

But Why the Pope?

Many who accept the value of apostolic succession still question why Catholics would rely so heavily on the pope.

In order to answer this question, we must complete a circle and return to the first mark of the Church—its oneness. The pope is the

"perpetual and visible source and foundation of the unity of bishops and of the multitude of the faithful."[19] As Catholics we believe that without the pope the unity of the Church would be severely threatened by local

churches and bishops addressing competing national and cultural issues. There have been many times in the history of the Church when such national issues did seem to compromise the unity and universal nature of the Church. In some of these instances, the personal, national ties of the reigning pope have contributed to the problem, yet the formal institution of the papacy has always stood for a unity which supersedes these ties. Even after the most troublesome periods of Church history, because of its institution by Christ, the papacy has always been maintained as an institution that is not subject to any one nation or culture, and as an institution that draws us into a unity which goes beyond national and cultural boundaries. As the successor of St. Peter and head of the college of bishops, the pope is the pastor who watches over the whole Church and each of its members throughout the world.[20] His jurisdiction is referred to as the Holy See.

Each diocese or "local church" is led by its own bishop, who has also been established by the Holy Spirit. This bishop has the primary responsibility for interpreting and handing on the apostolic tradition within his own diocese and also for keeping his diocese united to the universal Church.[21] His co-worker priests, who help to pastor parishes within the diocese, aid him in this task. Each bishop must adapt the Church's teachings to the particular culture and particular needs of his own diocese. Yet when these necessary and lawful adaptations are made, it is important that the unity of the Church be maintained. The fidelity of each individual bishop, and of all of the bishops together, to the bishop of Rome (the pope) helps ensure that unity is not lost.

The role of the pope is not limited to the preservation of the Church's unity. The pope also has the task of giving voice to the universal mission and vocation of the Church. The pope calls Catholics everywhere to remember their responsibility to all of

God's people and not just those in their immediate vicinity. The pope also calls Catholics everywhere to remember that there are certain Church teachings which cannot be adapted to suit the local culture. There are issues—such as the protection of the rights of the most defenseless—that are fundamental to the universal vocation of the Church; they must not be ignored or denied by any who wish to call themselves Catholic.[22]

STUDY QUESTIONS

- HOW IS THE CHURCH FAITHFUL TO ITS APOSTOLIC NATURE?
- WHAT HISTORICAL CIRCUMSTANCES LED TO THE CHURCH'S EMPHASIS ON APOSTOLIC SUCCESSION?
- WHAT IS THE ROLE OF THE POPE?

JOURNAL ASSIGNMENT

- WRITE A LETTER TO YOUR LOCAL BISHOP. DESCRIBE YOUR FAITH IN GOD AND THE CHURCH. TELL HIM SOME OF THE PLANS YOU HAVE FOR YOUR LIFE.

IN CONCLUSION

Interviewing newly baptized Catholics provides a great source for understanding why people choose to be Catholic.

Some choose the Catholic Church specifically because she stresses the value of continuity with the past. Many people know how easy it is to be caught up in the present and to ignore the wisdom of the past. One recent convert to Catholicism went so far as to say that his primary reason for joining the Catholic Church was her respect for the past: "The world wouldn't be in such a sorry state if more people followed the Catholic Church and paid attention to Tradition." Another expressed agreement and added, "If you won't build on the knowledge and understanding of the generations that went before you, you end up spending all your time reinventing the wheel. For the most part churches that want to reconsider the basics of faith in every generation never have time and energy for service to the rest of the world." No catechumen is naive enough to think that Catholics are perfect, but most do believe that a respect for and willingness to be taught by the past was part of a Catholic's identity, and they want to embrace it and pass it on.

Other new Catholics find comfort and security in the presence of the papacy. For them the papacy provided an assurance that the Catholic Church would not be reduced to a conglomeration of independent congregations who worked in opposition almost as often as they worked in cooperation. The papacy is a sign and source of mutual commitment, even in the face of discomfort, in a world in which commitment is increasingly disregarded.

At the Easter vigil, a multitude of catechumens express for all to hear, "I profess all that the Holy Catholic Church believes, teaches, and proclaims to be revealed by God." What they are saying is what all who remain in the Catholic Church are called to say daily through their words and actions. That is:

- I profess my faith in one God: Father, Son and Spirit. I surrender myself to that God and to the assembly which God has called to make his presence visible and tangible.

- I surrender myself to a Church that is one. I commit myself to working with, rather than separating from, other members of the Church with whom I may disagree. I commit myself to living in solidarity with those who are in need. I agree to worship with others in a manner suited to the community as a whole, not just to me as an individual. I accept the profession of faith which belongs to the Church as a whole. I accept the ethical framework of the Catholic community. I will allow others to challenge and shape me.

- I surrender myself to a Church that is holy. My faith will affect the way that I live. I commit myself to doing all that I can to reveal the presence of Christ. I will try to understand and follow Catholic ethical teachings. I will strive to incorporate the evangelical counsels of poverty, chastity, and obedience into my life. I will participate in the sacraments and accept the grace that Christ offers to me through those sacraments.

- I surrender myself to a Church that is catholic or universal. I will not discount anyone on the basis of race, culture, age, or financial situation. I will acknowledge the right of people from other traditions, cultures, and ways of thinking to shape the Church into something to which we can all belong as equals.

- I surrender myself to a Church that is apostolic. I know that I have been sent by God to make God's presence visible and tangible in my life. I accept this mission. I acknowledge the importance of the role of the pope and the bishops. I accept the pope and the bishops as the authoritative interpreters of Jesus' teaching.

LEARN BY DOING

Research each of the following Church heresies and explain what they involved. Tell how and when the Church responded to each of these heresies with authentic teaching.

- Gnosticism
- Arianism
- Nestorianism
- Monophysitism
- Pelagianism
- Novatianism and Donatism

PRAYER

BLESSING OF THE CATECHUMENS

Let us pray.

Almighty God,
Lord of all,
through your Son
you cast Satan from his throne
and freed mankind from its captivity
by breaking the chains that bound it.
We thank you
in the name of these catechumens
whom you have called.
Strengthen them in faith
that they may know you, the one true God,
and Jesus Christ, whom you sent to us.
Keep them clean of heart and make them grow in holiness
so that they may receive baptism
and share in the holy mysteries.

We ask this through Christ our Lord.
Amen.

—from the Rite of Christian Initiation of Adults

NOTES

1. #17
2. *Redemptoris Mater,* #14.
3. We will discuss this concept in greater depth in Unit 5 when we speak about the sacramental life of the Church.
4. *Catechism of the Catholic Church,* #750.
5. See Vatican II, *Lumen Gentium,* #48.
6. See *Catechism of the Catholic Church,* #810.
7. Ibid., #813.
8. Ibid., #816.
9. Ibid., #814.
10. Ibid., #815.
11. Ibid., #1201.
12. See 1 John 4:16.
13. See *Catechism of the Catholic Church,* #826.
14. Ibid., #827.
15. See *Lumen Gentium,* #48.
16. *Ad gentes,* #1 as quoted in *Catechism of the Catholic Church,* #849.
17. *Redemptoris Missio* as quoted in *Catechism of the Catholic Church,* #852.
18. See *Gaudium et Spes,* #58.
19. *Lumen Gentium,* #23.
20. See *Catechism of the Catholic Church,* #936–937.
21. Ibid., #938.
22. We will discuss papal authority in greater detail at a later point.

UNIT TWO

THE CHURCH IS MYSTERY

THE CHURCH IS MYSTERY

Though the Church is in historical time, she also transcends history. The Church is both part of human history and surpasses our human comprehension. Only in faith can one see the Church as the bearer of divine life along with her place in history.

The Church is both a visible and spiritual reality. As the Second Vatican Council documents teach, she is

- a society structured with hierarchical organs and the mystical body of Christ;
- the visible society and the spiritual community;
- the earthly Church and the Church endowed with heavenly riches (*Lumen Gentium*, 8).

The Church is also a mystery of man's union with God. "It is in the Church that Christ fulfills and reveals his own mystery as the purpose of God's plan: 'to unite all things to him'" (*CCC*, 772). God established the Church for the holiness of her members. Mary, the Mother of God, leads the Church as a model of holiness.

The Greek word for mystery—*mysterion*—was translated by two Latin terms: *mysterium* and *sacramentum*. A sacrament points out the visible sign of the hidden reality of Salvation offered by Jesus and the Church. Christ himself is the mystery of Salvation. The Church, too, is like a sacrament—"a sign and instrument, that is, of communion with God and of unity of all men" (*Lumen Gentium*, 1).

Unit 2 teaches that the Church is a mystery that can never fully be expressed from a single viewpoint. However, there are things within the Church which cannot and will not change and can be understood. The Church has a permanent body of dogma, a permanent ethic, and a permanent constitution. Chapter 2.2 demonstrates how through history the Church has remained permanent and unchanging. The chapter also points out how the Church has used different images to explain how the Church is relevant to the world and at the same time separate from the world.

When you have completed Unit 2, you will be able to:

- explain why we say the Church is mystery;
- illustrate some of the ways in which the mystery of the Church is reflected in the life of the Church;
- identify the place of the Church in Salvation History;
- demonstrate why and how the Church is necessary for Salvation;
- name and describe the three things in the Church which cannot and will not change;
- describe the role of the Magisterium within the Church;
- demonstrate a knowledge of the progression of Church history and the time frame of key events within the Church;
- identify the images or understandings of the nature of the Church that dominated different periods of Church history;
- appreciate the way in which the Church of today is informed and shaped by the Church of other periods in history;
- identify the images of the Church which you see in operation in your local community.

ENDURING and DEVELOPING

LET THERE BE UNITY IN WHAT IS NECESSARY, FREEDOM IN WHAT IS DOUBTFUL, AND CHARITY IN EVERYTHING.

—*Gaudium et Spes, #92*

WHAT'S REALLY CATHOLIC?

Tonia has been a Catholic youth minister for almost ten years. When she was asked what the statement, "the Church is a mystery," meant to her, she told the following story.[1]

I can still remember a particular incident after my very first youth group meeting. The pastor of the parish, Father Kelly, came down the stairs just as the door closed behind the last high school student. He growled out a loud "Hmph!" and then said, "I must say I was surprised to see Sara O'Rourke there today. She

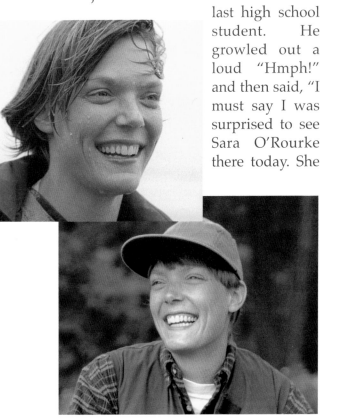

was one of the last kids I thought you'd get out for a youth group. Her parents haven't darkened the door of the church since my first month here. They are old Father Dave groupies who act as if I'm the devil incarnate. If I were you I'd be prepared for trouble. They may have ideas about using the youth group as a new platform for their wacky ideas."

His words didn't shock me. Even in my short time at St. Pius parish I had grown used to Father Kelly's "my way or the highway," talk. In fact, I'd come to realize that his gruff attitude was more a front than anything. But his final warning about Sara did start me thinking again. I had hoped to stay out of the ever present, rarely vocalized conflict in our parish, but Father Kelly's comments made me realize that was probably not possible. Everything I did was going to be interpreted as my taking one "side" or the other. I needed to do more thinking about what those sides were.

The problem was, Father Kelly and the pastor who had been at St. Pius before him—Father Dave—approached their ministries from very different perspectives. The parish was now divided between those parishioners who were angry that Father Dave had been transferred and those who were thankful that Father Kelly had come.

In one of our first conversations, Father Kelly explained his ministerial approach to me: "I'm the quarterback. I call the plays. Then I hand the ball off to someone else to run them. When I came here there were too many people trying to be the quarterback and not enough who were prepared to run, block, and receive. Nothing ever got done. Even worse, people were doing all kinds of crazy things in the name of the Church. Catholicism was equated with every half-baked idea that came through this town! My job is to make sure that what happens here is genuinely Catholic."

Father Kelly believed that the Church should call people to accept their responsibilities. He challenged people to live up to their commitments, beginning with their commitment to the Church. "Being a member of the Church isn't about feeling all warm and fuzzy inside," he told me when I interviewed for the job. "It is about making a commitment to God. You don't come to Mass because of what you get out of it. You come because Sunday worship is part of your commitment."

Father Kelly wouldn't baptize kids, except in emergencies, unless their parents were regular church-goers. ("How can they make promises for other people that they don't even keep themselves?") He also wouldn't let people receive their First Communion or be confirmed if he thought they weren't taking their responsibility to the Church seriously enough. Every kid in the parish school and every kid in religious education classes was given a set of envelopes. They were to put an envelope in the basket every Sunday, with or without money. If people were preparing for First Communion or Confirmation but weren't putting envelopes in the basket every Sunday, Father Kelly would tell them that they had to wait another year to receive the sacraments. He also refused to preside at weddings if the couple was already living together.

Father Kelly believed in rules, structure, and Church hierarchy. "If you take those things away people start thinking that 'anything goes.' And go it does, straight to Hell." He was fond of saying, "If you run the Church as a democracy, ignorance and sin will win every election."

Another Perspective on Church and Ministry

I never met Father Dave, but I know that his understanding of Catholicism was completely different. I can't count the number of times I heard people say to Father Kelly, "Father Dave always said that we are the Church. The Spirit moves in each one of us and all of us together. The Church is not the same thing as the **Magisterium**." According to Father Dave, the job of a pastor was to make people believe in themselves and their gifts. The parish council during Father Dave's tenure had been a large group with representatives from every segment of the parish. The council's primary focus had been on making St. Pius a welcoming community with opportunities for everyone to get involved.

When Father Dave was the pastor at St. Pius, homilies had been about love, acceptance, and forgiveness. There had been very few rules about who could receive the sacraments. Father Dave actually had a reputation for accepting weddings that other priests refused. His philosophy was, "Maybe the wedding will be the beginning of their return to the Church."

Father Dave believed that every person was a necessary part of the Body of Christ, the Church. When any person was separated from the Body, the whole Body suffered. Father Kelly also believed that every person was called to be part of the Body of Christ, but he felt that the greatest harm to the Body came not from the absence of some members, but from the presence of others who were not living and acting as they should.

The parishioners of St. Pius, like the parishioners of so many parishes in North America, were divided between these two

Magisterium—The bishops, acting in unison with the pope, by virtue of their ordination, constitute the magisterium. The Magisterium is the teaching authority of the Church.

viewpoints. There were people in each group who were hurt and angry because they felt that the true Catholic Church was being threatened. People from both groups turned to me as the newest member of the parish staff and ask me to support them and help move the Church and particularly the youth in the "right" direction, their direction.

I realized that if I was going to be effective I had to answer the questions for myself: "What is the 'right' direction?" And, "Who really represents the 'true' Catholic Church?" The more time I spent listening and praying, the more I realized that both Father Kelly and Father Dave represented the "true" Catholic Church. Both of them were right about who we are and who we are called to be. The Catholic Church has room for and need for both Father Kelly and his supporters and Father Dave and his supporters. That, for me, is part of the mystery of the Church!

JOURNAL ASSIGNMENT

- HOW DO YOU ANSWER THE QUESTION "WHO REALLY REPRESENTS THE 'TRUE' CATHOLIC CHURCH?"

WHY THE CHURCH IS A MYSTERY

In his opening address to the Second Vatican Council, Pope John XXIII said, "everything, even human differences, leads to the greater good of the Church." Although the tensions at St. Pius and in many other Catholic parishes are sometimes painful and uncomfortable, they can also enrich our faith and our understanding of the Church. In fact, a certain amount of tension among believers concerning the nature of the Church is inevitable. The Church is a mystery of faith that can never be fully expressed from any single viewpoint. It is only when we share and explore our different understandings of the Church that the mystery of the Church begins to unfold for us.

To say that the Church is a mystery is to say that her nature can never be grasped by the power of reason alone. The Church is a visible, tangible, historical reality, but it has been permeated by the Spirit of the invisible, intangible, and timeless God. The spiritual essence of the Church—her inner truth—is not something that can be scientifically observed or measured. It is something which can only be known because it has been revealed by God. God's Revelation allows us to see that the Church is different from other human institutions. Through the eyes of faith, we can see the hand of God accomplishing things in the Church that could not be done by humans alone.

As Catholics we believe that the Church is far more than the sum of all her members. The Church is a joining of the human and the divine, and is essentially both.[2] Although individual members and groups within the Church may act in a way that is contrary to God, the Church herself can never be in opposition to God. For this reason, we are never called to separate ourselves from the Church no matter what is being done by some in the name of the Church.[3] God may call us to challenge others within the Church or to disassociate ourselves from certain actions done in the name of the Church. God will not call us to abandon the Church, because the Church is not merely human; she is also divine.

The Church is a mystery because she holds apparent opposites together. Within the Church is the human and sinful, and the divine and holy. Within the Church is the visible and changeable, and the invisible and permanent. Within the Church is the earthly and the heavenly, the "already" and the "not yet."

The Church and God's Kingdom

Through the Incarnation of Jesus, the **Kingdom of God** broke into human history. The barrier between the divine and the human, which had been in place since Adam and Eve and the fall of humanity, was shattered. God's Kingdom, the realm in which God's will is done, was opened to humanity. In Jesus' Death and Resurrection earthly life was permanently linked to this Kingdom; but no one on earth will experience the Kingdom fully until Jesus' Second Coming. The Church is the focal point of the Kingdom's presence on earth. The Church is also the place where we are most acutely aware of the fact that we still await the fullness of the Kingdom.

The Church is the focal point of the Kingdom's presence because it is through the Church that the will of God—the foundation of the Kingdom—may be most reliably known. The Holy Spirit dwells in the hearts of the faithful and

speaks the will of God to them. The Spirit does not, however, speak to human beings in the same way that we speak to one another. The Spirit reveals God to us primarily through signs and symbols. The Church makes those signs and symbols available and helps us recognize and interpret them. So, for example, it is in the Church, and most particularly in the Eucharist, that we hear the call to be one with God and one with each other.

The Holy Spirit not only speaks to us through signs and symbols; the Spirit also transforms us through the power of those signs and symbols. Thus the Church not only calls us to reconciliation and peace, but also gives us the confidence to believe that reconciliation and peace are possible, and the Church gives us the strength and the courage to work for them. The Church is the focal point of the Kingdom's presence, because in the Church God's will is not only manifest, it is also accessible.

But even as God's will is made accessible to us we are brought face to face with the great distance between God's will and our behavior. Week by week we are asked to acknowledge our own failings and our own sinfulness and to seek forgiveness for the ways in which we have chosen to hinder God's plan for peace, justice, unity, and love. The Church is the place where forgiveness and hope are already present; it is also the place where we come to recognize how much we still need forgiveness and hope.

So we return to Tonia's question: "Who speaks for the 'true' Church? Those who remind

SURVEY OF OPINION

Interview at least five Catholics you know of different ages. Ask them their opinion on this dilemma:

A mother and father bring their infant child to your parish for Baptism. The father has never practiced a religion. The mother was baptized a Catholic but eventually stopped going to Church. If you were the pastor, would you allow the baby to be baptized? If not, why? If so, would there be any requirements you would ask of the couple? What would they be?

Write a summary of each person's opinion. Then offer your own opinion on what you would do in this situation.

Kingdom of God—The reign or rule of God. The Kingdom of God has begun with the coming of Jesus. It will exist in its perfect form at the end of time.

Rite of Christian Initiation of Adults (RCIA)—The process through which non-Catholic adults learn about and join in full communion with the Catholic Church by receiving the Sacraments of Baptism (if they have not already received Christian Baptism), Confirmation, and Eucharist.

mystagogia—Unfolding of the mystery. This is the name given to the period following the Baptism of adults. During this time, the newly baptized are to open themselves more fully to the graces received in Baptism.

us of our sins and our need to change? Or those who offer us unconditional acceptance, love, and hope?" The answer, as Tonia herself said, is "both do." The world must hear both voices if it is to be transformed. When Father Dave invited people to know God's forgiveness and acceptance and to embrace the hope which the Church offers, he was moving people in the "right" direction. He was helping them to understand that in the "true" Church the Kingdom of God—the Kingdom in which none will be outcasts—is already present. When Father Kelly called people to greater personal responsibility, when he challenged them to confess their sins and repent, he too was moving people in the "right" direction. He was helping them to understand that in the "true" Church we all must come face to face with our own need for forgiveness and the ways in which we personally have kept the Kingdom of God from being present in its fullness.

MYSTAGOGIA

The final stage of the **Rite of Christian Initiation of Adults (RCIA)** is known as **mystagogia**, that is, "the unfolding of the mystery." During this period, the neophytes ("newly baptized") and their sponsors continue to meet and to reflect upon their life in the Church. As they participate in the sacramental life of the Church, these new Catholics "taste more intimately the good word of God" and come to discover the goodness of the Lord in a new and more profound way. A deeper understanding of the faith, the Church, and the world becomes available to them, and they are invited to explore and embrace it.[4]

The Church recognizes that the process of becoming a Catholic is begun but not completed in the Sacraments of Initiation. Those who join the Catholic Church at the Easter Vigil commit themselves to the faith expressed in the creed and to life shared with a community that is "one, holy, catholic, and apostolic;" nonetheless it will take a lifetime of prayer and study to fully understand what this commitment means.

STUDY QUESTIONS

- WHAT DOES IT MEAN TO SAY THAT THE CHURCH IS MYSTERY?
- HOW IS THE CHURCH "THE FOCAL POINT OF THE KINGDOM'S PRESENCE"?

JOURNAL ASSIGNMENT

- WHO ARE SOME PEOPLE IN YOUR CHURCH COMMUNITY WHO HELP MOVE YOU IN THE "RIGHT" DIRECTION TOWARD GOD'S KINGDOM? HOW ARE THEY DOING THIS?

THE CHURCH IS THE CULMINATION OF SALVATION HISTORY

"The world was created for the sake of the Church." This phrase was used by Christians of the first centuries to express their understanding of the role of the Church in God's plan for the world.[5] The Church is the culmination of **Salvation History**. From the creation of the world, God has intended human beings to share in divine life. In the Church this sharing finally becomes a reality.

The call to "be the Church" highlights God's invitation to enter into dialogue with him. In the Church we are invited to relate to the Father, not merely as God's lowly creatures, but as his sons and daughters. The call to be the Church is an incredible gift and an incredible trust. The Church is the summation of all of God's gifts throughout history. She is the remnant foretold by the prophets. Despite our weaknesses and our many failings, God has never abandoned us or despaired of us. Despite the many times that human beings have violated God's trust, God has offered us the most precious gift of the Church. In order to better understand this, it will be helpful to consider some of the other ways God has invited and trusted humanity throughout the course of Salvation History.

At the beginning of human history God invited man and woman to be co-creators with him. In the name of all humanity Adam and Eve were given dominion over the earth (Genesis 1:28). All people are invited by God to use their own talents and efforts to perfect and complete the work of creation.[6] In spite of human sinfulness, God has never taken away our roles of co-creator or caretaker for the world. The story of Noah and the ark reveals this truth (and in fact the Church is prefigured in Noah's ark).

Later, God invited a particular people to do more than care for the earth. The Israelites were called to enter into a mutually binding, **covenant** relationship with God. God willingly bound himself forever to a group of people and gave them a unique and pivotal role in his plan for the world. Although the Israelites broke the covenant over and over again, God never gave up on them or abandoned them. In fact, God trusted them as the faith community from which God's own Son, Jesus, would be born.

Salvation History—The story of God's action in human history. Salvation history refers to the events through which God makes humanity aware of and brings humanity into the Kingdom of God. It begins with the creation of the world and will end with the Second Coming of Christ.

covenant—The partnership between God and humanity which God has established out of love. The new covenant is offered through Christ. The blood which Christ shed on the cross is a sign of the new covenant.

WE ARE CHRIST'S BODY

Do at least one of the following actions for Christ today:

- Invite a lonely classmate to join you for study or lunch.
- Help a classmate with special needs.
- Be extra courteous to a retail worker.
- Visit with an older neighbor or relative.
- Babysit a young child without charging money.

What are some other actions you can do for Christ today?

Pentecost—sometimes known as the "birthday of the Church." It was the day that the Holy Spirit descended on the Apostles and empowered them to preach the Good News to Jews gathered in Jerusalem for the harvest feast known by that name. Pentecost refers to the "fiftieth day" from Passover.

When the time was right, God himself became a member of that community. Jesus, the Son of God, was born as a helpless baby completely dependent upon the love, support, and care of the people around him. God entrusted his own Son, his very self, to human beings. What is more, in the person of Jesus God chose to bind the divine nature with human nature so that the two became one.

Body of Christ on Earth

Yet even the union of human nature and divine nature in the person of Jesus was not the final gift of God to humanity, nor was it God's final effort to unite humanity in partnership with God. Even after becoming human, even after living, suffering, and dying as a human and for the sake of humanity, God still had more to offer us. The depth and breadth of God's love for humanity and trust in humanity is revealed beyond Jesus' death—and even beyond the resurrection—in the establishment of the Church.[7] Following his Resurrection Jesus returned to the Father, but his Ascension did not mark the end of God's tangible involvement in history. A fifty-day period of preparation preceded **Pentecost**, the day a new era in God's relationship with humanity began. The Holy Spirit was given to the Church from the Father and the Son while bringing a variety of hierarchical and charismatic gifts so that the Church could continue the works of Christ in proclaiming and establishing God's Kingdom.

The Spirit's gifts help the Church fulfill her mission. The Church herself has become the Body of Christ on earth, and each member of the Church is a member of that Body. Now it is primarily through the Church that God chooses to be made known, present, and tangible. It is primarily through the Church that God communicates truth and grace.[8] The Church is the "Sacrament of Salvation," pointing people toward God and making God an accessible reality for them.[9] The miracle of the Church is that despite all of humanity's failings and weaknesses, God loves us so much and places so much trust in us that he is willing to act and to be known through us.

St. Teresa of Avila (1515–1582) calls us all to remember our role as Church:

> Christ has no body now on earth but yours,
> yours are the only hands with which he can do his work.
> Yours are the only feet with which he can go about the world.
> Yours are the only eyes through which his compassion can look upon the world.
> Christ has no body on earth, but yours.

- WHAT DID EARLY CHRISTIANS MEAN BY THE PHRASE "THE WORLD IS CREATED FOR THE SAKE OF THE CHURCH"?
- HOW DOES GOD REMAIN INCARNATE IN HUMAN HISTORY?

THE CHURCH IS NECESSARY FOR SALVATION

St. Teresa of Avila's words help us to understand the mystery of the Church's necessity. The official teaching of the Catholic Church has long stated that the Church is necessary for **Salvation** and that "outside of the Church there is no Salvation." Salvation comes to the world only through Jesus. Jesus remains present in the world through his Body, the Church. We say that the Church is necessary for Salvation because Jesus is necessary for Salvation. Without Jesus, who has chosen the Church as his Body, there is no Salvation.

All who recognize that the Church is the Body of Christ are called to be a part of that Church. If they reject the Church, knowing that she is the Body of Christ, they are rejecting Salvation. This does not mean that those who, through no fault of their own, do not know Christ or his Church have rejected Salvation. Jesus and the Church are necessary to God's plan for Salvation; however, through ways known only to God, the Holy Spirit can lead those who know

neither Jesus or the Church to unity with the Father.[10]

In order to be faithful to Christ and to truly be his Body on earth, the Church must reach out with compassion to everyone; the Church must also challenge her own members to live as Christ lived. The Church must be willing to say that certain things are not compatible with a total surrender to Christ. The Church is the sign and instrument of God's love for humanity. As the sign, the Church must strive for perfection; as the instrument, the Church must offer God's all-encompassing love. The true Church is critical and accepting at the same time. This is part of the Church's mystery.

What Is the True Church?

Return once more to Tonia's question. What attitude is necessary if we are to be the Body of Christ on earth and continue Christ's work of bringing Salvation to the world? Is it the attitude of Father Kelly or of Father Dave?

Truly, the answer is both attitudes. Jesus said, "As I have loved you, so you also should love one another"(John 13:34). Those who prefer Father Dave's approach have recognized the importance of showing everyone the love and acceptance which

Salvation—True, complete, and permanent unity with God and with one another. Salvation is the end goal of all creation. It refers to the fulfillment of the human desire for ultimate truth and goodness. Salvation is made possible by Christ's Death, Resurrection, and Ascension.

Jesus showed to sinners. They are speaking as the "true" Church when they share God's healing and forgiveness with others. They are truly acting as the Body of Christ when they place people above rules. Jesus also said, "Be perfect just as your heavenly Father is perfect" (Matthew 5:48). Furthermore, Jesus tells people that when members of the community sin they should be approached and corrected by one person; then, if necessary, by several; and finally, if still needed, by the whole Church. Any who refuse to listen to the Church should then be treated like outsiders (Matthew 18:15–20). Those who are more comfortable with Father Kelly's approach have recognized that being a member of the Body of Christ is a great responsibility. They are speaking as the "true" Church when they insist that one's membership in the Body of Christ should be evident in a person's priorities and behaviors. They are truly acting as the Body of Christ when they stress the importance of doing what God would have us do.

STUDY QUESTIONS

- EXPLAIN THE STATEMENT "THE CHURCH IS NECESSARY FOR SALVATION."
- NAME AN EXAMPLE FROM THE RECENT NEWS IN WHICH THE CHURCH HAS HAD TO SPEAK OUT BECAUSE IT WAS NOT COMPATIBLE WITH THE GOSPEL AND TOTAL SURRENDER TO CHRIST.

JOURNAL ASSIGNMENT

- DRAW A CIRCLE. PUT CHRIST IN THE CENTER. THEN ADD THE INITIALS OF SEVERAL PEOPLE YOU KNOW OR KNOW OF IN RELATION TO WHERE THEY ARE IN (OR OUT) OF THE BODY OF CHRIST. EXPLAIN YOUR REASONING.

THE CHURCH IS THE BRIDE OF CHRIST

The loving relationship of Christ and the Church also acknowledges a distinction between Christ (the head) and the Church (the body). The image of Christ as the bridegroom and the Church as the bride was prepared by the Old Testament prophets and announced by John the Baptist. In explaining why he wasn't the Messiah, John named Jesus as the bridegroom, "the one who has the bride" (John 3:29). The Church is Jesus' bride.[11]

In the letter to the Ephesians (5:29–32), St. Paul talks about the relationship between Christ and the Church by using the passage from Genesis which speaks of a husband and wife becoming one flesh. In Paul's understanding of marriage a husband and wife belong completely to each other.[12]

Although they remain separate people they have surrendered themselves to each other. Their marriage is a relationship as God intended it to be, to the extent that the husband and wife are no longer two but one—one in will and one in action. In choosing the Church to be his body on earth, Paul writes of the whole Church, the members of the Body, as a bride "betrothed" to Christ, the groom, so as to become one with him. Christ has entered a similar marriage covenant with the Church, and has filled the Church with his grace. Christ has surrendered himself to the Church, allowing the Church to express his will to the world.

The Church in turn must surrender herself to Christ. In order to be Christ's Body on earth, the Church must make Jesus' will its own. The Church honors its covenant with Christ and truly acts as his Body when her members live as Christ lived, following the principles of charity, humility, and self-denial.[13]

The Church that is not identical to Christ is nonetheless the Body of Christ because she has been joined to Christ in a true marriage covenant. The Church and Christ have become one. The true identity of both Christ and the Church can now be known only in the other.

JOURNAL ASSIGNMENT

- IN YOUR OWN WORDS, EXPLAIN HOW CHRIST'S RELATIONSHIP WITH THE CHURCH IS LIKE A HUSBAND'S RELATIONSHIP WITH HIS WIFE.

THE CHURCH IS UNCHANGING YET DEVELOPING

The Church is mystery in that she is unchanging and yet she doesn't look the same in every period in history.

Catholics believe that Jesus Christ is the absolute self-communication of God to humanity. Nothing new will be revealed to us that has not already been revealed in the Life, Death, Resurrection, and Ascension of Jesus, and in his sending of the Holy Spirit. We also believe that our understanding Jesus and the truth which he revealed is constantly growing and deepening.[14]

Apostle—"One who is sent." It is the name used for the twelve men whom Jesus chose and who the Church believes were given authority by Christ.

The role of the Church as the Body of Christ guided by the Holy Spirit is to continue to reveal the presence of God and to lead all people to unity with the Father just as Jesus did. It is the task of the Church to interpret what is going on in today's world in light of the gospel.[15] We reveal what has been revealed to us through who we are, through what we say, and through what we do. Though Revelation is complete in Jesus, our understanding and expression of the Revelation can and do develop and change.

According to a Catholic understanding of the Church, there are three things within the Church which cannot and will not change:

1. The Church has a permanent constitution.
2. The Church has a permanent ethic.
3. The Church has a permanent body of dogma.

We will examine each one of these in more detail and consider some of the implications of saying that these are permanent.

The Church Has a Permanent Constitution

When we speak of the **permanent constitution** of the Church, we are speaking about her basic form and makeup; we are referring to the structure that makes it possible for the Church to be the Church. This structure has been part of the Church from the beginning. It is not something which has been superimposed on the Church any more than our bodies are things which have been

permanent constitution—Those elements in the Church's structure which were established by Jesus. It includes the presence of the hierarchy.

superimposed on us. The Church's structure is an essential part of the Church's identity in the same way that our bodies are an essential part of our identity. Even as it changes and develops it remains fundamentally the same.

We believe that Jesus established the basic structure for the Church when he chose twelve **Apostles** from among his many followers. Because of human limitations some people were bound to know Jesus and his message more intimately than others. Jesus specifically selected some with whom he would share the most, and he made it clear that this selection came with responsibilities. Jesus gave the Apostles authority to teach and baptize in his name. He also made it clear that this authority was not to be used to gain power, but to serve others and help them grow spiritually.[16]

Given the power from Jesus to act in his person, the Apostles passed on their knowledge of Jesus, their authority from him, and their commitment to service in his name to their successors. In this way, the hierarchical structure of the Church was permanently established. The Catholic understanding of the Church is built upon the belief that this structure has been what Jesus intended. When Jesus commissioned the Apostles he also promised that he would be with them to the end of time (Matthew 28:20). He would guide them in their teaching and in who they baptized. Since the Apostles themselves did not live until "the end of time," the Catholic Church understands this promise to mean that Jesus will continue to guide those who will succeed the Apostles until the end of time.[17]

Bishops in union with the **pope** and with priests as their co-workers have the responsibility of carrying on this teaching role. They are called to protect the central truths of our faith from ideas and beliefs which are not compatible with the truth revealed by Jesus. Bishops are committed to passing on the truth which they have received from those who have gone before them, extending all the way back to the Apostles. Bishops can and must interpret that truth in light of current circumstances. They also can and must express that truth in language which makes sense to the people of the day. But they are not free to change or contradict the fundamental essence of that truth. Changing historical circumstances cannot change the nature of God or the nature of God's call to us. Since we believe that both of these things (God and God's call to us) were perfectly revealed in Jesus, changing historical circumstances should never cause us to accept things that contradict what has been passed to us from Jesus through his Apostles and their successors.

The Responsibility of the Magisterium

The bishops of the world, often referred to as "the college of bishops," are committed to maintaining continuity between the faith of today and the faith of the past. They help prevent us from reinterpreting what Jesus said and did in such a way that we can use it to justify anything we are doing or want to do. The bishops, acting in

unison with the pope, by virtue of their ordination, are the authentic teachers of the faith. They constitute the Magisterium, the teaching authority of the Church. The pope and bishops hand on the Deposit of Faith from generation to generation. Competent theologians and spiritual authors—both ordained and lay people—are able to help the pope and bishops in the area of teaching and preaching.[18] But it is the job of the pope and bishops to ensure that the teachings of Christ—the head of the Body—are not dissipated or corrupted before they reach the other various parts of the Body—the members of the Church. It is also the responsibility of the Magisterium to convey the messages that come from the head in such a way that they can be understood. The

bishop—Literally an "overseer." A bishop is a successor to the apostles and the head of a particular church (usually a diocese). All of the bishops together and united with the pope exercise leadership over the universal Church.

pope—The bishop of Rome. The pope is successor of Peter and as such holds the highest office of teaching and governance in the Catholic Church.

Magisterium is the authentic interpreter of Scripture and Tradition (the doctrinal and moral teachings which have been passed from generation to generation).

The Magisterium is not the Church. The Church is the whole Body of Christ: laity, clergy, and religious. However, the

Magisterium is essential to the Church. Without it the Church would not function as a single and unified Body. Furthermore, without the Magisterium of the Church, much of the truth which Jesus revealed about God and about God's call to us would be permanently lost or distorted.

A point of contention may be made that there are other Christian denominations which do not have a Magisterium and which nonetheless have remained faithful to Jesus. It must be noted, however, that the presence of the Magisterium in the Catholic Church has served non-Catholic Christians as well as Catholics in at least two specific ways. First, the very existence of the Catholic Magisterium has ensured that issues such as abortion, physician-assisted suicide, and justice for the poor will be discussed in relationship to Christian faith. Christians of many other denominations are aware of, and find it necessary to respond to, the

pronouncements of the Catholic Magisterium on these and other issues. Second, the Magisterium of the Catholic Church has ensured the preservation of certain beliefs and practices which many Protestant churches had ignored for a time but are now reclaiming.[19]

According to Catholic teaching, the Magisterium—the pope and bishops— were established by Jesus. They will always be, and should always be, part of the Church. Furthermore, the pope and bishops will and should always have the job of interpreting Scripture and Tradition in light of current circumstances. Theirs will always be the authoritative voice concerning what is genuinely Catholic at any particular point in history. This is one of the beliefs that most clearly distinguishes Catholics from those in other Christian denominations.

When An Individual Disagrees with the Magisterium

Each Catholic, in following the teaching of the Church, needs to keep in mind the good of the whole Church and of all persons. However, sometimes an individual faces a situation in which following the teaching of the Church seems particularly difficult. Only with appropriate study, reflection, prayer, and consultation with others knowledgeable about a teaching of the Church can one make an informed decision. A person should not seek to place individual conscience apart from the teaching of the Church. When after a process of fully forming one's conscience in this way, one concludes that he cannot follow the Church's teaching on a particular matter, he must realize he is disagreeing with the Magisterium. Despite this disagreement, one must contine to pray for conversion and strive to form his conscience in conformity with the teaching of the Church in that matter. When people disagree with the Magisterium, they must admit that they are not speaking as representatives of the Catholic Church, but as individuals. They must acknowledge that their opinions do not carry the weight of a universal Church, or of a teaching with an unbroken connection back through history to Christ. They must acknowledge the cultural biases of their opinions and admit that those opinions may not be open to the voices of people of faith from very different cultures.

They must admit that in taking a stand that is different from that of the Magisterium they are implying that the Holy Spirit has revealed things to them and to their group that have been withheld from many others who are equally committed to listening to the Spirit. In other words, Catholics should be very cautious when they hold opinions that differ from the teachings of the Magisterium, and they must always be open to the possibility that those opinions are wrong. Furthermore, Catholics are called to acknowledge the right of the Magisterium to say that certain beliefs and behaviors are so fundamentally opposed to the central truths of the faith that a person who publicly embraces or advocates them can no longer expect to be treated as a member of the Catholic Church.

We now return again to Tonia's question: Who represents the true Church? Father Kelly, who insisted that everyone obey the teachings of the Magisterium? Or Father Dave, who said that all of the faithful together make up the Body of Christ and that priests and bishops are no more important than anyone else? Once again we must answer that, in the great mystery which is the Church, both Father Kelly and Father Dave are right. All of the baptized are equally members of the Body of Christ. All are called to serve God and to make Jesus' presence known in the world. Father Dave is speaking of the true Catholic Church when he helps

people to understand that it is not the hierarchy alone that determines how the Good News will be shared with the world. Every Catholic has both the right and the responsibility of helping to shape the Church. On the other hand, the Magisterium is needed to ensure the unity of all of the individual efforts and to ensure that individual efforts do not separate Catholics from the essential truths revealed by Christ. Father Kelly is speaking with the voice of the true Catholic Church when he stresses the importance of knowing, understanding, and respecting the teachings of the Magisterium.

The Church Has a Permanent Ethic

In order to cope with the tremendous intermingling of different cultures and value systems, many North Americans have accepted the way of thinking which says that everything is relative. In other words, the view is held that there is no "right" way of relating to other people, no "right" religion, no "right" understanding of marriage and sexuality, any more than there is a "right" food, a "right" way to dress or a "right" type of music. In today's popular culture right and wrong are in the mind of the individual. Under this belief, each person follows his or her own conscience and respects the right of others to do the same.[20]

Catholic moral teaching agrees that we must respect the rights of others to follow their own conscience; God has given each one of us the freedom to choose between right and wrong, and we should do no less for one another.[21] Catholic moral teaching does not, however, agree that "right" and "wrong" are a matter of individual perspective. Fundamental to Catholicism is the belief that God is unchanging, and therefore there are certain things that have always been and will always be opposed to God. Certain behaviors always undermine our relationship with God and with God's people regardless of our

permanent ethic—Those moral teachings which are essential corollaries of the Church's understanding of God revealed in Jesus.

reasons for doing them. Rejecting God and God's plan for the world is always wrong and will always have negative consequences both for the individual and for his or her community, both local and global.

There are some elements of Catholic moral teaching which can never be changed, no matter how much the world changes. This is the meaning of the statement that the Church has a **permanent ethic**. This is because certain moral teachings are essential formulations of our understanding of the God who was revealed in Jesus. For example, we believe that every single human being has value because every single human being is made in the image and likeness of God. When human nature was permanently joined to the divine in the Incarnation of Jesus, the dignity of human life was underscored. In choosing to become human, to be born and to die, Christ revealed that human life has value from the moment of conception until death. Because of this basic belief, the Church is not free to decide that some human lives have ceased to have value. Similarly the Church does not have the right to decide that sexual behavior is morally neutral and therefore something that the Church should not comment on. Because in our sexuality we are offered the role of co-creators with God, we believe that our sexuality is a gift from God. The way we use our sexuality shapes the world. The Church has a responsibility for teaching and encouraging people to use their sexuality in a

way that is compatible with God's revealed intention for the world.

We are a Church made up of sinners. We recognize that throughout history many Catholics "have been disloyal to the Spirit of God."[22] The Church has not always upheld its own moral teaching. During historical periods such as the Inquisitions and the Crusades, the Church violated some of the basic principles of its ethic. Pope Leo X went so far as to claim that the burning of heretics was completely in accord with the will of God. Nonetheless, an ethic rooted in a belief in God's love for all people has never ceased to exist, and it has been passed on even through the darkest times of Church history.

Responsibilities to the Church's Permanent Ethic

The permanent ethic is part of what defines Catholicism. By definition, it is impossible to be a Catholic and to reject the permanent ethic of the Church just as it is impossible to be a Catholic and to reject the notion of a Church with a pope and bishops. It is the responsibility of the Magisterium to give voice to the permanent ethic of the Church. Every Catholic is responsible for learning and embracing this ethic. If a person knowingly rejects all or part of the permanent ethic of the Church; that is, if a person knowingly rejects all or part of the moral order which has been revealed by Jesus and chooses some other arbitrator of right and wrong; that person puts him or herself outside of the Catholic Church. On the other hand, if a person accepts the permanent ethic of the Church but rejects the Magisterium's interpretation of that ethic with regard to a specific set of circumstances, that person is not automatically separated from the Church.

The Magisterium not only gives voice to the permanent ethic of the Church, it is also responsible for observing and evaluating the common practices of the day in light of that ethic. It is the Magisterium's role to guide the faithful as it determines the behavior appropriate to specific situations. Every Catholic is called to pay close attention to the Magisterium's interpretation of the permanent ethic in light of specific current circumstances; however, there may be instances when a person, even after careful study, reflection, and prayer, accepts the permanent ethic of the Church but believes that putting that ethic into practice means behaving in a way that goes against a specific teaching of the Magisterium. This person may or may not be sinning, but he or she has not ceased to be Catholic.[23]

Even as we are called to give careful attention to the directives of the Magisterium, we are also to respectfully challenge the Magisterium when necessary. We must share with the Magisterium and with the rest of the body the experience, wisdom, and knowledge which are unique to our own segment of the Body. When various members of the Body ignore the teachings of the Magisterium, the Body acts like a person suffering from a severe spastic disorder who is unable to function in a coordinated manner. On the other hand, when members of the Body follow the directives of the Magisterium blindly without taking any responsibility for sharing their own wisdom and insight, it is like a body suffering from leprosy, with no sensation coming from the hands or feet to warn of problems or dangers. The Magisterium has the final authority for interpreting the permanent ethic of the Church which has been handed down to us through Scripture and Tradition. However, every member of the body of Christ is called to support and aid the Magisterium in carrying out this task.

The mystery of the Church can be seen in its moral teaching. The **hierarchy** and the laity work together to preserve a permanent ethic and to give it life. In a world in which wrong choices can blind us to the difference between right and wrong, the mystery of the Church lies in the fact that she has not lost sight of the "right" which was revealed by Jesus. The mystery of the Church is revealed in the fact that she has preserved an ethic rooted in love even through the darkest periods of her own history. Despite the sinful nature of some of her members, the Church has not allowed the ethic which she received from Jesus to be swallowed up by secular culture. In the permanence of the Church's ethic, the hidden presence of the eternal, unchangeable God is revealed.

DISCIPLESHIP

When Jesus chose the apostles, he gave them a mission. He also set the conditions of discipleship. Read Matthew 10:1–43. Then write ten goals you have for living your life as a disciple of Christ.

hierarchy—The structural order of leaders within the Church. The term is commonly used to refer to all of the ordained ministers in the Church: the pope, bishops, priests, and deacons.

permanent dogma—Those absolute truths which were revealed by Christ and are so essential to Christian faith that their essence can never be changed.

Once again Father Kelly is right when he speaks about the importance of listening to the teachings of the Magisterium on issues of morality. Once again Father Dave is right when he invites people to discuss issues of morality and when he says that their experience is relevant. The wisdom of the Magisterium's teachings is revealed most clearly in dialogue with human experience. All truth comes from God; therefore we must trust that if we are honestly attentive to both, the truth which the Magisterium speaks and the truth of human experience will be revealed to be the same truth. We cannot ignore the Magisterium's teachings but we also should not try to suppress or ignore human experience. It is not as if once the Magisterium has spoken the laity have nothing to contribute.[24]

The Church Has a Permanent Body of Dogma

"No one has a right to tell me what to believe."

"Everyone should be able to believe whatever they want."

"What I believe doesn't affect anyone but me; so it isn't anyone else's business."

"Church leaders are no better than me. I'm just as much a part of the Church as they are. Why should I believe something just because they tell me to?"

These and similar statements are often heard as soon as the subject of dogma is raised. Many people in our society rebel at the idea that there are certain things

which they must believe, and that there are certain things that are absolute and not a matter of individual choice. And yet, the Catholic Church insists that there are absolute truths.

Catholic theology teaches that there is a **permanent body of dogma** within the Church. That is, there are certain absolute truths which must be accepted because they have been revealed to us by Jesus and will never change. Furthermore, Catholic theology says that our knowledge of these truths allows us to infer other truths, both positive and negative, which we also must accept. If we fail to accept and live in accordance with these truths, we have separated ourselves from the Body of Christ—the Church.

The Church's understanding of truth and the development of dogma will be presented in greater detail in Unit 4. At this point it will suffice to say that it is the role of the Magisterium to help us understand that if we structure our lives around certain beliefs we will reveal God's presence to the world, and if we structure our lives around certain other beliefs we will be in danger of obscuring the presence of God in the world.

It is the task of the Magisterium to study the truths of faith which have been handed down to us through the ages, and to interpret those truths for the present generation. In carrying out this task the Magisterium speaks with one voice which unites people from all places, cultures, and walks of life. The Church is called to listen to the teachings of the Magisterium and to give them an assent of faith. In other words, as Catholics, we are called to do our best to structure our lives around those beliefs which the Magisterium has proclaimed to be true. Catholic faith is not the faith of a few individuals or groups, but of the whole body of Christ. That is why it is necessary for the entire Church to give heed to the teachings of the Magisterium.

STUDY QUESTIONS

- WHAT IS THE CONSTITUTION OF THE CHURCH?
- WHAT IS THE MAGISTERIUM?
- WHAT IS THE MAGISTERIUM'S ROLE IN INTERPRETING SCRIPTURE AND TRADITION?
- GIVE ONE EXAMPLE OF HOW THE PRESENCE OF THE MAGISTERIUM WITHIN THE CATHOLIC CHURCH HAS SERVED NON-CATHOLIC CHRISTIANS.
- WHAT ARE THE RESPONSIBILITIES OF SOMEONE WHO DISAGREES WITH THE MAGISTERIUM?
- WHY IS IT IMPOSSIBLE FOR CERTAIN MORAL TEACHINGS TO CHANGE?
- WHAT IS THE ROLE OF THE MAGISTERIUM WITH REGARD TO MORAL BEHAVIOR? WHAT IS THE ROLE OF THE LAITY?
- WHAT DOES YOUR KNOWLEDGE OF ABSOLUTE TRUTHS HELP YOU TO DO?

IN CONCLUSION

The Church is a mystery because it is the culmination of Salvation History. The Church is the permanent union of the divine and the human, and the permanent physical presence of God on earth. The Church is the Body of Christ which is in history and which also transcends history. Because the Church is human, she is in history; she is affected by history, and she must change in response to history. Because the Church is divine, she transcends history; she has aspects which are permanent and which will not change no matter how much the world changes. The aspects which do not change are what make it possible for the Church to be the Body of Christ and to function as the Body of Christ: the Church's basic structure (or constitution), her permanent ethic, and her permanent body of dogma.

The Church will always be an institution with a hierarchy. Often people talk as if one had to choose between belief in an institutional Church and belief in a Church which is truly a mystical body. In fact it is the institutional structure of the Church which facilitates the union of individuals in a mystical body. It is the Church's hierarchy— especially the pope and bishops—which enables the Church to function as one body.

Finally, God has given the Church a permanent ethic and a permanent body of dogma, a body of revealed truths around which we must structure our lives. The basic nature of the Church and the way in which she relates to the world are determined by the truths which God has revealed. If the dogma and moral teaching of the Church were to change and to become something other than what God has revealed, the Church would cease to be the Body of Christ.

LEARN BY DOING

Read and report on one recent pope. Use the Vatican website and this link at www.vatican.va/holy_father/index.htm.

Cover the following:

- biographical information on the pope,
- an itinerary of his travels,
- a summary of at least three of his teachings.

PRAYER

May the eyes of your hearts be enlightened, that you may know what is the hope that belongs to his call, what are the riches of glory in his inheritance among the holy ones, and what is the surpassing greatness of his power for us who believe, in accord with the exercise of his great might, which he worked in Christ, raising him from the dead and seating him at his right hand in the heavens, far above every principality, authority, power, and dominion, and every name that is named not only in this age but also in the one to come.

—Ephesians 1:18–21

NOTES

1. The names of the people and the parish in this story have been changed.
2. See *Catechism of the Catholic Church*, #771.
3. During certain periods of history non-Christians were tortured and killed in the name of Christ and the Church. This does not mean that Christ and/or the Church were evil at certain times in the past. It does mean that members of the Church were "disloyal to the Spirit of God" (*Gaudium et Spes*, #43). They used the name of Christ and the name of the Church to justify things that go against the very nature of Christ and the Church. In other words, they blasphemed. To abandon the Church or Christ because of the behavior of blasphemers is to accept the blasphemy as true.
4. See The Congregation for Divine Worship, "The Decree on the Rite of Christian Initiation of Adults," *The Rites of the Catholic Church* (New York: Pueblo Publishing Co., 1976), #38.
5. See *Catechism of the Catholic Church* #760.
6. See *Centesimus anno*, #37 and #51
7. The *Catechism of the Catholic Church*, #772 says, "It is in the Church that Christ fulfills and reveals his own mystery as the purpose of God's plan: 'to unite all things in him.'"
8. See *Lumen Gentium*, #8.
9. See *Gaudium et Spes*, #45
10. See *Lumen Gentium*, #14–15 and *Catechism of the Catholic Church*, #846–847.
11. See *Catechism of the Catholic Church*, #796
12. See 1 Corinthians 7:4.
13. See *Lumen Gentium*, #5.
14. See *Dei Verbum*, #4, 8.
15. See *Gaudium et Spes*, #4.
16. See Luke 22:24–30 and *Lumen Gentium*, #27.
17. See *Lumen Gentium*, #20.
18. See *Catechism of the Catholic Church*, #2033
19. Two examples of this would be the importance of ritual and an deep appreciation for the central role of Mary in Salvation History.

20. See Reginald W. Bibby and Donald C. Posterski, *Teen Trends: A Nation in Motion* (Toronto: Stoddart Publishing Co., Ltd., 1992), pp. 175–179.

21. We will consider the role of conscience in Catholic teachings in more detail in Unit 4.

22. *Gaudium et Spes*, #43.

23. What does this mean in practical terms? Let us consider a simple example. God has established marriage for the mutual support and love of the spouses and for the procreation and nurturing of children. This is a truth which has been revealed by God and is part of the permanent ethic of the Catholic Church. Any person who would claim that marriage and procreation or the raising of children are fundamentally separate and unrelated, is rejecting the Catholic understanding of family and community which are at the heart of Catholic life. Such a person has separated him or herself from the Church. On the other hand, a person who recognizes that one of the primary purposes of marriage is procreation and yet chooses to use birth control is certainly sinning in the eyes of the Church, but he or she has not separated from the Church.

24. Once again an historical example may help to illustrate the point. In 1864, out of a desire to protect and preserve Catholic belief in the truth of Catholicism, Pius IX condemned many elements of modern political society including freedom of the press and freedom of religion. It was the voice of human experience that eventually led the bishops at the Second Vatican Council to speak in support of these freedoms not because they rejected the goals or concerns of Pius IX but because they had come to believe that the very freedoms he condemned can in fact underscore the truth of Catholicism.

THEREFORE EVERY SCRIBE WHO HAS BEEN TRAINED FOR THE KINGDOM OF HEAVEN IS LIKE THE MASTER OF A HOUSEHOLD WHO BRINGS OUT OF HIS TREASURE WHAT IS NEW AND WHAT IS OLD.

—*Matthew 13:52*

FROM ALL SIDES OF THE CIRCLE

There is a way of teaching about God in some Native American communities that is known as "teepee" teaching. When the students are all sitting in a circle, an elder walks to the center and stands very still with her hands held close to her sides. The elder then asks a student on her right to describe the position of the fingers on her (the elder's) left hand. Since the student cannot see the elder's left hand, he can do what the elder has asked only if he first gets

information from someone who is on the other side of the circle. The elder then explains that this is how it is with God. God stands in the center of creation and we stand on its edges. Each one of us can see only "one side" of God. We must rely on others who sit in different places in the circle of creation if we wish to come to know God more completely.[1]

Crusades—The nine armed expeditions by Christians beginning in 1095 and ending in 1291 which were intended to drive the Muslims out of the Holy Land and in the process reunite Christians of East and West.

Applying this lesson to our broader experience, our understanding of God is limited not only by such things as our nationality and our culture, but also by our time in history. God stands outside of time; for God the past, the present, and the future are all the same. God is not changed by time; nor is God's call to us changed by time. On the other hand, our perception of God and our understanding of God's call do change with time. We, unlike God, stand within time. Our perspective is limited to the present, and the way we understand God is limited by the thought categories of our own period in history. Although we see and know the same God that our ancestors saw and knew, we see and know him very differently. In order to understand God more completely we must listen not only to the voices of other people in our own time, but also to the voices of our ancestors in faith.

Sometimes we would prefer to ignore or disown the voices of history, the voices of the Catholic Church of the past. There are moments in Church history which seem incomprehensible or horrible to us today on first inspection. Nonetheless, we must acknowledge that both our Church and our faith have been shaped by Catholics from every period in history, even those times which rightly make us uncomfortable—like the **Crusades** or Inquisitions. Furthermore, we should admit that we have something to learn from Catholics of every period of history. If we listen carefully to the voices of faith from every age—especially the voice of the Holy Spirit—we can develop a more complete understanding of what it means to be the Church.

Whether it is at its best or at its worst, the Church is both divine and human. This means that even when the Church is at her worst, she can provide us with glimpses of divine perfection; and even when she is at her best, the Church is not completely free from the influences of sin. It is only when we look honestly at the history of the Church that we can really begin to understand what this means. Knowledge of our past can keep us from arrogantly assuming that if the Church does something she must be right. Knowledge of our past can also bolster our faith that the Church is more than a human institution, and will always have a voice that is different from the voices of the secular world. Knowledge of our past can give us a better understanding of both sin and grace within the Church, and can make us less likely to repeat past sins and more likely to embrace grace.

The Church is a mystery because it is both part of the world and tempted by sin, and apart from the world and shaped by grace. This tension is created as the Church tries to make God visible and relevant to the secular world. The various images that have been used to describe the Church are all attempts to explain how the Church is relevant to the world and at the same time separate from the world. As we study the history of the Church we begin to see how these different images have shaped and continue to shape the lives of Catholics.

The focus in chapter 2.1 was on the ways that the Church remains unchanging even as the world around it changes dramatically. In this chapter we will focus on the ways in which the Church changes with history and the ways in which those very changes can help us to understand the permanent and unchanging mystery which is the Church. Pope John XXIII was known to refer to history as "the teacher of life." The history of the Church can teach us how to be the living Church today.

One Church, Many Viewpoints

In **Scripture** and throughout history a variety of images have been used to describe the Church. For example, the Old Testament images point us toward a deeper understanding of the Church as the "chosen People of God." In the New Testament, Christ is described as the head of this Chosen People; he has united God's People in himself and made them his Body on earth. The Church as the "Body of Christ" is its central and most complete image. Every other image of the Church—for example, a cultivated field or a city, a spotless spouse, or beloved bride—must be understood in light of the primary image of the Body of Christ. These secondary images are valuable for helping us to understand more fully what it means to be part of the Body of Christ and to make

Scripture—Literally, the "writings." The term Scripture is used to refer to those books which have been determined by the Church to be the Word of God and to be normative for faith and morals.

Christ's presence visible and tangible in the world. These images can become distorted and harmful when they are separated from the central image of the Body of Christ.

As we look back over the history of the Church we see that in different periods of history different images that express the Church's mystery seemed to dominate Church life. The events and attitudes of each period can help us to understand both the richness and the potential dangers of the image which dominated it. Several of these images will be explored in the sections that follow.

STUDY QUESTIONS

- WHAT IS THE CENTRAL IMAGE OF THE CHURCH?
- HOW DO ALL OTHER IMAGES OF THE CHURCH RELATE TO THIS IMAGE?

JOURNAL ASSIGNMENT

- IN WHAT WAYS IS YOUR OWN VIEW OF GOD LIMITED?
- HOW DO YOU RELY ON OTHERS TO HELP YOU TO BETTER UNDERSTAND GOD?

A CHOICE VINEYARD

The Second Vatican Council document, *Lumen Gentium*, describes the Church as a "cultivated field." The text goes on:

> On that land the ancient olive tree grows whose holy roots were the prophets and in which the reconciliation of Jews and Gentiles has been brought about and will be brought about again. That land, like a choice vineyard, has been planted by the heavenly cultivator. Yet the true vine is Christ who gives life and fruitfulness to the branches, that is, to us, who through the Church remain in Christ, without whom we can do nothing (Lumen Gentium,⁶).

Tracing the history of God's People helps us to understand more about this image.

When Israel was a tiny nation of people recently released from slavery, it was not too difficult to understand what being "chosen" by God meant. YHWH had freed the people and YHWH would ensure their survival. Likewise, when Israel was a small nation defeating more powerful enemies and later became a more powerful nation governed by a mighty king, it was not too difficult to understand what being chosen by God meant. But when Israel was a conquered and occupied land whose glory and prestige were little more than memories, it was much more difficult to understand what it meant to be a Chosen People. Furthermore, it also became increasingly difficult for the Jews to identify what it meant to be a *separate* people. As the period of foreign occupation grew longer, the pressures to assimilate and identify with those in power increased in some areas while the resistance to and fear of assimilation increased in other areas.

Thus during Jesus' lifetime there was a great deal of disagreement among Jews in Roman occupied Palestine concerning the meaning of being chosen by God, and the essential characteristics of God's Chosen People. The question that had to be answered was, "What is the proper relationship between the Chosen People and the rest of society?" This question had been asked in Israel since the Greeks under Alexander the Great conquered Palestine in the fourth century BC.

Part of the Greek policy for dealing with the people of conquered lands was to combine Greek customs and practices with the customs and practices of the people of the conquered territory. This included a policy of equating and mixing the gods of different nations. In other words, the Greeks allowed Jews to worship YHWH, though they considered YHWH to be a Greek god under a different name. To the Greeks, there was no point in arguing about which religion worshipped the true God; all worshipped the same God or gods, just under different names and in different ways.

This form of **religious syncretization** continued in Palestine when the Romans conquered the land in 63 BC. The Jews found it wholly unacceptable. To the Jews, YHWH was the one, true God. YHWH could not be seen as just one of the gods of the Greek Pantheon, even if described as the greatest god. Most Jews agreed that if they accepted the policy of religious syncretization it would be the equivalent of denying their God altogether. All Jews were not agreed, however, on what degree of assimilation short of equating gods would be acceptable. From the time of Alexander's conquest until the destruction of Jerusalem in AD 70 there was a constant struggle within Judaism between pressures to adopt the customs and culture of the rest of the empire and a desire to remain faithful to YHWH.

→ engraving of Alexander the Great by J. Chapman

religious syncretism—The attempt to reconcile or blend the beliefs and practices of various religions into one.

Hellenistic (Greek) rule was inaugurated by Alexander the Great. His sweeping conquests brought Greek culture to each new place he conquered. He died prematurely at the age of thirty-three at Babylon in 323 BC.

THE CHURCH: OUR STORY

Sadducees—Another of the religious groups of Jews in Jesus' day. The Sadducees were religiously conservative. They rejected all religious teaching which was not from the Torah, including belief in the resurrection of the dead. They were willing to accept many elements of Roman culture.

Pharisees—One of the four main religious groups of Jews in Jesus' day. The faith of the Pharisees was based on scripture and on Jewish oral tradition. The Pharisees believed that faith should shape everyday life. They were particularly concerned with making Judaism relevant under Roman rule.

Essenes—The strictest of the four main Jewish groups of Jesus' day. The Essenes lived celibately, interpreted every law in the strictest possible way, and separated themselves from all who did not live as they did.

Jewish Sects in the First Century

By the time of Jesus' ministry in the first century, there were at least three distinct Jewish sects, each of which understood faithfulness to God in a slightly different way.

The **Sadducees** were primarily members of the Jewish aristocracy who continued to hold positions of power even under Roman rule. For the Sadducees, the Temple was the focal point of all Jewish life. They believed that their identity as God's Chosen People was dependent upon maintaining the cultic purity of the Temple and a specific, narrow set of religious beliefs, such as a rejection of the concepts of angels and the resurrection of the dead.

The **Pharisees**, on the other hand, were a sect concerned not only with what people believed and how they worshipped, but also with how they lived from day to day. Their primary concern was to make the Jewish faith relevant even under Roman rule. They wanted to make it clear to Roman authorities that even though they were not in power, the Jewish

people still maintained an identity and a moral code that was different from those around them.

The **Essenes**, like the Pharisees, believed that Jewish faith and identity involved every aspect of life and not only those aspects which were specifically "religious." The Essenes, however, were far more extreme than the Pharisees. They separated themselves completely from all who did not live as they lived. They interpreted every law in the strictest way possible. The Essenes lived an ascetic life. They held all property in common and owned nothing unnecessary; if one person had two coats he was expected to give one away. Furthermore, all members of the community, whether married or single, were expected to live celibately.

It is possible that John the Baptist was influenced or even a member of the Essene sect. John lived an ascetic life as did the Essenes.

Most members of the Essene community appear to have been opposed to war. There were, however, some Essenes who were also Jewish **zealots**. The zealots believed that God had chosen Israel to be a great and powerful political entity. According to the zealots, it was God's will that the Jewish people fight and overthrow the Roman oppressors. Because they were "chosen," the belief went, they would succeed.

It is within the context of a Judaism defined and disputed by these groups that Jesus lived and taught, and that the early Church began. Initially, no one seems to have thought of Christianity as a new or distinct religion. Christian and non-Christian Jews and **Gentiles** all appear to have regarded Christianity as one more Jewish sect. The earliest Jewish Christians believed that their faith was the fulfillment of Judaism. They still kept the Jewish sabbath on the seventh day of the week and added a celebration of the resurrection Sunday.

Also, Christianity expanded throughout the Roman empire because of the presence of Jewish communities within every major city of the empire. These Jewish communities maintained strong ties to Palestine. As Jewish Christian merchants traveled to these places, they shared the good news of the "new way" (one of the earliest names for Christianity). St. Paul, known as the "Apostle to the Gentiles," used this network of Jewish communities to aid his mission of evangelization.

Non-Christian Jews viewed Christianity as heretical and as something that could destroy the essence of Judaism. Vicious disputes arose between Jewish Christian and non-Christian Jews. In fact the dispute between Christian and non-Christian Jews became so disruptive that many scholars cite it as the reason that all Jews, Christian and non-Christian alike, were expelled from Rome in the first century.

It was only gradually, as the number of Gentile converts to Christianity increased and as Jewish nationalism increased, that the link between Judaism and Christianity disappeared. But before it did, an image of the Church that was rooted in the Jewish tradition and practice was firmly established.

JESUS AND THE JEWISH SECTS

Research and report on one of the Jewish religious sects active in Jesus' time—the Pharisees, Sadducees, Essenes, or zealots. Include the following information:

· main beliefs of the sect that distinguished it from other elements of Judaism

· at least one New Testament reference

· Jesus' interaction with the sect

· Christian beliefs or practices shared with the sect

zealots—Jews living in Jesus' time who believed that God called them to overthrow the Roman government in Palestine.

Gentiles—A term for non-Jews.

Justin the Martyr was one of the early Christian apologists who defended the faith against the hostile attitudes of the Roman government. He was killed in Rome around 165 AD under the prefect Rusticus.

Grafted to the Vine of Christ

Of all the first century Jewish sects, the Christians most closely identified with the Pharisees, since membership in the early Church also involved a radical dependence on God. Perhaps the image which most clearly describes the Church's self-understanding in the biblical period is that of a vineyard planted by God and grown from a single true vine (John 15:1ff). This understanding was thoroughly Jewish in character. The prophet Isaiah had spoken of Israel as the vineyard which was left to grow wild until it eventually would die back to no more than a stump. According to Isaiah, from that stump, a new shoot would sprout and the messianic age would be ushered in (Isaiah 5–11). Christians believed that a new shoot had sprouted in Jesus, the true vine. The Church was the new vineyard. This new vineyard, however, was unlike the old in one important way. It would never go wild and produce what God did not desire because God himself, in the person of Jesus Christ, was its root stock and main vine. All the shoots (people) of the vineyard drew their life from Jesus.

The image of the Church as the vineyard of God helped answer the question of how Gentiles could become members of God's Chosen People without first becoming Jews. They could be "grafted" to the vine of Christ. The image also served as a reminder that everything Christians do must be directly rooted in Christ or it will have no life and no meaning. This principle was crucial during the initial development of the Church. In the early years of the Church people used Christ to justify and promote all types of behavior without making any attempt to connect those behaviors to Christ himself. According to some, Christ had set them free to do whatever they chose. According to others, the Spirit sent by Christ had given them a secret knowledge of right and wrong. The Church survived because its apostolic leaders drew their inspiration and teachings from the image of the vine and the branches and insisted upon a direct and demonstrable connection to Christ in what they said and did.

The vineyard image ceased to be a dominant image in the Church only as the Church moved farther from its Jewish origins and became less concerned with the relationship between Jewish and non-Jewish Christians. As new issues came to dominate Christian life, new images of the Church became more prominent.

STUDY QUESTIONS

- DEFINE RELIGIOUS SYNCRETISM.
- EXPLAIN THE DIFFERENCES IN HOW THE PHARISEES, SADDUCEES, ESSENES, AND ZEALOTS UNDERSTOOD THEIR ROLE AS GOD'S CHOSEN PEOPLE.
- HOW DID THE PRESENCE OF JEWISH COMMUNITIES THROUGHOUT THE ROMAN EMPIRE HELP CHRISTIANITY TO EXPAND?
- HOW DID AN UNDERSTANDING OF THE CHURCH AS THE VINEYARD OF GOD SHAPE THE LIFE OF THE EARLY CHURCH?

JOURNAL ASSIGNMENT

- WRITE YOUR OWN DESCRIPTION OF THE CHURCH AS A VINEYARD. OR, DRAW AN IMAGE THAT REPRESENTS CHRISTIANS AS GRAFTED TO THE VINE OF CHRIST.

THE DWELLING PLACE OF GOD

The Church is also called the *building* of God—the house in which God's family dwells. The Church is the place where God dwells with humankind. This image represented the Church well in the first three centuries when Christians were shunned or persecuted in the Roman empire. Yet the Church continued to attract new members. If we are to understand the Church of this period, there are two questions which we need to answer.

First, why were Christians hated and persecuted?

And second, what was it about the Church that continued to attract new members despite this widespread abhorrence?

Christians were despised for many reasons. A common belief of the time was that Christianity was antisocial; some went so far as to call it barbaric and cannibalistic. Christians were considered antisocial for many of the same reasons that Jews were. Christians, like Jews, refused to participate in many social events because they involved worship of the Roman gods. They would not go to the gymnasium or attend the theater. Many refused to attend banquets or eat food purchased in the market which had first been sacrificed to idols.

The stories of barbarism and cannibalism were largely based in wild rumors. For example, it was widely known that Christians gathered every week to celebrate an agape or "love feast" to which only the baptized were admitted. It was also known that all Christians called all other Christians, even their spouses, "brother" and "sister." From these two facts, rumors spread that Christians met for regular orgies. And, since Christians spoke of being nourished by the Body and Blood of Christ, stories circulated that Christians cut and ate from a loaf of bread with the newborn Christ child concealed inside. Though Christian writers pointed out that these rumors were ridiculous and incompatible with the way in which Christians lived, the rumors persisted among the uneducated.

Among the learned Roman citizens, Christianity was rejected for being "intellectually wanting." Some of this criticism was rooted in class prejudice. Christianity could not be a very profound religion, it was held, if it could be taught by so many who were without culture or education. Some (including St. Augustine before he became a Christian) rejected

Though worship of Roman emperors was more patriotic than religious, Christians found such worship incompatible with allegiance to Christ.

Christianity because Scripture was "poorly written" and showed a lack of literary finesse.

Most of the detractors of Christianity, however, focused on what they saw as the laughable nature of the Christian God. The detractors wondered why, for example, Christians seemed afraid of anything connected with worship of the Roman gods if they believed that those gods were false and impotent? Didn't their fear prove the fragility of their own God? How could there be any logic to accepting martyrdom and leaving this life which was certain to go to another which was uncertain? And, how could anyone take the resurrection of the body seriously? They cited Christ's Death as proof that the Christian God was hardly "all-powerful" as claimed. Questions and arguments went on in this vein as scholars tried to demonstrate that Christianity had logical inconsistencies and therefore could not be true.

Many of the earliest Christian doctrines were developed as Christian apologists responded to these and similar critiques. Unit 4 traces the development of many of these doctrines.

Christian Persecutions

The objection to Christianity with the most serious consequences for Christians came from those who believed that the Roman gods were angered as more and more Roman citizens abandoned their old faith and became Christians. Many of the worst and most systematized persecutions of the Christians were rooted in a belief that Christianity was nothing short of treason. Christians were blamed for all of the misfortunes of the empire, ranging from floods and epidemics to military invasions. Although Christians tried to demonstrate that they were good citizens, they had no real answer to the charge that they had angered the Roman gods.

Because of the tenuous position of Christians in the empire, in the first three centuries Christians were often persecuted and put to death. The severity of these persecutions, however, varied considerably from decade to decade and from region to region. The persecution of Christians in the city of Rome under the emperor Nero (AD 64–68) was extremely cruel. Christians were not just killed, they were tortured in a wide variety of ways to provide entertainment for the populace. On the other hand, through most of the second century, although Christianity was outlawed, Christians were not sought out for persecution. They were

only punished if someone specifically brought them before the courts. In the first half of the third century Christians were rarely persecuted for their faith. But then in

The emperor Nero blamed a large fire in Rome in AD 64 on the Christians, deflecting the rumor of arson from himself. Hundreds of Christians were tortured and killed in the Vatican gardens after this incident.

AD 249 Decius came to power. He believed that many of Rome's problems were punishments because people had stopped worshipping the old gods and those gods had responded by abandoning Rome. Decius enacted a law that required everyone to offer sacrifices to the gods of the empire. Any who did not have a certificate to prove that they had offered the necessary sacrifices were to be shunned and treated as outlaws with no rights. Decius did not want to kill the Christians outright because he believed that martyrs only attracted more people to Christianity.

By the end of the third century Christians were rarely being threatened. But then a controversy erupted involving the military. Church leaders began to teach that Christians should not be part of the military. In approximately AD 295 a number of Christians were killed for refusing to join or for attempting to leave the army. The emperor became convinced that Christians were a threat to the army and he ordered that all Christians should be expelled from the Roman legions. Rather than see their ranks dwindle, many officers tried to force Christians to abandon their faith. Those Christians who refused were executed.

In 303 an order was issued that Christians should be removed from all positions of responsibility and that all Christian buildings and books should be destroyed. Some Christians were tortured and killed when they refused to hand over their copies of Scripture. When a fire broke out in the imperial palace, Christians were accused of setting it. Finally a decree was issued ordering the arrest of all Church leaders. A second decree ordered all Christians to offer sacrifice to the Roman gods under pain of death.

Despite the verbal and physical hostility aimed at Christians in the first four centuries, converted new Christians were not only religious, but in many places were quite open about their Christian identity. These Christians wanted to conquer the prejudice and misinformation which abounded and make it clear through the witness of their lives that they could be good citizens. One example of this can be found in the second century in Asia Minor. When a certain governor began to persecute Christians from the poor and lower classes, all of the Christians of the region—including those in positions of power—paraded in front of his home. They wanted to make it clear that the Christian faith was not something limited to a small group of social outcasts.[2]

The Appeal of Being Christian

What was it that made membership in the Christian Church attractive despite the obvious dangers? Of course a clear answer is "the power of the Holy Spirit." But since the Spirit works through human beings, the question should be probed a little deeper. The Christian Church offered the presence of a loving and caring God. Within the community of the Church, God's presence was a tangible reality. The Church was the "house of God in which his family dwells; the household of God in the Spirit; the dwelling-place of God among men. . . ."[3] Those living in the Roman empire experienced God's love which was given equally to all regardless of social standing. Christianity cut across social boundaries in a way that no other religion did.[4] Within the Church, women and slaves were considered as deserving of respect as free men. Women as well as men were understood to have rights in marriage, and men as well as women were expected to be faithful to their spouses. Furthermore, although according to Roman law slaves could not contract a legal marriage, within the Church a marriage involving a slave was considered as indissoluble as any other.

Also, Christians were noted for their kindness and their charity toward those who were in need. In a world that was often hostile and uncaring, in a world in which people had little control over their fate, Christians offered hope, love, and practical assistance in dealing with misfortune. People converted to Christianity even when it was punishable by death to do so, because they wanted to be in the presence of God and experience Christian charity.

From the beginning there was an expectation that life within the Church would be countercultural, reflecting God's standards, not human standards. Because of this, the process of becoming a Christian was a long one, usually extending over a period of several years. When people became Christians they committed themselves to living a life of generosity and love. They committed themselves to permanently avoiding sin.[5] They committed themselves to being part of a community that was the dwelling place of God, a community whose life together revealed God. What is more, Christians became known for living up to their commitments to such an extent that their numbers grew among people from all walks of life.

STUDY QUESTIONS

- WHAT WERE THE MAIN REASONS THE MAJORITY OF ROMAN CITIZENS REJECTED CHRISTIANITY?
- EXPLAIN THE CONTROVERSY INVOLVING CHRISTIANS AND THE MILITARY.
- WHY DID CHRISTIANITY REMAIN ATTRACTIVE TO SO MANY PEOPLE IN SPITE OF PERSECUTIONS?

JOURNAL ASSIGNMENT

- HOW DO YOU FIND YOUR LIFE AS A CHRISTIAN AS COUNTER-CULTURAL AMONG PEERS, NEIGHBORS, AND SOCIETY AT LARGE?

THE CITY OF GOD

The final and worst persecution of Christians occurred when Galerius was emperor of Rome. Galerius himself was the driving force behind the persecutions. He blamed Christians for all of the problems in the empire. Then in AD 311 Galerius was stricken with a very painful disease. Apparently he became convinced that his illness was a punishment from the Christian God, for in April of 311 he issued an edict stating that Christians would be allowed to practice their faith. A second edict demanded that in return for this tolerance Christians would be required to pray to their God for the well being of the emperor and the empire.

The persecution of Christians ended but Galerius died five days later. The Christian historian Lactantius voiced the belief of many Christians when he said that Galerius's repentance came too late.

Following Galerius's death, the Roman empire was divided among Licinius, Maximinus Daia, Constantine, and Maxentius. Constantine began a campaign to take control of the Empire. In a surprise attack Constantine marched on Rome, Maxentius's capital city. Although Constantine's forces were inferior, Maxentius was unable to defend his strongholds. He was forced to fall back to Rome with his troops. Then, rather than fight from within the well-fortified city, Maxentius chose to go out and fight.

With the prospect of a new battle looming, Constantine ordered his soldiers to place a Chi-Rho symbol on their shields and

IN THIS SIGN CONQUER

standards. In Greek *chi* and *rho* are the first two letters in the name Christ. According to two Christian historians who knew Constantine, this order was prompted by a revelation from God. Eusebius wrote that Constantine saw a vision of the Chi-Rho symbol in the sky along with the words "in this you shall conquer." Lactantius wrote that Constantine was told in a dream to place a Christian symbol on his soldiers' shields. At any rate, Constantine's army defeated Maxentius and Constantine became ruler of the entire western half of the Empire. After this Constantine formed a new alliance with Licinius. Part of their agreement was that all persecution of Christians would stop and all confiscated properties would be returned to the Christians.

Many have seen the use of the Chi-Rho symbol in the battle for Rome, and the subsequent Edict of Milan agreed upon by Constantine and Licinius as the signs of Constantine's conversion to Christianity. But the truth is, Constantine did not join the Church until he was on his death bed. For most of his life he continued to worship the

Constantine had a dream the night before the battle where he saw the first two letters of Christ's name with the words "By this sign you will conquer." He had the Chi-Rho painted on the helmet and shields of his soldiers.

Unconquered Sun, even as he showed respect for the Christian God. Nonetheless, from about AD 313 on Christianity became not only legal, but accepted.

Positive and Negative Results of Legalized Christianity

A downside of Christianity's legalization was that religion and secular politics began to be intermingled. Constantine came to think of himself as the bishop of bishops. He believed that he had the right to intervene in the life of the Church whenever he deemed it necessary. It was Constantine who called the ecumenical council at Nicaea because he was tired of the fighting among Church leaders and wanted certain issues settled once and for all. Many Christians saw the change in the official attitude toward Christianity as a sign of divine intervention. Their attitude is clearly expressed by the Church historian Eusebius who believed that Constantine had been chosen by God to help Christianity to develop fully. Many Christians who thought like Eusebius stopped focusing their hopes on Jesus' Second Coming and began to look at how the Kingdom could be effected in the present.

One of the results of this new attitude was a dramatic change in how Christians viewed wealth and possessions. In the first three centuries, the poor took precedence. One of the big theological concerns in those years had been how the rich could be saved. When Christianity became a state religion, concern for those in need no longer dominated Christian thought. Clerical positions became important political positions, and a clerical aristocracy with little connection to the poor began to develop. The distance between the clergy and the poor was underscored by

the building of large ornate churches and the adoption of "imperial protocol" within the liturgies; that is, many of the things which were used as signs of respect for the emperor, such as incense and specific gestures, began to appear within the Church liturgies. The images and symbols used in the Church also pointed to connections between God and those in power within the empire. For example, the image of Christ as a universal ruler (*pantokrator*) sitting on a throne much like the throne of the emperor became very popular.

The dominant image of the Church became that of the "city of God," a city that when described resembled the city of Rome. The city of God image for the Church described a Church with an established order and hierarchy. Laws and common codes of belief and behavior were central. This image allowed for a great deal of diversity within the Church, but it also underscored the need for significant points of unity in the form of a common philosophy and moral code. Whereas in the first three centuries of Christianity the Church had been a source of challenge for society at large, now the Church became the place where society flourished. Many things that had a place in culture now found their way into the Church.

This had both positive and negative effects. On the positive side, Christian leaders and Christian values became more imbedded in the public consciousness. On the negative side, many people sought Church membership only because they were seeking power and prestige. Furthermore, because change was occurring so rapidly, some of the societal attitudes and practices which were brought into the Church were not sufficiently reinterpreted and transformed by the message of Christ. A social stratification began to

In 330, Constantine transferred the capital of the Eastern empire to a city he constructed and named for himself, Constantinople. The religious consequences of this move would be significant.

develop in the Church paralleling that of society; the poor became increasingly disenfranchised and the rich were emulated.

Christianity's new focus did not go unnoticed by the common person. Although most welcomed the end of persecution, a significant number of Christians saw Constantine's conversion as a disaster. They believed that the Church was falling into **apostasy**. The narrow gate into the Kingdom of Heaven was becoming a wide highway. Baptism was no longer a commitment that might end in martyrdom; it was becoming a stop on the road to luxury. Because of this, thousands of Christians fled to the desert as Christ had done to take up the hermit life, embracing poverty. With this phenomena, two different images of Church began to exist side by side. Those in the desert continued to view the Church as the dwelling place of God, a place in which all must act as Christ acted. Those in the city saw the Church as the city of God in which different things were expected of different people. Those Christians who did not become hermits were nonetheless attracted by those in the desert. However, poverty and charity were no longer seen as Christian norms. Instead they were seen as commitments of a select few who lived these ideals in the name of the entire Church.

Symbol of Civilization, Protector of Order

From the fifth to the eighth centuries Europe was swept by a series of invasions. As various barbarian tribes overran the Roman Empire, the image of the Church as the city of God took on new importance. The intention of most of the tribes was for the most part not, as many Romans perceived it, to destroy civilization, but rather to participate in the benefits of civilization.[6] Many of the tribal leaders adopted the Christian faith of those they had conquered because that faith was both a sign and a means of civilization. When a leader converted, all of those under him also converted.

The Church was not only a symbol of civilization for the invaders. She was also the hope of many of the conquered. As Roman civilization crumbled, the Church became the guardian of order and justice.

Three incidents in particular underscore the growing importance of the papacy as the protector of hope and order. In AD 452 Attila the Hun invaded Italy. The road to Rome was open before him. There was no army to stop him and the western emperor was too weak and too poor to do anything. Pope Leo the Great left Rome and went to meet with Attila. After the meeting, Attila turned north and spared Rome. In a similar incident three years later, Pope Leo negotiated with the Vandals and kept their

THE RICHNESS OF POVERTY

Some of the great Christian saints who embraced monasticism also expressed their love for poverty. Read their words. Then write one paragraph on how it is possible for you to find richness in poverty.

The more you use moderation in your life, the more you are at peace, for you are not full of cares for many things.
—St. Anthony the Great

Poverty was not found in heaven. It abounded on earth, but man does not know its value. The Son of God, therefore, treasured it and came down from heaven to choose it for himself, to make it precious to us.
—St. Bernard

He is rich enough who is poor with Christ.
—St. Jerome

apostasy—A total denial of Christ and a disavowal of the Christian faith.

St. Gregory the Great was born into a wealthy family in Rome about 540. When his parents died, he converted their estate into a monastery. But he was only able to lead the monastic life for about four years before being elected pope.

army from burning the city. In the sixth century it was the Lombards who were united and poised to conquer all of Rome. At the time, floods had destroyed much of the Roman food supply and an epidemic had broken out in the city itself. Gregory the Great, a monk, worked with Pope Pelagius II to organize sanitation and food for those in need. Later reluctantly named pope, Gregory organized food distribution within the city of Rome, and oversaw the rebuilding of the city's aqueducts and defenses. He also negotiated a peace with the Lombards. Although he continued to think of himself as only a religious leader, he was, by default, the political leader of Rome, too.

STUDY QUESTIONS

- TRACE THE EVENTS THAT LED TO THE LEGALIZATION OF CHRISTIANITY IN THE ROMAN EMPIRE.
- NAME THREE WAYS THE PRACTICE OF CHRISTIANITY CHANGED AFTER THE EDICT OF MILAN.
- WHO CALLED THE FIRST ECUMENICAL COUNCIL? WHY?
- DURING THE BARBARIAN INVASIONS, HOW DID THE CHURCH HELP PRESERVE ORDER AND JUSTICE?

THE CHURCH AS A SHEEPFOLD

After the death of Gregory the Great the papacy lost some of its effectiveness as a moral leader. The emperors of the eastern empire in Constantinople began exerting their influence over the western Church as well. The popes became little more than puppets of the state. It was only when the east fell under Moslem rule that Constantinople and its emperors lost their control of the western Church.

About that same time, another image to describe the Church became most prominent. The Church was known as a "sheepfold," a place in which one was protected from the "wolves"

Purgatory—The final purification of all who die in God's grace and friendship but remain imperfectly purified. Purgatory is the final cleansing away of all sin and of all the consequences of sin.

of evil and damnation. As Roman civilization crumbled and Europe seemed to be slipping into anarchy, protection and security took the place of culture and learning as priorities in society. The Church was increasingly valued for her ability to be able to provide protection and security, not only for the dangers of this world, but for the uncertainties of the next world.

During the time of Pope Gregory the Great, the belief in **Purgatory** became firmly rooted in Catholic teaching. Pope Gregory was particularly concerned with how people could make amends to God for their sins. He reaffirmed the necessity of priestly absolution. He also encouraged the practice of offering Masses to assist those who were in Purgatory into Heaven. In a world where danger and punishment seemed to be everywhere, the Church offered its faithful protection from eternal suffering.[7]

The image of the Church as sheepfold was given a slightly different twist beginning in 800 when Pope Leo III crowned Charlemagne, king of the Franks, as emperor of the West at the Christmas Day Mass. Charlemagne came to use the Church for his own ends; in fact he appears at times to have thought of the Church as a branch of his government, passing a number of laws regarding the life of the Church. He used the Church as a means of subduing his enemies. Conquered people were given a choice of Baptism or death. Those who chose Baptism believed that they had angered their old gods and had no choice but to turn to the Christian God for protection, and to earn that protection by accepting the Christian God's leaders.

Charlemagne appointed bishops just as he appointed generals. He reiterated that Sunday was to be a day of rest and worship. He ordered that preaching be done in the language of the people. He made tithing mandatory and instituted the collection of tithes as a tax. He mandated monastic reform, decreeing that all monasteries should be brought into compliance with the Rule of Benedict. He supported a revival and reform of Church schools. Charlemagne saw the Church as a sheepfold which protected but also confined and controlled the sheep.

The image of the Church as sheepfold remained prominent through the Middle Ages as fear remained a constant presence, especially as the bubonic plague struck Europe in the fourteenth century. In many ways the Church offered lasting comfort, peace, and a sense of security to those who were afraid, as Jesus intended when he said,

> *But whoever enters through the gate is the shepherd of the sheep. The gatekeeper opens it for him, and the sheep hear his voice, as he calls his own sheep by names and leads them out. When he has driven out all his own, he walks ahead of them, and the sheep follow him, because they recognize his voice (John 10:2–4).*

When we look back on the Middle Ages we tend to see a Church whose primary focus was on death and arbitrary suffering. We neglect the fact that death and arbitrary suffering were the dominant images of life because of events outside of the Church's control. It was not the Church that created the prevailing sense of an angry and judgmental God, it was the events of the time. The Church responded by helping people find a way to trust, rely on, and respond to God even in the face of apparent chaos.

Charlemagne means "Charles the Great." He was the son of the Frankish king Pippin. By the time of his death, he had doubled his father's possessions. He extended Christianity by his conquest of the Saxons.

STUDY QUESTIONS

- WHY DID THE CHURCH'S IMAGE AS A SHEEPFOLD TAKE PROMINENCE?
- HOW DID CHARLEMAGNE ACT AS THE PROTECTOR OR GUARDIAN OF THE SHEEPFOLD?

JOURNAL ASSIGNMENT

- COMPARE YOUR IMAGES OF CHURCH WITH SOMEONE WHO DOES NOT SHARE YOUR SAME SOCIAL, CULTURAL, RACIAL, OR ECONOMIC EXPERIENCE.

A CULTIVATED FIELD

In all periods of history the good and the bad are inextricably mixed within the Church. This does not mean that the Church has ceased to be holy at any time, any more than the farmer's crop in the parable of the weeds among wheat (see Matthew 13:24–30) had ceased to be good. It does mean, however, that those within the Church must listen carefully to hear the voice of God in the midst of all the confusion. Our faith assures us that God's voice will always be present within the Church. It will be recognizable just as the good wheat in the field will be recognizable amidst the weeds.

The Church of the Middle Ages certainly fits the image of this cultivated field. Following Charlemagne's death the empire began to struggle. Trade was interrupted because of conflicts with the Arabs. Money almost stopped circulating. Kings and lords paid for services by giving

away land. The result was the development of **feudalism**, a strict division among social classes, nobility, clergy, and serfs who farmed the land. Europe became increasingly fragmented both politically and economically. The papacy itself became a prize fought over by various rival groups in Rome and the popes were accused of various corruptions. Church offices and Church property were frequently being used to further the ends of the rich and powerful. Things got so bad that in 897 Pope Stephen VI presided over what came to be known as the "cadaveric council." The body of a previous pope was disinterred, dressed in papal robes and exhibited on the streets. This dead pope was then tried and found guilty of a variety of crimes. His body was mutilated and thrown into the Tiber River.

Nonetheless, in the midst of all of this turmoil there were also strong pressures for reform. In 909 the monastery of Cluny was founded. The monastery was led by Berno, a monk who was well

feudalism—The governing system which prevailed in Europe in the Middle Ages in which a superior or lord granted land to a vassal in return for the services (primarily military) of that vassal. The vassal did not own the land but he did receive its income as long as he remained faithful to the lord he served. Under this system all land was owned by a few powerful people. The vast majority of the population worked the land in return for food, shelter, and protection.

known for his efforts to reform monasticism and restore adherence to the Rule of Benedict. Although Cluny began simply as a place where the Rule was actually followed, it soon became the center of a large monastic reform movement. After reforming and reordering hundreds of monastic communities many Cluniacs hoped for a general reform of the Church along similar lines.

A primary goal of the reformers was to free the Church from her obligations to kings and nobles. One way to do this was to put an end to simony (the buying and selling of Church positions). A second goal was to enforce clerical celibacy so that Church positions could not be hereditary and Church property could not be dissipated by heirs. The Cluniac reformers also stressed the importance of obedience within the Church. Just as according to the Rule of Benedict all monks were expected to be obedient to their superiors, the reformers believed that all of the faithful should be obedient to the pope.

Perhaps the weakest point in the Cluniac reform movement was in its attitude toward wealth. For although the reformers said that individual monks should not own property, they insisted on the right of the monastery and the Church to accumulate wealth for the glory of God and to aid in service to the poor. This accumulation of wealth and property, however, meant that abbots and bishops were powerful feudal lords. This in turn maintained the practice of simony and made Church involvement in politics almost unavoidable. Because of this flaw in the Cluniac movement, it was eventually replaced by other movements which were more insistent upon simplicity and poverty. The most well known of these was the Cistercian movement led in particular by St. Bernard of Clairvaux.

Efforts for Church reform also came from the papacy itself. In 1048 Bruno of Toul was offered the papacy by the emperor. He said that he would only accept it if the people and the clergy elected him. He then traveled to Rome as a barefoot pilgrim and was acclaimed by the clergy and the populace alike.[8] He took the name of Leo IX and embarked upon a series of reforms. The central elements of his reforms were the same as those of the monastic reforms: clerical celibacy and an end to simony. The efforts of these many reforms succeeded for the most part, but not without significant opposition.

War and Division

An attitude persisted in the Middle Ages that the time was coming when the wheat would be separated from the weeds, that is, non-Christians and Christian heretics from Christians in good standing. This is one of the reasons why, when Pope Urban II announced the First Crusade in 1095, so many were willing and anxious to join. The goal of the

One of the Cluniac reforms was the "Truce of God" begun in 1040. Its aim was to limit wars between nobles from Wednesday evening until Monday morning in memory of Christ's passion. It had only partial success.

Crusade was to "win Heaven" by taking back the Holy Land from the Muslims and by saving the Eastern (Byzantine) Church from the Muslim threat and thus facilitating possible unification between the east and west.

The crusaders saw themselves as the army of God, and the army of the apocalypse. Their job was to begin the final separation of the wheat and the weeds. The unmerited killing of Jews and Muslims was for them the beginning of that process.[9] The crusader's attitude led to action in Christian Europe as well. A crusade against heresy was begun in many parts of Europe. In 1209 noblemen from the north of France invaded the south to slaughter a Christian sect which believed that God's role as creator was shared by another power. In 1215 the Fourth Lateran Council established the Inquisition, declaring that every bishop was responsible for looking into any potential heresy within his diocese and destroying it.

Awareness of the cultivated field image of the Church helped people of the Middle Ages to maintain their faith in and commitment to the institution of the Church, in spite of the sins of Church leaders. However, there are two potential dangers in viewing the Church (or the world) as a cultivated field in which the wheat and the weeds—sin and grace—are intermingled. The first is that we will become indifferent to the presence of sin and may do nothing to challenge it. The second is that we may begin to think of ourselves as harvesters whose job it is to identify and destroy both sin and sinners.

STUDY QUESTIONS

- HOW DID THE CULTIVATED FIELD IMAGE APPLY TO THE CHURCH IN THE MIDDLE AGES?
- WHAT WERE SOME GOALS OF THE REFORMERS DURING THE MIDDLE AGES? WHAT WAS THE WEAKEST POINT OF THE REFORM MOVEMENT?

JOURNAL ASSIGNMENT

- EXPLAIN HOW YOU HAVE WORKED TO OVERCOME THE DANGERS ASSOCI-ATED WITH THE CULTIVATED FIELD IMAGE—INDIFFERENCE TO YOUR OWN SIN AND WILLINGNESS TO POINT OUT THE SINS OF OTHERS.

There were six Crusades, which were a political and religious disaster. The so-called Children's Crusade of 1212 was led by a pair of ten-year-olds. Groups of pre-teens set out for the Near East by foot. Most died on the way. Others were enslaved in Moslem countries.

ST. CATHERINE OF SIENA

At a time when women were usually considered vastly inferior to men, when women were almost never permitted to study, and when women were expected to follow the lead of men in everything, one thirty-year-old woman helped change the life of the Church.

St. Catherine was born in 1347 in Siena, Italy. She was the twenty-fourth of twenty-five children in a middle-class merchant family. At age sixteen Catherine took the Dominican habit and cloistered herself in her bedroom. She spent three years praying and fasting, eating just enough to survive. She left the room only for Mass and to go to confession. At the end of the three years she felt called to rejoin her family and the world. She began to tend the sick, especially those with the most repulsive diseases. She also ministered to the poor and to those who were in prison, in particular, those who had been sentenced to die.

In the summer of 1370 Catherine experienced a series of visions and a call to become actively involved in the public life of her world. She began to write letters to people of all walks of life, encouraging and/or chastising them to live their lives according to gospel principles. She entered into a correspondence with the princes and republics of Italy and she was often consulted by the papal legates. She began a concerted effort to convince Pope Gregory to return the papacy from Avignon (where it had been since 1309) to Rome. She also called upon him to reform the clergy and the administration of the papal states.

In June of 1376 Catherine volunteered and was sent as an ambassador from Florence to the Pope in Avignon. At the time Florence was under interdict. No priest was allowed to celebrate the sacraments in Florence, and no Christian was allowed to do business with a Florentine under pain of excommunication. For a variety of political reasons Catherine's attempts to negotiate a settlement were unsuccessful. She did, however, make a profound impression on Pope Gregory. He announced his intention to move the papacy back to Rome.

When the pope returned to Rome, Catherine returned to Siena and established a monastery of cloistered Dominican Sisters. She began having a series of mystical experiences which she wrote down in The Dialogue.

When trouble began bubbling up once again in Florence, the newly elected pope, Urban VI sent Catherine to mediate. Catherine negotiated with the people of the city during the day and dictated her book at night. In August an agreement was reached between Florence and the papacy and the interdict was lifted. Catherine returned to Siena.

Catherine was an enthusiastic supporter of Pope Urban and his efforts to reform the Church and care for the poor. Therefore it is not surprising that shortly after her return to Siena, Pope Urban once again called upon Catherine, this time to support him against the cardinals who had elected a second pope. Catherine went to Rome along with a group of her followers. She remained there for the rest of her life serving the poor, working for reform within the Church, and writing letters in support of Pope Urban to people from every walk of life.

OUR MOTHER

A chronology of the **Protestant reformation** is far too complex to totally cover here. Suffice it to say that by the time Pope Paul III convened the first session of the **Council of Trent** in 1545, the rift between Protestants and Catholics was permanent. Eventually the sessions of the Council led to a predominant image of the Church as mother, offering care and protection to her flock.

Although the reformation may have begun as a response to the corruption and abuses within the

Protestant reformation— An effort to reform the Catholic Church in the sixteenth century which led to the separation of large numbers of Christians from communion with Rome and with each other.

Council of Trent—The sixteenth century ecumenical council held in response to the challenges of the Protestant reformation. The Council clearly outlined Catholic doctrine on such matters as authority, sin and justification, and the role of Mary and the saints.

REFORM

The Council of Trent was part of the Catholic reformation, a period in history where the Church reflected on its words and actions and reformed them in the truth of Christ and the gospel.

Write a personal plan for reforming your own life in the following areas:

· Your relationship with your parents

· Your efforts in school work

· Your attitude toward people of other races, religions or cultures

· Your prayer life and relationship with God

Catholic Church, it rapidly became a movement challenging not only the abuses, but also significant elements of Catholic theology and practice.[10] Among the issues raised by the protesters were: the role of

the Bible in determining orthodox theology, the cause and nature of sin and justification or redemption, the number and nature of the sacraments, how liturgy is celebrated, the theology of Eucharist, the authority of the hierarchy, the proper relationship between the Church and the state, the role of Mary and the other saints, and the existence of free will. The Council of Trent (1545–1563) responded to the reformers by formalizing the Catholic position on all of these issues and making it clear that any who disagreed with the council's pronouncements were separated from the Church.

The Council of Trent had a more significant impact on the life

of the Catholic Church than any other event for the next four hundred years. The Council linked orthodoxy with uniformity, requiring Catholics everywhere to do and say the same things with respect to faith. This was in part a reaction against Protestantism which seemed to welcome and embrace diversity in both theology and worship.

Underlying many of the declarations of the Council of Trent was a fundamental belief that both ordained ministry and the hierarchical structure of the Church had been established by God and were absolutely necessary. This was a central element in the council's discussion on the role of Scripture. The council fathers rejected the assertion of Martin Luther, whose ninety-five theses initiated the reformation by saying that only Scripture (*sola scriptura*) was necessary. The Council said that Scripture and Tradition must both be considered for a proper understanding of theology.

According to the Council, the Tradition of the Church cannot be set aside. (Recall that the Tradition of the Church refers to the faith which was handed by Christ to his Apostles and by those apostles to their successors.) Scripture cannot be separated from Tradition, because scripture was part of the Tradition of the Church before it was Scripture; furthermore, it was the Church who decided that it would be considered Scripture. Scripture is a written account of the earliest understanding of the faith, and it is the core on which all subsequent understandings are built. Nonetheless, Tradition cannot be reduced to only what is in Scripture. The Council made it clear that, as it was in the beginning, so it continued to be: the Word of God must be interpreted by the Church, and more explicitly by the bishops of the Church in order that it might be properly understood and applied in each generation.

The Council further declared that the Latin translation of the Bible (the Vulgate) was to be considered the authoritative version of the Bible, because it was the translation which had been used by the Church for one thousand years and therefore was part of the Tradition.[11] With this declaration, the Council reinforced the idea of a "teaching Church" and a "learning Church." Lay people were part of the learning Church and were not to attempt to read and interpret Scripture for themselves, but should rely on the wisdom and knowledge of the bishops and priests—the teaching Church.

More Teachings of the Council of Trent

The Council of Trent also emphasized the importance of the hierarchy in the administration of the sacraments. The Protestant reformers had raised questions about the number and nature of the sacraments; for the most part, they had rejected all but Baptism and Eucharist. The Council of Trent decreed that there are Seven Sacraments and that the clergy have a significant and necessary role to play in all of them.

The Council reinforced the thinking of the day which distinguished between the power of ordination and the specific role as leader of a church. In the early Church a priest could only be ordained if he had been called by a particular local church community, and his ordination was understood in terms of his service to that church. By the eleventh century, however, ordination itself was understood to confer special powers on the man ordained, powers which were independent of the priest's role in the community. The Council also pointed out the distinction between the "priesthood of all believers" and the ordained priesthood. The Council stressed that even as Baptism changes one's character, ordination changes it further. Because of his ordination a priest is able to stand in the person of Christ and celebrate Eucharist. He has the power to speak the words which change the bread and wine into the Body and Blood of Christ. The priest has the power to offer the one, true sacrifice, the only sacrifice which is acceptable to God, the sacrifice of Jesus. The priest also has the power to stand in the person of Christ and speak words of forgiveness and healing. The emphasis on priestly powers gave the ordained a status in the Church that was higher than that of the laity and supported the claim that the laity should defer to the ordained in all religious matters.

The Council of Trent outlined the way that Catholics must live and the faith that they must profess. It declared marriages between Catholics and non-Catholics to be invalid. It established a list of forbidden books, and it established guidelines for the education and training of clergy, which was to occur in seminaries set apart from the rest of the faithful.

The Council of Trent created an Index of forbidden books to keep Catholics from radical and heretical ideas. Negatively, the Index kept Catholics from reading some important intellectual works and authors like Milton, Descartes, and Kant. The Index was formally abolished by Pope Paul VI in the 1960s.

The main image of the Church which emerges from the Council of Trent is that of the Church as "mother." In other words, the Church, through its leaders, will feed, educate, and protect her people. The Church will feed them the bread of life and teach them the truth about God, human nature, and salvation. The Church will also rescue them when they fall into sin and offer them protection from hell and damnation.

The Church's image as mother may have been necessary to move the Catholic Church beyond the Protestant reformation. The Catholic Church needed to offer a clear and unified response to the various theologies and practices of the reformers if she was to maintain a clear identity. The Council of Trent not only established the Church's response to the reformation, she also established who had the right to speak for the Church. Any who aligned themselves with the hierarchy were demonstrating their right to call themselves children of the Catholic Church.

The understanding of the Church as a mother who protected and cared for her children, and who also held all the right answers and solutions to her children's problems, also affected much of the Church's missionary work which was taking place simultaneously in the New World.

STUDY QUESTIONS

- NAME THE MAIN ISSUES RAISED BY THE PROTESTANT REFORMERS.
- HOW DID THE COUNCIL OF TRENT VIEW THE RELATIONSHIP BETWEEN SCRIPTURE AND TRADITION? BETWEEN THE PRIESTHOOD OF ALL BELIEVERS AND THE ORDAINED PRIESTHOOD?
- WHAT WAS MEANT BY THE DISTINCTIONS "LEARNING CHURCH" AND "TEACHING CHURCH"?

JOURNAL ASSIGNMENT

- NAME AN INCIDENT THAT HAS OR COULD HAPPEN TO YOU THAT WOULD LEAD YOU TO SEEK OUT THE CHURCH AS YOUR MOTHER.

POPE PAUL III'S INSTRUCTIONS TO CHURCH MISSIONARIES

Recent history has looked with a critical eye at the missionary work of the Church from the fifteenth to the early twentieth century. In many cases Catholic missionaries suppressed native cultures as they presented the gospel from a European perspective. Many missionaries could not or did  not separate Catholic faith from European culture. Pope Paul III, the pope who convoked the Council of Trent, spoke out against the culturally insensitive and often exploitative treatment of the native peoples by Church missionaries. In his apostolic letter, *Sublimus Dei*, he wrote:

> We define and declare by these our letters . . . the said Indians and all other people who may later be discovered by Christians, are by no means to be deprived of their liberty or the possession of their property, even though they be outside the faith of Jesus Christ; and that they may and should, freely and legitimately, enjoy their liberty and the possession of their property; nor should they be in any way enslaved; should the contrary happen, it shall be null and have no effect.

ONE BODY, MANY PARTS

When in January, 1959, only three months after his election, Pope John XXIII announced his plan to call an ecumenical council, many were unsupportive. Some felt that councils should only be called to deal with pressing questions or particularly dangerous heresies; others believed that since papal infallibility had been declared in the nineteenth century, councils had become a thing of the past and the pope could rule the Church alone. Nonetheless, Pope John XXIII called the Second Vatican Council, expressing his view that the Church needed to be "updated" so that it could respond more effectively to the modern world.

The Second Vatican Council was by far the largest of any ecumenical council, attended by over 2,600 bishops, of which 42 percent came from Latin America, Asia, and Africa.[12] This large attendance of non-European bishops for the first time at an ecumenical council brought concerns for the poor and oppressed to the forefront. This council brought the most wide-sweeping changes to the Church since the Council of Trent. Some of the changes affected by the documents of Vatican II are summarized below:

- *The Constitution on the Sacred Liturgy* emphasizes the importance of the full participation of both the clergy and the laity in the liturgy. For this reason, all the liturgy is now said in the common language of the people, not in Latin. Latin, however, remains the official language of the Church.
- *The Dogmatic Constitution on the Church* speaks of the Church as a mystery. This document gave special attention to the image of the Church as the People of God—lay, religious, and clergy. It said that all members of the Church bear a responsibility for carrying out the Church's mission.

- *The Decree on Ecumenism* calls for the restoration of Christian unity. Many new divisions—sects and cults—have arisen since the time of the Protestant reformation. The division among Christian churches is a sad reality and a breach in the unity for which Christ prayed that "all be one, as you, Father, are in me and I in you, that they also may be in us" (Jn 17:21). The decree acknowledges that the Church is already joined in many ways to other properly baptized Christians. The decree also states that Christians of today cannot be held responsible for divisions in the Church which occurred centuries ago, especially since those divisions were the result of errors committed by people on both sides. In a similar vein, the *Declaration on the Relationship of the Church to Non-Christian Religions* says that the Church does not reject truth and holiness that can be found in other religions. All people were created by God and form a single community. Christians are called to share their own faith with those of other religions, but they are also called to "acknowledge, preserve and encourage the spiritual and moral truths found among non-Christians, also their social life and culture" (#2). *The Declaration on Religious Freedom* states that the Church recognizes the inherent right of all people to choose and practice their own religion.

- *The Pastoral Constitution on the Church in the Modern World* makes it clear that the Church is part of the world and is called to serve the world. Every member of the Church is called to bear witness to Christ and to help bring about the transformation of the world in his or her social and professional life.

Since Vatican II, a new image of the Church has emerged. We have returned to the image of the Church described by St. Paul in 1 Corinthians 12:12–26. The Church is a single body with many parts. Every member of the Church has an important role to play. Also, although the Catholic Church regrets the fact that all Christians are not in full communion with one another, it recognizes that Christians of other denominations are also part of the one Body of Christ. Furthermore, it understands that every person in the world is in some way connected to the Body of Christ because all people are called to Salvation.[13]

Born Angelo Roncalli, Pope John XXIII was thought only to be a "transitional pope" because of his advanced age. The Second Vatican Council opened on October 11, 1962. Pope John XXIII gave the opening address. Though he died on June 3, 1963, before the Council closed, he had already put his stamp on its outcome.

The dominant image of Church as mother has shifted again to that of a Body of which Christ is the head and we are all part. This image has had several discernible effects on the life of the Church. Lay involvement in the internal life of the Church and in the mission of the Church to the world has dramatically increased. Dialogue between all members of Christ's Body is a strength of this image. Lay people have taken more ownership of the Catholic Church since Vatican II. This, in turn, has contributed to a certain amount of uncertainty within the Catholic Church, as Catholic identity is no longer as clearly defined as it once was.

STUDY QUESTIONS

- SUMMARIZE THE MAIN TEACHINGS OF THE FOLLOWING DOCUMENTS OF THE SECOND VATICAN COUNCIL: CONSTITUTION ON THE SACRED LITURGY, DOGMATIC CONSTITUTION ON THE CHURCH, DECREE ON ECUMENISM, AND PASTORAL CONSTITUTION ON THE CHURCH IN THE MODERN WORLD.

JOURNAL ASSIGNMENT

- READ 1 CORINTHIANS 12:12–26. DESCRIBE YOUR PARTICIPATION IN THE BODY OF CHRIST.

IN CONCLUSION

The Church is a mystery.

Her nature can never be grasped by the power of reason alone. Her essence can never be captured by a single image. Each of the images that has been used to describe and understand the Church conveys something of the truth of the Church; none of them capture the whole truth. The Church is indeed the *choice vineyard* grown from the rootstock which is Christ; the Church has no life or purpose apart from Christ. At the same time, the Church is the *dwelling place of God*. The Church and Christ are not identical, and yet to be a member of the Church is to accept the responsibility for making God's presence visible. The Church is also the *city of God* in which the laws of God are made known. The Church is the city of God in which people love and serve God in many diverse ways. The Church is a *sheepfold* offering shelter from the evil that threatens us. Christ himself is the gate to the sheepfold; if we are in the Church nothing should cause us to despair. This does not mean, however, that the Church is free from problems or even dangers. The Church is a *cultivated field* in which both good and bad can be found. God has planted the seeds of the kingdom in the Church, but others have planted the weeds of sin. The Church will be perfected only at the time of the harvest.

As much as these images help us to understand the Church, they can never be sufficient. The Church is far more than an inanimate object. The Church has a personal quality. Each one of us is called to build a personal relationship with the Church. So it is that we also call the Church *our mother*. The Church watches over us, protects us from harmful influences, and teaches us the things that we need to know. We are called to respond with love and obedience. And yet, love and obedience alone are not enough. We are also called to take responsibility for the Church. Each one of us is part of the one Body that is the Church.

History reminds us over and over that the Church is indeed a mystery. Within the Church seemingly incompatible opposites are held together. The Church is our mother and yet we have a role in parenting others. The Church is one vine that strikes down all differences between people, and yet the Church is the city of God in which structures and hierarchies and distinctions between the roles of different people are both necessary and important. The Church is the dwelling place of God which should house nothing profane, and yet the Church is a field in which the weeds of sin must be allowed to grow side by side with the good seed of grace until the harvest.

Most people tend to be most comfortable with one or two images of the Church. Sometimes we act as if our images for Church are the only ones that are correct. We grow angry or impatient with other Catholics who do not think of the Church in the same way we do. The challenge in being Church is to remember that there are many different "true" images of the Church, and each of those images has something important to teach us. Because we are limited, we need to choose one or two images of the Church to guide and shape our interaction with the Church. At the same time we need to listen to and learn from other Catholics who prefer other images.

LEARN BY DOING

Chapter 1 of the Second Vatican Council document *Lumen Gentium* (Dogmatic Constitution on the Church) describes the mystery of the Church, using many of the images from this chapter along with some others. Read Chapter 1 of *Lumen Gentium*, paragraphs 1–8 (see www.vatican .va/archive/hist_councils/ii_vatican_council/documents/vat-ii_const_19641121_lumen -gentium_en.html). Choose one of the images for Church described in the chapter. Using any art medium of your choice, depict the image in a unique way. For example, use tile, ceramics, paint, pencil, photography, or any other medium or combination to depict an image of Church.

PRAYER

Prayer for Christian Unity

Good and gracious God,
We pray for all of our brothers and sisters
   who profess faith in Jesus Christ.
May our peace and unity increase
   as we show the world our love for each other,
   and that we are your faithful friends.
We ask this in the name of your Son, Jesus Christ.
Amen.

NOTES

1. I am indebted to Terry Widrick of Selkirk, Manitoba, for this teaching. A similar teaching is implied although never made explicit in many Catholic Churches. In many older churches and in many European and Latin American churches, there are shrines and statues of various saints all around the outer perimeter of the Church. Each of these saints is known for a particular way of understanding and relating to God. Many of these saints are extremely different from one another, and yet all are honored because God has been visible in their life and work. The placement of the shrines and statues reminds us that there are many different ways to relate to God and even to understand God. Each person, even the most holy, is limited in his or her ability to see God. Only when we look together as the whole Church, the whole communion of saints on earth and in heaven, do we begin to see God clearly.

2. The earliest surviving Christian apology, *To Dogenetus* 5:1–11, summed up the message which Christians wished to convey to their pagan neighbors. "Christians are no different from the rest in their nationality, language or customs. . . . They live in their own countries, but as sojourners. They fulfill all their duties as citizens, but they suffer as foreigners. They find their homeland wherever they are."

3. *Lumen Gentium,* quoted in the *Catechism of the Catholic Church,* #756.

4. See Henry Chadwick, *The Early Church* (Middlesex, England: Penguin Books, Ltd., 1967), p. 59.

5. Within the early Church those who committed a serious sin had to serve a very long, public penance before being readmitted into communion with the Church. Furthermore, they could only be readmitted once. If they sinned again they were permanently banned.

6. See Justo L. Gonzalez, *The Story of Christianity*, Vol. 1 (New York: Harper Collins Publishers, 1984), p. 231.

7. Many saw the barbarian invasions as punishment from God for the moral laxity and more particularly the indifference to the poor which had entered the Church when it was embraced by the empire.

8. In 1059 the Second Lateran Council declared that popes should be elected by cardinals who were also bishops.

9. Although the Crusades were officially against the Arabs who controlled the Holy Land, the crusaders killed thousands of Jews as they marched across Europe.

10. One of the main abuses which Martin Luther attacked at the beginning of the Reformation was the sale of indulgences to raise money for the Church. In particular Luther was protesting against the sale of indulgences in Germany which was being led by the Dominican John Tetzel. Tetzel had gone so far as to say that his indulgences would make people "cleaner than when coming out of baptism," and that "the cross of the seller of indulgences has as much power as the cross of Christ." He also promised that when indulgences were purchased for someone who had died, "as soon as the coin in the coffer rings, the soul from purgatory springs." (Statements of Brother J. Tetzel quoted in Gonzalez, *The Story of Christianity,* Vol. 2, p. 21.

11. The Second Vatican Council in The Dogmatic Constitution on Divine Revelation said that while the Church honors ancient translations of Scripture such as the Septuagint and the Vulgate, suitable and correct translations of the Bible must be made available in different languages, and these translations should be based upon the original Greek and Hebrew Texts. *Dei Verbum,* #22.

12. See Gonzalez, *The Story of Christianity,* Vol. 2, p. 352.

13. See *Catechism of the Catholic Church,* #836.

UNIT THREE

THE CHURCH IS THE PEOPLE OF GOD

THE CHURCH IS THE PEOPLE OF GOD

God calls people to be holy and to Salvation not as individuals but as a people with a link between them. In history, God first called the Israelites to be his people. God gradually instructed them in preparation for the new and perfect covenant which was ratified in Jesus Christ.

In the New Covenant of Christ, God formed a new people who are made up of Jews and Gentiles of every race and place.

The Church is called the People of God because in the Church Jesus has offered a new communal identity, one which inclines us to live as one, and to work in partnership with God, sharing in the unity of the Holy Trinity.

The Church is the People of God in seven basic ways:

1. God calls those who belong to the Church to be "a chosen race, a royal priesthood, a holy nation" (1 Pt 2:9).
2. We become members of the Church through faith in Christ and Baptism.
3. Christ is the head of the Church. The Holy Spirit flows from Christ into the body.
4. The Holy Spirit dwells in us as in a temple of God.
5. The new law of love—love others as Christ loved us—is given to the Church.
6. The mission of the Church is to be salt to the earth and light of the world.
7. The destiny of the Church is the kingdom of God, which will be extended by God to perfection until the end of time.

In chapter 3.1 you will explore the necessity of communal identity as we come to approach God. You will examine the similarities and differences between Christian communal identity and Jewish communal identity. You will learn to describe the specific characteristics that identify you as a Christian and Catholic.

Chapter 3.2 traces the various requirements and implications of Church membership through the centuries, beginning with the first admission of Gentiles to the Church following the decision of the Council of Jerusalem, to the response of the Church to the Protestant Reformation, to a renewal of Catholic attitude toward non-Catholics expressed at the Second Vatican Council.

When you have completed Unit 3, you will be able to:

- understand the basic human and religious truth that human beings were not created to live in isolation;
- identify the similarities and differences between the Christian communal identity and the Jewish communal identity;
- explain why an understanding of our communal identity is essential to an understanding of the doctrines of original sin and salvation through Christ;
- name and describe the specific characteristics which define the People of God and the specific attitudes and behaviors which are a necessary part of our communal identity;
- evaluate their own acceptance of Christian communal identity;
- describe the requirements and implications of Church membership at various times in history;
- explain the decisions made at the Council of Jerusalem regarding the role of Jewish laws within Christianity;
- describe the problem which the "lapsed" Christians presented for the church and the Church's response to them;
- explain the relationship between Penance and Baptism;
- explain how the Church attempted to exert control over all people during the Middle Ages;
- summarize the Council of Trent's response to the Protestant reformers;
- identify the changes in the Catholic attitude toward non-Catholics as expressed in the Vatican II document *Lumen Gentium*;
- define religious indifferentism and explain its danger to society.

TOGETHER as ONE

IN YOUR NATURE, O ETERNAL GODHEAD, I SHALL KNOW MY OWN NATURE.

—*Saint Catherine of Siena*

ONE FOR ALL, ALL FOR ONE

W"here we go one, we go all."

The words, written on the ship's bell of the Albatross, sound the central theme for the movie *White Squall*.[1] These words represented a theme of the movie: hope, happiness, and the ability to cope with difficulties all depend on a person's willingness to live in solidarity with others. In many ways these words could also sound the theme for the Catholic life. Recall that one of the meanings of the word "catholic" is "of the whole." To be Catholic is to recognize that we are part of a whole, a community of faith.

The boys who sailed on the Albatross demonstrated that they had found the maturity they had been sent away to find, when they stood in solidarity and refused to let any one person take the blame for a terrible tragedy that befell their voyage. Similarly, Saint Paul writes that being a mature Christian means accepting the grace which God offers. Being a mature Christian does not mean we can explain the complete body of Church theology, nor have the faith to work all miracles. Rather, being a mature Christian means standing in solidarity with those who are in need, freely offering our love and compassion to them, and responding to their needs and their hopes as our own.[2]

There is a basic human truth which is easily forgotten in our very individualistic society: our lives are meaningless unless we are connected to one another. This observable human truth rests upon a basic religious truth which is summed up God's declaration: "It is not good for the man to be alone" (Genesis 2:18). God did not create human beings to live in isolation, and God does not choose to save us as disconnected individuals. God created us to be one with others, and God offers us Salvation as a people who are one.[3] From the beginning God intended that human nature would be one, and human beings would be united with one another and with God. It was only when sin entered the world that humanity became divided in itself and from God.

Adam and Eve

The story of Adam and Eve found in Genesis 2 traces the beginning of this division. This creation account says that after God created the earth, but before there were any plants or animals, God created a human being from the mud. Only after this human was made did God complete the work of creation. God created plants and trees as part of a beautiful garden which he gave to this first human to live in and to care for. Then God watched Adam ("man") and decided that he needed a helpmate. But God did not immediately make another human being. Instead God made all of the animals and brought them to Adam one by one to see if

they would be the right companion for him.

The Scripture says that God brought all of the animals to Adam, and Adam named each one, "but none proved to be the suitable partner for the man" (Genesis 2:20). A message of the Genesis story is that God wanted Adam to be involved in creation. God chose Adam to be involved in the divine work of naming the animals—and creating the perfect companion.

Eventually God puts Adam into a deep sleep and creates Eve, a woman. When Adam sees this new human, he is full of enthusiasm. He recognizes himself in this new person: "This one, at last, is bone of my bones and flesh of my flesh" (Genesis 2:23). Adam and Eve are perfect companions because they are one, just as they are also one with God.

Of course, the serpent is the foil in the story, questioning, tempting, and sowing the seeds of division. The serpent asks the woman why she remains dependent on God when she has the opportunity to do something that would make God unnecessary: ". . . the moment you eat of [the fruit] your eyes will be opened and you will be like gods." The serpent convinces the woman that unity with God is a hindrance. And so, the woman and the man decide that they would rather live without God; they deliberately do what God has told them not to do.

As soon as they choose to disobey what God has told them and taste the forbidden fruit, the unity which God intended is destroyed. The man and the woman no longer see themselves in one another, instead they see someone who is totally other. Where unity once dominated their relationship, now they see only incompatible differences which they must try to hide. What is more, where they once understood themselves and their actions as one, now they wish to disassociate themselves from one another. Adam says, "The woman whom you put here with me—she gave me the fruit." The woman is no longer "flesh of my flesh"; she has become someone unrelated to Adam.

Likewise, Adam and Eve's unity is broken with God. Adam once understood himself to be in partnership with God. He worked with God to find a suitable helpmate for himself, but now that helpmate has become the one whom "you [God] put here with me." The human beings whom God made in his own image no longer view God as a companion; now they see only the huge gulf which separates them from God.

HANDLING CONFLICT

How do you usually respond to conflict

- with your mom?
- with your dad?
- with your teachers?
- with other adults?
- with female peers?
- with male peers?
- with close friends?
- with boyfriends/ girlfriends?

There are several negative ways to handle conflict. For example, shouting, lying, being physically aggressive, pouting, or blaming. There are more positive ways to handle conflict. For example, dialoguing, apologizing, cooling off, or talking over the situation with a trusted third party.

With a partner, talk over how you handle conflicts. Share one negative example and one positive example.

After you have both shared, discuss how forgiveness can play a positive role in settling conflicts. Also discuss how forgiveness played a crucial role in ending the broken unity between God and mankind.

STUDY QUESTIONS

- WHAT BASIC HUMAN TRUTH IS OFTEN FORGOTTEN?
- WHAT IS THE RELIGIOUS TRUTH THAT CORRESPONDS WITH THIS HUMAN TRUTH?

JOURNAL ASSIGNMENT

- READ GENESIS 2. DESCRIBE IN YOUR OWN WORDS THE UNITY GOD INTENDED FOR HUMANITY IF THERE HAD BEEN NO SIN.

A COMMUNAL IDENTITY

Salvation History tells the long story of humanity's return to unity with God and with one another. When God called Abraham, it was to make of him a great nation, a unified people. When God called Moses, it was to free the descendants of Abraham from bondage and to lead them to a place where they might know and serve God as one. The story of the Exodus is the story of how God called one people to be a sign to the world of the unity which God desires.

The escape from Egypt, the miraculous crossing of the Red Sea, the forty years spent wandering in the wilderness, and the conquest, against all odds, of a land controlled by foreigners, bonded twelve tribal groups into a single nation with a common identity. To be an Israelite was to be one of God's Chosen People.

The Passover celebration reminded **Israelites**—known as Jews in succeeding generations—that they were the people whom God led out of Egypt. Every Israelite has been shaped by the experience of the Exodus regardless of when or where he or she lived.[4] Religious law built upon the Exodus experience and taught the people that because God had acted in a particular way they should respond in a particular way. Religious law gave the Israelites the continued strength to live as a people. The Law was not only a demand but also a precious gift from God. The Law held the Israelite community together so that together they could do what none could do alone—obey God's will and avoid the bondage of sin. The Israelites believed that God had saved them as a people and continued to relate to them as a people (see Deuteronomy 14:2; 26:16–19), blessing or punishing them in accordance with their communal

Israelites—The Chosen People of God. The Israelites are the descendants of Abraham through Isaac and Jacob, also known as Israel.

fidelity or infidelity to the Law. Each Israelite was therefore called to fidelity to God not only for his or her own sake, but for the sake of the whole people.

The early Christians inherited this sense of a communal relationship from the Jews. Establishing communal identity became an integral part of Christian faith. Significant aspects of Christian theology are rooted in the belief that Christian identity is not simply one's personal possession. A Catholic understanding of community is that regardless of what we intend or desire, we are shaped by others and we shape others. Our relationship with God is dependent on how our community—the Church—relates to God.

Catholic Doctrine Rooted in Community

Unless we understand and accept our rootedness in community, some basic Catholic doctrines will not make sense to us. The doctrine of **Original Sin** is related to our communal identity. This doctrine says that because Adam and Eve sinned, all human beings are born in a state of sin. Because of our communal identity with all people, the sin of two individuals affects the entire human race. Human nature itself was changed by Adam and Eve's rejection of God.

The doctrine of Salvation through Christ is also tied to our communal identity. Because Jesus was human, he shared community

with all humans. His life of complete fidelity to the Father affected every other person. His life brought life to the whole world.[5] As soon as there was one human being who conquered death, the possibility of avoiding the clutches of death was open to all humanity.

The Israelite people shared a communal identity rooted in sinfulness that they inherited from Adam and Eve. The Law helped them to understand this inclination to sin and to recognize sin for what it was. The Law also encouraged them to draw together in their efforts to resist sin. The Law could not, however, free them from the sin which separated them from God. It could call people to unity with God, but it could not establish that unity.

In other words, the Law alone could not restore human nature; all it was able to do was prepare people for the one who could. The actual restoration of human nature had to wait until the coming of Jesus. It was only in Jesus that human beings once again became capable of a life of unity. Jesus

Original Sin—The absence of holiness and justice given by God to the first people. Because of the sin of Adam and Eve, humans are inclined to sin and are subject to ignorance, suffering, and death.

offered a new community identity—an identity which inclines us to live as one,[6] to work in partnership with God, and to share in the unity of the Trinity.[7] Christ's fidelity did not change human nature in the same way that Adam and Eve's infidelity did. Adam and Eve's legacy of sin is still passed on. We are born with a wounded nature of Original Sin. Now, however, healing is

possible. Sin is no longer unavoidable and hopelessly cumulative.[8] Human beings now have a choice between the life of sin in unity with Adam and Eve and the life of grace in unity with Christ.

Jesus established a new people whose lives are governed, not by an external law, but by a law that was written on their hearts,[9] a law that is a part of their very nature.

STUDY QUESTIONS

- HOW DID THE LAW SHAPE ISRAEL'S COMMUNAL IDENTITY?
- HOW DOES OUR ROOTEDNESS IN COMMUNITY HELP US TO UNDERSTAND CHRISTIAN DOCTRINE?
- WHAT IS THE COMMUNAL IDENTITY THAT JESUS OFFERS?

JOURNAL ASSIGNMENT

- IN WHAT WAYS HAVE YOU WITNESSED THE MULTIPLICATION OF SIN? HOW DOES THE GRACE OF CHRIST HELP YOU TO AVOID SINFUL BEHAVIOR?
- HOW ARE YOU ABLE TO MAINTAIN YOUR INDIVIDUALITY WHILE STILL SEEKING OUT COMMUNAL IDENTITY IN YOUR FAMILY, PEER GROUP, SCHOOL, AND CHURCH?

REBORN THROUGH BAPTISM

The Church is this new People of God. All the baptized are reborn as members of this people. Catholics believe that all sins—both personal sins and Original Sin—are forgiven in Baptism. Baptism makes a person a part of the Body of Christ, and therefore a "partaker of the divine nature." Those who are baptized have been changed; they have become "new creature[s]."[10] A baptized

person's potential is determined by the grace of Christ, not the sin of Adam and Eve.

In Baptism a person is given a new character, which is one of belonging to God and to other people through God. Once people have been baptized, their whole being is defined first and foremost by the fact that they belong to God. Their identity as members of the People of God is more important to who they are and to what they do than their gender, their family, their talents, their race, their nationality, or anything else that shapes them.

Unless a person belongs to God and is a member of the People of God, he or she will not know Salvation. Salvation, indeed, is a belonging to, or a unity with, God. The opposite of Salvation is a total separation from God. As Christ himself affirms, Baptism is necessary for Salvation.[11] Baptism is the only way we know of giving oneself to God and of being incorporated into the People of God; we believe that Baptism is necessary for Salvation. We realize, however, that God is free to make people his own through other means.[12] The Church has long recognized what is known as the **baptism of desire**. We believe that God makes his own all who sincerely seek the truth and follow the will of God as they understand it, even if they are ignorant of the Christian faith or the necessity of Baptism.[13]

When we are baptized into the People of God we become a member of a community of faith and take on a new communal identity. Our old identity separated us from one another and left us content to see only our differences; our new identity draws us into community. We are called to defer to one another and make our choices based on our communal needs and desires, and not just on our individual needs and desires. We are now part of a whole, our individual well-being is inseparable from the well-being of the community. As the letter to

the Ephesians says, we must learn to be "subordinate to one another out of reverence for Christ" (5:21).

In medieval art the Church was often depicted as a ship because a ship's crew must live and act as one if they are to survive and get where they are going. The entire crew, acting in communion with one another, has an impact on the ship's day to day operation. In the same way our communal identity as the People of God must be the deciding factor in all that we do. The individual members of the People of God must live and act as one if they are to fulfill their role as the Body of Christ on earth. Each person must be prepared to care for every other, and all must be willing to follow the leadership of those whose role it is to coordinate and direct the activity of the people as a whole.

In our society, the concept of living in solidarity and

baptism of desire—Seeking the truth and doing the will of God to the best of one's understanding, even though the person may not understand the gospel or the necessity of the Church. The Church teaches that God allows those people who would have explicitly desired baptism if they understood its necessity to share in the benefits of the baptized.

NEW LIFE FROM LIVING WATER

Read each of the following Scripture passages that deal with water and new life:

- Genesis 6–8 (the Great Flood)
- Exodus 14 (the crossing of the Red Sea)
- Luke 3:21–22 (Jesus' baptism in the Jordan River)

Write about how each example describes the transition from death to new life. Also, write or share an example from today that shows the power of water to bring new life.

communion with others is often challenged. There is a sense that communal identities erase or obscure individuality. Another notion is that communal identities can result in discrimination, when individuals are treated unfairly because they belong, or don't belong, to a particular group. It is important to recognize that the Christian call to form community is not meant to bring to the fore either of these pitfalls. The People of God are unlike any other people. They are not an ethnic, political, or cultural group. There is no particular physical bond which defines the People of God; it is the presence of the Holy Spirit in our midst that makes us who we are. The People of God are the people in whom God's Spirit dwells. They are one because the Spirit within them is one. All people are called to be members of the People of God. None are to be excluded.

Membership in the People of God does not obscure individual identity. Even after a person has been incorporated into the Body of Christ, that person maintains his or her unique identity. What membership in the People of God does do is make it clear that God gave us individual personalities, not as a means of separating us, but as a means of uniting us. The more we work together as one, the more we will come to see that our differences are complimentary. Just as the variety of functions of the various parts of the human body (arms, legs, feet, hands, etc.) increase what the body can do as a whole, so too the variety of gifts among the Christian Body increase our effectiveness as the whole Body of Christ. Incorporation into the Body of Christ enhances a person's individuality, it does not destroy it. We believe that it is only in giving ourselves to others that we can discover our true selves.[14] We will find meaning and value in our individuality only if we are living in a community.

STUDY QUESTIONS

- HOW DOES BAPTISM CHANGE A PERSON'S INDIVIDUAL IDENTITY? COMMUNAL IDENTITY?
- EXPLAIN THE NUANCES OF THE STATEMENT "BAPTISM IS NECESSARY FOR SALVATION."
- EXPLAIN HOW THE IMAGE OF THE SHIP DESCRIBED THE CHURCH IN MEDIEVAL TIMES.
- WHY DOESN'T MEMBERSHIP IN THE PEOPLE OF GOD OBSCURE OUR PERSONAL IDENTITY?

WE ARE A CHOSEN RACE

Like the Israelites of the Old Testament, Catholics believe that we have been chosen by God. When we speak about being chosen by God, we are not implying that God has chosen some people while ignoring or dismissing others. We are not saying that we believe in a God who in some figurative sense lines up all humanity and selects those who would make the best "team." As Catholics, we are not chosen as separate individuals set against one another. We are chosen as we were created, as one. When we speak about being chosen we are referring to the fact that God chose to be one with humanity, that God chose to offer us a partnership with the Trinity, that God chose to love us. God did not have to give humanity another chance after we rejected him. God chose to do all these things. We are chosen because we share in the human nature in which Jesus chose to share.

Since we have been chosen because of God's great love for us and not because of our merit, our lives should be lived in gratitude rather than demand. We are not entitled to the blessings we receive; they are the free gift of God. The worship life of the Catholic Church reflects this. The liturgy is the source and summit of Catholic life; the eucharistic prayer which is a prayer of thanksgiving is the heart and summit of that liturgy.[15] Daily, but especially on Sundays, our worship forms us as a people who count our blessings. If gratitude does not play a significant role in both our individual and communal lives we will be living at odds with our nature.

FINDING OUT ABOUT THE HOMELESS

Homelessness is a national problem. Most cities have homeless shelters that appreciate citizens volunteering their time or contributing food and other necessary items. Read about the complexity of homelessness at the following website. Write about a way you can help combat the problem and how you will enact your plan.
National Coalition for the Homeless:
www.nationalhomeless.org/help.html

STUDY QUESTIONS

- WHAT ARE SOME THINGS THAT BEING A "CHOSEN RACE" DOES NOT IMPLY FOR CHRISTIANS?
- WHY SHOULD CHRISTIANS LIVE THEIR LIVES IN GRATITUDE?

JOURNAL ASSIGNMENT

- NAME FIVE THINGS THAT HAPPENED IN THE PAST TWENTY-FOUR HOURS THAT YOU ARE THANKFUL FOR.

WE ARE A ROYAL PEOPLE

In our world, members of royal families are often portrayed as little more than props for parades and pageantry, or as sources of titillating scandal. This, however, is not how royalty is understood in the Judeo-Christian tradition. Rather, in this understanding, royalty means "to be anointed by God." Christians are a royal people. We have been anointed by God to provide others with that which is most necessary for life—God's love. We have been chosen, not as servants, but as children who will one day be full partners in the "family business" of God's Kingdom. We are called royal because our status, dignity, and freedom are those of the children of the most high, the King of Kings. No matter what possessions, prestige, or talents we may or may not have, as Christians, we are inferior to no one. Within the Church we are called to a radical equality, in which each person regards every other as a fellow ruler.[16] Each one of us is also called to take on the responsibilities of leadership by revealing God's presence to others.

Leading Through Service and Self-Sacrifice

Christians are to rule as Jesus did, through service and self-sacrifice. As children of God we are called to imitate God who committed himself to humanity even when humanity offered nothing in return. We fulfill our royal duty when we commit ourselves to those who are most in need and can offer us the least.

Again, our worship both forms our identity and reminds us of this challenge. The Eucharist explicitly commits us to the poor.[17] When we share the Body and Blood of Christ, we are reminded that there is nothing that we should refuse to share. In fact, to refuse to share anything else after we have shared the Body and Blood of Christ is to dishonor the Eucharist by acting as if something else were more precious. The Eucharist not only reminds us of our commitment to the poor, it also strengthens that commitment. When we share in the Body of Christ we become what we eat. When we share in the Eucharist, we are more firmly united to one another as the Body of Christ. Rich and poor, strong and weak, all become more completely one.

STUDY QUESTIONS

- HOW IS ROYALTY UNDERSTOOD IN THE JUDEO-CHRISTIAN TRADITION?
- HOW DO CHRISTIANS FULFILL THEIR ROYAL DUTY?

JOURNAL ASSIGNMENT

- PUTTING A FACE ON POVERTY, WRITE ABOUT A PERSON YOU KNOW WHO IS MOST IN NEED AND COULD USE YOUR HELP THE MOST. WHAT CAN YOU DO TO HELP THE PERSON?

WE ARE A KINGDOM OF PRIESTS

All Christians are also **priests**. Every Christian, male or female, young or old, religious, lay, or ordained, is called to consecrate the world to God in his or her daily life.[18] We do this by asking the Holy Spirit to be part of everything that we do. We also do this by offering all that we do to God along with the Body and Blood of Christ in the Eucharist. This priesthood of the baptized is different than the ordained priesthood. Ordained priests consecrate the bread and wine during Eucharist and preside at the other sacraments. When the priest offers Christ's Body and Blood during the Mass, the assembly adds to it the offering of their work, their play, their prayers, their struggles—their entire lives. Every person present acts in a priestly way by offering a sacrifice that is pleasing to God. Furthermore, just as the ordained administer sacramental forgiveness, healing, and strength within the Church, every Christian is called to carry God's presence, forgiveness, healing, and support to the world.

The saving mission of the Church cannot be carried out by the ordained ministers alone, by religious alone, or by the laity alone. The saving work of the Church can only be done by the Church as a whole: lay, religious, and clerical. The ordained priesthood is directed to life within the Church, while the priesthood of all believers is directed toward life within the secular world. The hierarchical structure of the Church enables the People of God to carry out the mission of the Church in the world. The power of ordination is a power to serve.[19] The ordained priesthood serves the priesthood of all believers by guiding, supporting, and strengthening it, and by acting as a living sign of what it should be. Without the laity much of the world would remain untouched by the Church. Without the ordained priesthood the laity would not have the spiritual resources and grace which they need to work on behalf of the Church in the world.[20]

priest—Every Christian, male or female, young or old, religious, lay, or ordained, who by virtue of their Baptism is called to consecrate the world to God in his or her daily life. This priesthood of the baptized is different than the ordained priesthood. Ordained priests consecrate the bread and wine during Eucharist and preside at the other sacraments.

STUDY QUESTIONS

- LIST SEVERAL WAYS THE ORDAINED PRIESTHOOD IS DIFFERENT FROM THE PRIESTHOOD OF ALL BELIEVERS.

WE ARE A NATION OF PROPHETS

We are the People of God. Our identity is that of the Body of Christ on earth. Unless we act in accordance with Jesus, our head, we are denying that we are Christ's Body. Jesus is "the way, and the truth, and the life" (John 14:6). We must be the same. All who encounter the People of God should encounter the truth of God, the way which God established for humanity, and the life God intended for all human beings. In other words, all who encounter the People of God should encounter a nation of true prophets.

What is a **prophet**? Simply, a prophet is someone through whom the will of God is made known. Prophets speak and live the truth in such a way that others are able to hear and recognize God and God's will for the world. Remember, God created human beings to live in unity with each other and in partnership with God. Prophets are those who echo God's call to live in unity and who show us how to live in unity.

Prophets are also the voices of freedom. Freedom is one of the first gifts from God. Freedom is the power to make the choices which will enable us to fulfill our potential and become the people we were created to be. Anything which makes us less than God intended us to be is not really freedom. Since God intended all people to live as one, true freedom will always be "directed toward communion."[21] By challenging us to live in communion and accept our responsibility for one another, prophets lead us to freedom.

It is the nature of the People of God to be prophetic. We are a visible sign established by God. People outside the communion of the Church take note of the behavior of Christians. Our lives will influence both their behavior and their understanding of God.

An informal study done several years ago underscores the truth of this statement. A car was stopped at the side of the highway with its hood up. The driver stood looking down at the car, obviously at a loss. About ten miles down the highway another car was stopped, once again the hood was up and the driver was looking forlorn, but this time there was a second car which had obviously stopped to offer assistance. Just a mile beyond this second disabled car was a third car. Once again the hood was up and a puzzled driver stared down at the engine. The object of the study was to see if the example of someone helping the second driver had any effect on the number of people who would stop to help the third. Over the course of the day the number of people who stopped to offer assistance to the third driver was many times greater than the number who stopped for the first. The Church is to be a similar prophetic example for others to stop, examine their lives, and come in contact with the holy.

prophet—Someone through whom the will of God is made known. Prophets speak and live the truth in such a way that others are able to hear and recognize God and God's will for the world.

STUDY QUESTIONS

- WHAT IS A PROPHET?
- WHAT DO PROPHETS DO?
- DEFINE FREEDOM.

JOURNAL ASSIGNMENT

- WHO HAS BEEN A PROPHETIC EXAMPLE FOR YOU? HOW SO?

A VERY PUBLIC CATHOLIC

Mike Sweeney, a major league all star who began his career with the Kansas City Royals, is also very public about his Catholic faith. In fact, he serves as a spokesman for the Catholic youth ministry organization, Life Teen (www.lifeteen.org).

There are many temptations having to do with money, power, and fame that come with being a professional athlete. Mike admits as much. In an interview with Life Teen he admitted, "It's tough following Jesus daily. Sin is easy—sin is the easy thing to do. Most of the guys will go out and have some beers after the game and chase girls at the bar. Do you want to go follow them? NO! That's the toughest part, just saying no. You have to rely on the Holy Spirit. But the good part is when you get back in your room and you say, 'Yes, I made it.' Then you feel like Jesus has given you a big hug and is saying, 'Son, I love you. Great job. I'm proud of you.' And then you open up the Bible before you go to bed and his word just seems so rich and personal."

Mike grew up in a Catholic family as the second oldest of eight children. "I really didn't know there was any other church but the Catholic Church. My family had their faith in Jesus Christ through the Church that brought them up."

Nowadays, Mike is a husband and a father as he continues his career in baseball. In spite of being an all star and someone blessed to be paid a great deal of money to play a game that he loves, Mike's faith comes first. He explains, "In major league baseball a lot of people say, 'You have money, you can drive a nice car, you can live in a big house.' Yet people have all of that but they're still empty inside. And I've known since I was a teenager that having Jesus in my life equals joy, and that's something no one can take from me. Joy is something that the world can't rob me of if I go 0 for 10 or make four errors in one inning. Joy comes from Jesus and I don't need to buy a huge house or bring home a big paycheck or drive a fancy car or wear flashy jewelry to make me feel good."

IN CONCLUSION

God created people to live in community. Unfortunately, although we were created to be one, our ability to live in unity with one another was damaged by the sin of Adam and Eve. Adam and Eve's sin separated them from God and altered human nature. Now human beings are born with an inclination to distance ourselves from one another and from God. Even when we recognize the error of our ways we do not have the power to restore human unity on our own; our wounded nature will always lead us astray.

Jesus came so that our nature could be healed and we could take on a new corporate identity that is not marred by Original Sin. Jesus established a new people freed from Original Sin. Now human beings have a choice: we may share in the corporate nature defined by the sin of Adam and Eve, or we may become part of the People of God and share in a new corporate nature defined by the grace offered by Jesus.

When we choose to become part of the People of God we are joined to Christ and to one another. Our identity is no longer our own personal possession; it is tied up with the identity of the whole People of God. Who we are is now defined first and foremost by the essential characteristics of the People of God. Once we are united to God through Baptism our nature is shaped by the fact that we are a chosen people. We will be at odds with ourselves unless our lives are marked by gratitude. We also recognize that once we have been united with Christ, our identity is tied up with his identity as priest, king, and prophet. We must begin to understand ourselves as priests, called to consecrate the world to God; as rulers, called to lead and govern others through love and service; and as prophets, called to be a living witness to the truth and a living sign of God's presence. This is our new nature, the nature of the one baptized in Christ.

LEARN BY DOING

Use concentric circles to list all the communities you belong to. (The circles which share common membership will overlap in part.) Some of the communities to include are:

- Catholic Church
- global community
- nation
- state
- parish
- school
- extended family
- nuclear family

Write a brief report about how the individual is essential to each of these communities.

PRAYER

For the Church

Gracious Father,

we pray to you for your holy Catholic Church.

Fill it with your truth.

Keep it in your peace.

Where it is corrupt, reform it.

Where it is in error, correct it.

Where it is right, defend it.

Where it is in want, provide for it.

Where it is divided, reunite it;

for the sake of your Son, our Savior Jesus Christ.

—William Laud, Archbishop of Canterbury (1573–1645)

NOTES

1. This 1996 movie was based on a true incident which occurred in 1961 on a sailing vessel that combined nautical instruction and regular high school academics. It tells the story of the teachers and the students, their life together, their fight against death when their ship sank, and their efforts to protect their captain against those who wanted to take his license and hold him responsible for the terrible tragedy.
2. See 1 Corinthians 13:1–3.
3. See *Lumen Gentium*, #9, and *Catechism of the Catholic Church*, #781.
4. This remains true of the Passover celebration for Jews today.
5. See Romans 5:17.
6. See John 17:21.
7. See John 14:20, and *Lumen Gentium*, #4.
8. Before Christ, each sin drew people further into sin; there was no way out. Without the grace of Christ, sin was hopelessly cumulative. Religious law could help people avoid falling deeper into sin, but it could not undo the effects of past sins, and the more people violated the law, the harder it became to follow it.
9. See Jeremiah 31:33.
10. *Catechism of the Catholic Church*, #1265.
11. See John 3:5
12. See *Catechism of the Catholic Church*, #1257.
13. Ibid., #1260.
14. See *Gaudium et Spes*, #24.
15. *Catechism of the Catholic Church*, #1352.
16. Canon 208 states: "In virtue of their rebirth in Christ there exists among all the Christian faithful a true equality with regard to dignity and the activity whereby all cooperate in the building up of the Body of Christ in accord with each one's own condition and function." Although we are called to lead people in different ways and in different places no one of us is more or less valuable as a person or more or less deserving of basic human respect.
17. See *Catechism of the Catholic Church*, #1397.
18. See *Lumen Gentium*, #34, and *Catechism of the Catholic Church*, #901.
19. See *Lumen Gentium*, #18.
20. The role of the religious in this particular context is similar to that of the laity. Religious, like the laity, work to consecrate the world to God. Because of their vows, their lives are a unique sign of what it means to be consecrated to God.
21. *Veritatis Splendor*, #86.

"I HAVE OTHER SHEEP THAT DO NOT BELONG TO THIS FOLD. THESE ALSO I MUST LEAD, AND THEY WILL HEAR MY VOICE, AND THERE WILL BE ONE FLOCK, ONE SHEPHERD."

—*John 10:16*

UNIT   1   2   **3**   4   5   6   7   8

DID LYNNE LEAVE THE CHURCH?

Almost two hundred people were gathered on the covered bridge in western Maine. The bridge was an historic

site, but they were not there for the history. Their attention was focused on a wedding canopy which stood in the middle of the bridge. Beneath the canopy, Lynne and Alan had already exchanged vows and rings; now the groom was bending down to place a wine glass wrapped in a linen napkin on the ground. He straightened up and stamped his foot down on the glass.

Cries of "Mazeltov!" rang through the gathering and the wedding ceremony was over.

As the bride and groom walked together toward one end of the bridge, some of the bride's relatives were visibly distraught. They wondered how her parents, two very committed Catholics, could be pleased with this marriage. One aunt was even heard whispering to another, "Doesn't it make them sad to know that their daughter has just left the Church? It's such a shame. I think Lynne used to be a eucharistic minister and a religious education teacher; now she can't even be a godmother for her nieces or nephews because she was married outside of the Church."

It never even occurred to Lynne's aunt that Lynne might not have "left the Church." As far as she knew, Catholics who were married outside of the Church were no longer considered Catholics in "good standing" and could not serve in any Church position in which others might look to them as an example.

What Lynne's aunt and several of her other relatives failed to realize was that Lynne wasn't married outside of the Catholic Church. Yes, her wedding to Alan was a Jewish wedding. But it was also a Catholic wedding. Both a rabbi and a Catholic deacon participated in the ceremony. The Catholic Church recognizes Lynne's marriage as every bit as valid as any other marriage.

Understanding What It Means to be Catholic

The Catholic position on interfaith marriages has changed since the 1950s—when Lynne's aunt was married. In those days, a Catholic was allowed to marry a non-Catholic only if the non-Catholic agreed to be married in a Catholic church (or rectory) with a Catholic priest officiating. Non-Catholic ministers were not allowed to participate in the ceremony. Furthermore, the non-Catholic had to promise that the future children of the couple would be baptized and raised as Catholics (even if his or her spouse died). Today, Catholics can be given a dispensation to be married in another church.[1] What is more, although a Catholic priest or deacon may be present at the wedding, a minister of another faith may be the primary official.

When Lynne and Alan were married, Lynne had to state that she intended to continue practicing her Catholic faith. She also had to promise to do all that was reasonably in her power to share her faith with their children (baptizing them and raising them in the Catholic Church if possible.) Alan had to state that he agreed with the teaching of the Catholic Church about the two ends of marriage, the good of the spouses and the bearing and raising of children, but he did not have to promise anything. He retained his right to share his own faith with their children and to encourage them to choose Judaism. When Lynne's pastor talked to her about the promise she was making, he stressed the fact that her marriage to Alan was as indissoluble as any other. Although the Church hoped that the children would be raised as Catholics, the issue of how the children would be raised was something that she and Alan would have to work out between themselves.

The change in the rules concerning interfaith marriages reflects the development in the Catholic understanding of what it means to be a member of the People of God and of the proper relationship between members of the Church and those who are not part of the Church.

Since the earliest days of Christianity, marriage has been recognized as the total and permanent commitment of a woman and a man to each other. Because of this the Church has been concerned with making sure that a marriage commitment will not pull a person away from God. A Christian must not be bound to someone who will pull him or her away from the People of God.

From the moment that Jesus instructed his followers to "go and make disciples of all nations, baptizing them in the name of the Father, and of the Son, and of the Holy Spirit" (Matthew 28:19), Baptism has been recognized as the primary means of entering the Christian community and becoming a member of the new People of God. Over the centuries, however, there have been significant disagreements over the requirements of Baptism, the effects of Baptism, and the status of those who are not baptized. In other words there have been significant disagreements over the questions of who could become a member of the People of God, what it takes to remain a member of the People of God, and whether or not the mere presence of certain groups of people posed a threat to the People of God.

The last chapter examined the characteristics of the Church—the innate traits that have become part of our identity since we have been named as God's own. In this chapter we will look at the requirements of becoming and remaining a member of the Church.

STUDY QUESTIONS

- NAME TWO CHANGES IN THE CATHOLIC VIEW OF INTERFAITH MARRIAGES.
- IS LYNNE STILL A CATHOLIC? EXPLAIN.

JOURNAL ASSIGNMENT

- IN JUST ONE OR TWO SENTENCES, SUMMARIZE WHAT YOU KNOW TO BE THE "REQUIREMENTS" FOR BEING A MEMBER OF THE CHURCH.

THE GENTILE QUESTION

When St. Stephen preached the Gospel, he was condemned to death by the Jewish authorities (Acts 6:8–7:60). Earlier, Peter and John had been brought before these same Jewish authorities for the same crime. Their punishment was different: they were flogged, ordered to stop preaching (an order which they stated that they would not obey), and released (Acts 4:1–21). Why the differences in punishment? Peter and John were among the group of Jews referred to in the New Testament as **Hebrews**, while Stephen was one of those known as a **Hellenist**. The Hebrews were those who insisted on maintaining the purity of Judaism, strictly adhering to all of the customs of their ancestors. The Hellenists were Jews who were more open to Greek influences.[2] The Jewish authorities in Jerusalem were primarily Hebrews. Although they objected to all forms of Christianity, they objected most strongly to those forms which were more Hellenized and therefore seemed to be an even greater "perversion" of the Jewish faith.

The differences between the Hebrews and Hellenists brought to the fore tensions that had become present in the Christian community. The first question was whether or not Christianity was open to Gentiles as well as Jews. Other related questions that needed to be answered were: Which elements of Judaism were necessary to Christianity? Which elements of Judaism could Christians abandon? Which elements of the Greco-Roman culture were acceptable and which were not?

According to Acts, it does not seem to have occurred to the early Church that the Salvation offered by Jesus was intended for Gentiles as well as Jews. Only after God spoke to Peter in a vision did he become convinced that Salvation in Christ was to be offered to Gentiles as well as Jews. Then, on his return to Jerusalem, the other Apostles demanded that Peter explain why he had shared a meal with the uncircumcised (the Gentiles). Only after hearing of Peter's vision and of the descent of the Spirit on the Gentiles were the other Apostles willing to accept the possibility of non-Jewish members of the People of God (see Acts 10–11).

After Gentile converts were accepted, the question of which elements of Judaism were essential to Christianity became even more pressing. For example, did Gentile Christians need to obey all of the Jewish dietary laws? Was it necessary for Christians to worship in the Temple? Was circumcision—the sign of the covenant between God and Abraham and his descendants—necessary for Gentile converts to Christianity?

When Paul and Barnabas were completing their first mission to the Gentiles there were many Jewish Christians who were saying that all of their converts would have to be circumcised if they wished to be saved (see Acts 15:1).

Hebrews—A term sometimes used to refer to all Jews. More specifically Hebrews were those who insisted on maintaining the purity of Judaism, strictly adhering to all of the customs of their ancestors.

Hellenists—Those Jews who were more open to Greek and Roman influences and who were more willing to allow their faith and religious practice to be shaped to some extent by the culture around them.

Paul and Barnabas went to Jerusalem to discuss the issue with the Apostles there. After a long debate Peter reminded everyone of the vision God had shown him which had first led them to preach to the Gentiles. Peter said that if God had accepted the Gentiles and blessed them with the Spirit when they were uncircumcised, a council made up of human beings had no right to declare circumcision to be necessary.

The Council of Jerusalem

Church leadership gathered at the Council of Jerusalem. The Council ruled that Gentile Christians did not have to follow the entire Jewish law. Rather there were only three basic laws which they needed to keep. First, no Christian should eat meat that had been sacrificed to idols because to do so would be to give honor to false gods. Second, no Christian should eat the meat of strangled animals or eat blood. Because God had given this law to Noah, the ancestor of all people, the Jews believed that it should be binding on Gentiles as well. Finally, the Council said that all Christians, Gentile or Jew, must avoid illicit sexual activities. No matter what the practices were in

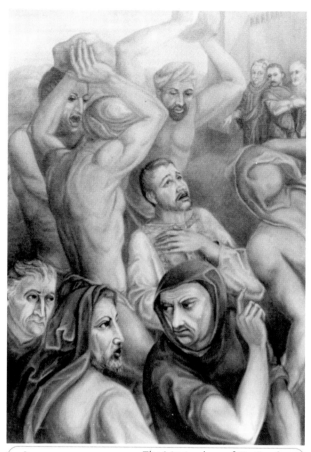

→ *The Martyrdom of St. Stephen*

the world around them, Christians were to understand that sex belonged only in marriage.

Although the Council of Jerusalem released Gentile Christians from many of the other more difficult obligations of Jewish law, the Council also made it clear that Christianity, like Judaism, was a religion of the body and not just the spirit. Church leaders had a right to tell people how to behave both in public and in private.

By the end of the first century the Church had accepted the idea

Q&A

Interview an adult who has been affected by prejudice or racism. If possible, record the interview on tape and write a transcript of your questions and the person's responses.

Consider the following questions:

· Why were you the object of prejudice or racism?
· Were individuals, groups, or societal structures mainly responsible?
· Tell about some incidents that caused you pain.
· Tell about some incidents that brought healing.
· How have you noticed society changing in the area that caused you hurt?
· What are some practical things teenagers can do to combat prejudice and racism?

St. Stephen was the first Christian martyr. While he was being stoned to death, the cloaks of the perpetrators were being minded by "Saul," known more commonly after his conversion as St. Paul (see Acts 7:58).

that the Good News was to be shared with all people, including Gentiles. They also agreed that anyone who was moved by faith to become a Christian could do so without first converting to Judaism or learning the details of Jewish law. Yet the Church continued to insist that law still had a place in Christian life. It was not enough for Christians to

believe in Jesus Christ, they must also behave in a way that reflected that belief. All Christians—whatever their origin—were required to reject anything in their own culture which would undermine or contradict faith in the one, true, creator God.

STUDY QUESTIONS

- DIFFERENTIATE BETWEEN THE HEBREW AND HELLENIST MEMBERS OF THE EARLY CHURCH.
- WHAT ELEMENTS OF JUDAISM DID THE APOSTLES BELIEVE WERE ESSENTIAL TO CHRISTIANITY?
- WHAT WAS THE PRIMARY ISSUE BEFORE THE COUNCIL OF JERUSALEM? HOW WAS THIS ISSUE RESOLVED?
- WHAT DOES IT MEAN TO SAY THAT CHRISTIANITY IS A RELIGION OF THE BODY, NOT JUST THE SPIRIT?

CHURCH MEMBERSHIP: PERMANENT OR CONDITIONAL

confessors—Those Christians who refused to respond to Decius's decree to offer sacrifices to Roman gods.

When Decius became Roman emperor in 249 his primary goal was to restore Rome to her former glory. He was convinced that Christianity bore much of the responsibility for the empire's troubles. He felt that the ancient gods had been angered by the loss of so many of their people; they had responded by turning their backs on all. Decius was

determined to restore the worship of Roman gods. He declared that all who refused to worship the ancient gods were guilty of treason.

Decius decreed that every person in the empire must offer sacrifice to the Roman gods. All who did not have a certificate to prove that they had offered the required sacrifice were to be treated as criminals. Few Christians were sentenced to death because of this law but many were arrested, threatened, and tortured. Christians who refused to respond to this decree were known as **confessors**.

The Council of Jerusalem took place in AD 49. The decision at the Council showed that Christianity was destined to be a catholic (universal) religion, intended for all people at all times.

Decius's policies not only produced confessors, they also resulted in many other Christians who gave in to his demands. Some Christians offered sacrifices to the pagan gods. Others falsified certificates without actually offering sacrifices. When the persecutions ended in 251, the Church had to answer the question of what to do with these "lapsed" Christians. Could a person still be considered a member of the Church if he or she had reneged on the promises of Baptism?

The city of Carthage in North Africa became the focal point for much of the dispute. Cyprian, the city's bishop, had fled during the persecutions and ruled his diocese during that time through written correspondence.[3] When the persecutions ended, some Christians of Carthage felt that the confessors who had stayed and faced the persecution had more right to govern the local church than a bishop who had fled the persecutions. When the confessors began to readmit the lapsed who had offered sacrifices but now admitted and expressed sorrow for their error, many bishops were upset. They insisted that only a bishop had the authority to admit or readmit anyone into the Church.

Cyprian called a **synod** and gathered all of the regional bishops in order that they might establish a uniform ruling for responding to the lapsed Christians. Cyprian believed that a uniform ruling was essential because no one could

have God as his or her Father without also having the Church as his or her Mother. Cyprian believed that the Church must be a community of saints with no room for those who could reject the most fundamental elements of their faith.

In the end the synod chose a compromise position somewhere between Cyprian and the confessors. Those who had offered sacrifices to the pagan gods and repented would only be allowed back into the Church on their deathbeds. Those who had not repented would never be allowed back into the Church. Those who had obtained false certificates without actually offering a sacrifice could be readmitted immediately.

The Debate Continues

This controversy brought out a more central issue. Was one's status as a member of the Church permanent or conditional? If certain characteristics defined a Christian, could a person who failed to demonstrate those characteristics and instead demonstrated their complete opposite still be a member of the Christian community? In other words, could sin separate a person from God if he or she had already

synod—A representative body of bishops assembled periodically by the pope to advise him on important Church concerns. It is not a legislative body.

Cyprian was born in Carthage about 200. He was a man of wealth and education. About 246 he converted to Christianity and two or three years after he became bishop of Carthage. He fled from persecutions in 250, but in 258 he stood his ground and suffered a martyr's death by beheading.

THE CHURCH: OUR STORY

Penance—The name for the sacrament that allows a sinner to return to communion with Christ and the Church.

been united to God in Baptism? As the answer to these questions was both "yes" and "no" we are able to better understand why Christ instituted the Sacrament of **Penance**.

Baptism involved a radical reorientation of a person's life. It inclined one toward God and away from sin. Baptism erased the sin inherited from Adam and Eve, but it did not erase the freedom to sin. Just as Adam and Eve rejected God before original sin existed, so the baptized person is able to reject God even after Original Sin has been washed away. When Adam and Eve rejected God, however, there was no way to restore their broken relationship. When baptized people reject God, the grace of Christ that healed them once still remains to heal them again if they request it. Just as the catechumenate was developed to help a person prepare for a life with Christ and the Church, so the Sacrament of Penance helped prepare any sinner for a life reunited with Christ and the Church.

The problem of responding to lapsed Christians did not disappear after the third century synod in Carthage. It came to a head again in the fourth century, also in the city of Carthage. Following the conversion of Constantine, when Christianity was not only no longer a persecuted religion but, in fact, a desirable religion, there were many who thought that the Church should not be too quick to welcome back those who had abandoned the faith during more difficult times. Many of the confessors began to argue that the lapsed Christians who needed to accept a long penitential process before being welcomed back to the Church included not only those

who had offered sacrifices to idols, but also all those who had cooperated with the authorities by handing over the Bible to be destroyed.

While the debate over this issue was going on, Caecilian was elected bishop of Carthage. He did not agree with those who were calling for greater strictness for the lapsed Christians, so a stricter group within the Church elected another bishop, claiming that Caecilian's consecration was invalid. According to Caecilian's opponents (who came to be known as Donatists, named after the bishop they elected), one of the bishops who had consecrated Caecilian had been among those who had handed over the Scripture. The Donatists claimed that since this bishop was a traitor to the faith, any sacrament conferred by him was invalid. They also said that, since Caecilian was not validly ordained a bishop, any priest he ordained was not really a priest. What is more, they added that any other bishop or priest who sided with Caecilian also became a traitor to the faith; his ordination could no longer be considered valid nor could any sacrament that he administered.

Caecilian and those who supported him argued that the bishops who had ordained him were not traitors, but even if they had been, his ordination would still be valid. They said that the validity of a sacrament did not and could not depend on the purity of the one administering it. If it did, people would be in constant doubt concerning the validity of their own Baptisms and of any Eucharist they participated in.

The emperor Constantine, followed by the western (Latin) bishops, and finally the eastern (Greek)

bishops, declared that Caecilian was the true bishop of Carthage. Thus it came to be understood that the grace of the sacraments could not be destroyed by the sin of those administering or receiving them and that a person's past sins alone should not be the cause of permanent disassociation from the Church.

Leading to Unam Santam

In the fourth century, the actions of Ambrose, the bishop of Milan, foreshadowed an attitude that would become prevalent in the Church in the Middle Ages, that those who were "outside" the Church could not be saved. Ambrose was a wise man and gifted theologian. He was outspoken on the duty of Christians to help the poor and unfortunate. His concern, however, was for Christians only. When some Christians in the town of Callinicum were ordered by the emperor to rebuild a synagogue which they had burned down, Ambrose intervened. He insisted that a Christian emperor should not force Christians to build a Jewish synagogue. A sad precedent was set of placing the rights of Christians above the rights of any others.

The Church continued to exert or approve of various controls over people. There was a growing sense that membership in the People of God (or more specifically, the Catholic Church) was what entitled people to basic human rights. When Charlemagne decided that the only way to gain permanent control over the barbarians was to baptize or slaughter them, there were no significant protests from within the Church. Church leaders did not question the validity or appropriateness of Baptism at sword point.

The Church's claim to absolute authority over all people reached its climax in 1302 in

the papal bull *Unam Sanctam*, written by Pope Boniface VIII. According to Boniface, when Jesus told Peter to "tend my sheep," he was giving him authority over all people. This authority was a temporal, as well as a spiritual,

authority. Therefore, Pope Boniface concluded, "We declare, we proclaim, and we define that it is absolutely necessary for salvation that every human creature be subject to the Roman Pontiff." In essence the letter supported those who believed that the lives of any who rejected the pope and the teachings of the Catholic Church were already forfeit.

Ambrose was governor of a large portion of northern Italy when the death of the Milan bishop occurred in 374. The cry of "Ambrose Bishop!" arose when he entered the church. Though unbaptized, he was elected bishop of Milan. Ambrose gave up his wealth and power to become a Christian.

STUDY QUESTIONS

- WHAT HISTORICAL EVENTS RAISED THE ISSUE OF WHAT TO DO WITH "LAPSED" CATHOLICS?
- IS MEMBERSHIP IN THE CHURCH PERMANENT OR CONDITIONAL?
- WHAT ISSUE WAS RAISED IN THE CONTROVERSY BETWEEN CAECILIAN AND THE DONATISTS? HOW WAS IT RESOLVED?
- WHAT INCIDENT WAS AMBROSE INVOLVED IN THAT PLACED THE RIGHTS OF CHRISTIANS ABOVE THE RIGHTS OF NON-CHRISTIANS?
- WHAT WAS THE SIGNIFICANCE OF *UNAM SANCTAM*?

JOURNAL ASSIGNMENT

- HOW HAVE YOU RECEIVED AND GIVEN UNCONDITIONAL LOVE?

FAITH VS. WORKS

By the late Middle Ages, the only people who could not be members of the Church were sinners who refused to repent and those who openly rejected Christianity. Yet, the Church continued to do everything possible to convert people in each of these groups.

The sacrament of Penance continued to take on prominence as Christians were reminded that even though they had been cleansed of Original Sin through Baptism, their personal sins committed after Baptism could result in eternal damnation unless they demonstrated true repentance and were absolved of their sins in the Sacrament of Penance.

The Protestant reformers, led by Martin Luther, questioned the penitential system. Luther argued that since God saved humankind as sinners, the gift of Salvation belongs to all who remain sinners. Luther maintained that the Sacrament of Penance placed too much emphasis on human works and too little emphasis on the unmerited grace offered by God. Luther said that no person could possibly keep all of the commandments of God; everyone would be condemned if salvation hinged upon human behavior. The wonder of the Gospel for Luther was that God offers us Salvation despite our behavior. Luther was not indifferent to sin and realized that sinful behavior was to be taken seriously. But,

On October 31, 1517, Martin Luther posted his Ninety-Five Theses on the church in Wittenberg, Germany, to protest the selling of indulgences in connection with the Sacrament of Penance. Luther was raised a Catholic and became an Augustinian priest.

Luther argued, every effort to avoid sin should be in response to the free gift given by God and not because of a fear of punishment. Luther and his fellow reformers believed that the key to Salvation was found in a person's faith and not in his or her actions. According to Luther, penance (satisfying or making up for one's sins) and indulgence (payment for sins that have already been forgiven) served no purpose; they only encouraged people to place their trust in human effort rather than in God.

The Council of Trent agreed with the Protestant reformers: people are saved because of the grace of God and the sacrifice of Jesus Christ, not their own merit. The Council reemphasized the fact that one receives this saving grace first and foremost in the Sacrament of Baptism. The Council agreed that a person cannot be justified (reunited with God) without faith. However, the Council pointed out that Baptism, not personal faith, is the first step toward Salvation. Baptism is "the sacrament of faith." Baptism is not only the sign but also the instrument of a faithful relationship with God. In other words, catechumens do not come to the Church because their faith in God is so strong that they have special knowledge that they are members of the People of God. Rather, catechumens come to the Church because they want the faith which the Church can offer them. When they receive that faith, they also receive the gifts of hope and Christian love (charity): "For faith, unless hope and charity be added

thereto, neither unites man [and woman] perfectly with Christ, nor makes him [or her] a living member of [Christ's] body."[4]

Post-Baptism Behavior

All who are baptized are members of the People of God. They have been united to God and offered the gift of Salvation. That does not mean, however, that the behavior of the baptized no longer matters. What has been freely given by God can also be taken away. Baptism makes a faithful relationship with God possible, but it does not take away a person's free will. If a person chooses to continue sinning even after receiving God's grace, his or her faith will become meaningless and the gift of Salvation can be lost. According to the Council of Trent, it is nothing short of arrogant to presume that one was a member of the Body of Christ even when one's behavior harmed that body or was in opposition to the head of the Body—Christ.

Luther believed that God's law could never really be kept. To Luther, the primary purpose of the law was to make us aware of the great gulf which separates us from God, and to show us just how dependent we are on God's mercy. The Council of Trent insisted that God does not ask the impossible. If a person has been united with Christ, that person is able to keep God's commandments. The Church holds that anyone who says the commandments are impossible to keep is separated from the Church.

THE COUNCIL OF TRENT ON JUSTIFICATION

Read the text of the sixth session of the Council of Trent (see http://history.hanover.edu/texts/trent/ct06.html). Write five teachings of the council related to what is necessary for justification of the soul. Rework these statements as questions and answers. Take turns quizzing a classmate on the teachings you uncovered.

The teaching of Trent means that anyone who fails to keep the commandments after receiving God's grace through Baptism can lose that grace. Once lost, grace can only be regained as it is given by God. To facilitate this Jesus gives us the Sacrament of Penance. As the Council of Trent made clear, Catholics hold that grace is mediated. In other words, we receive the grace of God through physically tangible signs and celebrations. The sacraments make the invisible visible and the intangible tangible; that is, the divine is put on a human plane. The Sacrament of Penance, like the Sacrament of Baptism, is a gift from God which enables us to perceive and receive God's forgiveness and grace. The Sacrament of Baptism makes a person a member of the People of God. The Sacrament of Penance restores a person to the People of God after he or she has been separated due to personal sin.

In summary, the decrees of the Council of Trent made it clear that membership in the Church depends on both faith and works. Because the Council of Trent was in many ways a response to the Protestant reformation, the phrase "faith" and "works" came to be understood as implying adherence to the doctrine and practice of the Roman Catholic Church.

STUDY QUESTIONS

- WHAT WAS LUTHER'S OBJECTION TO THE CATHOLIC SYSTEM OF PENANCE?
- THE COUNCIL OF TRENT AGREED WITH THE REFORMERS ON ONE SIGNIFICANT POINT. WHAT WAS THAT POINT?
- ACCORDING TO THE COUNCIL, WHAT WAS THE FIRST STEP TOWARD SALVATION?
- HOW WAS THE COUNCIL'S UNDERSTANDING OF DUTIES REGARDING THE COMMANDMENTS DIFFERENT FROM LUTHER'S?

JOURNAL ASSIGNMENT

- SHARE EXAMPLES OF HOW GOD'S GIFT OF FAITH HAS LEAD TO YOUR DOING GOOD WORKS.

INCLUSION AND EXCLUSION

The Council of Trent reinforced the position taken by the Council of Florence in 1442: "[The Holy Roman Church] . . . firmly believes, professes, and preaches that 'no one remaining outside the Catholic Church, not only pagans,' but Jews, heretics, or schismatics, can become partakers of eternal life; but they will go to the 'eternal fire prepared for the devil and his angels' (Matthew 25:41), unless before the end of their life they are received into it."[5]

This remained the basic Catholic position for over four hundred years. In 1864, in his Syllabus of Errors, Pius IX said that the Catholic religion should be the only religion permitted by the state. From a Catholic perspective, membership in the Church was synonymous with adherence to the Pope and reliance on the Seven Sacraments of the Church, particularly the Sacrament of Penance which the Protestants had abandoned. A person had rights because he or she belonged to God; therefore, the rights of those who were not Catholic and could not claim to belong to God were not equal to the rights of Catholics.

Pope Leo XIII gave the first hint of a coming change in 1885 when he said that no one should be forced to become a Catholic against his or her will. Pope Leo also acknowledged that in certain circumstances concern for the greater good might make it necessary for governments to tolerate non-Catholic beliefs and practices.

Catholic attitude toward non-Catholics changed dramatically with the Second Vatican Council. This change is epitomized by a revision in the wording of paragraph 8 in the Vatican II document *Lumen Gentium*. An early draft of this document said that the Church of Christ—the People of God—is the Catholic Church; the final draft says that the Church of Christ subsists in the Catholic Church. As Catholics we still believe that the Catholic Church is complete in herself. The Church does not need anything or anyone from outside of herself to complete her identity as the People of God. We also believe, however, that membership in the People of God is not limited to those who have been baptized or received into the Catholic Church.

The Declaration on Religious Liberty issued by the Second Vatican Council states that no one should be compelled to be a Christian or to act against his or her own religious convictions either in public or in private. Children should not be required to attend classes that contradict their parents' religious convictions. The right to freedom of religion stems from the basic human dignity which belongs to all people because they have been created in the image and likeness of God. The declaration stresses that no one should be penalized in any way for his or her religious convictions.

The Second Vatican Council stressed that since God desires all people to be one, we must recognize that everyone belongs to or is related to the People of God to some degree. The Catholic faithful who participate in the sacramental life of the Church and who obey the teachings of Christ are fully incorporated into the People of God. All Christians, even if they are not in unity with the pope, have been united to Christ through Baptism. They, too, are members of the People of God, and they, along with Catholics, are called to work for the unity of all Christians. Those who have not accepted the gospel are also joined to the People of God in different ways. The Jewish people remain very dear to God. They are the people with whom God first established his covenant, and God does not go back on his word. Furthermore, all people who believe in the creator are joined to the People of God because they too are part of God's plan for Salvation. First among these are the Muslims

BEING INCLUSIVE

Spend a week breaking from your usual routine of friends, activities, and interests. Do some or all of the following:

- listen to a different style radio station
- hang out with at least one person from a different peer group
- attend Mass at a parish with a different cultural or economic base than yours
- read about people in need from a different region of the world
- say "hi" to at least five people you've never met and note their reactions

Write a report summarizing your week of "being inclusive" of others.

religious indifferentism—The attitude which holds that all religions and all ways of expressing one's faith are equal or essentially the same.

who share the faith of Abraham and who with us worship the one, all powerful, and merciful God. Finally, those who do not know God but who seek truth and goodness with a sincere heart may also share in the Salvation promised to the People of God.[6]

According to Church teaching today, all people of good will have the hope of Salvation. All people deserve to be treated with respect. Non-Catholics should enjoy the same rights as Catholics. What is more, Catholics need not separate themselves or their children from people whose religious beliefs are different from their own. Although the Church today warns Catholics that marrying someone who is not Catholic will place additional burdens on their marriage and on their ability to understand one another and determine the proper education of their children, the Church does not forbid such marriages.

The Church does still warn people against the dangers of **religious indifferentism**—thinking that all religions are the same. Catholics continue to profess that the truth which God has revealed to humanity exists most completely in the Catholic Church. We recognize, however, that we do not have a monopoly on the truth. Those who are not Catholic may also know, love, and serve the one true God. Over the centuries we have come to understand that although God is not indifferent to our beliefs and our behavior, and although God expects certain things of those of us who have been blessed with the faith of the Catholic Church, God understands the faith of others in ways that we cannot. It is not our place to declare that others have been excluded from the People of God for following the best judgments of their own consciences.

STUDY QUESTIONS

- WHAT DOES IT MEAN TO SAY THAT THE PEOPLE OF GOD "SUBSISTS" IN THE CATHOLIC CHURCH?
- ON WHAT GROUNDS DID THE SECOND VATICAN COUNCIL SAY THAT ALL PEOPLE HAVE A RIGHT TO RELIGIOUS FREEDOM?
- WHO BELONGS TO THE PEOPLE OF GOD?

Muslims accept Jesus as a prophet born of Mary, but they do not believe he was the Messiah or God's Son. Muslims believe that God sent prophets in all ages and that Muhammad was the final and greatest prophet God will send to the world.

JOURNAL ASSIGNMENT

- HOW DOES YOUR GENERATION ENCOUNTER AND RESPOND TO RELIGIOUS INDIFFERENTISM?

IN CONCLUSION

As history has unfolded, the Church's understanding of what it means to be a member of the chosen People of God has changed and expanded. At times in our history Catholics have mistakenly assumed that they were chosen by God because of certain characteristics, attitudes, beliefs, or responses. We have believed that any individuals or groups who did not demonstrate the proper qualifications were not among the chosen. Over time we have come to understand that our being chosen is God's unmerited gift. It is an expression of God's love and not a reward for being who we are or for doing what we have done. Furthermore, we have come to understand that God has not just chosen select individuals or groups, but all of humanity. With infinite love and mercy God has chosen to offer himself to and unite himself with the whole human race.

God's free election cannot be negated by characteristics of birth such as race or gender. It cannot be negated by human weakness, sin, or ignorance. God has chosen every person and blessed every person with the dignity of God's own image and with the rights that accompany that dignity.

LEARN BY DOING

Research beliefs and practices of three other worshiping communities: Jews, Muslims, and any Christian denomination other than Roman Catholic. Summarize beliefs and practices in the following areas:
- God
- Jesus Christ
- Salvation
- prayer and worship
- initiation and membership requirements

When completed, write a short essay comparing Roman Catholic belief in these areas of belief and practice to those you researched.

PRAYER

O glorious St. Michael, guardian and defender of the Church of Jesus Christ, come to the assistance of this Church, against which the powers of hell are unchained, guard with especial care her august Head, and obtain that for him and for us the hour of triumph may speedily arrive. O glorious Archangel St. Michael, watch over us during life, defend us against the assaults of the demon, assist us especially at the hour of death; obtain for us a favorable judgment, and the happiness of beholding God face to face for endless ages. Amen.

—Pope Leo XIII

NOTES

1. Or, if they are marrying a non-Christian, in a neutral place not attached to any one religion.
2. See Gonzalez, *The Story of Christianity,* Vol. 1, p. 18.
3. Cyprian insisted that he fled not out of cowardice but because he believed that he could do more good guiding the Church from a distance than he could remaining and being arrested. In fact, he demonstrated his courageous commitment to his faith only a few years later when he was martyred.
4. The Council of Trent, Decree on Justification, chapter 7.
5. The Decree for the Jacobites, cited in Richard P. McBrien, *Catholicism* (San Francisco: HarperSanFrancisco, 1994), p. 387.
6. See *Lumen Gentium*, #13–16, and *Catechism of the Catholic Church*, #836–842, 847.

UNIT FOUR

THE CHURCH IS TEACHER

THE CHURCH IS TEACHER

The Catholic Church is a Teacher of truth.

The truth the Church teaches is about God's plan for the world that is intimately linked with the Salvation offered by Jesus Christ. Christ, himself, said to Pilate, "For this I was born and for this I came into the world, to testify to the truth. Everyone who belongs to the truth listens to my voice" (John 18:37).

Pilate then asked Jesus, "What is truth?"

What Pilate and others before and since failed to grasp is that the heart of truth is that God is love. And through Jesus Christ, God has made it possible for each person to participate in that love.

The truth of God's love is meant to be shared with others. Jesus sent his Apostles out with the mission to "Go, therefore, and make disciples of all nations" (Matthew 28:19). Through Jesus, the Apostles were united to the mission Jesus received from God the Father and given the power to carry it out.

The bishops are the successors of the Apostles. Together with the pope they share the authority to teach in Jesus' name. The teaching office of the Church is called the Magisterium. The magisterial teaching of the pope and bishops can be found in creeds, laws, dogmas, and doctrines which build up the Church, administer the sacraments, and correctly proclaim the gospel for the current age.

Chapter 4.1 examines the truth taught by the Church. Chapter 4.2 reminds us all of our challenge to share the revelation of God's truth with others.

When you have completed Unit 4, you will be able to:

- explain how Church dogma influences our everyday experiences;
- define the term "revelation" and the role of Revelation in Christianity;
- understand the similarities and differences between religious truth and scientific truth;
- articulate the role of scripture in Catholic teaching;
- trace the development of the canon of Scripture;
- explain how "Tradition" is understood to contribute to our understanding of Jesus;
- define dogma and heresy;
- identify some of the challenges which Catholic dogma presents to the world today;
- explain the role conscience plays in decision making;
- define what is meant by "good" evangelization;
- explain the Christian witness of widows and virgins in the early Church;
- outline the development of the Christian monastic movement;
- critique the different approaches used by Catholic missionaries in the New World;
- summarize some of the main events in the history of the Catholic Church in the United States.

CREEDS, LAWS, DOGMAS, and DOCTRINES

DOGMAS ARE LIGHTS ALONG THE PATH OF FAITH; THEY ILLUMINATE IT AND MAKE IT SECURE.

—*Catechism of the Catholic Church, 89*

dogma—Those truths which the Church teaches have been specifically revealed by God. Acceptance of dogma is essential for complete faith and the deepest possible relationship with God. Denial of dogma is heresy.

WHO NEEDS DOGMA?

A grandmother who loves roller-coasters, a priest who's a baseball fanatic, and a young father whose adopted son must always be on a respirator: not one of them would strike you as the kind of person who would be particularly concerned about how Church **dogma**—core teaching issued with the highest authority— is being taught. They are all very down-to-earth people who are more concerned with everyday life than they are with great intellectual questions. They all insist that Christianity is rooted in love, not rules. So why do Joan, Father Pete, and Toby bemoan the fact that Catholics are too unaware of their own dogma?

All three of these people are hospital chaplains. They spend their days and often their nights talking with and listening to people who are in pain, people who have

Trinity—The central Christian mystery that one God is in three Persons: Father, Son, and Holy Spirit.

been injured and can no longer do the kind of work they've always done, and people who are dying or whose parent, spouse, or child is dying. Toby works in Missouri, Father Pete in southern New Jersey, and Joan in Maine. There are days when all of their conversations are about God, faith and prayer. There are other days when the main topic of discussion is grandchildren or sports or life in India; God is scarcely mentioned. Regardless of which kind of a day it is, all three of them would agree that the majority of their conversations are shaped by dogma.

Father Pete explains it this way, "People who are suffering aren't interested in discussing the finer points of theology. They don't want to debate the nature of the **Trinity** or the relationship between Jesus' humanity and his divinity. However, most of the really important things that they do want to talk about are connected in some way or another to their understanding of God and of human nature—the main topics of dogma."

Toby adds, "As hospital chaplains, we spend a lot of time helping people to cope with the sense of complete isolation that often comes with illness. When people believe that in the person of Jesus God himself suffered and faced anxieties just as they are suffering and anxious, they often feel less abandoned. They can take comfort in the fact that God understands what they are going through, even if no one else does."

Joan nods and says, "Parents who think of Mary as their own mother, or who have reflected on the fact that God is the Father of Jesus, often cope with the suffering of their child in a very different way from those who have no relationship with Mary or who have never thought about the relationships within the Trinity.

"Pope John Paul II once said that the current ecological crisis stems from an 'anthropological error.' People don't understand their proper place in the order of creation. Instead of cooperating with God, they try to take God's place. A lot of the emotional crises which I see stem from similar 'errors.' People expect doctors or hospitals to take the place of God. They define ultimate good and bad by medical standards instead of by Christian standards."

Joan, Toby, and Father Pete all agree that what we believe about God influences the choices we make. Dogma forms the framework for a Christian worldview. It shapes our understanding of good and bad. It shapes our attitude toward suffering and setbacks in life. It helps us determine what we should try to change and what we should leave to God.

Joan says, "I see a lot of committed Catholics whose faith is threatened as soon as tragedy strikes. I also see an increasing number of Catholics who are ready to join the secular world and say that suffering should be eliminated at all costs. I feel like these people haven't understood some of the basic truths of our faith."

Toby agrees and adds, "I would draw an analogy between many of the people I meet in the hospital and myself the first time I went hiking in the Himalayas. I was completely unprepared for the effects of very high altitude on my body. I could not understand why I was so weak and uncoordinated. I felt as if my body had betrayed me. I was so upset and worried that I never had a chance to enjoy myself. If I had understood a little bit more, I could have coped with everything much better. In the same way, many of the people in the hospital are completely unprepared for suffering and loss. They feel like God has betrayed them. If they understood theology a little bit better they would have more of the tools that they need to cope.

"Of course you can explain altitude sickness to a person who is suffering from it. But when a person's faith is shaken because he or she has misunderstood the nature of God or of humanity, a quick lesson in theology isn't the cure."

"But time spent sharing faith might be part of the cure," Father Pete observes. "One of the things I've come to appreciate over the years is just how much of a difference parish eucharistic ministers who bring communion to the sick can make. Some of the eucharistic ministers from our church are very good at sharing their own faith with those they are visiting. Without being preachy they can give the people they are visiting some new insights and some new hope. Of course it only really works if the eucharistic ministers live a life rooted in a proper understanding of Christian truth. So we're back at the beginning—looking for a better way to help people connect dogma with everyday life. As Catholics, we need to take more time to talk about some of our most basic beliefs before crises arise."

STUDY QUESTIONS

• TELL TWO WAYS THAT CHRISTIAN DOGMA IS RELEVANT TO EVERYDAY LIFE.

JOURNAL ASSIGNMENT

- HOW IS CHRISTIAN DOGMA RELEVANT TO YOUR LIFE? SHARE TWO EXAMPLES.

THE GOOD NEWS IS ROOTED IN THE TRUTH

WHAT IS TRUE?

Given that each of the following statements are true, how would you describe the kind of truth in each statement?

- It is 110 miles from San Diego to Los Angeles. (e.g., *geographical truth*).
- Ronald Reagan was elected President of the United States in 1980.
- 12 x 12=144
- I have known Mary for years. I can attest she is an honest person.
- Water is made up of two parts hydrogen and one part oxygen.
- It is wrong to steal.
- My mother loves me.
- It is raining cats and dogs.
- God loves me.

Which type of truth named above is most present in Scripture and Church Tradition?

Jesus said, "you will know the truth, and the truth will set you free" (John 8:32). In our society we often interpret this to mean, "the more you know, the more freedom you will have." There is no disputing that knowledge is a good thing; indeed, it is one of the gifts of the Holy Spirit. Knowledge alone, however, will not lead a person to the truth and to freedom. Knowledge needs to be systematized and categorized before it can reveal the truth. The way that we systematize and categorize our knowledge can vary significantly, depending upon the type of truth that we are seeking. In the scientific world we categorize knowledge based upon observation and measurements. Things which cannot be observed or measured, such as the purpose or meaning of life or the essence of right and wrong, are outside of the realm of scientific truth. In the religious world we categorize our knowledge based upon Revelation. Everything that we learn must be related to the things which God has made known to us. From a religious perspective, anything which would deny, contradict, or change what has already been revealed cannot be true.

Both religious truth and scientific truth are objective. They come from outside of us; we cannot shape them to suit ourselves. Both help us to order our lives so that we will be in harmony with the world around us. Religious truth does not deny scientific truth, but it does carry us beyond scientific truth. Observation and measurement will not contradict Revelation because God is the source of both. Observation and measurement alone, however, will never tell us all that there is to know. Scientific truth alone will never make people free.

Only those who know the truth about God and God's plan for the world can ever really be free. People who have a false understanding of reality make choices based on misinformation. These choices result in things they never desired or even anticipated. Sin itself is a rejection of the truth. It multiplies as people continue to embrace a false understanding of the world. Freedom from sin and an understanding and acceptance of the truth go hand in hand.

The Catholic Church is an apostolic church. Catholics have been sent to proclaim the Good News to the world. That Good News is a message of "glad tidings to the poor . . . liberty to captives and recovery of sight to the blind" (Luke 4:18). It is a message of liberation, and therefore it is a message of truth.

Two things go hand in hand with our sharing of the Good News. The first is a relationship with God; the second is an understanding of reality. We are called to share and live the Good News in such a way that those who meet us are aware of God's presence and gain a clearer understanding of the truth.

Through the centuries the Church has encountered God and passed on a knowledge and understanding of the truth through both Scripture and Tradition.

STUDY QUESTIONS

- HOW ARE RELIGIOUS TRUTH AND SCIENTIFIC TRUTH DIFFERENT? HOW ARE THEY THE SAME?
- WHAT MESSAGE DO WE SHARE WHEN WE SHARE THE GOOD NEWS?
- WHAT ARE TWO THINGS THAT GO HAND IN HAND WITH OUR SHARING OF THE GOOD NEWS?

JOURNAL ASSIGNMENT

- WHAT IS WRONG WITH DETERMINING TRUTH BASED ON STATEMENTS LIKE "AS LONG AS [FILL IN THE BEHAVIOR] DOESN'T HURT ANYONE ELSE, IT IS OKAY"?

PASSING ON THE TRUTH THROUGH SCRIPTURE

The Bible is normative for all of Catholic faith and theology. As Catholics we believe that Scripture is the word of God, and as such it should guide us in all that we do. We believe that the Holy Spirit inspired the authors of the various books of the Bible so that they wrote what God desired them to write.[1] Because all of Scripture is inspired by the Holy Spirit, it is free from error. That means that Scripture is true in its essence. Properly understood, Scripture can never give us a false understanding of God or of the world and can never lead us to do things that God does not desire. The key words here are "properly understood."

The Catholic Church teaches that Scripture must always be interpreted.

Scripture is inerrant because it is the Word of God, but it is the Word of God expressed in human words. Like all human words, therefore, it has been shaped and limited by human weaknesses and limitations. Scripture is the Word of God for all times and places, but it was written in words that were appropriate to the people of a particular time and place. In order for us to understand Scripture fully, we must consider how it would have been understood by the people for whom it was originally written. When we say that Scripture is inerrant, we are not saying that the authors of Scripture were inerrant. They remained human even as they wrote the word of God. They were not deprived of their particular personalities, strengths, or weaknesses, but their personal characteristics, biases, and limitations did not interfere with the message which they were to convey to the people of their time. Some of the biases and limitations may interfere, however, with our understanding of the message. If we read things too literally and

fail to recognize the changes which have occurred between their time and our own, we may confuse the message of God with the culture of biblical times.

For example, Scripture was used for years to justify slavery because it speaks about how slaves and masters should relate. What was overlooked was the fact that the entire Bible was written in a time when slavery was not even questioned. The New Testament authors did not challenge the concept of slavery itself, but they did challenge the attitude which said that people should be valued and treated differently depending upon whether they were slaves or free. The essence of the message had nothing to do with either the acceptability or unacceptability of slavery; the essence of the message was that all people were of equal importance before God regardless of their social standing. The fact that the authors of Scripture accepted slavery did not affect the ability of their contemporaries to hear their essential message, but it can affect our ability to hear the essential message if we fail to recognize the social climate in which the words were written.

The Bible is the Book of the Church

The Catholic faith is not a faith of "the book." It is a faith of the living Word of God.[2] Because we are different people from our ancestors, God does not speak to us in exactly the same way that he spoke to them, even though he speaks through the same Scripture. Each generation must use the critical tools which are available to it in order to read and interpret Scripture in light of its own knowledge and experience. This reading and interpretation should take place first and foremost within the community which is the living body of Christ.[3] This does not mean that individuals should not read and study the Bible; it does mean that they should allow their study to be guided by the teachings of the Church.

The community of the Church has been an integral part of Scripture since the beginning. The Gospels were created from oral accounts of the Life, Death, and Resurrection of Jesus. When they were written down, they were written for specific communities with specific needs and concerns. The different styles and emphases of the four Gospels reflect the different natures of the groups for whom they were written. The very fact that we have four Gospel accounts instead of only one, is an indication of the fact that God enters into a dialogue with the Christian community; God does not simply dictate absolutes to us. In a similar way, most of the epistles were written to specific communities and they addressed the issues which were most relevant to those communities.

It is part of our Catholic tradition to give equal attention to all four Gospels. Over a three year period of Sundays the lectionary takes us through each Gospel; it also takes us through most of the rest of the New Testament. Because we hear the same message presented in different ways with different emphases, we are reminded that Scripture is something that must be discussed, interpreted, and applied. It is not something that is intended as a step-by-step instructional manual. We recognize that each scriptural event or passage can have a range of meaning because each event and each passage points to a truth which is much greater than itself.

The Canon of Scripture

Often we think of the Bible as the starting point of Christianity. We talk as if the Church developed in response to Scripture. In fact, in many ways it is more accurate to say that it was Scripture which developed in response to the Church. The **canon** of Scripture—the list of writings which the Church considers sacred and normative—did not drop from the sky. It was not simply handed to the Church. The Church herself had to decide which of the many letters, Gospels, and instructions about Jesus and Church **doctrine** it would consider authoritative. The Church may have taken much longer to make its decision if it had not been for a significant threat to Christianity which arose in the middle of the second century in the person of Marcion.

Marcion saw himself as a Christian leader and teacher. Indeed, he was a man who could attract a significant following, but whether that following could be considered Christian was a matter of debate. Although Marcion called himself a Christian he did not embrace the doctrines of the majority in the Church; instead he developed his own "Christian doctrine" to suit his anti-Jewish and anti-material biases. He tried to purge Christianity of everything Jewish and everything which might incline a person to see good or value in the physical world. Like the gnostics, Marcion believed that Jesus had been sent

canon—A name for those books which have been accepted by the Church as normative for faith.

doctrine—An official teaching of the Church.

to free human beings from the prison of their physical selves so that they could live as pure spirits.

In AD 144 Marcion went to Rome. Though he was able to attract a sizable following, eventually Church leaders and the majority of Christians decided that Marcion's teachings contradicted several fundamental principles of Christianity. Marcion was labeled as a heretic. He then established his own church with his own bishops, doctrine and scripture.

During this entire Marcion controversy there was no official list of sacred Christian writings. When Christians of that time referred to Scripture they usually meant the Septuagint, a Greek translation of the Old Testament.[4] Marcion rejected the entire Septuagint, along with all of the New Testament books which he thought had been influenced by Judaism. Marcion's canon included only the Gospel of Luke and the letters of Paul. He justified his acceptance of these books despite their numerous Old Testament quotations by saying that the

quotations were the work of Judaizing editors and should be ignored.

Marcion's church was a serious rival to the apostolic Church; other Christian leaders could not ignore the challenge which Marcion's teachings presented. The Apostles' Creed and the canon (the official list of Christian scriptures) were both developed in response to Marcion and his followers. No council was called to determine which books should be considered sacred, but a consensus gradually developed over time.[5]

Scholars generally agree that three main criteria were used to determine the sacredness of a particular book: apostolic authorship, orthodox content, and catholicity. In order to be selected a book had to have come from the Apostles, either directly or through those who had known them; it had to portray Jesus in a way that was compatible with the faith of the majority of Christians; and it had to enjoy widespread and frequent use in the worship and teaching of the Church—in other words it had to be genuinely catholic.

STUDY QUESTIONS

- WHY DON'T CATHOLICS BELIEVE IN A LITERAL INTERPRETATION OF SCRIPTURE?
- WHAT QUALIFICATIONS GO WITH THE STATEMENT "CATHOLICS BELIEVE THAT SCRIPTURE IS INERRANT"?
- WHAT DOES IT MEAN TO SAY THAT CATHOLICISM IS A FAITH OF "THE LIVING WORD OF GOD"?
- WHAT IS THE RELATIONSHIP BETWEEN THE COMMUNITY OF FAITH AND THE BIBLE?
- WHY ARE THERE FOUR GOSPELS IN THE BIBLE AND NOT JUST ONE?
- BRIEFLY SUMMARIZE THE MARCION CONTROVERSY.
- DEFINE THE "CANON OF SCRIPTURE."
- WHAT CRITERIA WERE USED TO DETERMINE THE CHRISTIAN CANON?

JOURNAL ASSIGNMENT

- HOW OFTEN DO YOU READ THE BIBLE? WHAT IS YOUR FAVORITE BIBLICAL PASSAGE?

INTERPRETING SCRIPTURE

The Second Vatican Council made it clear that there is a way to read Scripture which is neither overly literalistic nor overly subjective. In the "Dogmatic Constitution on Divine Revelation" (*Dei Verbum*), the council outlined the principles for governing the reading and interpretation of scripture. Several points deserve special attention.

Whenever we are reading any scriptural book or passage we must determine the intentions of the authors. It is also necessary to consider the literary form of the book or passage. For example, is it an historical account, a hymn or a prayer, a myth or allegory, a legal document or a list of household rules? How did the author expect it to be read and understood?

Once we have identified the literary form we must consider the historical period in which the text was written. We recognize that historical circumstances affect the way we hear and interpret different things. In interpreting scripture we need to consider the way that the authors and their original audiences would have understood the meaning of particular phrases or passages.

Finally, we need to read each individual passage and book in the context of the canon as a whole. The truth of Scripture is to be found above all in its unity. The message and meaning which we derive from any single passage can only be accurate if it is in agreement with the message and meaning which we find in the rest of the Bible and in the **Tradition of the Church**. As *Dei Verbum* points out, there is only one God and only one truth (#12).

TRUTH THROUGH TRADITION

Scripture is the written account of God's self-revelation to humanity; it is normative for all of Catholic theology. Nothing we say or do can contradict what has been written in the word of God. Nonetheless, Scripture alone will not necessarily lead us to the truth. As mentioned before, ours is a living faith, not a "dead letter" faith. Before Scripture became the written word, they were the lived experience and knowledge of the apostles and other early Christians. Even after they were written, they continued to be interpreted and explained by the Apostles and their successors.

From generation to generation the Church has handed on both the written account of Revelation and its own understanding of that Revelation. When we speak of the Tradition of the Church, we are speaking of all of the ways in which we have passed on our understanding: our creeds, doctrines, governmental structure, liturgies and patterns of prayer, and service. These are the things that truly make our faith apostolic. These are the things that create continuity between the apostles' understanding of Jesus and our own understanding of Jesus.

Tradition of the Church— The faith which the Church has received from Christ through the apostles and all of the ways the faith has been passed on: in creeds, doctrines, decisions of the magisterium, liturgies, and patterns of prayer and service.

TEACHERS OF DOCTRINE IN THE EARLY CHURCH

Throughout the second century the policies of the Emperor Domitian were followed. Although Christianity was illegal, Christians were not sought out. They were punished only if someone actually brought them before the court. For this reason Christians depended heavily on the goodwill of their neighbors. Christian **apologists** worked hard to dispel the false rumors about Christianity and to make Christianity appear both reasonable and acceptable to non-Christians. In the second half of the second century, Christian apologists also found it necessary to respond to the gnostics and the Marcionites, who were making heretical statements in the name of Christ.

Several of the apologists were particularly influential in defining and explaining the basics of Christian doctrine. Among these were Irenaeus, Clement of Alexandria, Tertullian, and Origen.

STUDY QUESTIONS

- WHAT DOES THE TRADITION OF THE CHURCH REFER TO?

FULLY ALIVE

"The glory of God is a human person fully alive."
—*St. Irenaeus*

Create some artwork, take a photo, write a poem, or design another way to describe what it means to be fully alive.

Irenaeus

Irenaeus, the bishop of Lyons (in present day France), was born in AD 130. He was not particularly interested in joining in on all of the philosophical speculation of the day, especially about the nature of God. He was first and foremost a pastor, who wrote because he wanted the people in his care to understand the basics of Christian faith. Above all, he wanted them to know that God is a loving God, a Good Shepherd who desires what is best for all of creation, especially human beings.

Irenaeus also took a firm stand against all who would claim that the physical was either evil or undesirable. God not only deliberately created humans to be physical beings, but from the beginning God also intended to join

our physical nature with his spiritual one. Irenaeus outlined several beliefs which have remained central to Catholic theology. First, human beings are good. We have been created in God's image and given freedom so that we might draw ever closer to perfection. Second, because God values both our physical and spiritual selves, what we do with our bodies is significant to our relationship with God. Finally, a history which unfolds and changes over time is something that God desires. Human progress is part of God's plan for creation.

Clement of Alexandria

While Irenaeus was concerned with expressing the simple truths of Christianity, Clement of Alexandria (in Egypt) attempted to establish connections between Christianity and Greek philosophy. Clement was born in Athens about AD 150. He wanted to show pagans that much of Christian doctrine could be supported by Plato. Plato and Socrates both criticized the ancient gods and their petty disputes, while teaching about a perfect, unchangeable, supreme being. Clement emphasized that this was the God of the Christians. Clement argued that the law which had been given to the Jews and the philosophy which had been given to the Greeks both pointed to the same ultimate truth, which had now been revealed in Jesus Christ. Clement helped establish a way of thinking which continues to characterize Catholic thought and theology, a way of thinking which sees faith and reason as part of a single whole.

Tertullian

In many ways, Tertullian (born in North Africa about AD 160) was radically different from Clement. Whereas Clement encouraged Christians to be open to the truth present in philosophy, Tertullian said that Christians must reject everything that wasn't explicitly Christian.

In Tertullian's *Prescription Against Heretics*, he insisted that the Church is the rightful owner of Scripture. He based this on the fact that the Church had both claimed and used the Bible for several generations without any challenge from the heretics. He went on to write that, since Scripture belongs to the Church, heretics have no right to use it or to interpret it in a way that contradicts the Church. Tertullian further argued that since the Church's interpretation of Scripture can be traced in a direct line back to the Apostles while the interpretations of the heretics cannot, it should be obvious that the Church's interpretation is the true one.

Tertullian's argument that Scripture belongs only to those who are in union with the legitimate successors of the Apostles has been used repeatedly against dissidents in the Church. It formed the foundation for the rejection of Protestantism in the sixteenth century. In fact, it is only since the Second Vatican Council that the Catholic Church has officially acknowledged that Scripture belongs to Protestants as well as Catholics, and that Protestants too have a right to interpret Scripture. But even as the Catholic Church acknowledges that all Christians have a right to use the Bible, it still insists that no legitimate interpretation can directly contradict the teaching of the Catholic Magisterium which has been passed down from the Apostles. Catholics believe that the Holy Spirit has been active in the Church since her beginnings and do not accept an interpretation of Scripture that would overturn or radically alter the faith which the Church has held through the centuries.

Origen

In most respects Origen (born about AD 185 in Egypt) was more like Clement of Alexandria than he was like Tertullian. This is not surprising since he was, in fact, one of Clement's disciples. Like Clement, he sought

Son of God—A title for Jesus that refers to his relationship with the other Persons of the Trinity.

Incarnation—Becoming human. The event and process in which the eternal Son of God took on flesh and entered human history.

divine—Literally, "of God."

to explain Christian doctrine to the pagans and to relate Christian theology to pagan philosophy. He was, however, more concerned than Clement in making sure that Christian doctrine was not set aside in favor of pagan philosophy. He stated that "nothing which is at odds with the traditions of the Apostles and the Church is to be accepted as true." He then went on to outline those things which were essential to Christianity. First was the belief that there is only one God who is the creator and ruler of the entire universe. Second, he stated clearly that Jesus Christ is the **Son of God** and that he became fully human in his **Incarnation**, but he also remained fully **divine**. The third essential was that the Holy Spirit shares in the glory and divinity of

the Father and Son. Finally, according to Origen, there will be a final judgment and a final resurrection of the body. Origen insisted that Christians must not change or alter the teachings of the Apostles in any way, but he also believed that in those areas for which there was no specific apostolic teaching, Christians were free to speculate.

Origen's position has remained the position of the Catholic Church throughout the centuries. Catholics are expected to adhere to those things which have been definitively taught, but they are free to speculate in other areas. In fact, it is prayerful speculation and study which often leads to a deeper understanding of Revelation and to the development of new doctrines.

STUDY QUESTIONS

- DEFINE APOLOGISTS.
- WHAT WAS IRENAEUS'S MAJOR CONTRIBUTION TO CHRISTIAN THEOLOGY AND DOCTRINE? CLEMENT OF ALEXANDRIA'S? TERTULLIAN'S? ORIGEN'S?

FUNDAMENTALS OF DOGMA

Recall that syncretism refers to selecting and combining bits and pieces from various religious and philosophical systems. Syncretism was very common in the early Church, when many people used the name of Christ to justify a wide variety of beliefs and practices, some of which had little

or no relationship to the gospel of Christ.[6] Syncretism is common again today, as many people substitute popular philosophies or spiritualities for traditional Catholic or Christian faith.[7]

Origen and Tertullian, in particular, worked against the tendency toward syncretism. They insisted that there are certain beliefs and principles which are central to Christian faith. If these are altered or contradicted in any way the resulting belief system is no longer Christian.

Those beliefs which are essential to Christian faith are called dogmas. Dogmas are truths which we believe have been specifically revealed by God. A person who deliberately rejects the dogmatic teaching of the Church falls into **heresy**. The word heresy means "division" or "choice." A heretic is someone who has chosen to divide Christianity and make it into something that it is not. Heretics are people who have separated themselves from the Church because they are unwilling to organize their lives in accordance with the truth which the Church teaches.

There is no universally accepted list of Catholic dogmas, however, there are certain dogmas which are universally recognized as important. These are, first and foremost, the beliefs which are stated in the two primary creeds of the Church, the **Apostles' Creed** and the Nicene Creed. The basic text of the Apostles' Creed was formulated in Rome around AD 150. It was called a "symbol of faith." In other words, it was a means of recognizing the faith of the Church. Catholics believe that it is not possible to remain a member of the Church and reject any of these creedal statements.

Thus it can be said that anyone who is truly part of the Church will believe in "one God, the Father almighty, creator of heaven and earth." This first assertion of the early Church made it clear that Christianity was rooted in the faith of the Jews and not the philosophy

or religion of the pagans. It was a rejection of Gnosticism and Marcionism, both of which claimed that the physical world is undesirable. Basic to Catholic faith and a Catholic's interaction with the world is the belief that everything that exists was created by God and therefore serves a purpose. Catholics reject the idea that any part of the created order is either evil or a mistake. Catholics also reject any theology, philosophy, or way of life which would imply that there are two equal powers, one good and one evil, which are involved in a cosmic battle. There is only one all-powerful God.

Second, to be a Catholic is to believe in Jesus Christ, the Son of God, who existed with the Father from the beginning, was begotten not made, was born of the Virgin Mary, and became human. Catholics believe that Jesus Christ, although he is one person, has two natures. Jesus is fully human and fully divine. This belief is a rejection of several different heresies which threatened the early Church. Arianism said that though the greatest of all God's creatures, Jesus was created and not begotten. Docetism said that Jesus was not human at all; he only appeared human. **Apollinarianism** claimed that although Jesus had a human body, he had no human soul. **Monophysitism** allowed that Jesus had been born fully human; it states however that his human nature had been completely absorbed by his divine nature.

Although we rarely hear the names of these heresies used

heresy—The term literally means "choice." A heresy is a conscious, deliberate, and persistent or public denial by a member of the Church of one or more of the truths of faith (dogma).

Apostles' Creed—One of two great creeds, or statements of belief, of the Church. It is considered to be a summary of the Apostles' faith. It is the ancient baptismal symbol of the Church of Rome.

Monophysitism—A heresy of the late fifth and early sixth centuries that taught that there is only one nature in the Person of Christ, the divine nature. Following the Council of Chalcedon in 451, those who accepted the Monophysite position formed what are called the Oriental Orthodox churches.

Apollinarianism—A false belief that claimed that although Jesus had a human body, he had no human soul.

today, they continue to surface in various forms in some of the beliefs and practices which the Church rejects. For example, popular society sees little worth in suffering. This view has manifested itself in a call for assisted suicides and even euthanasia in the name of "death with dignity." When Christians respond that a person's suffering is valuable because Christ's suffering was valuable they are often met with the reasoning that Christ suffered because he had no choice (he was not divine—Arianism) or that Christ's suffering was different from ours because he was divine (he was not human—Docetism). The teaching of the Church stresses the value of human life and experience: God accepted every aspect of human life and so should we. The teaching of the Church also makes it clear that in Jesus God has become completely one with us and has made it possible for us to become completely one with God. In Jesus' two natures, human and divine, God is revealed as both absolutely immanent and absolutely transcendent; that is, absolutely present to us and absolutely beyond us. God is absolutely immanent because in Jesus all of human experience is taken up in the divine. God is absolutely transcendent because there is nothing, not even death, which is outside of God's power. The fact that Jesus is both fully human and fully divine ensures us that no situation is ever hopeless. This belief also ensures us that no human experience, even the most negative or the most difficult, is outside of the reach of grace. God himself accepted suffering and helplessness, therefore we can be sure that neither suffering nor helplessness can deprive our lives of value or meaning.

STUDY QUESTIONS

- WHAT IS DOGMA?
- WHAT ARE THE MAJOR CATHOLIC DOGMAS?
- IDENTIFY TWO COMMON MISUNDERSTANDINGS OF THE TRINITY AND EXPLAIN WHY THEY ARE INCORRECT.

JOURNAL ASSIGNMENT

- CHOOSE ONE DOGMA AND EXPLAIN HOW IT IS SIGNIFICANT TO YOUR EVERYDAY FAITH.

The Holy Trinity

At the time the creeds were formulated, the Church also defined the central mystery of the Christian faith—the belief that the one God is in Three Persons, the Holy Trinity. A Catholic Christian is someone who believes in and interacts with the Holy Trinity.[8]

Throughout the centuries the Church has struggled to find words to express its understanding of the Trinity. Over and over again those words have proved problematic either because they were inaccessible to the majority of Christians or because they implied things about God that were not true. One help in defining what the Holy Trinity is is to explain what the Trinity is not.

To say God is one in Three Persons does not simply mean that God has three different ways of interacting with people or that we perceive God in three different ways. Rather, we believe in a God whose very nature is relational. Our belief in the Trinity helps us to understand that "God is love," since all love flows from the love which exists between the Father, Son, and Holy Spirit. When we are called into communion with God, we are called to participate in the love of the Trinity. We are not called to simply love God as one who is totally separate from us; instead, we are called to become one with the Persons of the Trinity who are already one among themselves.

Also, belief in the Holy Trinity does not mean that we believe the three persons of the Trinity have three distinct roles which together complete the "role of God." For example, refering to the Three Persons of the Trinity as Creator, Redeemer, and Sustainer, rather than Father, Son, and Holy Spirit, is highly problematic because it implies that the Three Persons of the Trinity can be distinguished by what they do. In fact, we believe that God in all Three Persons created the universe, God in all Three Persons redeemed humanity, and God in all Three Persons sustains us from day to day. Whatever one does, all three do. The Council of Florence stressed this when it declared that the Father, Son, and Holy Spirit are one in everything. There is no opposition within God.[9] It is essential to understand the Trinity if we are to understand the Church. Because the Trinity is one, God was made accessible to humanity in the person of Jesus Christ and God continues to be accessible in the Church in which the Holy Spirit lives.

Mary, the Mother of God

Another of the foundational Church dogmas is that Mary is the Mother of God. In fact, this belief is the corollary to the belief that Jesus is fully human and fully divine. In AD 428, Nestorius, the patriarch of Constantinople, declared that Mary should not be called the mother of God (*theotokos*) but should be referred to only as the mother of Christ (*Christotokos*). Nestorius believed that it was necessary to draw a distinction between Christ's humanity and his divinity. He said that some of Jesus' traits and experiences were purely human, while others were purely divine. According to Nestorius, God could not be totally dependent upon a human being, thus we must say that it was only Jesus'

human self which was born of Mary; his divine self was not. Many people immediately recognized the dangers in dividing Christ into two persons. If the human and the divine were not really joined in Christ, there would be no possibility of being freed from original sin and being born into a new human nature which was fully united to God, because no such nature would exist.

In AD 431 the Council of Ephesus denounced Nestorius. It stated clearly that Jesus is one person with two natures. Everything which Jesus experienced was experienced by his whole person. From the moment of his conception, Jesus was both fully human and fully divine. Mary, therefore, can rightly be called the Mother of God. In Mary, the divine and the human were eternally joined. Following the Council, those churches that followed Nestorius and established separate churches returned to union with Rome.

The fact that Mary is the Mother of God shapes Catholic understanding of what it means to be human and how God relates to human beings. Indeed, our understanding of the role of the Church in mediating God to the world is tied up with our understanding of Mary's role. Catholics are often asked by other Christians why they honor Mary as they do. The Church honors Mary because God made her immanently important. God depended on Mary to bring Salvation to the world in the person of Jesus Christ, the only Son of the Father. Catholics believe that God continues to depend on and act through human beings.[10]

STUDY QUESTIONS

- WHAT IS DOGMA?
- WHAT ARE THE MAJOR CATHOLIC DOGMAS?
- IDENTIFY TWO COMMON MISUNDERSTANDINGS OF THE TRINITY AND EXPLAIN WHY THEY ARE INCORRECT.

JOURNAL ASSIGNMENT

- CHOOSE ONE DOGMA AND EXPLAIN HOW IT IS SIGNIFICANT TO YOUR EVERYDAY FAITH.

ARIANISM

Arianism was one of the most pervasive and tenacious heresies in the early Church. In fact, the persistence of Arianism in Spain and in many parts of Northern

Africa into the seventh century may have eased the Moslem conquest and allowed for the acceptance of the Islamic faith by many who had been Christians. The Arians, like the Muslims who followed them, believed that Jesus was not divine. Arianism held that Jesus was created by God as the first of all creation. The first proponent of this belief was a priest named Arius, who argued that to say that Jesus was anything other than one of God's creatures would be to deny **monotheism**, that is, a belief in one God.

Arius's own bishop argued against him, saying that if what Arius claimed were true, Christians would either have to stop worshiping Christ, or admit that they were breaking the first commandment and worshiping a creature. The bishop removed Arius from all posts in the Church, but Arius, who was very popular, appealed to the people and to other bishops. This resulted in demonstrations in the street and a conflict which threatened the unity of Christianity in the eastern empire.

The emperor Constantine had a vested interest in maintaining Christian unity, so he called all of the bishops to meet at the Council of Nicaea to settle the dispute. The Arian side was presented by the bishop of Nicomedia. He was so convinced that monotheism necessitated Arianism that he expected everyone else to agree with him as soon as they heard a clear presentation of his case. The Nicomedian bishop was apparently completely unprepared for the reaction he received when he called Jesus a creature. The other bishops shouted him down and his speech was ripped from his hands, shredded, and trampled on.

The Council of Nicaea issued a statement which forms the basis of the Nicene Creed. Most of the bishops present signed the statement. Those who did not were denounced as heretics by the other bishops and then banned from their cities by the emperor, who had agreed to govern by the council's decision.

monotheism—The belief that there is only one God.

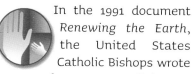

RENEWING THE EARTH

In the 1991 document *Renewing the Earth*, the United States Catholic Bishops wrote of our responsibility to reflect and then act on environmental issues. While the understanding of the earth and its place in the universe has changed in the years since Galileo, our responsibility to the environment has not. The document offered the following suggestions for ecological responsibility:

· a God-centered and sacramental view of the universe, which grounds human accountability for the fate of the earth;

· a consistent respect for human life, which extends to respect for all creation;

· a worldview affirming the ethical significance of global interdependence and the common good;

· an ethics of solidarity promoting cooperation and a just structure of sharing in the world community;

· an understanding of the universal purpose of created things, which requires equitable use of the earth's resources;

· an option for the poor, which gives passion to the quest for an equitable and sustainable world;

· a conception of authentic development, which offers a direction for progress that respects human dignity and the limits of material growth.

Read more selections from the document at www.nccbuscc.org/sdwp/ejp/bishopsstatement.htm#3. Write a personal mission statement for your own proper relationship with God's creation.

DOGMA RELATED TO DOCTRINE

Dogmas are truths which we believe have been specifically revealed by God. A person's acceptance of Church dogma is essential to a complete faith and the deepest possible relationship with God. Dogmas are infallible and irreformable. They cannot change in their essence since the truth which has been revealed by God remains for all eternity. This does not mean that the way in which we express dogmas cannot change. All infallible teachings are expressed in human language. Every statement of dogma is limited by the concerns which motivated its expression. Every statement of dogma is also limited by the context of human knowledge at the time when the dogma was framed. People in different time periods have different thought categories and conceptions and different ways of perceiving and responding to the world. As these change, the way we express and respond to dogmas will change.[11]

Portrait of Galileo

The story of the Church's response to Galileo is a prime example of how a dogma can be true and at the same time be expressed in a way that proves inadequate and in need of change. When Galileo declared, in the sixteenth century, that the earth revolved around the sun, many Christians were horrified. According to the way of thinking of the time, if the earth was not the physical center of the universe, then neither the earth nor those who live on it could be central to God's plan for creation. In the sixteenth century it seemed obvious to the Magisterium that one could not affirm the centrality of Christ to the universe without also affirming the centrality of the earth, Christ's home, within the universe. Thus the Magisterium of the Church declared that it was heresy to say that the earth revolved around the sun. As human thought categories changed and the understanding of the difference between scientific and religious truth developed, it became clear that one could accept Galileo's teachings without rejecting Christianity. Although the essence of the Church's dogma regarding the centrality of Christ and the importance of the earth and its human inhabitance to God's plan has not changed, the way we express this dogma has changed completely.

Each time the Magisterium declares that a particular statement or concept is part of the Deposit of Faith, Catholics are obliged to accept their assertion as true. It is a basic tenet of Catholicism that every dogmatic statement protects an essential truth which is in danger of being lost. Because we believe in a mediated grace—that is to say, because we believe that God works in concrete ways through the world around us and not simply through abstract concepts—we believe that truths must be expressed with practical implications. Thus we understand that even though it seems ridiculous to us today, in Galileo's day it may have been necessary for the Church to insist that the sun revolved around the earth. Because of the thought patterns in use at the time, if Christians had been told that the earth revolved around the sun, the belief that Christ's Incarnation was central to God's plan might have been lost.

However, not everything that the Church teaches is dogma. There are many Church teachings which have not been directly revealed by God but which reflect our best understanding of that which has been revealed. These are part of the Church's doctrine, not her dogma.

Doctrine refers to any belief or teaching which has the official approval of the Magisterium. Doctrines establish the boundaries for preaching and catechesis. All of the Church's doctrine is based upon the Revelation of God in Christ which is expressed in dogma. Doctrine helps us to understand the implications of dogma.

As Pope John Paul II wrote in his encyclical letter *Veritatis Splendor*, "the Magisterium does not bring to the Christian conscience truths which are extraneous to it; rather it brings to light the truths which it ought already to possess, developing them from the starting point of the primordial act of faith."[12]

infallibility—A spiritual attribute possessed by the Church as a whole ensuring that the Church will never cease to be the body of Christ on earth. Infallibility is more commonly used to refer to the special attribute possessed by the pope and by the college of bishops in communion with the pope which ensures that when they speak on matters of faith and morals they are free of error.

STUDY QUESTIONS

- WHAT IS THE DIFFERENCE BETWEEN DOCTRINE AND DOGMA?
- NAME TWO CHARACTERISTICS OF DOGMA.
- EXPLAIN HOW THE CHURCH'S UNDERSTANDING OF DOGMA CAN AND DOES CHANGE.
- WHAT OBLIGATIONS DO CATHOLICS HAVE WITH RESPECT TO THE TEACHINGS OF THE MAGISTERIUM?

JOURNAL ASSIGNMENT

- WRITE ABOUT A BELIEF (E.G. IN THE AREA OF POLITICS, SOCIAL REFORM, RELATIONSHIPS, THEOLOGY) YOU HAVE THAT HAS EVOLVED FROM ONE POINT OF VIEW TO ANOTHER. WHY DO YOU THINK YOU HAVE HAD THIS CHANGE?

ADHERENCE TO CHURCH TEACHING

Catholics believe that the pope has the authority to proclaim something as dogma. If, in his capacity as "supreme pastor and teacher of all the faithful," he proclaims with a definitive act that a doctrine of faith or morals is to

be accepted as part of God's Revelation and thus as an infallible dogma, then it is indeed an infallible dogma. **Infallibility** refers to a teaching that is free from error. (Likewise, the gift of indefectibility guarantees that the Church will always teach the Gospel of Christ without error, even in spite of the defects of her members, both ordained and lay.)

The college of bishops also has infallible teaching authority when

ecumenical council—A gathering of all the Catholic bishops of the world. The word "ecumenical" pertains to a theological recognition of and willingness to learn from those of different faith traditions. Ecumenical councils determine those things which all the local churches (dioceses) will hold in common.

it exercises its teaching office in an **ecumenical council** and declares for the universal Church that a doctrine of faith or morals must be definitively held.[13] Furthermore, even if a doctrine has not been proclaimed with a definitive act, Catholics are still called to respect the teaching of the Magisterium and avoid everything that is not in harmony with it.[14] This is because Catholics believe that the Holy Spirit guides the Church through the Magisterium.

The Magisterium's role in preaching the Gospel and applying it to the lives of Catholics is to help us to do God's will and to bring about God's Kingdom. The pope and bishops are pastors, a word that means "shepherd." They fulfill their role in imitation of Jesus, the Good Shepherd.

There are many competing voices that seek to influence our thoughts and actions, including in the area of morality. On the other hand, Jesus speaks through the Magisterium, offering the voice of truth. The Magisterium not only preserves the saving truth of Jesus but also expounds upon it regarding contemporary issues and the circumstances of everyday modern life. Practically this is done through papal enclyclicals—official letters of the pope to the universal Church and all people of good will. It is also done through pastoral letters written by bishops for people in their own countries. In these many ways the Church functions as our Teacher.

excommunication—The most severe penalty within the Church. A person who is excommunicated is separated from the communion of other Catholics. He or she cannot receive the sacraments or hold certain positions within the Church.

EXCOMMUNICATED

A person who has been excommunicated is no longer considered to be a member of the Catholic Church. He or she cannot receive any of the sacraments nor hold any Church position which is restricted to Catholics. Once a person has been excommunicated, only the pope, a bishop, or a priest who has been given specific authorization can grant absolution and reinstate him or her into the Catholic communion. (If the person is in danger of death any priest can grant absolution.)

When the code of canon law was revised in 1983, the number of sins for which a person would automatically be excommunicated was significantly reduced. Today, automatic or *latae sententiae* **excommunications** are imposed on the following people:

- apostates (those who openly reject the faith of the Church as a whole)
- heretics (those who openly reject the truth of one or more dogmatic statements)
- schismatics (those who refuse to respect the authority of the pope)
- a person who throws away the consecrated species or uses them for sacrilegious purposes
- a person who uses physical force against the pope
- a priest who absolves an accomplice of sins against the sixth or ninth commandments
- a bishop who consecrates someone without a pontifical mandate and the person who receives consecration without a pontifical mandate
- a confessor who directly violates the seal of confession
- a person who procures a successful abortion.

STUDY QUESTIONS

- HOW DOES THE MAGISTERIUM ACT IN JESUS' ROLE OF THE GOOD SHEPHERD?

JOURNAL ASSIGNMENT

- NAME SOME COMPETING VOICES IN TODAY'S WORLD THAT CONTRADICT JESUS' CALL TO TRUTH.

IN CONCLUSION

There is an old Jewish story about a pagan doctor who feels called by God but who does not feel that he can devote his life to study. He goes to speak with Rabbi Shammai and says, "I will become a Jew and faithfully serve your God for the rest of my life, if you can tell me all that I need to do while standing on one foot."

Rabbi Shammai is annoyed. He says that God would not want the service of a person who was so frivolous and so unwilling to take the time to learn all that God had to teach. He sends the pagan on his way.

The pagan returns to his old life, but he continues to feel that God is calling him. As soon as he can get away from his patients he goes to speak with Rabbi Hillel. Once again he says, "Rabbi, I will become a Jew and faithfully serve your God for the rest of my life, if you can explain the law to me while standing on one foot."

Rabbi Hillel looks in the pagan's eyes and knows that God has indeed called him. Slowly he lifts one foot off the ground and says, "Love God with all of your heart, mind and strength; and love your neighbor as yourself. All the rest is commentary."

The pagan became a Jew and devoted the rest of his life to caring for those who were most in need. Each day, before going to work, he would spend an hour in prayer and study so that he would know how he was called to love that day.

If a person were to come to us and say, "I will become a Christian if you can explain the truth which will set me free while standing on one foot," what would we say? The Church's task is to tell the world the truth which has been revealed in Christ. At the heart of this truth is the fact that God is love. And through Christ God has made it possible for humanity to participate in that love.

Although in some ways this truth is quite simple, in others it is very complicated. Before Christ revealed the truth to the world, humanity lived in the falsehood of sin. Starting with the Original Sin which was manifested in the belief that we did not need God and that we could become like gods ourselves, human beings wove an intricate web of sins, lies, and misunderstandings.

Like all webs, the web of sin tends to cling to us, even as we try to take it down. Even when people have recognized Christ as the Son of God who offers the gift of Salvation, they may still be ensnared by many of the old lies and misunderstandings which led people to sin and despair. For this reason the Church must present the Good News of Christ in such a way that people are able to recognize each strand of falsehood for what it is. The scriptures, creeds, dogmas, and doctrines of the Church all help us to understand the truth of Christ and what it means to structure our lives around that truth. Those who know and live by the truth will experience freedom and joy even in the midst of the worst that life has to offer.

LEARN BY DOING

Write a report on one of the Christian apologists named in this chapter: Irenaeus, Clement of Alexandria, Tertullian, or Origen. Include in the report:
- a brief biography of the person
- background on the heresy(ies) the person disputed
- the person's response to the heresy
- some of the actual written words of the apologist

PRAYER

God the Father,
origin of all that is divine,
good beyond all that is good,
fair beyond all that is fair,
in you is calmness, peace, and concord.
Heal what divides us from one another
and bring us back into the unity of love,
bearing some likeness to your divine nature.
Through the embrace of your love
and the bonds of godly affection,
make us one in the Spirit
by that peace of yours
that makes all things peaceful.
We ask this through the grace, mercy, and tenderness
of your only begotten Son, Jesus Christ our Lord.
Amen.

—St. Dionysisus of Alexandria

NOTES

1. See *Catechism of the Catholic Church*, #106.

2. See *Catechism of the Catholic Church*, #108.

3. The community must allow the Magisterium to guide it in its interpretation.

4. It has become common practice in many places today to refer to the Old Testament as the "Hebrew Scriptures" out of sensitivity to the Jewish community for whom these scriptures are not "old." Unfortunately, this terminology presents a certain difficulty for Catholics and for the Orthodox. The Old Testament of the Catholic and Orthodox bible includes several books and parts of books which were written in Greek not Hebrew. These books were part of the Septuagint, the Greek version of the Jewish Scriptures which was used by the majority of early Christians. When the Jewish community officially closed its canon, at the end of the first century AD, those books which were part of the Septuagint but not part of the Hebrew Scriptures were excluded. During the reformation Protestants adopted the shorter version of the Jewish canon as their Old Testament. The Jewish Bible and the Protestant Old Testament are therefore properly called the "Hebrew Scriptures," but the Catholic Old Testament is not.

5. The official Roman Catholic decision about which books should be included in the canon did not come until the Council of Trent in the sixteenth century.

6. See Gonzalez, *The Story of Christianity,* Vol. 1, p. 58.

7. It is important to note that there is a difference between syncretism and inculturation. Syncretism refers to the combination of Christianity with practices and philosophies which actually undermine or contradict basic Christian truths. Inculturation refers to the presentation of basic Christian doctrine using symbols and language which are familiar to people of a particular culture. In many areas of North America Native American Catholics are working to reincorporate traditional Native American prayers into their own Catholic worship. This is inculturation. They are not challenging or changing basic doctrines; they are making their worship a more powerful sacramental sign for their community. On the other hand, there are Catholics who choose to wear crystals or pay close attention to their horoscopes, as if rocks and stars had more power over their lives than the Holy Spirit. This is syncretism.

8. It should be noted that the beliefs expressed in the Nicene and Apostles' creeds are not unique to Catholics. The majority of churches which call themselves Christian embrace these creeds. However, not all of these churches would say that a person who denied one or more of the statements of these creeds had by definition separated him or herself from the Church.

9. See the Council of Florence, 1442, Decree for the Jacobites.

10. We will discuss this in more detail in Unit 7.

11. See *Mysterium Ecclesiae*, Congregation for the Doctrine of the Faith, June 24, 1973.

12. #64.

13. See Canon 749 § 1–2.

14. See Canon 752.

15. See *Veritatis Splendor*, #32.

4.2

"GO, THEREFORE, AND MAKE DISCIPLES OF ALL NATIONS, BAP-
TIZING THEM IN THE NAME OF THE FATHER, AND OF THE SON,
AND OF THE HOLY SPIRIT, TEACHING THEM TO OBSERVE ALL
THAT I HAVE COMMANDED YOU."

—*Matthew 28:19–20*

evangelization—Sharing the Good News. Evangelization involves proclaiming the Gospel in such a way that people's hearts and lives are changed. In the same spirit, Pope John Paul II first described a "new evangelization" that calls each Catholic to first deepen his or her own faith before taking on the missionary task of sharing the Gospel with others.

GOOD EVANGELIZATION

When Pope John Paul II announced that **evangelization**, that is, the sharing of the **Gospel** with the world, would be part of the focus for beginning the new millennium, the Florida parish of St. Luke's established an evangelization subcommittee of its pastoral council to look at ways

Gospel—The "Good News." Gospel refers to the good news of Jesus' life, death, resurrection, and ascension. The word "gospel" is always used specifically for the first four books of the New Testament—Matthew, Mark, Luke, and John— which tell the story of Jesus and his message.

that their parish might become more actively involved in evangelization. One young woman, Elizabeth, was appointed to the subcommittee in the hope that she might have some ideas on how to attract other young adults. Instead, at the first meeting, Elizabeth shared what she described as an "evangelization horror story" with the other committee members. This is how her story went:

I'm here because I get nervous every time people start saying that

we need to do more evangelizing. The first thing that comes to my mind is an "evangelization team" that visited my dorm room in college. I never actually met them, but I saw the damage they did. I came back to our room on the day they visited to find my roommate, Lee, a practicing Jew, literally shaking at the end of her bed. When I asked what was wrong she told me that two people from one of the Christian groups on campus had just left.

"They said such horrible things," Lee told me. They told her she was going to hell if she didn't accept Jesus as her personal Lord and savior. They said that the blood of Jesus was on her and all those who persisted in rejecting him. They said all she had to do was look at history to see how people "like her" had suffered.

I didn't want to hear any more. I remember saying, "They're wrong! Stop torturing yourself by repeating things that never should have been said!"

Lee didn't even look up at me as she asked, "Do you really think they're wrong? They said that all Christians know that non-Christians are damned, it's just that some don't care enough to try and warn us. They implied that you haven't said something because you just want to keep the peace."

I felt like throwing something. Instead, I told Lee what those people had said was garbage. I added, "Lee, I hope that after a year of sharing a room with me you know that I care about you. If I thought you were about to walk over a cliff you can be sure I'd try to stop you. But you're not about to walk over a cliff!

"All Christians do not believe that nonsense they were spouting! Personally, I don't see how anyone who knows anything at all about Jesus could imply that the holocaust, AIDS, or any other horrible tragedy is a punishment for lack of faith. Our God doesn't work that way."

Lee persisted, "But you're a Christian. You believe in Salvation through Christ, right?"

I explained that I do believe in Salvation through Christ. And I told her that for me being a Christian and a Catholic is essential. I have been given faith. I have known Christ. I have felt the presence of the Holy Spirit within me. If I threw all that away, I would be rejecting God. But I told Lee that it was different for her. She had not thrown away faith in Christ. It just wasn't a gift she'd been given.

"Besides," I said to her, "You are one of God's Chosen People. God will not abandon you. That's what the Catholic Church teaches."

I tried to explain a little more about my faith, how my life would be missing something without Jesus. If I wanted Lee to be a Christian, my only reason would be so that she would know the joy and the peace that I know.

Elizabeth concluded, "The point that I'm trying to make with all this is that I think we need to be very careful about not equating evangelization with going door to door and forcing our faith on other people.

The other people on the committee agreed.

When Elizabeth finished, an older woman spoke directly to her. "I agree with what you said. However, truly good evangelization took place in your story. The real evangelizer was you! Evangelization is about helping people see the good in Christianity. You did that for Lee."

The committee decided that its primary task was to remind the parish of the teaching of the Second Vatican Council which stated in its "Pastoral Constitution on the Church in the Modern World" (*Gaudium et Spes*) that when it comes to overcoming unbelief, the witness of mature faith is more important than a proper presentation of dogma.[1] Evangelizing the world means, first and foremost, becoming aware of what our actions are teaching others about Christ and the Church.

BEING A GOOD LISTENER

Good evangelization goes hand in hand with good listening skills. Really getting to know a person is a an excellent first step at being a witness for the gospel. Look for ways to practice the following good listening skills:

- Give your full attention to the speaker. Make eye contact. Eliminate other distractions (music, television) while you are listening.
- Focus on what the person is saying. Usually, this doesn't involve remembering facts and details. Rather, it involves focusing on a central theme or feelings behind what the person is saying.
- Show your interest. For example, ask clarifying questions. Also, nod or say things like "I see" or "I understand" as the person is speaking.
- Summarize what the person has said. Recap the highlights of the conversation. For example, say "As I understood it, you were saying...."

JOURNAL ASSIGNMENT

- IN YOUR OPINION, WHAT IS A MORE POWERFUL TOOL OF EVANGELIZATION, A CHRISTIAN'S WORDS OR ACTIONS? EXPLAIN.

APOSTLE TO THE GENTILES

St. Paul led an exciting and varied life. Raised a Pharisee, Paul studied to be a rabbi in Jerusalem under the famous teacher Gamaliel. He later participated in the persecution of Christians. After Paul converted to Christianity, he used many of his life experiences to help him evangelize the Gentiles. Research and report on the following elements of Paul's life and explain how each would have helped him preach the Good News to Gentiles.

• He received an excellent Greek education in Tarsus. He was familiar with Gentile religions, philosophies, and customs.
• He supported his missionary activity with a job as a traveling tent maker.
• He was a Roman citizen.

Also, read Paul's words in 1 Corinthians 9:19–27. How did this translate to a style of evangelization? How would you utilize this style in your own life? Give at least one example.

HOW THE GOOD NEWS WAS FIRST SHARED

Initially, the Gospel was shared in Jewish synagogues. The Roman empire had an elaborate system of roadways. As Jewish Christians traveled throughout the Roman empire they shared their new understanding of Judaism in local synagogues. Also, Jewish Christian merchants told about the "new way" as part of their business conversations. In their own words, Jewish Christians gave the same explanation that Peter gave on the day of Pentecost: in the person of Jesus, God had fulfilled his promise to David. The Messiah had come.

Likewise, Christianity initially was shared with Gentiles in the marketplace and in casual conversations. Christianity was especially appealing to those who were trapped at the bottom of a rigid social structure. It offered them both hope and dignity. On the other hand, one of the most com-mon objections to Christianity within Roman society was that it was a religion of the lower classes and of the uneducated. Recall that St. Augustine initially rejected Christianity because of the inelegance of Christian Scripture. He could not bring himself to believe that an all powerful God would reveal himself in such mundane and uneducated terms.

It was only gradually that Christianity came to be seen as a religion that was not beneath the dignity of the educated and cultured. Apologists like Clement, Origen, and Justin Martyr were instrumental in establishing connections between Christianity and the philosophy of the pagans. Christianity also gained a greater acceptance through the witness of the many martyrs. Many were so intrigued by a faith which could give women and slaves the courage to stand up to the worst kinds of torture that they began to ask questions and to study the faith for themselves.

STUDY QUESTIONS

• WHERE WERE THE PRIMARY PLACES THE GOOD NEWS WAS INITIALLY SHARED?
• WHAT WERE ELEMENTS OF CHRISTIANITY THAT PEOPLE IN THE FIRST AND SECOND CENTURIES FOUND ATTRACTIVE?

Origen was an Egyptian who was the most brilliant theologian of the third century. Ordained a priest in 230, one of his greatest fields of expertise was the study of Scripture.

PERPETUA AND FELICITAS

The witness of Perpetua and Felicitas in AD 203 was one of the most dramatic of all Christian martyrdoms. Perpetua and Felicitas were condemned to death when they entered the Christian catechumenate. Perpetua was a wealthy young mother from an educated family. When she was asked to abandon the Christian faith and save her life, she said that everything had a name and an identity that could not be changed by mere words; her name and identity were Christian. Felicitas was a slave. She was pregnant when she was arrested and gave birth to a daughter while she was still in jail. When she cried out because of the pain of childbirth, the jailers asked her how she expected to face being torn apart by wild beasts. She answered: "Now my sufferings are only mine. But when I face the beasts there will be another who will live in me, and will suffer for me since I shall be suffering for him."[2]

THE WITNESS OF WIDOWS AND VIRGINS

Other teachers of the faith in the early Church were widows and virgins. In the early days of the Church widows were cared for in accordance with the instructions of the Old Testament. A widow without support would ordinarily have been forced to remarry or to depend upon her children. If either her children or her new husband were not Christian, her Christian life would be severely limited. In order to protect the faith of its widows, the Church supported them and gave them particular responsibilities. Soon the word "widow" came to refer to a particular class of respected women within the Church who performed special functions.[3] The class of widows also included some women who chose to remain unmarried in order to better serve the Lord. There were specific commissioning prayers for widows. Widows and deaconesses were responsible for much of the pastoral care of other women. They anointed women at Baptism and were sent to lay hands on those who were sick. Widows were given a specific place to sit in the front of the church during the celebration of the Eucharist.

Ancient documents such as the Didache, Origen's Homily on Luke 17, and Tertullian's On Monogamy make it clear that those women who chose celibacy, poverty, and a life of service in response to the Gospel were regarded as leaders in the early Church. The Church recognized that they taught the truth of Christ by example. In a society where women were generally expected to be followers, Christianity provided a way for women to lead with dignity. In a society where leaders were generally those with positions of power, the Church recognized that some of the strongest leadership came from those who were without power.

STUDY QUESTIONS

- WHAT DID THE TERM "WIDOW" REFER TO IN THE EARLY CHURCH?
- SUMMARIZE THE ROLE OF WIDOWS IN THE EARLY CHURCH.

The Church supported widows to keep them from living in poverty. St. John Chrysostom estimated that at the end of the fourth century there were 3,000 widows and virgins supported by the Church at Antioch.

JOURNAL ASSIGNMENT

• DESCRIBE SOMEONE YOU KNOW WHO WAS AN EFFECTIVE LEADER EVEN THOUGH HE OR SHE WAS "WITHOUT POWER."

THE DESERT FATHERS

monasticism—A style of Christian life which stresses communal living and communal worship along with private prayer, silence, poverty, chastity, and obedience.

In the fourth century a phenomena of desert **monasticism** arose. These **desert fathers** were people who wanted to get away from the distractions of society and live in solitude. They did not choose the desert because they wanted to live a difficult life. They chose it because they wanted to be isolated away from distractions that drew their attention from God. Yet their life of isolation was itself a way of proclaiming the Good News. When Christianity was legalized in 313 and martyrdom became rare, monasticism became the most extreme way to live out a Christian vocation.

desert fathers—Christians of about the fourth century who chose to live an ascetic life of prayer, fasting, and abstinence. The teachings of these men (and women) had a profound impact on the theology and spirituality of the Church and on the development of monasticism.

No one person can be credited with founding desert monasticism. It appears that thousands saw it as an obvious response to the Gospel's call to sell one's possessions, to pray constantly, and to stop worrying about the future. However, St. Anthony of Egypt best illustrates the nature of monasticism and the way that it shaped Christianity.

Anthony of Egypt

Anthony was born into a wealthy Roman family. His parents died when he was still young, leaving him enough money that he did not need to worry about the future. Anthony planned to live an easy life, enjoying the good things which

society had to offer. Then one day he heard the Gospel story of the rich young man who was instructed by Jesus to sell everything and give to the poor. He knew the story was intended for him. Anthony disposed of all of his property and all of his security and went into the desert to learn monastic discipline from an old man who was already living there. Each time that Anthony longed for the pleasures of his former life he would impose stricter discipline on himself.

After a few years, Anthony moved off on his own. He survived on bread which was brought to him every few days by kind-hearted people. Although he was far from the cares of the world, Anthony's life was neither easy nor peaceful. He was tormented by visions of demons who came to tempt him. At first his struggles with the demons seemed almost impossible to endure, but over time he became convinced that God would never abandon him and his faith grew even stronger.

Although Anthony longed for solitude, he was constantly sought by others who wanted to know God even as Anthony did. No matter how far into the desert Anthony retreated, people found him and begged him to teach them prayer, discipline, and wisdom. For years Anthony tried to avoid them. He did not want to be a teacher, but eventually he realized that his very experience of God made him one. Anthony made an agreement with those who wanted to learn from him. He would remain in one place and they could live nearby. If they agreed to leave him in solitude most of the time, he would visit them periodically to share his understanding of prayer, contemplation, and spiritual discipline.

COMMUNAL MONASTICISM

When Christianity was illegal, persecution and the threat of persecution honed the faith and helped ensure that few became Christian for frivolous reasons. This wasn't so after Christianity was legalized. Many

who were very serious about their faith were afraid that it would be corrupted by ease if they did not do something drastic. Some travelers reported that there were as many as twenty thousand women and ten thousand men living the monastic life in one area of the desert.[4] Although these numbers are obviously exaggerated, it is clear that many believed that Christianity needed to be separated from the lure of power and wealth in order to be authentically preserved. Many saw the strict life of desert living as the only true form of Christianity.

As the number of people in the desert grew, solitary monasticism was replaced by communal monasticism. The final shape of

this communal monasticism was heavily influenced in the early fourth century by a former pagan named Pachomius. Before his conversion, Pachomius was conscripted into

STUDY QUESTION

- HOW DID DESERT MONASTICISM COME TO PROMINENCE IN THE FOURTH CENTURY?

the Roman army. He was miserably unhappy, and, when several Christians came to comfort him and his companions, he was very moved. He vowed that if he ever got out of the army he would dedicate his life to loving and serving others even as they had done. When he was allowed to leave the army, Pachomius remembered his vow and sought out a Christian teacher. After a few years he felt called to go to the desert, first to study with an older monk, and then to live on his own.

There, Pachomius joined with other men living in the desert to form a community of monks. When discipline broke down and the monks refused to care for one another, Pachomius expelled them all. A short time later he tried to start another community, but this time he was far stricter with those who wished to join. All who came had to give up everything they owned and promise absolute obedience to their superiors. The most basic rule of the community would be mutual service. Every person would be expected to serve every other person. No one, from the newest member to the highest superior, would ever be allowed to say that any task was beneath him. The community modeled a life of prayer without ceasing. They gathered for common prayer twice a day; during the rest of the day they prayed as they worked, sang psalms, meditated on scripture, and recited prayers both aloud and in silence. Over the course of his lifetime, Pachomius founded nine communities of several hundred monks each. His sister, Mary, founded similar communities for women. All of the communities founded by Pachomius and by Mary were under the leadership of Pachomius and his successors.

Gradually communal monasticism replaced individual monasticism as the "ideal witness" to the Christian life. Many bishops and Church leaders recognized the value of the monastic witness for the daily life of the Church. Many of the great teachers of the Church used the stories of the desert to illustrate the call and the blessings of Christianity.

STUDY QUESTIONS

- WHY WAS THE STRICT LIFE OF DESERT LIVING ONCE VIEWED AS THE ONLY TRUE FORM OF CHRISTIAN LIVING?
- DESCRIBE THE BASIC FORM OF COMMUNAL MONASTICISM AS DEVELOPED BY PACHOMIUS.

JOURNAL ASSIGNMENT

- HOW DOES YOUR FAMILY PRACTICE MUTUAL SERVICE OF BOTH FAMILY MEMBERS AND THOSE OUTSIDE OF THE FAMILY?

Other monasteries imitated the practices of St. Pachomius. St. Basil the Great (329–379) in the East required monks to engage in works of charity for the poor and unemployed. St. Martin of Tours in France required the monks to preach to the barbarians.

THE CONVERSION OF THE BARBARIANS

From the fifth through the eighth century, around the same time communal monasticism was taking root, western Europe was hit by wave after wave of barbarian migrations from various tribes. The Asiatic Huns pressured the western tribes that began to invade the Roman empire. The Visigoths invaded Gaul and Spain, the vandals moved into North Africa, and the Ostrogoths and Lombards headed into Italy. By and large, the barbarian invaders were taught the faith and converted by the quiet and persistent witness of the thousands of Christians whom they had conquered.

Some of the conversions of barbarians had to do with a legitimate faith experience, other conversions were primarily a means of establishing political stability. The conversion of the Visigoths is a prime example of this. The Visigoths defeated the Romans at the battle of Adrianople in 378. They then took control of the Balkans and moved into Spain. The Visigoth King Recared quickly realized that the support of the Christians there would be necessary if he was to achieve any level of stability in the region. He officially embraced Christianity at an assembly in Toledo in AD 589.

The majority of the Franks accepted Baptism shortly after their leader, Clovis, was converted to Christianity. Clovis's wife was already a Christian. She told her husband about the all powerful Christian God, so, on the eve of a very important battle Clovis promised that he would become a Christian if the Christian God gave him victory. He won the battle, and on Christmas day in AD 496 Clovis and many of his nobles were baptized.

ST. PATRICK

St. Patrick was not the first Christian missionary to Ireland, but he was the first to meet with any significant success. Patrick was the son of a deacon and the grandson of a priest from the village of Banavem Taberniae. (Obviously this was a period of history before mandatory celibacy for priests was required. The exact location of Patrick's village remains in debate; most scholars believe that it was near Dumbarton in Scotland.) Patrick was captured and taken to Ireland when he was sixteen. He spent six years working as a herdsman before he managed to escape. He sailed on a ship to Gaul, but after a few years he returned to Britain.

Patrick believed that God had called him to return to Ireland. After being consecrated as a bishop he was sent on a mission to Ireland. Patrick's success was probably the result of several factors. He had an extraordinary personality and he was an exceptional preacher. He was also willing to accommodate himself to the language and culture of the people he wished to convert. He would assemble the people by standing in an open field and beating a drum. When they had gathered he would tell them the story of Jesus' life, death, and resurrection, accompanied by music and song. Over the course of two generations he was primarily responsible for converting an entire nation. Patrick's success was due in great part to the fact that he did not associate Christianity with his own culture. He did not try to bring other missionaries from outside of Ireland to work with him. Instead he chose his successors from among the Irish people. Many of the priests and bishops who carried on the work which Patrick began were themselves descended from the kings and chieftains whom the clans venerated.

Prior to his death in 511, Clovis took most of the land north of the Pyrenees Mountains (the area which became France) from the Visigoths. Some even regard Clovis as the "founder of France."

WESTERN MONASTICISM

The first monastic communities were in the Egyptian desert, but it wasn't long before they spread to other areas of the empire. When the barbarians—most of whom were either pagans or Arians—migrated to the western half of the empire, they were influenced in their conversion to orthodox Christianity by those monastic communities in the west.

Benedict of Nursia was the person most influential to western monasticism. His family was from an area that was controlled by the Ostrogoths, though they were part of the Roman aristocracy. Sometime around AD 500, at the age of twenty, Benedict decided to become a hermit and withdraw from the trials of a society in constant conflict. He chose to leave his home and take up a life of extreme **asceticism** in a cave. Over time, others became aware of what he was doing and came to see him. Like many of the monks of the desert, he soon had a community of disciples who lived with him. When the cave was no longer suitable for the community, Benedict and his followers moved to a hill with a grove between Rome and Naples. This was to be the site of Monte Cassino, the monastery that became the cradle of Western monasticism. Benedict's sister, Scholastica, soon joined her brother in Monte Cassino and founded a monastic community for women.

asceticism—Strict self-denial as a means of spiritual discipline. Christian ascetics imitate Christ's life of self-sacrifice in order to live the gospel more faithfully.

Monte Cassino was located halfway between Rome and Naples. The Lombards destroyed the monastery in 570 and the monks fled to Rome, taking the Rule of Benedict with them.

Benedict's most significant contribution to the monastic life and to the life of the Church in general was in the establishment of his Rule, which was based on strict discipline without unnecessary harshness. At the heart of Benedict's rule was prayer. Specific times were set aside for prayer eight times each day. During these prayer times the monks would recite the psalms and read other parts of Scripture. Over the course of a week, the entire book of Psalms would be recited. Eventually the monks and many lay people who adopted the devotional practices of the monks learned the psalter by heart and developed a great familiarity with large portions of the rest of the Bible. Benedict's community—the Benedictines—attracted the attention of other devout Christians.

The eight periods of prayer established by Benedict came to be called the "canonical hours" and their celebration was called the "divine office." Even today canon law requires that all who have been ordained as deacons or as priests to pray the divine office, or as it is known today, the **liturgy of the hours**. Furthermore, the Second Vatican Council encouraged lay people to also make this prayer their own.

The second pillar of Benedict's Rule was physical labor. Every member of the community who was physically able was to share in the work of the community. Additionally, every member of the community was to take a turn at every task. An exception could be made in the case of a monk with a unique gift who could serve the community best by doing something that he alone could do. From the monastic discipline of work Catholics have developed the concept of "offering up" the difficult or unpleasant physical chores which are part of our daily life or part of our commitment to others.

Prayer and work are the foundation of the Benedictine Rule. They are reinforced by two other significant elements of the Rule: the requirements of obedience and permanence. Benedict did not permit the monks in his community to move from one monastery to another. If a monk was unhappy he had to stay and work things out. Furthermore, Benedict insisted that all monks owed their superiors as much willing and instant obedience as possible. Benedict believed that the surrender of a monk's will to his superiors was a first step in surrendering oneself to God.[5]

The example of monastic obedience has shaped the Catholic understanding of what it means to truly say "yes" to God. Catholics in and out of a monastery are expected to accept the discipline of obedience.

liturgy of the hours—The prayer of the Church; it is also known as the divine office. The liturgy of the hours utilizes the scriptures, particularly the psalms, for specific times of the day from early morning to late evening.

STUDY QUESTIONS

- WHO WAS BENEDICT OF NURSIA?
- WHAT WERE THE TWO PILLARS OF BENEDICT'S RULE? WHAT WERE TWO OTHER SIGNIFICANT ELEMENTS OF THE RULE?
- HOW DID THE MONASTIC DISCIPLINE OF OBEDIENCE INFLUENCE THE CHURCH AS A WHOLE?

JOURNAL ASSIGNMENT

- NAME TWO WAYS YOU ACCEPT THE DISCIPLINE OF OBEDIENCE IN YOUR OWN LIFE. HOW CAN THIS DISCIPLINE HELP YOU TO SAY "YES" TO GOD?

PRAYING THE PSALMS

The liturgy of the hours, also called the divine office, is the official daily prayer of the Church. The use of "hours" implies that certain periods of the day will be set aside for prayer around the clock. The book of Psalms is a primary source of the prayers of the liturgy of the hours. Browse through the book of Psalms. Record verses of several psalms that you can use to pray on these occasions:

- morning prayer
- noon prayer
- prayer for success in school
- prayer for the poor
- prayer for family and friends
- prayer in praise of God's goodness
- night prayer

TWO MENDICANT ORDERS

In the Middle Ages, more and more people—especially the poor—moved from rural areas into towns and cities. Simultaneously, in response to the needs of the poor and migrant people, mendicant ("begging") orders developed to travel with the poor and minister to their needs, including teaching them the faith through words and actions. Mendicants took strict vows of poverty, renounced all worldly possessions, and had a willingness to beg or work for their own food.

The Franciscans

St. Francis of Assisi, one of the most popular saints of all-time, was the founder of the first mendicant order.

Francis was the son of a well-to-do merchant, Peter Bernardone. While still a young man, Francis had a profound religious experience which led him to give everything that he had to the poor and dress himself in rags. Each time his parents gave him more money and possessions, Francis would give them away. Francis found a deep joy in his poverty that he had never experienced before; all those who knew him commented on his extreme happiness. He told them that his was the joy of a newly married man. He had married the most beautiful lady in the world, lady poverty. His parents decided that he had gone mad. They locked Francis in a cellar and called upon the local bishop for help. The bishop decided that since Francis was obviously incapable of using his family's wealth wisely, he must give it up. As soon as the bishop made his pronouncement, Francis publicly disinherited himself. Then, in a gesture that remained etched on the minds of many, he took off the clothes that he was wearing, clothes which had been purchased with his father's money, and walked away naked.

For a while Francis lived the life of a hermit, but in 1209 he decided that, like the first disciples who were sent to share the Good News with no money and no provisions, God was calling him to combine poverty with preaching. He decided that his poverty should not just be a means of self-discipline, but also a way of relating to those who were poor.

Gradually a community of men formed around Francis and

eventually he received permission from the pope to found a new monastic order—the Franciscans. His friend from Assisi, St. Clare, founded a sister order for women.

The Dominicans

A second major mendicant order, the Dominicans, was founded by St. Dominic (1170–1221). Dominic was disturbed by the use of force to convert the Albigensians in southern France. He was convinced that the sword was not the best way to eliminate heresy, so he established an order which combined the rule of poverty and the practice of mendicancy with careful study and informed preaching. For the Dominicans, poverty was a way of gaining the attentions of the Albigensians who had rejected Christianity because they thought it was too worldly. In addition, the Dominicans (and also the Franciscans) preached not only to Christians, but also to the Moslems and Jews.

The Dominicans were different from other mendicant orders. The teaching aspect of their ministry was a defined focus. Rather than reside in monasteries, they lived among the people. Also, instead of focusing on manual labor, their main focus was education. Dominicans connected themselves with major universities, and they became well-known for excellence in scholarship and theology.

The Church's greatest theologian, St. Thomas Aquinas, was a Dominican. His work still shapes Catholic understanding on the relationship between faith and reason, and between the natural order and the divine order. He also formed a Catholic understanding of **natural law**. According to Aquinas, the basic

FRANCIS AND THE LEPER

Francis understood his task to be that of bringing the joy of the gospel to those who had nothing. A famous story of Francis recounts a time when he was walking down the street and came face to face with a leper. He was both terrified and repulsed, but he remembered the example of Jesus. Although his whole body was crying out for him to cross the road and get away, he embraced the leper and wished him the peace of God. In that instant he knew that it was Jesus himself that he embraced. From that day on he never allowed another's illness or disfigurement to offend his sensibilities or make him turn away.

→ *St. Thomas Aqinas*

natural law—The universal moral law which God has given to all people and which can be known by the power of reason alone.

St. Thomas Aquinas was born in 1225 in Aquino, Italy. He defied his parents by joining the Dominicans. In fact, they had two of Thomas's brothers kidnap him and imprison him in the tower of the castle in the hope he would change his mind. Thomas didn't, and studied in Cologne under St. Albert the Great. Because of his heavy weight, his classmates called him "the dumb ox." Albert defended him and said, "This dumb ox will fill the world with his bellowing."

principle of natural law is that the will of God has been given a voice in creation. All who use their powers of reason to try to understand creation will be guided by God's voice whether they know it or not. Every person who seeks the truth by carefully studying and observing the world will eventually come to see and desire the balance and order which God desires. The natural world cannot reveal everything. It tells nothing about the purpose of creation or God's plan for humanity, but if we pay close attention to the natural world, it will teach us how God wants us to behave.

STUDY QUESTIONS

- DEFINE MENDICANT.
- COMPARE AND CONTRAST THE FRANCISCAN ORDER WITH THE DOMINICAN ORDER.

JOURNAL ASSIGNMENT

- SPEND SOME TIME ALONE, OUTSIDE, OBSERVING A NATURAL SCENE. RECORD ANY LESSONS THE SCENE TEACHES YOU ABOUT GOD AND HOW YOU ARE TO BEHAVE.

CHRISTIANITY IN THE NEW WORLD

The Church expanded rapidly as Spanish and Portuguese settlers traveled to Mexico and Central and South America during the sixteenth century. Popes Alexander VI and Julius II had given the kings of Spain the right of "royal patronage" over the Church in the new world. That meant the kings had the right to nominate bishops in the Americas. This made the bishops more beholden to the monarchy than to the Church or the native people.

Fortunately, these questionably appointed bishops were not the only official Catholic presence in the new world. Many Franciscans, Dominicans, and Jesuits also were involved in missionary efforts in the Americas. These religious lived with the native people and were aware of the negative colonial policies of their governments. In many cases these missionaries argued strongly in support of the natives and against the European settlers.

In Argentina, Uruguay, and Paraguay, the Jesuits were the most successful missionaries. Roque Gonzalez, one of the best known Jesuit missionaries, grew up in Asuncion and spoke the language of the local population. Gonzalez knew and respected the customs of the natives and was able to gather the natives to live in several villages. Gonzalez taught European agricultural methods and the basics of Christianity. To a significant extent these villages operated as small theocracies ("governments ruled by religious authorities"). The members of the village elected their own leaders, but the missionary had final say on the appropriate Christian way to do things. In most of the villages property was held in common and the people lived according to the monastic disciplines of communal work and prayer.

The worst enemies of these mission villages were the Spanish and Portuguese colonists who were angered by the fact that the Jesuits would not allow them to enslave the natives. In 1625 some of the Portuguese in Sao Paulo began attacking the Jesuit missions and taking the inhabitants as slaves. At first the Jesuits responded by moving their villages farther away. When the attacks continued they began to arm the native people. They complained to Pope Urban VIII and he agreed to excommunicate any who hunted the native people in Jesuit territories.

By 1731 there were more than 140,000 native people living in Jesuit mission villages. But the Jesuit defense of the native people against their fellow Europeans angered many. In 1767 the Spanish government ordered the Jesuits to leave the Spanish colonies. As soon as they were gone the colonists began taking slaves again. By 1813 only about 50,000 native people remained in mission villages.

In Mexico, the Franciscans had great success. After Spain's conquest of the Aztecs, the explorer Hernando Cortez requested that Charles V send mendicant friars to "set a good example" for the native people, insisting that he did not want secular priests whose luxurious habits would scandalize the people. In response to Cortez's request, twelve Franciscans were sent to Mexico. At first they were resented by the native people.

Nonetheless, many natives believed that since the Christian God had clearly defeated their own gods they should seek Baptism. The Franciscans baptized any who could recite the Lord's Prayer and the Hail Mary, and who knew that there was only one God, and that Jesus was the Redeemer.

The Franciscans and the Jesuits also established missions in the southwestern portion of what is now the United States. The Jesuit Eusebio Kino made detailed maps of the southwest as he moved through the areas of Texas, Arizona, New Mexico, and California, baptizing Native Americans and establishing a large number of missions. Father Junipero Serra, a Franciscan, established and named the communities of such places as San Diego, San Juan Capistano, Santa Barbara, and San Luis Obispo.

The primary aim of both the Jesuit and the Franciscan missionaries was to establish permanent native settlements with European organizational structures. The missionaries established schools, markets, and churches. They taught basic Christianity along with European agricultural techniques, trades, and domestic skills. Rather than adapt Catholicism to the culture of the native people, the missionaries in the southwest tried to adapt the native people to the European culture. For example, the Franciscans expected newly baptized Native Americans to speak only Spanish. Because of this, any Native American who became a Catholic was required to remain in the mission community where he or she could live in a way deemed "suitable."

Missionary activity in the Far East was different than in the West. For example, Jesuit Matteo Ricci (1552–1610) in China tried to adapt the native culture to Christianity. Ricci learned the Chinese language, wore Chinese garb, and won over a great many Chinese because of his knowledge of astronomy.

Missionaries in Canada and the Northeastern United States

While the Franciscans in Mexico and in the southwestern United States disallowed the traditional religious practices of the native peoples, the French missionaries of the northeastern United States and Canada quickly realized that the only way to have any influence on the Huron tribes was to live with them and learn their languages and customs.[6] One of the first and most respected Jesuit missionaries was Jean de Brébeuf. In his first three years among the Hurons he baptized only one person, but he demonstrated a remarkable physical endurance which impressed many in the Huron tribe who had come to view Europeans as weak.

Although the Native Americans gradually gained a grudging respect for the Jesuits who lived among them, many still believed that the missionaries were responsible for the evils which had befallen them. The native communities were decimated by European diseases. Although these diseases were primarily carried by traders, many of the Huron people believed they were caused by the Jesuits. This belief was exacerbated by the fact that the Jesuits typically only baptized healthy people if they were convinced they had completely committed themselves to Christianity and were genuinely prepared to change their lives. The majority of Baptisms, therefore, were of those who were on the brink of death. As a result many of the Huron people believed that Catholic rituals caused death. As more and more of the Huron people succumbed to disease some Huron leaders began to call for the execution of the Jesuits.

Probably the only reason Jesuits were allowed to remain in the Huron communities during the first two decades of their missionary effort was that the Hurons wanted to preserve good trading relations with the French.[7]

Following the example of de Brébeuf, the Jesuit missionaries learned the language and customs of the people among whom they were living. They did not try to set themselves apart. They did not live like people in exile who longed for the day when they could return home to Europe. In fact, nineteen of the twenty-four Jesuits who went to live among the Hurons during the seventeenth century remained in their adopted tribes until they died or the tribe was destroyed by war.

To some extent, the Jesuits not only accepted Huron culture and lifestyle, they also accepted the rituals of the Huron religion. The Jesuits focused on the many similarities between Christianity and the religion of the Hurons. They tried to build upon the things that the two faiths had in common in order to gradually move the Huron people into Christianity. For example, they emphasized the similarity between the sacramental view of the world Catholics held and the Huron understanding of a supernatural power who acted through day to day events and religious ceremonies. They drew parallels between Huron spiritual quests and their own spiritual exercises,[8] and they pointed out the similarity between the Huron spirits (oki) and the Christian understanding of angels. The Hurons believed in the importance of proper worship. The Jesuits worked patiently and persistently to convince the Hurons that Catholic worship was the most effective. In all cases the Jesuits used the points of intersection between Christianity and the Huron religion as a starting point from which to persuade the Hurons that some of their beliefs and practices—such as easy divorce, blood feuds, and eating the flesh of their enemies—were unacceptable.

Like the Jesuits in South America, the North American Jesuits tried to create a hybrid culture, blending Christianity with those elements of Huron culture which were compatible with Christian beliefs. They tried to shelter the Hurons from all European influences except Christianity. In fact the Jesuits did what they could to ensure that French traders had minimal contact with the Huron people. They wanted to establish a Christianity which could survive because it was truly indigenous.

In fact, Jean de Brébeuf himself died much like a Huron warrior. On March 16, 1649, Brébeuf and his fellow Jesuit Gabriel Lalemant were captured by the Iroquois as they ministered to Huron villagers who were suffering with war injuries. Rather than kill them outright, the Iroquois captors stripped Brébeuf and Lalemant, tore out their fingernails, and then led them to a nearby village for ritual slaughter. No matter how much he was tortured, Brébeuf refused to flinch or cry out. His only words were words of concern for his fellow captives and calls for his captors to repent. The Iroquois did all that they could to break his spirit and make him beg for mercy. All of their efforts were unsuccessful; when Brébeuf died his tormentors were so impressed by his bravery that they ate his heart, as they would the heart of an enemy warrior, in order to acquire his courage. Brébeuf died as he lived, doing all that he could to earn the respect of those he hoped to convert.

In some ways the Jesuits succeeded in their efforts to establish the Christian faith among the Hurons. In other ways they were instrumental in destroying the very culture which they were trying to preserve. The missionaries encouraged baptized Hurons to believe that their destiny was different from that of their unbaptized neighbors. For this reason, many of the baptized said that they did not wish to be buried in a common grave with non-Christians. The mingling of the bones of all the people was considered the ultimate sign of communal identity. When some people refused to be buried with others, it was seen as a rejection of the solidarity which had made the Huron people strong. As the Huron sense of a single communal

STUDY QUESTIONS

- HOW DID THE JESUITS RESPOND TO THE ATTACKS BY THE SPANISH AND PORTUGUESE COLONISTS IN SAO PAULO?
- WHAT WAS THE PRIMARY AIM OF THE JESUIT AND FRANCISCAN MISSIONARIES IN SOUTH AMERICA, MEXICO, AND THE SOUTHWESTERN UNITED STATES? HOW DID THEY ACHIEVE THAT AIM?
- WHY DID THE HURONS BELIEVE THAT CATHOLIC RITUALS CAUSED DEATH? WHY DID THEY ALLOW THE JESUIT MISSIONARIES TO REMAIN WITH THEM NONETHELESS?
- WHY WERE THE HURONS IMPRESSED BY THE EXAMPLE OF JESUIT MISSIONARY JEAN DE BRÉBEUF?

Between 1642 and 1649 eight Jesuit missionaries were murdered by the Iroquois and Mohawk tribes. These are the North American Martyrs. Often the Jesuits were forced to "run the gauntlet" between club-wielding tribal members.

identity began to disintegrate, Huron society began to unravel. This unraveling was compounded by the death of large numbers of people through disease. When the Iroquois League launched a military campaign against the Hurons in 1648, the Huron confederacy was unable to mount a unified defense. By the summer of 1650 the Huron nation was little more than a number of small groups, each trying to save itself. Christian Hurons remained with Jesuit leaders and gradually established small native Christian communities along the Saint Lawrence River.

JOURNAL ASSIGNMENT

- WHAT HAVE YOU LEARNED ABOUT THE REWARDS OF PATIENCE AND PERSISTENCE IN YOUR OWN LIFE?

THE GROWTH OF CATHOLICISM IN THE UNITED STATES

Historians tend to portray the thirteen original colonies as places where people came to find freedom, particularly religious freedom. This is not entirely accurate. Many did leave Britain because they had been persecuted for their faith and they longed for a place where they could worship freely. However, they did not necessarily long for a place where others could worship equally freely. Anti-Catholic biases ran deep among many of the first European settlers. In most of the colonies the Catholic Church was not allowed to own property or establish schools or churches. In some places Catholicism itself was outlawed and no Catholic was allowed to own property or participate in the political system.

Although Catholics had been opposed to the concept of religious freedom in European countries in which they were in the majority, Catholics in the American colonies took a very different stance, supporting religious freedom wholeheartedly. In 1649 the Maryland colony—founded by Catholics—passed the Act of Toleration, granting freedom of religion to all people. Ironically, one hundred years later, when Catholics were no longer in the majority within Maryland, Catholicism was outlawed there.

Gradually, some of the prejudices against Catholics began to subside. The colonialists needed the help of Catholic France in order to win the revolution with Great Britain. Moreover, the witness of Catholics like Charles Carroll, a prominent statesman and signatory of the Declaration of Independence, and John Barry, the commander of the American navy, influenced many. These men were not evangelists in the traditional sense of the word, but they were people who did not separate their Catholic faith from the rest of what they did. Others knew that they were Catholics and began to look upon Catholicism differently because of them.

After the American Revolution many people, particularly in Maryland, began to

John Carroll was one of the most influential Catholics during the Revolutionary War. He wrote that Catholic blood "flowed as freely [as others'] to cement the fabric of independence as that of their fellow citizens."

petition the pope for an American bishop. In 1789 John Carroll, the cousin of Charles, became the first bishop of Maryland and the United States. Throughout his life Carroll worked to convince everyone that it was possible for Catholics to be loyal Americans even while maintaining allegiance to the pope. (Archbishop Carroll himself was invited to preside at the laying of the cornerstone for the Washington Monument in Washington, D.C., though he had to refuse the invitation because of poor health.)

Catholic Education in the United States

John Carroll also shaped the United States Catholic Church herself. Carroll was a strong believer in education. He believed that if the Catholic Church was going to flourish in the new nation there would be a need for Catholics who were well-educated in faith as well as in other matters. There would also be a need for American-educated clergy who understood and respected the political system in the new nation. Even before he was named bishop, Carroll convinced his fellow clergy to fund Georgetown College (later University). He also invited the Sulpician Fathers to come to Baltimore to found St. Mary's Seminary.

Carroll also supported the work of Mother Elizabeth Seton and the Sisters of Charity as they worked to establish Catholic elementary schools. In 1829 the Plenary Council of Baltimore agreed with Carroll's assessment that Catholic schools were "absolutely necessary" to teach Catholic faith and morality and to make Catholics equal members of society. The insistence on a

John F. Kennedy

Catholic school system arose, at least in part, out of a concern that large numbers of Catholics were not being educated at all. Although the United States Constitution did not designate a "national Church" and although Catholics and Protestants shared the same basic rights, Protestants continued to dominate both the political scene and the educational scene. As a result, many of the texts which were used in public schools were unacceptable to Catholics. Schools in New York, for example, used only Protestant prayers and hymns and only the King James version of the Bible. Furthermore, many of the texts for courses in history and literature presented the Catholic Church in a very unfavorable light. Many immigrants refused to send their children to such hostile schools. When Catholics complained and called for change they were often answered with an increase in anti-Catholic rhetoric and sometimes even with violent demonstrations. Many came to believe that parochial schools were the only viable alternative. At the Third Plenary Council of Baltimore in 1884, the bishops declared that every parish must establish a school for its children.

As successive waves of Catholic immigrants came to the United States, Catholic schools and parishes played a major role in integrating these new immigrants into American society. They taught basic skills to the uneducated and helped those who had come from very different cultures to understand and become participants in the American political system. The efforts of many—particularly religious sisters and brothers—to educate and assist Catholic immigrants throughout the late 1800s and early 1900s resulted in an ever increasing acceptance of Catholics by the populace. As more and more Catholics were able to participate fully in every aspect of life in the United States, anti-Catholic sentiments began to fade. Nonetheless, some groups, most notably the Know Nothings and the Ku Klux Klan, continued to believe and promote the idea that Catholicism was a threat to the United States. When the Catholic Al Smith ran for president in 1928, the Klan warned Americans that if a Catholic were elected democracy would disappear and Smith would have allegiance to Rome. It was not until the 1960 election of John F. Kennedy as president of the United States that the last traces of blatant anti-Catholic bias in national politics were overcome.

STUDY QUESTIONS

- HOW WERE CATHOLICS DISCRIMINATED AGAINST IN THE AMERICAN COLONIES?
- HOW DID THE ATTITUDES OF CATHOLICS IN THE AMERICAN COLONIES DIFFER FROM THE ATTITUDES OF EUROPEAN CATHOLICS WITH REGARD TO RELIGIOUS FREEDOM?
- WHAT WERE SOME OF THE WAYS ARCHBISHOP JOHN CARROLL HELPED SHAPE THE CATHOLIC CHURCH IN THE UNITED STATES?
- WHY WERE ANTI-CATHOLIC BIASES SO STRONG IN AMERICA? HOW WERE THEY OVERCOME?

JOURNAL ASSIGNMENT

- WHAT DO YOU BELIEVE IS THE PRIMARY PURPOSE OF THE CATHOLIC SCHOOL SYSTEM IN THE UNITED STATES TODAY?

Born in Italy, Mother Cabrini (1850–1917) was naturalized an American citizen in 1909. She is the first non-martyred American saint. She is known for her tireless work among American immigrants. She founded the Missionary Sisters of the Sacred Heart.

ST. ELIZABETH SETON

Elizabeth Ann Seton, the first American born saint, was a single mother who dedicated her life to helping the poor and educating the young.

She was born Elizabeth Bayley into a wealthy Episcopalian family in New York City in 1774. Although she had plenty of material possessions, her mother's death when Elizabeth was very young hurt her greatly. Young Elizabeth then spent a great amount of time with her father and grandfather. Elizabeth's grandfather was an Episcopalian priest who assisted black slaves who came to New York. Her father was a professor and a doctor who also helped the poor. In fact, he died from yellow fever which he contracted while caring for Irish immigrants.

When Elizabeth was twenty she married a wealthy merchant named William Seton. They had five children of their own and they took in William's six brothers and sisters when his father died. Elizabeth was kept busy with her family and with her charitable works. Then tragedy struck again. William lost the family fortune and became ill. The family traveled to Italy in the hopes that the warmer climate would help him, but he died within a few weeks of their arrival.

Elizabeth remained with friends in Italy for a few months. During that time she learned to see the strength and beauty of Catholicism. When she returned to New York she joined the Catholic Church. She was happy with her choice, but many of her old friends and acquaintances were not. She felt the sting of anti-Catholic prejudices and began to think about moving to Canada, where Catholicism was more acceptable. However, when she was invited by Father Louis DuBourg to come to Maryland and establish a school for girls near Saint Mary's seminary she accepted his invitation.

In 1808 she and her family moved to Baltimore. The following year she moved her school to Emmitsburg, Maryland. She did not want the school to be completely dependent on her or to die when she did. Therefore, she requested permission to establish an order of religious women who would commit themselves to teaching and to caring for the poor. Archbishop Carroll gave her the permission she requested. He witnessed her vows and gave her the title "Mother Seton."

Her order, the Sisters of Charity of Saint Joseph, followed the rule of the French Sisters of Charity. They established a network of schools which became the model for parochial schools throughout the United States. They also founded hospitals, clinics, child-care centers, and homes for the elderly that are still in operation today.

Elizabeth Seton died on January 4, 1821. She was declared a saint by Pope Paul VI in 1975.

IN CONCLUSION

Evangelization is the sharing of the Good News in such a way that it touches people's hearts and inspires them to reorder their lives. Evangelization is intended for those who have yet to hear the Good News. Evangelization is a mandate for all Catholics from the teaching office of the Church, the Magisterium. Throughout the years Catholics and other Christians have used several methods as they evangelized, from the extreme of forcing Baptism on individuals or nations at the point of a sword to a visible persuasion exercised through the witness of men and women, living out their Christian faith in the midst of non-Christian communities.

Initially, Christianity was shared through preaching in Jewish synagogues and in places of business where Jewish Christians conducted trade. When Christianity was illegal in the Roman empire, Christianity was at once a risky proposition but also an appealing one, as Christians exhibited great courage and strength to the point of being martyred for their faith. Many were attracted to Christianity because of this powerful example.

Monastics took up where martyrs left off in dramatically witnessing to the faith. Originally, desert hermits like Anthony of Egypt offered a living witness to the vows of poverty and chastity associated with Gospel living. Later this was taken up in the founding of Christian monasticism, where work and obedience to a religious superior also came to the fore. Prayer and work became the motto of Western monasticism as founded by Saint Benedict of Nursia.

As the population shifted and many poor peasants migrated from place to place and into cities and towns, two mendicant or begging religious orders, the Franciscans and Dominicans, were founded to accompany them. St. Francis himself exhibited a great love for poverty and embraced it in the name of the Gospel. St. Dominic and the Dominicans combined preaching with solid theology and scholarship appealing to reason rather than the sword to combat heresy.

Interesting twists to evangelism were tried in the New World. Whereas bishops and Church hierarchy were appointed and associated with colonialism, religious missionaries, especially the Franciscans and Jesuits, tried to various degrees to incorporate native religious customs with Catholic rituals and practices. Missions in South America, Mexico, and the southwestern United States provided places where native peoples could be safe from colonists as well as learn the religion of the newcomers.

As in other places and eras, acceptance of Catholicism in the United States was furthered more by actions than by words. Catholicism was accepted as Catholics proved themselves to be educated and loyal Americans. Throughout history it has been the actions of Christians which have inspired others and made them stop and listen to the good news. This is the meaning of "good" evangelization.

LEARN BY DOING

Research and report on one of the following:
- a typical contemporary day in the life of one of the religious orders mentioned in this chapter;
- St. Thomas Aquinas's five proofs for the existence of God;
- key elements of the rule of St. Benedict;
- the North American Martyrs;
- prejudice against Catholics in the United States.

PRAYER

Prayer of St. Francis

Lord, make me an instrument of your peace:
where there is hatred, let me sow love;
where there is injury, pardon;
where there is doubt, faith;
where there is despair, hope;
where there is darkness, light;
and where there is sadness, joy.

Grant that I may not so much seek
to be consoled as to console;
to be understood as to understand;
to be loved as to love.

For it is in giving that we receive,
it is in pardoning that we are pardoned,
and it is in dying that we are born to eternal life.

NOTES

1. See #21.
2. Martyrdom of Perpetua and Felicitas, 5:3.
3. See Gonzalez, *The Story of Christianity*, Vol. 1, p. 98.
4. See Gonzalez, *The Story of Christianity*, Vol. 1, p. 142.
5. It is important to note that surrendering oneself to one's superiors never meant agreeing to do that which one believed was genuinely wrong, but only agreeing to do that which was perceived as best for the community rather than as best or most comfortable for the individual monk.
6. See Henry Warner Bowden, *American Indians and Christian Missions: Studies in Cultural Conflict* (Chicago: The University of Chicago Press, 1981), p. 52.
7. Bowden, *American Indians*, p. 78.
8. The Spiritual Exercises of Saint Ignatius, the founder of the Jesuits, consist of systematic meditations and prayers aimed at helping a person discern the will of God in his or her life.

UNIT FIVE

THE CHURCH IS SACRAMENT

THE CHURCH IS SACRAMENT

Sacraments are sacred and visible signs of God's loving grace active in the world. Jesus Christ is the original sign and the primordial or prime sacrament. Jesus is not only the sign of God the Father in our midst, he is the very presence of God.

Like Christ, the Church is also a sacrament. The Church is a sign of our inner union with God. The Church is also a sign of our unity with others. As the *Catechism of the Catholic Church* teaches further, "The seven sacraments are the signs and instruments by which the Holy Spirit spreads the grace of Christ the head throughout the Church which is his Body. The Church, then, both contains and communicates the invisible grace she signifies. It is in this analogical sense, that the Church is called a "sacrament" (774).

Liturgy is the "work" of the people. By participating in the sacramental life of the Church, we participate in the work of God in the world. The sacraments define us as a Church which frees the captives, strengthens the lame, feeds the hungry, heals the sick, brings forgiveness to sinners, serves the poor, and unites those who were separated.

In chapter 5.2, sacrament and liturgy are defined and their roles in the Church are explained. The second part of the chapter offers more depth as to how the sacraments shape the Church. In other words, each time a sacrament is celebrated, the Church becomes more fully the community which makes Christ's presence tangible. Even when the sacraments are over, Christ remains with the Church in some tangible form. This is known as the lasting effect of the sacrament. Each of the Seven Sacraments has its own unique, lasting effect.

Chapter 5.2 covers in more depth the historical development of the sacraments following their institution by Christ. In each century the sacraments have been a source of grace, and in each century the theology and practice of the Church has prepared many to cooperate with the grace of the sacraments.

The chapter focuses especially on the Sacraments of Initiation—Baptism, Confirmation, and Eucharist. It will help you to understand how the Eucharist allows you to be present at both the saving events of the past (the Last Supper and Crucifixion) and the saving events of the present (the Second Coming.)

When you have completed Unit 5, you will be able to

- define the term "sacrament" and explain the ways in which Christ and the Church are sacraments;
- explain how the sacraments are shaped by the worldview and dominant culture of the day;
- articulate how the Church, particularly the liturgical life of the Church, is the focal point for the world;
- express the importance of the communal nature of the sacraments;
- understand the "lasting effect" of each sacrament and discuss how belief in a lasting effect of the sacrament shapes Catholic religious practices;
- name the aspects of the sacraments that can change and those that cannot;
- explain the diversity in the celebration of the sacraments from culture to culture;
- trace the history and development of the Sacraments of Initiation;
- understand Jesus' baptism to all subsequent Christian Baptisms;
- understand how the Eucharist allows its participants to be present at both the saving events of the past (Last Supper and Crucifixion) and the present (Second Coming);
- express an understanding of the Eucharist as both meal and sacrifice;
- summarize the historical circumstances which led to the promulgation of the doctrine of transubstantiation and to the particular language used to explain the doctrine;
- name all Seven Sacraments.

A SIGN and SOURCE
of GOD'S GRACE

WHAT ELSE ARE THE SACRAMENTS (ALL OF THEM!), IF NOT THE ACTION OF CHRIST IN THE HOLY SPIRIT? WHEN THE CHURCH BAPTIZES, IT IS CHRIST WHO BAPTIZES; WHEN THE CHURCH ABSOLVES, IT IS CHRIST WHO ABSOLVES; WHEN THE CHURCH CELEBRATES EUCHARIST, IT IS CHRIST WHO CELEBRATES IT: "THIS IS MY BODY." AND SO ON. ALL THE SACRAMENTS ARE AN ACTION OF CHRIST, THE ACTION OF GOD IN CHRIST.

—*Pope John Paul II*
Crossing the Threshold of Hope

FORGIVE US

Kathleen was working in Rwanda when the resettlement of Hutu refugees began. She noted that while people often criticize the Church and its leaders, saying that they have not done enough or that they have done the wrong thing during a time of crisis, it is rare

to hear the stories of how the Church made it possible for people to survive and maintain their sanity during times of absolute horror. "The truth is, despite its imperfections, the Church has been a sign and source of hope and healing during the very worst situations." Kathleen shared the following story[1] to illustrate her point:

In April of 1994, the plane carrying the President of Rwanda was shot down. Like many people in Kigali, Sylvère heard the explosion from his home. He had enough political savvy to know that there was no time to spare. War had been on the horizon for months. The explosion signaled its arrival. Within the hour Sylvère sent his wife, his two sons and his three daughters to take shelter in the Catholic church of St. Paul's. He chose to stay at the house and pray by the

family shrine. Sylvère tried to convince his mother to go with the rest of the family, but she insisted that she was too old to fear death; she would stay by his side.

Sylvère was on his knees when his neighbors came armed with bow and arrows. A man on his knees is an easy target, and a neighbor who has become an enemy has no mercy. The very first arrow pierced Sylvère's chest. He did not die immediately, but death was inevitable. Sylvère knew it, and so did those who had shot him. They saw no point in wasting a second arrow. They turned to Sylvère's mother, Marie. She shook as she waited for death, but no one shot. Instead one spat and sneered at her, "You're too old to be worth an arrow. Sit and watch your son die. That should be death enough for you."

Marie said nothing, but after the Hutu neighbors had left, she promised her son that they would suffer from every kind of revenge. Sylvère told her that she needed to pray for them, not curse them. "Our faith tells us to forgive. 'Forgive us our trespasses as we forgive others.' That's what we say at Mass. That's what Jesus and Mary would do. We must too." Then, struggling for each breath, Sylvère began to sing hymns. Gradually his voice faded into silence. Marie began to weep.

When the neighbors returned, Marie thought her son was dead. She called down curse after angry curse upon those who would shoot a neighbor. Then she saw that Sylvère's eyes were open again and he was looking at her. He whispered again: "Forgive them."

Sylvère died shortly after that. Against all odds, Marie made it to the church alive. Sylvère was well loved and respected in his community. When Marie told people of his death there were many who wanted to do something. Under the cover of darkness, a small group went back to the house to reclaim his body. They brought it to the church for a funeral and a proper burial. All of the people who were sheltering in the church participated in the funeral Mass. In those days of slaughter, Sylvère was one of the only people in the whole country to have a decent burial. He was also one of the only ones who had someone to tell his story. God had surely blessed him for his faithfulness.

Sylvère's family and the rest of the community spent almost three months in the church. They had minimal rations of food and drink. They kept their minds from their hunger and found a way through their fear by praying and studying the Bible. A family motto became "The Church sheltered us, the faith we rediscovered in the Church kept us alive."

After Sylvère's murder, both of his sons spent a lot of time reflecting on the way their father had lived and the way he had died. One son took his father's call for forgiveness to heart. Josué said that he could never fight the Hutus no matter what they had done. When the United Nations began trying to persuade Hutus to leave the refugee camps and return to Rwanda, Josué worked with a team from the U.N. whose primary goals were to encourage refugees to return to Rwanda and to make those who did return feel welcome.

Sylvère's other son, Christian, was far less moved by his father's final words. He remained bitter about what had happened and he longed for the opportunity to fight the Hutus and give them some of what they "deserved."

A little over two years after Sylvère's death, Kathleen attended Mass with his family in Kigali. During the homily the priest spoke about the unity of the Body of Christ, which included both Hutus and Tutsis. Christian was deep in thought as people filed by him on the way to communion. The rest of his family moved forward to receive but he remained where he was. Finally he too went forward. When the liturgy was over, he made only one comment to Kathleen, "That was a very good message. It was also my father's message."

This story has much to do with the Church as **sacrament**, the main subject of Unit 5. Kathleen's observation that the Church is often a sign and source of hope and healing during the most unbearable situations is correct. For Sylvère, the Church was a sign of God, constantly reminding him of the person whom God was calling him to be. In a similar way, the Church was both the sign and source of God's protection and comfort for Sylvère's family. They took shelter in the church because it was God's Church. Those who took shelter in the church experienced the presence of God, both in the Blessed Sacrament reserved in a special chapel off the main sanctuary and in the very lives of the community that spent

sacrament—A sign and instrument of God's presence in the world. Jesus is the first sacrament. Jesus is the sign of God's presence in history and the means or instrument through which God's presence in history is made accessible to human beings. The Church is the first sacrament of Christ. The Church is the sign and instrument of Christ's continuing presence in the world. The Church herself has Seven Sacraments through which it makes the grace of Christ's Death, Resurrection, and Ascension available and accessible to the faithful.

grace—The free and undeserved help that God gives us to respond to his call to become children of God and partakers of the divine nature and of eternal life

three months not only living together but also praying together. Finally, the Eucharist, celebrated weeks after his father's death, was the sign and the means for Christian to let go of his anger and forgive.

Sylvère's family continues to believe that God is present in the Catholic Church. As the priest in Kigali said, the Church belongs to all people: Tutsis, Hutus, and all others. All pray one prayer. All share in one body. All become one body in the Spirit. Eventually all may learn to be one people in the flesh. The Church is the dream of a better, more peaceful future. Each person who has been helped by the Church has been touched by God. Through his Body, the Church, Christ constantly offers the gift of **grace**. Each encounter with the Church is a grace-filled invitation to enter into a deeper relationship with God. The physical aid which the Church gives is a reflection of the spiritual aid which is being offered. During Jesus' time on earth, all who looked closely at him saw God. In our day, all who look closely at the Christian community which offers them help see Christ.

JOURNAL ASSIGNMENT

- HOW WAS THE CHURCH A SIGN OF GOD'S PRESENCE TO SYLVÈRE AND HIS FAMILY?

CHRIST IS THE FIRST SACRAMENT

We are physical beings. We use our five senses to perceive and relate to everything around us. Even when we want to speak about our understanding of that which is not physical—for example God or spirituality—we use analogies to the physical world. We speak of God the Holy Spirit as a fire or a wind. We say that we "feel the warmth of God surrounding us." As Catholics we believe that God interacts with us through the physical world. Our God, who is incomprehensible, chooses to be present to us through things which we can comprehend. We are not summoned to a relationship with God in spite of the fact that we are rooted in the material world; we are summoned through the material world itself. God uses everything around us to draw us into the relationship of the Trinity.[2]

Our experience of God who is outside of history is mediated by people, events, and things which are rooted in history.[3] The people, events, and things which always make God present to us are known as sacraments. Jesus is the first sacrament because in Jesus God is fully present to us. The God who is beyond the reach of human understanding, the God whose thoughts and ways are as high above ours as the heavens are high above the earth (see Isaiah 55:9) has become accessible and comprehensible to us by becoming a human being. The infinite Trinity has been mediated to humanity in the person of Jesus.

Jesus is a sacrament. He is the sign of God's love and care for us: "For God so loved the world that he gave his only Son . . ." (John 3:16). But Jesus is more than just a sign pointing to God's love. Jesus is also the instrument of God's love. It is in Jesus that God's love becomes a physical part of human history. All who encounter Jesus have encountered God, whether they realize it or not.

The Church Is the First Sacrament of Christ

Every other sacrament derives its nature from the nature of Christ. Each sacrament is a sign, which, like Jesus, points to something beyond itself. (Jesus is the sign which points to the Trinity.) Each sacrament is also an instrument which brings the grace of God into our world and into our lives. The traditional teaching of the Catholic Church says that sacraments are "perceptible signs (words and actions) accessible to our human nature."[4] What is more, sacraments are signs which cause what they signify. That is, they reveal something about God and they make what they have revealed reality.

When Jesus ascended into Heaven, he left us with other tangible signs which, like Jesus himself, allow finite human beings to relate to an infinite God. The first of these signs, the first sacrament of Christ, is the Church. The Church is the continuing presence of Christ on earth and in history. Jesus has ascended to the Father, but in his Body the Church he continues to be accessible to us and to work with us.

The Church makes God's continuing actions in the world both visible and tangible. The very nature of the Church is the sign of what God desires for the world. The Church is one just as the world was created to be one. The Church is holy. It is united to God just as the world was created to be. The Church is catholic. It is of all people and for all people even as God is the God of all people whose actions are for all people. And finally, the Church is apostolic. All authority in the Church comes from God the Father, through Christ, by the power of the Holy Spirit. In a perfectly restored world, all authority and power will come from God and will take the form of the authority and power of Jesus, who got on his knees to wash the feet of his followers. But the Church is more than just a sign of how the world should be; the Church is also the tool which God is using to remake the world.

STUDY QUESTIONS

- HOW IS HUMANITY'S EXPERIENCE OF GOD MEDIATED?
- WHAT IS THE FUNCTION OF A SACRAMENT?
- WHY IS JESUS THE FIRST SACRAMENT?

JOURNAL ASSIGNMENT

- WHAT ARE SOME WAYS THAT GOD INTERACTS WITH HUMANITY THROUGH THE PHYSICAL WORLD? WHAT ARE SOME WAYS YOU HAVE EXPERIENCED GOD'S INTERACTION?

WHAT IS AN EFFICACIOUS SYMBOL?

The Church is an efficacious symbol. That means that it is a symbol that not only points to a reality—in this case, salvation—but it also causes it. An efficacious symbol is different from other symbols or signs. For example, the peace sign of the 1960s was a symbol for an effort, mainly by young people, to end the war in Viet Nam. But the peace sign itself did not cause the war to end. From your understanding of "efficacious symbol," explain how each of the seven sacraments of the Church are themselves efficacious.

Cut out a several symbols from magazine photos that are common today (e.g. product symbols, team symbols). Explain why these symbols are not efficacious.

liturgy—The public worship of the Church which includes the celebration of the Eucharist and other sacraments and the liturgy of the hours. The word liturgy literally means "public work." In Christian tradition liturgy means the participation of the People of God in the work of God.

THE LITURGICAL LIFE OF THE CHURCH

The Church, particularly the liturgical life of the Church, is the focal point of God's action in the world.[5] Catholics believe that the Eucharist is the source and summit of all of the Church's activity.[6] In the **liturgy**, all that Christ has done, is doing, and will do for us is made part of the present moment. The liturgy is the sign of the redemption and transformation of the world which was begun in Christ and which will be completed at the time of the Second Coming. When the universal Church gathers to celebrate the Lord's Day, the world is symbolically restored. The Church uses ritual to enact the world as God intends it to be.[7]

Every element of the liturgical life of the Church directs us toward the world that God has envisioned for us. Through Christ's Passion the world itself has been redeemed. The Church can be understood as the "workshop of the world."[8] The Church is the place to which we bring the activity of the world so that it may be reshaped by the mystery of Christ and then returned to the world as something new. In the liturgical life of the Church all of the basic elements of our life together take on new meaning. Birth and death, eating and drinking, bathing, comforting, greeting, leading, sexual intercourse in marriage—they are all transformed in the presence of Christ. The liturgical life of the Church helps us to see and understand that transformation; what is more, it gives us the grace to live that transformation in the world.

What Happens in Liturgy

What we do in our worship is a sign of the people we are becoming. Our liturgy is the sign and source of our new identity in Christ. We begin the liturgy in the name of the Father, and of the Son, and of the Holy Spirit because we are becoming a people who act out of our commitment to God. What we do at our liturgy reminds us that unless our lives are lived in the name of the Trinity, unless all that we do is done with an awareness of God's presence and an acceptance of God's guidance, we will never find true fulfillment. In our everyday world we compete with, alienate, and hurt one another. During our liturgy we confess our sins and ask for forgiveness. We become a people who can transform our conflict into healthy growth. We are becoming a community which can carry Christ's reconciliation to the world. In our daily lives we are bombarded by cries for help. In our liturgy we pray for the world because Christ is transforming us into a people who accept responsibility for one another. In our life in the world we eat and drink for ourselves. In our liturgy we eat from one loaf and drink from one cup and God transforms us into one body. We are becoming a people who live, not for ourselves, but for each other. We are becoming a people who are united, even as the Three Persons of the Trinity are united. In our liturgy we are becoming a new creation so that we may also become a new creation in our world.

In the liturgy, people are not separated by race, gender, nationality, or any other characteristic of birth. Furthermore, time is suspended and distance becomes meaningless. In the liturgy, there are no divisions among people of different generations or from different periods in history. In the liturgy, there is no separation between people celebrating the Eucharist in different parts of the world. In the liturgy, death is not something horrible. Death is not something which divides; it is something which allows us to live a new life of true unity. Finally, in the liturgy, the peace and perfect communication with God and with one another that were lost at the time of the fall are symbolically restored, and we are assured that one day they will be completely restored. The liturgy makes us participants in a world in which all that is wrong has been righted.

Liturgy Is the Work of the People

As Catholics we believe that God acts through our liturgy, so that when we do something ritually we receive the grace to do that same thing in our everyday lives. When we are reconciled ritually, we are given the ability to reconcile in day to day life. When we are ritually cleansed from sin, we are given the grace to turn away from all that is harmful or evil in our everyday lives. When we are ritually united in the liturgy, we receive the grace to live in unity in the world. This is the essence of our belief that sacraments cause what they signify. This is why the liturgy is "the work of the people."

As we participate in the sacramental life of the Church, we are enabled to participate in the work of God in the world.[9]

The priest in Kigali reminded the congregation that their communion was a communion with the whole Body of Christ. In doing so he was calling their attention to the ritual unity which was being enacted in the Eucharist. When Sylvère's son, Christian, received communion, that ritual unity took on a new reality in his life. His attitude toward the Hutus shifted, however slightly. God acted through the Church and the Eucharist to unite Christian with his enemies in a new and more profound way. The complete transformation of the world moved one step closer.

As Catholics, we believe that in the Church, and particularly in the Eucharist, God offers enemies the grace which they need to set aside their hatred and to find true peace. The Church and the Eucharist are not just symbols of human unity, they actually make unity possible. Likewise, the Church and the Eucharist are not just symbols of human unity with God; they also make that unity possible. The Church is "the great sacrament of divine communion."[10] Because the Holy Spirit dwells in the Church, all who are part of the Church are both symbolically and genuinely united to God.[11] The world is restored internally, and the proper relationship of the world to the One who created and sustains it is also restored.

RESHAPING WORDS, GESTURES, AND RITUALS

According to Catholic doctrine, the grace which God gives through the sacraments is not altered when those sacraments are poorly understood, or when they are celebrated in a way that confuses rather than enlightens. This does not mean, however, that the sacramental signs are unimportant. Sacramental grace bears fruit according to the disposition of the individual who receives that grace. A person who does not understand a sacrament may be poorly prepared to embrace the grace which it offers.

The connotations of certain words, gestures, and symbols can vary dramatically from one culture to another. If the same words or the same symbols are used to teach and nurture faith in two very different cultures, two very different faiths may result. If there is to be only one faith, there must be many different ways of presenting and celebrating it. As cultures and worldviews vary, the way in which sacramental signs are used may also vary; indeed in some cases they must vary if they are to remain intelligible and assist people in receiving the grace which God offers.

An historical illustration may clarify this. When the Jesuit missionaries worked with the Hurons in North America they never spoke of the Eucharist as the body of Christ. They did not talk about eating Christ's body and drinking his blood because they knew that for the Hurons such phrases would mean something that was far removed from Christianity. The Huron people practiced a form of ritual cannibalism. It was their custom to eat their bravest enemies in order to absorb the courage of those enemies.

The Jesuit missionaries believed that speaking of the Eucharist as the Body and Blood of Christ would have given a wrong impression of the Christian view of cannibalism and a wrong impression of Jesus. Jesus was not an enemy who proved himself worthy by enduring torture. Jesus did not accept suffering to prove his strength. Furthermore, although courage is a gift of the Holy Spirit, it is by no means the ultimate gift which Jesus offers. Finally, we do not eat the Eucharist in order to absorb Jesus' power and make it our own. Yet all of these things would have seemed self-evident to the Huron people if they had been told that Catholics ate and drank the Body and Blood of Christ.

The Sunday Obligation

"Why should I go to Mass if I don't get anything out of it?"

"I don't want to go. It's boring."

"People go to Church and talk about love and then they won't even let each other out of the parking lot. It's all so hypocritical. Why should I bother?"

These are some refrains that can be heard in houses around the country and probably around the world. Many Catholics of all ages know that they are "supposed to" go to Mass each week, but they do not see any benefits of going or any real consequences of not going, so they stay home.

If we begin to view our liturgies as the "work" of our community, as the thing which we must do in order to participate with God in the transformation of the world, we will begin to understand the value of every liturgy regardless of the quality of the homily, the singability of the music, or even the interactions in the parking lot. God has chosen to be present in our liturgical celebrations and to act through those celebrations to give us grace. Our liturgies are not just about God, they are of God.[12] Because of this, every liturgy has the power to transform us, and through us to transform the world. Refusing to go to Mass because it's boring might be compared to a hospital patient who refuses intravenous feeding because it doesn't taste good. One goes to Mass in order to come face to face with, and be transformed by, the living God. The music, the visual environment, and the homily can all help us to open ourselves up to that transformation, but the transforming grace which God offers to us is not dependent on the quality of any of those things.

The liturgy, and particularly the Sunday liturgy, makes it possible for us to be the Church. We are able to be the Body of Christ on earth only because we receive the Body of Christ. Without the Eucharist, we would remain isolated individuals, impotent in the face of an infinite universe.

SACRAMENTS: ROOTED IN THE PASCHAL MYSTERY

The **Paschal Mystery**—Christ's Death, Resurrection, and Ascension—is a gift from God which can transform the life of the faithful. Through the Death, Resurrection, and Ascension of Christ we have been given the opportunity to share in a new life in union with the Trinity. But knowing we can be transformed is not enough to lead us to transformation. We need God's help to make the Paschal Mystery a part of our lives to such an extent that we will be remade.

The *Catechism of the Catholic Church* states that the Church exists in the time of the "dispensation of the mystery,"[13] that is, the time between Christ's Ascension and his return at the end of time. It is the task of the Church to enable the faithful to participate in the Paschal Mystery and be transformed by it so that they will be fully prepared to receive Christ when he comes again. The Church does this through the sacraments. In the celebration of the sacraments the historical events of Christ's Death, Resurrection, and Ascension become part of our present moment and we are invited to participate in them. Each of the sacraments of the Church unites those who receive it to the saving acts of Christ and enables them to share in the blessings which flow from those acts.

The sacraments are "the masterworks of God in the new and everlasting covenant."[14]

CHRIST'S PRESENCE

Draw (or use any other art medium) a symbol for young children who are preparing for First Communion that expresses how Christ is present in the Eucharist. Arrange to share or display your artwork in the religious education classroom where the children attend.

Paschal Mystery—Christ's Passion, Resurrection, and Ascension. Christians participate in the Paschal Mystery through Baptism, Eucharist, and the other sacraments.

STUDY QUESTIONS

- DEFINE LITURGY.
- WHAT DOES IT MEAN TO SAY THAT "SACRAMENTS CAUSE WHAT THEY SIGNIFY"? GIVE AN EXAMPLE.
- HOW DOES UNDERSTANDING THE LITURGY AS THE "WORK OF THE COMMUNITY" EXPLAIN THE NECESSITY OF ATTENDING SUNDAY MASS?

JOURNAL ASSIGNMENT

- FINISH THE FOLLOWING SENTENCES: "THE BEST MASS I EVER CELEBRATED WAS . . ." AND "IF I COULD PLAN THE SUNDAY MASS AT MY PARISH I WOULD. . . ."

THE SACRAMENTS SHAPE THE CHURCH

Jesus is the focal point of God's activity in history. The Church is the focal point of Jesus' continuing presence on earth; and the Eucharist is the focal point of the Church's work. All of the other sacraments of the Church are ordered to the Eucharist as their end.[15] When we receive the Body of Christ in the Eucharist, we become the Body of Christ. The Second Vatican Council document, *Lumen Gentium,* quoted St. Leo Martyr as saying, "The sharing in the body and blood of Christ has no other effect than to accomplish our transformation into that which we receive."[16] The Eucharist draws us into the mystery of Christ; each of the other sacraments sheds light upon that mystery and helps us to live particular aspects of it more fully.

The sacraments give definition to the Church. The sacraments ensure that the Church does what Christ would do in the world. They guarantee that we will act as the true Body of Christ, at least in our public work of worship. The sacraments define us as a community which frees the captives, strengthens the lame, feeds the hungry, heals the sick, brings forgiveness to sinners, serves the poor, and unites those who are separated. Each of the sacraments gives shape to our communal identity as the Body of Christ. Although there have been times in our history when people have spoken of the sacraments as if their primary purpose was to give individuals more grace, the fruit of the sacraments is both for individuals and the community. As Paul stresses in the first letter to the Corinthians, all that we do in our worship should be aimed at the building up of the Body of Christ. Anything that is more for the individual than for the community as a whole belongs in the privacy of our homes (see 1 Corinthians 14). The sacraments do benefit individuals, but that is because the sacraments bond individuals more completely to the community which is one with Christ and through Christ with the Trinity.

How the Sacraments Transform the Community

Unless we understand the fundamentally communal nature of the sacraments we may doubt their power to really transform, and we may be tempted to regard them as nothing more than symbols. As Catholics, we believe that the words which God spoke through the prophet Isaiah—"Just as from the heavens the rain and snow come down and do not return there till they have watered the earth . . . so shall my word be that goes forth from my mouth; it shall not return to me void, but shall do my will, achieving the end for which I sent it" (Isaiah 55:10–11)—may be applied to the sacraments. The sacraments are acts of God, and, therefore, they are always effective. Nonetheless, the sacraments will not automatically transform individuals. Baptism frees us from the clutches of sin and orients us to God, yet a baptized individual may still do horrible things. The Sacrament of Reconciliation gives us the grace to turn away from sin, yet an individual who has received the sacrament may still fall right back into the same sin. The power of the

sacraments to transform individuals depends on the disposition of the individual.

The power of the sacraments to transform the community, on the other hand, is not dependent on any human act or attitude. Each time a person is baptized, the brokenness and separation of Original Sin is defeated and the Church becomes more catholic, more universal. Each time a person receives the Sacrament of Reconciliation, the Church becomes a more reconciling community. Each time a person is ordained, the Church becomes more fully a community which is ordered according to God's will. Each time the Eucharist is celebrated, Christ's Death and Resurrection, Christ's sacrifice, and Christ's triumph become part of our present moment;[17] the Church is joined to Christ and becomes more fully the community which will be broken and poured out for the sake of the world.

Each time a sacrament is celebrated, the Church becomes more fully the community which makes Christ's presence tangible. In the absence of the sacramental signs, Christ would not be as clearly revealed through the Church. Without the sacraments, grace might be present, but we could not take hold of it in the same way. Without the sacraments, the Church might become more like a letter mailed from Christ to the world and less like the visible, accessible presence of Christ on earth.

STUDY QUESTIONS

- HOW DO THE SACRAMENTS GIVE DEFINITION TO THE CHURCH?
- WHAT IS NECESSARY FOR THE SACRAMENTS TO BE ABLE TO TRANSFORM INDIVIDUALS?
- WHAT WOULD THE CHURCH BE LIKE WITHOUT THE SACRAMENTS?

JOURNAL ASSIGNMENT

- DESCRIBE THE QUALITIES OF A FAVORITE PRIEST YOU HAVE KNOWN IN YOUR LIFE.

WHO NEEDS A PRIEST?

Many of the Protestant reformers of the sixteenth century were former Catholic priests. They claimed to know by experience that priests have no special "character," and they insisted that the responsibility for serving others in the name of Christ belonged equally to all Christians. Since the time of the reformation, Protestants have continued to question the meaning of the Catholic priesthood. Many have asked why Catholics need an "intermediary" between themselves and God. They use the term "intermediary" to imply a sort of "front office person" who prevents direct access to "the boss." Many Protestants have grown up feeling either pity or disdain for Catholics "who are unable to go straight to God with their needs and concerns."

The notion that Catholics cannot have a direct relationship with God stems from a misunderstanding of Catholic theology. Catholic theology regarding ordination can only be understood in the context of Catholic sacramental theology. We believe that God uses sacraments for our benefit. Human beings rely on their senses to perceive and communicate with the world around them. Through the sacraments, God, who is intangible and invisible, becomes visible and tangible. Through the sacrament of ordination Christ takes on visible, humanly perceptible leadership of his body, the Church.

By the grace of the sacrament of Holy Orders, when the priest presides at a sacramental celebration, he does so "in the person of Christ." Just as Baptism marks all Christians as the instruments through which Christ will make his presence known in the world, so ordination marks the one who is ordained as the instrument through which Christ will be present to lead the Church. When a priest (or deacon) baptizes, it is not the priest who baptizes, but Christ who baptizes through him. Likewise, it is Christ who consecrates the Eucharist, Christ who forgives our sins, Christ who offers us healing, and so on. The priest does not distance us from Christ. He brings us closer to Christ by allowing us to perceive Christ in human form.

To say that the priest allows us to perceive Christ in human form is not to say that everything that the ordained minister does is representative of Christ. Through the Sacrament of Holy Orders God gives the priest the grace to be conformed to Christ; but as with every other sacrament, this grace will bear fruit only if the one who receives it allows it to. An ordained minister may remain a very sinful and un-Christlike person, nonetheless God can and will act through him when he is functioning in his sacramental role and doing those specific things which have been handed down through apostolic succession.

As St. Augustine said, "As for the proud minister, he is to be ranked with the devil. Christ's gift is not thereby profaned: what flows through him keeps its purity, and what passes through him remains clear and reaches the fertile earth. . . . The spiritual power of the sacrament is indeed comparable to light: those to be enlightened receive it in its purity, and if it should pass through defiled beings, it is not itself defiled."[18]

THE POWER AND LASTING EFFECT OF THE SACRAMENTS

In the twelfth century, Peter Lombard, the bishop of Paris, and Hugh of St. Victor, a theologian and scholar, helped the Church clarify and systematize the way that it talked about the sacraments, their power, and their effect. They explained that each sacrament is to be thought of on three different levels: as a sign alone, as an event or rite by which grace is transmitted, and as something with a lasting effect which extends beyond the celebration of the sacrament itself.[19]

Christ instituted the sacraments. Christ himself is at work in the sacraments. It is Christ who acts in the sacraments in order to communicate the proper grace each sacrament signifies.[20] Because of Christ's action, the sacraments help us to understand what Christ has done for us and how he wants us to respond. Christ may act and be present to us in whatever way he chooses to, but for our sake he has promised to always act and be present in certain events, and those are the sacraments. Because of the sacraments, we do not need to ask if or when God will help us. We have been assured that the Father always hears the prayer of his Son's Church and helps us through the sacramental events of the Church. The sacraments do what their rites and signs signify. Each time a sacrament is celebrated, God gives us the grace to live as members of the Body of Christ. That grace will not change our lives unless we embrace it and conform our lives to it, but it is ours nonetheless.

Finally, all of the sacraments represent the saving works of Christ. When the sacraments are celebrated, time and space are transcended. Christ is as present to us as he was to his Apostles two thousand years ago. When the sacramental celebration is over, Christ remains with us in some tangible form. This is the lasting effect of the sacrament. Each of the Seven Sacraments has its own unique lasting effect, its own particular way of making Christ's presence accessible to us who cannot transcend time and space.

HOW WE "PUT ON" CHRIST

Pray this prayer of praise from the *Rite of Baptism*:

You have put on Christ
in him you have
been baptized.
Alleluia, alleluia.

Write five ways you have put on Christ today through your loving service of others.

Each Sacrament Has A Lasting Effect

The lasting effect of the Eucharist is the Real Presence of Christ in the consecrated elements of bread and wine. The Eucharist is above all of the other sacraments because in the Eucharist, Christ is present, both in his humanity and in his divinity. In the Eucharist Christ makes himself entirely present. During the Mass Christ comes to us even as he came to the Apostles after his Resurrection. What is more, he remains with us in the consecrated elements even after the rite itself is over.

The lasting effect of Baptism, Confirmation, and Holy Orders is an "indelible spiritual mark" or "character."[21] When we say that someone has been sealed with an indelible spiritual mark we are saying that God has changed his or her identity in some way. We may draw an analogy between being marked in such a way and becoming a parent. Once a person has become a parent, parenthood is part of his or her identity. A child may die or may be raised by someone other than his or her biological parents, but the biological parents are still a mother and a father. Nothing can ever change that aspect of who they are. Nothing they do can ever obliterate their particular connection to that other human life. So it is with the spiritual character given in the Sacraments of Baptism, Confirmation, and Holy Orders. Nothing that we do can ever obliterate our particular connection with God in Christ. Nothing we do can ever erase the sacramental character from our identity.

Christ joins himself to all who are baptized. Following a person's Baptism, he or she belongs to Christ and to his Church. Nothing can ever alter that fact. Those who have been baptized have become members of Christ's Body, capable of acting in his name. Similarly, those who have been confirmed have been sealed with the Holy Spirit and given the power to be witnesses for Christ,

and to be a voice for his Body, the Church. Even if they refuse to use this power, it is theirs.

Ordained ministers are also given a new character. They have become instruments used by God to give grace to the world. Bishops, presbyters (priests who are not also bishops), and deacons have been entrusted with the responsibility of serving the Church in the name of Christ. This responsibility is not just a task they are called to do, it is something that has become part of their identity. If they fail to carry out their responsibility, they deny their own true selves. We believe that Christ's presence is accessible to us in the person of those who have received Holy Orders. This does not mean that we believe that the ordained are holier or more Christ-like than anyone else. It does mean that we believe that Christ has marked certain people as channels through which he will give us grace.

In marriage, the lasting effect of the sacrament is the permanent bond between a husband and wife which is also the living symbol of the bond between Christ and the Church.

The lasting effect of the Sacrament of Reconciliation is a complete reunification of the sinner with the Church community and with God. Another lasting effect is the revitalization of the Church herself. Christ the reconciler is present in the bonds which reunite us.

The lasting effect of the Sacrament of Anointing is a deeper union between the one who is suffering and the suffering of Christ. The person who is ill is now able to participate in the saving work of Christ through his or her suffering. The suffering becomes a means of bringing Christ's redemptive suffering into our immediate presence. In the Sacrament of Anointing, suffering is transformed into something that can bring about good, even though suffering itself is not good.

Just as each of the Seven Sacraments of the Church acts on three different levels—as a sign which reveals God; as an event during which grace is given; and as the lasting presence of the One who forgives, heals, redeems, sustains, strengthens, leads, unites, and loves us—so, too, the Church as a sacrament may be understood on three levels. As a community that is one, holy, catholic, and apostolic, the Church is a sign of God's plan for the world. As a community which celebrates the Eucharist and the other sacraments, the Church is the means by which God gives grace and transforms the world. As the Body of Christ on earth, the Church is the continuing presence of Christ in history.

STUDY QUESTIONS

- WHAT DOES IT MEAN TO SAY THAT EACH SACRAMENT HAS A "LASTING EFFECT"?
- WHAT ARE THE LASTING EFFECTS OF EACH SACRAMENT?

JOURNAL ASSIGNMENT

- WRITE ABOUT A PERSON WHO HAS HAD A POSITIVE, LASTING EFFECT ON YOUR LIFE.

THE MATERIAL ELEMENTS OF THE SACRAMENTS

When St. Cyril of Jerusalem described the oil used in the sacrament of anointing, he said,

Beware of supposing that this ointment is mere ointment. Just as after the invocation of the Holy Spirit the Eucharistic bread is no longer ordinary bread, but the body of Christ, so this holy oil, in conjunction with the invocation, is no longer simple or common oil, but becomes the gracious gift of Christ and the Holy Spirit. . . . With this ointment your forehead and sense organs are sacramentally anointed, such that while your body is anointed with the visible oil, your soul is sanctified by the holy, quickening Spirit.[22]

The material elements of the sacraments do not have magical power. They cannot bind or manipulate God. Nor can they accomplish that which is unrelated to their material reality. The material elements of the sacraments have power because God has chosen to be welded to them and thus to extend their material reality into the spiritual realm. Christ has chosen to make the material elements of the sacraments carriers of his presence; for this reason these elements are able to affect our spiritual lives even as they affect our physical or our social lives. So it is that the waters of Baptism cleanse our soul. The imposition of hands at Confirmation strengthens our faith. The bread and wine of the Eucharist supplies the nourishment which is necessary for us to live as one with Christ. The words of absolution reunite us with God and with the community. The words of commitment make spouses of a man and woman before God. The oil of ordination marks the minister as an instrument of Christ at the deepest level of his being. And the community of people which is the Church becomes one body, just as the community of persons which is the Trinity is one God.

IN CONCLUSION

Catholics believe that God chooses to be present to us through the people, events, and things of this world. Those people, events, and things which always and in every circumstance make God present to us are called sacraments. A sacrament is a sign and instrument of God's presence in history.

Jesus is the first sacrament. Every other sacrament derives its nature from the nature of Christ. The infinite Trinity has been made accessible to humanity in the person of Jesus. After his Ascension, Jesus gave us other sacraments which would continue his role of mediating God to humanity until humanity is able to perceive God as he is at the end of time.

The first of these sacraments of Christ is the Church. The Church is the sign and instrument of God's presence because the Church is the Body of Christ. The Church is the continuing presence of Christ on the earth and in history. The Church is more than just a sign of how the world should be; it is also the tool which God uses to remake the world in his image.

The Eucharist is the source and summit of all the Church's activity. Jesus is the focal point of God's activity in history, and the Eucharist is the focal point of the Church's work. The liturgy is the sign of the redemption and transformation of the world which was begun in Christ and will be completed at the time of the Second Coming. The Church uses ritual to enact the world as God intends it to be. The liturgy makes us participants in a world in which all that is wrong has been righted.

All of the other sacraments are part of the one sacrament of the Church. The Seven Sacraments of Baptism, Confirmation, Eucharist, reconciliation, anointing, marriage, and Holy Orders all enable the Church to act as the Body of Christ in the world.

Each sacrament is to be thought of on three different levels: as a sign alone, as an event or rite by which grace is transmitted, and as something with a lasting effect which extends beyond the celebration of the sacrament itself. The lasting effects of the sacraments each have their own ways of making Christ's presence accessible to us who cannot transcend time and space.

LEARN BY DOING

Read chapter 1 of the Second Vatican Council Document *Lumen Gentium* ("The Dogmatic Constitution on the Church"). Choose and write five quotes that express for you how Christ lives in the Church. Write one or two sentences for each quote, explaining why you chose it and what it means to you.

PRAYER

God Be in My Head

God be in my head and my understanding.

God be in my eyes and in my looking.

God be in my mouth and my speaking.

God be in my heart and in my thinking.

God be at my end and my departing.

—Sarum Primer

NOTES

1. This story has been modified slightly to protect the people involved. Members of the rescape (survivor) community in Rwanda have been frequent targets of violence since the resettlement of refugees began.
2. Aidan Kavanaugh, *Liturgical Theology* (New York: Pueblo Publishing Co., 1984), p. 50.
3. See McBrien, *Catholicism*, p. 11.
4. *Catechism of the Catholic Church*, #1084.
5. Liturgy is the "official, public worship of the Church."
6. *Constitution on the Sacred Liturgy*, #10.
7. It is worth noting that the Second Vatican Council's document on the liturgy is called a "constitution." A constitution is something which addresses the essence of the Church's identity and understanding of its mission. What the Church does in its liturgy is as important to the Church's identity as its dogmas are.
8. Kavanaugh, *Liturgical Theology*, p. 43.
9. See *Catechism of the Catholic Church*, #1069.
10. *Catechism of the Catholic Church*, #1108.
11. The relationship between Christ and the Church has often been compared to the intimate relationship between a wife and husband. Those who are married are symbolically joined through the marriage. They are physically joined through the sexual intercourse which consummates the marriage (or makes it complete). Christ and his people are symbolically joined in the Church. They are physically joined in the Eucharist which makes the body of Christ an integral part of our own physical bodies (and thus completes the Sacraments of Initiation.)
12. See Kavanaugh, *Liturgical Theology*, p. 113.
13. *Catechism of the Catholic Church*, #1076.
14. *Ibid.*, #1116.
15. See *Catechism of the Catholic Church*, #1211.
16. *Lumen Gentium*, #26.
17. See *Catechism of the Catholic Church*, #1165.
18. St. Augustine, in *Evangelium Johannis Tractatus*, 5,15:PL 35, 1422. As quoted in the Catechism of the Catholic Church, #1584.
19. These concepts are usually referred to by their Latin names. The term used for the sign alone is *sacramentum tantum*. When we speak of the sacrament as an immediate reality, or a rite in which grace is transmitted, we are talking of the *res tantum*. And when we speak of the lasting effect of the sacrament, we are referring to the *res et sacramentum*.
20. See *Catechism of the Catholic Church*, #1127
21. *Catechism of the Catholic Church*, #1272, 1304, 1582
22. *Mystagogical Catechesis*, 3.3.

SACRAMENTS
for GOD'S FAITHFUL

AND BEHOLD, I AM WITH YOU ALWAYS, UNTIL THE END OF THE AGE.

—*Matthew 28:20*

TRANSCENDING TIME

What if there were a fold in the time-space continuum? What would happen if the past and the future were really accessible to us? How would our lives be changed if we could participate now in the events that happened long before our time, or in the events that will not actually take

place for many more years? These questions are favorite topics of science fiction books and movies, but they also involve real-life events in the Church.

As Catholics we believe that time is transcended in sacramental moments. When we celebrate the sacraments, the moment of creation, the saving acts of God recounted in the Old Testament, the past acts of Christ, and the end times are all brought together in the present moment. Furthermore,

in each sacramental moment, the experience and the faith of members of the Church from every age are brought together. Everything that God has done and will do is present in the "now" of the sacraments. Everything that the Church has done and will do in loving response to God is also present in the "now" of the sacraments.

Jesus did not give us the sacraments primarily for individuals, but for the community as a whole. The sacraments ensure the unity between Christ and his Body, the Church. Our individual ability to benefit from the sacraments depends in large part on our connection with the entire Body of Christ across all cultures and through all ages. As we increase our understanding of, and our appreciation for, the faith life of Catholics in other times and places, our connectedness to the body as a whole is strengthened and our ability to participate in the richness of the sacraments is increased.

The mystery of the sacraments, like the mystery of the Church herself, is something that is too great to be contained in any single culture or period of time. The people of each age and each culture will explain and celebrate the sacraments in a manner which is in keeping with their own particular needs and worldview. Those in other times and places may view the world differently and may therefore explain and even celebrate the sacraments differently. This is acceptable, even in a Catholic context, because the unchangeable essence of a sacrament is neither the theology which explains it, nor the ritual according to which it is celebrated. The essence of each sacrament is a particular graced encounter with God which occurs in and through the sacrament. The ritual and the theology of the sacrament are the outward signs which point us to the encounter with God. They guide us on our journey, but they are not themselves our destination.

One of the central beliefs of Catholic theology is that the Holy Spirit has been present and active in the Church and in the sacraments since the beginning. Although individual popes, bishops, clergy, religious, and members of the laity may have strayed from the truth, the Church as a whole has never lost the truth or the ability to bring the grace of God to the world. We believe that in each century the sacraments have been sources of grace, and in each century the theology and practice of the Church has prepared many to receive and cooperate with that grace.

Each of the different ways of explaining and of celebrating each sacrament through the years has emphasized certain characteristics of both the particular sacrament and the Church, while making only passing reference to other characteristics. It is only when we look at the different ways of celebrating and understanding the sacraments together that we begin to comprehend their incredible depth and breadth.

As we said earlier, Catholics believe that when we celebrate a sacrament, we are celebrating not only with those who are physically present, but also with all members of the Church throughout the world and with all who have been members of the Church in other times and places. An historical understanding of the sacraments, therefore, is not something which remains an interesting fact buried in the past; it is something that becomes a living part of our worship.

This chapter examines the history of the **Sacraments of Initiation**—Baptism, Confirmation, and Eucharist—as representatives of all Seven Sacraments of the Church, covering the different emphases in sacramental theology and practice in the early Church, in the Middle Ages, in the years following the Council of Trent, and in the Church of today. This study is intended to point out the insights which each period has to offer for our understanding of the sacraments.

Sacraments of Initiation—Baptism, Confirmation, and Eucharist. It is through participation in these sacraments that one is fully initiated in the Catholic Church.

- HOW IS TIME TRANSCENDED IN THE SACRAMENTS?
- WHY IS IT IMPORTANT TO UNDERSTAND THE SACRAMENTS IN THE CONTEXT OF HISTORY?

BAPTISM AND CONFIRMATION

On coming up out of the water he saw the heavens being torn open and the Spirit, like a dove, descending upon him. And a voice came from the heavens, "You are my beloved Son; with you I am well pleased."

—Mark 1:10–11

Jesus' baptism is the prototype of all Christian Baptisms. From the beginning, Christian Baptism has been linked to the descent of the Holy Spirit and to the permanent marking of the newly baptized Christian as God's own. Jesus' baptism transforms Baptism from a ritual gesture of human repentance and self-purification, to a sign of the divine purification which God offers through Jesus. The baptisms or ritual washings held by John the Baptist and others prior to Jesus' baptism involved only a human promise made to God. Christian Baptism involves both a human promise to God and God's promise to human beings.

From the earliest days of Christianity, Baptism has been linked to both death and life. The waters of Baptism were seen as both a tomb and a womb. In Baptism Christians are given new life, but a new life which will be fully realized only through the faithful acceptance of suffering and death.

According to Scripture, Jesus equated Baptism and death. When James and John asked Jesus if they could be given places of honor in heaven, Jesus asked them, "Can you drink the cup that I drink or be baptized with the baptism with which I am baptized?" (Mark 10:38). Also, Jesus said, "There is a baptism with which I must be baptized, and how great is my anguish until it is accomplished" (Luke 12:50). Similarly Paul says,

"Are you unaware that we who were baptized into Christ Jesus were baptized into his death? We were indeed buried with him through baptism into death, so that, just as Christ was raised from

The baptisms of John were unlike those previous Jewish washings in that they were not self-administered and they had connections with repentance, forgiveness of sins, and judgment. Jesus' baptism by John around the year 29 is the foundation of Christian Baptism.

the dead by the glory of the Father, we too might live in newness of life" (Romans 6:3–4). Each of these examples equates acceptance and reception of Baptism with a willingness to accept suffering and even death.

The early Christians trusted that the Holy Spirit who was given in Baptism would give them the strength to remain faithful in the face of temptation—the same grace to resist **sin** that Jesus had received. The early Christians retained the Jewish notion of baptism as a turning away from sin and a turning toward God. But unlike the Jews, they did not see this repentance (or returning to God) as something that a person would have to do over and over again. They believed that all who turned to God in the name of Jesus did so accompanied by the strength and grace of Jesus. Mere human weakness would no longer be enough to return them to a state of sinfulness. They could only fall back into serious sin through a deliberate rejection of God and of their newfound identity.

Reception of Baptism

The reception of Baptism in its earliest form seems to have been a four step process. A person heard the Gospel, believed it, repented, and was baptized. Initially this Baptism seems to have been only in the name of Jesus (see Acts 8:16), but before the end of the first century Baptism was done in the name of the Trinity (see Matthew 28:19). It seems that Baptism was coming to be understood not only as a participation in the Death and Resurrection of Jesus, but also as a participation in the life of the Trinity.

The *Didache* provides some details on the actual celebration of Baptism in the early Church. After a person had been taught and had accepted the basic principle of Christian faith and morality, he or she fasted for one or two days before being baptized. Other members of the community were called to join in the fast. The Baptisms themselves were done with "living" or running water (as from a stream, spring, or river) as possible. If this was not available, any cold water was the second choice, and finally even warm water could be used. The water was poured over the person's head three times. He or she was baptized in the name of the Father and the Son and the Holy Spirit.

Development of the Initiation Process

According to Scripture, Baptism was not always immediately linked to the reception of the Holy Spirit. On some occasions the Spirit was given before Baptism

Didache—Also called the "Teaching of the Twelve Apostles." The *Didache* is a moral, disciplinary, and liturgical text written in the later first or early second century. It includes teachings on Baptism, Eucharist, fasting, and prayer.

sin—An utterance, deed, or desire contrary to the eternal law. Sin is a failure to love God and neighbor. Sin harms both the sinner and the unity of the human family. Sin is an offense against God.

The *Didache* is the earliest known Christian writing other than the Old Testament, dating from approximately AD 60. It is a manual of Christian living in sixteen chapters, contrasting the way of life with the way of death.

(see Acts 10:44–48). Paul (or Saul) received the gift of the Spirit through the laying on of hands immediately before his Baptism with water (see Acts 9:17–18). On other occasions the Holy Spirit was given some time after Baptism. Philip baptized many new believers in Samaria, but they did not receive the Holy Spirit until Peter and John went to Samaria, prayed for the new converts, and laid hands on them (see Acts 8:14–17). In each case, the Holy Spirit was given through representatives of the apostolic Church in Jerusalem. The Spirit descended only when there was some manifest connection to the Apostles.[1] Nonetheless it was presumed that all who had received the Holy Spirit would be baptized, and all who had been baptized would receive the gift of the Spirit. Even when the two events were separated by time, they were never separated by theology.

Initially, the majority of new Christians came from the Jewish tradition. They were familiar with the saving acts of God and with the promise of a Messiah as recounted in the Old Testament. They

catechumenate—The period of preparation for Baptism.

understood monotheism and they believed that their relationship with God should shape everything that they did. As soon as they understood Jesus as the fulfillment of Scripture, they were prepared to become Christians. But as time went on and more and more Gentiles were attracted to Christianity, there was a need for a detailed process of initiation and for symbols that more clearly expressed the total change of life which Baptism entailed.

The process leading to Baptism and the ritual of Baptism itself had developed significantly by the beginning of the third century. The Apostolic Tradition of Hippolytus written around AD 217 presents a fairly clear picture.

The process began when the person was first attracted to the Gospel. Next, his or her life was examined by the Church. Any whose lifestyle or chosen profession were incompatible with Christianity were eliminated. (This included all members of the military and all who were involved in theater since the theater was closely tied to worship of the Roman or Greek gods.) All others were invited to join the **catechumenate**. On Sunday they gathered with the rest of the Christian community to listen to the Scripture and the sermon, but

Because of the rigor of the catechumenate and the strict approach to forgiveness of sins in the second and third centuries, many delayed Baptism until the time near death so that their sins would be forgiven and they would go safely to heaven. This superstitious practice was ended by the end of the fourth century when there were more infant Baptisms and bishops scrutinized more carefully the intentions of the catechumens.

before the community began its prayers and its celebration of the Eucharist they were dismissed, as they were not deemed ready to do the priestly work which the community undertook on behalf of the world. Instead, the members of the catechumenate met apart from the rest of the community for instruction and prayer.

Each year some members of the catechumenate were proclaimed ready for the final preparation for Baptism. These catechumens would be named as members of the elect, and would begin a period of intense prayer. Once again their lifestyles would be examined closely. Did they live piously while they were catechumens? Did they serve the poor and honor widows? If the answers were "Yes," they were given the prayers, creeds, and Gospel of the Church. In the days leading up to Easter the elect participated in daily exorcisms as the community prayed that all evil and all desire for evil would be removed from them. During the final three days before Easter the elect fasted and spent their time in prayer.

At the Easter vigil the elect gathered at the water basin near or inside the entrance of the church. There they publicly renounced the devil and were anointed with the oil of exorcism. (In the fourth century in Jerusalem, this renunciation was done facing west—to the place of darkness. It was followed by a turning toward the east and a claiming of the light of Christ.) For Baptism, the elect undressed and descended naked into the water.[2] While in the water they were questioned about their acceptance of the basic beliefs of Christianity and were immersed three times. When they came out of the water the newly baptized were dressed in a white garment, anointed with the oil of thanksgiving, and led inside the main body of the church, where the bishop would lay hands on them and pour the oil of thanksgiving over their heads.

The newly baptized Christians were welcomed as members of the Christian community with the kiss of peace. (This was the first time that they were allowed to share in the Christian kiss of peace, since before their Baptism their kiss was not yet pure.[3]) Finally, the new Christians were invited to join the rest of the community in the celebration of the Eucharist. During the celebration they were given three chalices from which to drink. One was the cup of the Eucharist. Another was a cup of milk and honey, symbolizing entrance into the promised land; the third was a cup of water, which symbolized their inner Baptism. In the fourth century, when converts flocked to the Church after the decree of Constantine, it became increasingly difficult to provide extended baptismal preparation or careful guidance for all new Christians. It also became increasingly difficult for a bishop to be present at each Baptism. This led to two distinct trends within the Church. The first was to have a priest serve as the minister for Baptism—including laying on hands and anointing—so that all of the elements of Christian initiation could be kept together. This was the practice which grew in the eastern Church. In the western Church the bishop kept a ministerial role in Christian initiation. In the west, the final anointing and laying on of hands was left to be done by a bishop whenever he was able to be present in that local church. This practice resulted eventually in a separation of the sacraments of Baptism and Confirmation.

Rise of Infant Baptisms

In the fifth century, adult Baptisms and the connection between Baptism and Easter also began to wane. In his arguments against Pelagius, who claimed that human beings could reach God on their own merits, Augustine stressed the absolute necessity of God's grace to free a person from original sin. Since the Church believes that grace is first given in Baptism, the corollary, as Augustine taught, was that Baptism was essential for

Salvation. Soon Baptism of infants came to be the norm, since parents feared the dangers of a newborn dying while still in Original Sin. Few parents would risk postponing their child's Baptism until Easter. (A fourteenth century decree required all infants to be baptized within eight days of their birth.)

Baptism came to be understood as the claiming of an infant by God. The relationship of the infant and the infant's parents to God and to the Church community was not considered relevant to the sacrament. No one questioned the parents as to whether the child would be brought to church regularly. No one expected the parents or the godparents to attend special classes to learn more about the sacrament. All that mattered was that each child be washed clean of the stain of Original Sin so that he or she would be eligible to enter the kingdom of heaven. In 1493 in The Decree for the Armenians the Church declared that Baptism was so important that it could be done by anyone, even a pagan or heretic, as long as that person used the form of the Church and intended to do what the Church does. The essential form was "I baptize you in the name of the Father and of the Son and of the Holy Spirit."

Christian Initiation Today

Neither a priest nor a profession of faith were considered essential for Baptism. However, both a bishop (or, with permission, a "simple priest"[4]) and a profession of faith were seen as essential elements of Confirmation. Confirmation was originally understood as the seal which completed and authenticated Baptism, much like a seal on a document completes and authenticates the legality of the document. Eventually, new understandings of

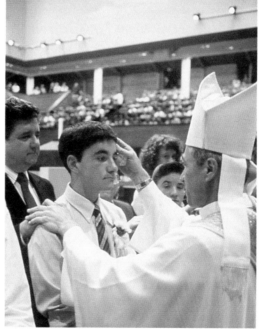

Confirmation arose. The *Catechism of Trent*, published in 1566, said that the Confirmation of Baptism must wait at least until the age of reason (age seven), at which point a person might be aware of what he or she was doing. Confirmation gave strength to the grace of Baptism and gave a person the strength to fight evil. Although Confirmation was seen as important for those who were trying to live out their faith in the world, it was not understood as essential for Salvation. Confirmation eventually came to be celebrated some time in adolescence. It was thought of as the sacrament of maturity which gave the grace that one needed to live as a faithful adult.

Up until the twentieth century the order of the Sacraments of Initiation remained as it had been from the earliest days: Baptism, followed by a seal on Baptism later known as Confirmation, and finally reception of the Eucharist. Then, in 1905, in an attempt to encourage people to receive communion more frequently, Pope Pius X moved reception of first Eucharist from early adolescence to age seven (though Confirmation remained in adolescence). Because of this change, Confirmation lost its identity as the sacrament which admitted a person to the eucharistic table and to full unity with the Church. The Eucharist lost some of its identity as the sign of total commitment to Christ and to his body, the Church. When Confirmation replaced the Eucharist as the culmination of the process of Christian initiation, it seemed to imply that both the sign of total commitment to Christ and his Church and the source of strength for that commitment now came from the unrepeatable

Sacrament of Confirmation rather than from the weekly (or even daily) celebration of the Eucharist. Many wrongly understood Confirmation as something like a "graduation" from Church. Some seemed to think that once a person had been confirmed, he or she had received the fullness of grace and no longer needed the Church in order to live as a Christian. As the RCIA (Rite of Christian Initiation of Adults) has come to be seen as more normative, the primary emphasis in Christian initiation has shifted so that it is first and foremost a process of uniting people with God in heaven and with the body of Christ on earth, not just a means of "washing away" the stain of Original Sin as quickly as possible. Greater emphasis is being placed upon the commitment of those receiving the sacraments or, in the case of infants, on the commitment of their parents and godparents.

Today there is a strong push in some places to restore the Sacraments of Initiation to their original order, so as to help reemphasize the Eucharist as the high point of Christian initiation and Christian life. In other places there is a push to move Confirmation closer to adulthood. Those who wish to see the sacraments restored to their original order, with Confirmation occurring sometime around age seven, often emphasize the Church teaching that the grace

given in the sacraments is a free gift of God and does not need to be ratified by human beings. Those who wish to see Confirmation moved to a later age tend to emphasize the Catholic teaching that the grace of the sacraments bears fruit according to the disposition of the individuals who receive it. They believe that Confirmation will be a more effective sign of the power of the Spirit in the Church and in the world if it is received by those who are truly prepared to commit their lives to Christ and to his body the Church. Both groups point to the RCIA to support their claims. Reception of the Eucharist is the high point of the RCIA. Adults who join the Church know intellectually and ritually that the Eucharist is the summit of Christian life and commitment. On the other hand, some stress the importance of adult commitment as a prerequisite of participation in the RCIA process.

The Church's experience over time teaches us that we are a community that constantly strives to find a balance between emphasizing God's free grace and emphasizing the importance of individual commitment if one is to benefit from that grace.

For those baptized as infants, canon law teaches that the sacrament of Confirmation should be conferred around the age of reason (about seven years old), unless the bishops determine another more appropriate age or the person is in danger of death. In the United States, the bishops have determined Confirmation to be between "the age of discretion and about sixteen years of age."

PENANCE

The grace received in Baptism has "not abolished the frailty and weakness of human nature, not the inclination to sin."[5] For that reason, the Sacrament of Penance has been called a "second Baptism."

In the early centuries Penance was understood as a communal process of reconciliation and healing. By the seventh century the sacrament was increasingly viewed as a time of judgment and satisfaction (prayer, almsgiving, and fasting as payment for the sin). A specific formula of **absolution** was developed, and the words of absolution came to be seen as efficacious themselves. People were readmitted to the Eucharist once absolution had been given, even if they had not completed their penance.

In 1215, the Fourth Lateran Council said that a person must receive absolution in the Sacrament of Penance at least once a year in order to receive communion. The Council of Florence in 1439 declared that the Sacrament of Penance was to be understood as a sacrament whose effect is forgiveness. Valid sacramental penance required contrition of heart, confession of serious sins to a priest, satisfaction, and absolution by a priest. The Council of Trent reiterated the teachings of the Council of Florence, stressing that the grace of God's forgiveness was always present in the Sacrament of Penance. At the same time, the council taught that a person could not benefit from that forgiveness unless he or she had the proper disposition, which included true repentance. Trent agreed with the Protestant reformers that forgiveness was a free gift from God, but the Council insisted that one's behavior affected one's ability to receive the gift.

The Second Vatican Council sought to restore the communal dimension of the Sacrament of Penance. In fact, the sacrament has become known by one of its rites as reconciliation. The document *Lumen Gentium* states that those who receive the sacrament obtain pardon from God and are reconciled with the Church which has been injured by their sin.[6]

absolution—The release of repentant sinners from their sin in the Sacrament of Reconciliation. Even after receiving absolution sinners must still do what they can to make amends for their sin in order to recover their full spiritual health.

Private, individual, and devotional confessions to a priest were introduced by Irish missionaries in the seventh century. This practice opened the possibility that the Sacrament of Penance could be repeated often.

STUDY QUESTIONS

- HOW IS JESUS' BAPTISM THE PROTOTYPE OF ALL CHRISTIAN BAPTISMS?
- HOW DOES CHRISTIAN BAPTISM DIFFER FROM THE EARLIER JEWISH RITUAL WASHINGS?
- WHAT ARE THE BASIC ELEMENTS OF BAPTISM AS DESCRIBED IN THE *DIDACHE*?
- WHAT WERE SOME REASONS FOR THE RISE IN INFANT BAPTISMS AFTER CHRISTIANITY WAS LEGALIZED?
- WHAT ARE THE ARGUMENTS FOR EARLIER AND LATER RECEPTION OF THE SACRAMENT OF CONFIRMATION TODAY?

JOURNAL ASSIGNMENT

- ASK YOUR PARENTS ABOUT YOUR OWN BAPTISM. WHO ARE YOUR GODPARENTS? WHAT CHURCH WERE YOU BAPTIZED AT? WHAT ELSE HAPPENED ON THAT DAY? WHY DID YOUR PARENTS CHOOSE YOUR NAME?

EUCHARIST

The Eucharist is "the source and summit of the Christian life."[7] It is "the culmination both of God's action sanctifying the world in Christ and of the worship [we] offer to Christ and through him to the Father in the Holy Spirit."[8] In addition, every celebration of Eucharist anticipates Christ's return.

In the early Church, the Eucharist was something that kept Christians from being too rooted in the present. Like the Jewish Passover, the Eucharist is a meal which allows participants to be freed from the constraints of time so that they can be present at both the saving events of the past (the Last Supper and crucifixion) and at the future

time of the second coming. The Eucharist took the community out of time and bonded the members of the community into a people who were "Not of this world."

The first-century text of the *Didache* also highlights the early Church's understanding that the Eucharist is a meal that forms Christians into the new People of God: "Even as this broken bread was scattered over the hills, and was gathered together becoming one, so let your Church be gathered together from the ends of the earth into your kingdom."[9] No one was to come to the Eucharist without having resolved any disagreements which might prevent the community from being truly united in the Lord (see Matthew 5:23–24). In a similar fashion the *Didache*

liturgy of the word—The part of the Mass which includes the "writings of the prophets" (the Old Testament reading and psalm), and the "memoirs of the Apostles" (the New Testament epistle and the gospel), the homily, the profession of faith, and the intercessions for the world.

HOW THE EARLY CHURCH CELEBRATED THE EUCHARIST

Write an essay with the title above, detailing how the early Church celebrated the Lord's Supper. Include an explanation of the following elements of the Eucharist from the first century:

· the breaking of the bread;
· how the entire community was welcomed;
· how it was held every day in homes;
· why Sunday was the special day for Eucharist;
· the prayers of thanksgiving that were offered;
· how participants must be cleansed before partaking;
· that those who ate the bread and drank the cup became one with Jesus and the community.

says, "But every Lord's day gather yourselves together, and break bread, and give thanksgiving after having confessed your transgressions, that your sacrifice may be pure. But let no one who is at odds with his fellow [neighbor] come together with you, until they be reconciled, that your sacrifice may not be profaned."[10]

Eucharistic Rites in the Early Church

In the first century, all of the Christians in one community would gather together, primarily in private homes, for the celebration of the Lord's Day. As congregations grew, some homes became churches. Eventually, even these churches were too small and it became impossible for all of the Christians in the same city to worship together. Although the Eucharist was still the meal which united all Christians, the visible sign of this unity—the single gathering of all in one place— seemed to be lost. In order to preserve and symbolize the bond of unity among all the separate churches of an area, the custom of "fragmentation" arose. A piece of eucharistic bread from the bishop's church was sent to each of the other churches in the same city to be mingled with their eucharistic bread.

Preaching, prayer, and the breaking of the bread were essential elements of Christian worship from the very beginning. The early format of the Eucharist is outlined

in the Gospel story of Jesus' appearance on the road to Emmaus (Luke 24:13–35). The Emmaus story follows the pattern of the earliest liturgies: Jesus traces Salvation History from the saving act of the Father in the Old Testament to the saving events of the Paschal Mystery. Jesus then offers a prayer of thanksgiving and breaks the bread. When the bread is broken, the presence of Jesus is revealed.

By the middle of the second century there was an identifiable fixed pattern for the Eucharist. In approximately AD 155, Justin Martyr wrote the first surviving outline of the rite of Eucharist. It began with a **liturgy of the word** in which the memoirs of the Apostles or the writings of the prophets were read. These readings, which at times were quite lengthy, were followed by a sermon. After the sermon everyone stood and offered their prayers, and then greeted one another with a kiss of peace. The bread and wine (and water on the occasion of Baptism) were brought in and the presider offered prayers of thanksgiving. These prayers were not fixed, but were dependent on the ability of the presider. The congregation gave their assent by saying, "Amen," the Hebrew for "so be it." Then the consecrated elements were received. Justin Martyr made it clear that the bread and wine were no longer "common" bread and wine. "We have been taught [that they are] the flesh and blood of the incarnate Jesus."[11]

Developments in Understanding and Practice

The understanding of the Eucharist as a sacrifice appears very early in Christian tradition. Early Christians understood Malachi 1:11—"And everywhere they bring sacrifice to my name, and a pure offering"[12]—as a reference to the Eucharist.[13] The Eucharist is the sacrifice which the letter to the Hebrews says is offered by Christ the High Priest. It is the acceptable sacrifice which pleases the Lord and puts those who offer it in right relationship with God.

PRAYERS OF THE FAITHFUL

In the early Church, the prayers of the faithful were so important that catechumens and penitents were not allowed to participate in them. The prayers of the faithful themselves usually took the form of a "bidding" prayer. The people would be called (usually by a **deacon**) to pray for a specific group or a specific need. This would be followed by a period of silent prayer during which the people frequently knelt or prostrated themselves. Then the presider would lead the congregation in specific prayers for the group named. The prayers of the faithful used in the Good Friday service in Catholic churches today follow this structure.

Many parts of the eucharistic prayers used today (for example, "The Lord be with you" and "Lift up your hearts") are found in Justin's account. The Apostolic Tradition, generally believed to have been written by Hippolytus around AD 215, outlines prayers and an order of worship that are even closer to our own liturgy, lacking only the Sanctus ("Holy, holy") and the preface of the **eucharistic prayer** (the prayer which precedes the account of Christ's saving work).

---

deacon—One who is ordained "not unto the priesthood, but into ministry." Deacons are ordained to serve by assisting bishops and priests in sacramental celebrations and by dedicating themselves to the various ministries of charity.

SAYING "AMEN"

When you say "amen" to the Body of Christ at holy communion you are really answering "yes" to questions like the following. Rate your willingness to answer yes to these questions on a 1 to 5 scale (5=strongest; 1=weakest).

- Do you believe this is the Body Christ?
- Do you want to believe this is the Body of Christ?
- Do you accept the people celebrating Mass with you as the Body of Christ?
- Do you want to belong to the Body of Christ?
- Are you willing to live like the Body of Christ?
- Will you do the work of the Body of Christ?
- Would you be willing to die like the Body of Christ?

Share with a partner or write an explanation of your highest and lowest response.

---

eucharistic prayer—The heart and summit of the celebration of the Eucharist. The eucharistic prayer follows the offering of the unconsecrated bread and wine to God. It begins with the preface in which the Church gives thanks to the Father, through Christ, in the Holy Spirit, for all his works. It includes the *epiclesis* (the request for the Spirit to descend), the institution narrative, the anamnesis (in which the Church remembers the passion, resurrection, and promise of Christ's return), the intercessions, communion, and a final prayer of thanksgiving.

Hippolytus came to Rome about the year 205 and was eventually chosen bishop. His writings give us a clue to Christian liturgy in the third century. He died a martyr's death in 235.

In the early centuries of Christianity the basic form of the liturgy was standardized, but the actual prayers of the liturgy varied from region to region. There was no serious effort made to regularize liturgical prayers and form, although the liturgy of Rome was sometimes used as a model for churches in other regions.

By the early Middle Ages, pilgrims who traveled to Rome to visit the resting places of martyrs often imitated the Roman style of worship when they returned home. In the ninth century, Charlemagne tried to mandate the Roman liturgy as a means of unifying all those under his reign. Church leaders in Rome, however, did not share his belief in the importance of a single liturgy and they gave very little support to his efforts. It was only with the invention of movable type in the fifteenth century that liturgical centralization really began and the Roman rite became the rite of the western Church.

As the Middle Ages progressed, the laity's role in the Mass became less participatory. The altar table was moved farther and farther away from the people until it was pressed against the east wall of the sanctuary. The priest turned his back on the people and toward the altar in order to emphasize the fact that he was offering a sacrifice on their behalf. A rood screen appeared, separating the nave (where the people were) and the chancel (where the priest and choir were). The high

point of the Mass was the elevation of the consecrated host. When the host was raised, if it couldn't be seen, the people in the nave would shout, "heave it higher sir priest!"[14]

The prayers of the Mass were all said in Latin, which by the Middle Ages was no longer the common language of the people. Furthermore, most of the prayers were said so quietly that even those who understood Latin could not hear them. The laity were connected to the celebration not by what they heard and understood, but by what they did: whether that was standing, kneeling, or adoring. As time passed, less and less active participation was expected from the laity. By the late Middle Ages their presence was considered unnecessary and private Masses were common.

As the communal aspects of the liturgy disappeared, a new sense of Christian spirituality developed. The piety of the Middle Ages tended to emphasize individual sins and pleas for mercy. The laity were expected to be present during the Sunday liturgy, but they were not expected to be overly involved in the Mass. Instead, they were to occupy themselves with silent prayer and individual penitential practices. A variety of private devotions became popular, and small side chapels at which people could offer their prayers while the Mass was going on multiplied.

It was in the twelfth century that the word **transubstantiation** came to be used to explain how bread and wine became the Body and Blood of Jesus. As the laity had become farther and farther removed from the celebration, and the consecration had become more and more a thing of mystery, superstitions involving the sacred species began to take life (for example, that the consecrated hosts would actually bleed).

The doctrine of transubstantiation corrected these misunderstandings. Transubstantiation is a term which is rooted in Aristotelian physics. According to Aristotle, every object could be defined by its essence (or substance) and by its accidents. The essence was what gave something its true identity and determined the impact that it would have on those who interacted with it. The accidents were those things which were perceptible to the senses. According to the doctrine of transubstantiation, during the consecration, the essence of the bread and wine was changed while the accidents remained the same. In other words, the bread and wine continued to appear as ordinary bread and wine when observed by any of the five senses, but their true identity became the identity of Jesus. Moreover, they carried the impact of the Son of God, not of ordinary bread and wine.

The consecrated bread and wine do not bleed. Nor do they physically inflict pain on someone who has committed an atrocity (another rumor circulating about the Eucharist during the Middle Ages). However, the Eucharist does change the lives of all who receive it faithfully. The doctrine of transubstantiation is intended to help people understand that as the bread and wine are incorporated into the one who receives them, that person's relationship with Christ is strengthened. The doctrine also helps people to understand that even though the consecrated elements appear like all other bread and wine, all who offer prayers before them are offering prayers before the incarnate Jesus himself. There is no need for people to search out a church in which the host has behaved miraculously. Every celebration of the Eucharist puts people in the presence of a miracle.[15]

A Sacrifice of Praise and Thanksgiving

By the Middle Ages, much of the Jewish understanding of sacrifice had been lost to Christians. The Jewish sacrifices described in the Old Testament were offerings which were a sign of one's total commitment to God. Sacrifices were also originally seen as payment to God of a debt owed. A person who had repented of a sin still had to make a payment. The early Christians understood Jesus'

transubstantiation—The change of the essential nature of the bread and wine into the Body and Blood of Christ during the consecration.

In the Middle Ages, practices that focused on eucharistic devotion sprang up, including the Feast of Corpus Christi, the Solemnity of the Body and Blood of Christ, on the Sunday following Trinity Sunday in June. The feast originated in the diocese of Liège, France, in 1246, based on the revelations of Sister Juliana of Mont-Cornillon.

Death as both a sacrifice of commitment and as payment of a debt. By the Middle Ages, however, the notion of sacrifice was influenced by pagan concepts. Many thought of a sacrifice as something to propitiate an angry God or as something that would put God in human debt, obliging God to do what those who had offered the sacrifice desired.

The Council of Trent sought to correct these misunderstandings, calling the Eucharist the true sacrifice of praise and thanksgiving and an expiation for the living and the dead. The cross was a bloody sacrifice and the Eucharist an unbloody sacrifice, but otherwise the two are the same. The Eucharist is not a sacrifice which binds God to us, it is a sacrifice which binds us to God.

The Council of Trent did not alter the theology of the Mass, but it did alter its practice. The Council of Trent standardized the liturgy and made specific texts and actions mandatory. The Roman rite became the rite of all the western churches. In 1661, Pope Alexander VII prohibited the translation of the missal to the vernacular (commonly spoken language) under penalty of excommunication. He feared that if people knew what the words of the Mass meant, the aura of mystery which surrounded it would be lost. From the Council of Trent until the Second Vatican Council, the celebration of the Mass remained virtually unchanged, no matter where in the world it took place. Unfortunately, fewer of the laity were able to perceive the many layered richness of the Eucharist. The Second Vatican Council attempted to correct this.

As Catholics, we believe that a sacrament causes what it signifies. The more clearly people understand what a sacrament signifies, the better prepared they will be to receive and benefit from the grace which it gives. Vatican II's Constitution on the Sacred Liturgy allows for legitimate variations in the liturgy from culture to culture, as long as those variations are in harmony with the true spirit of the liturgy. It also allows for the possibility of a more radical adaptation of the liturgy in certain places and under certain circumstances.

Although the liturgical texts of the Mass today are still standardized, there is much more opportunity for variation in the liturgy than there has been in any time since before the Council of Trent. For example, there are several options to choose from for each of the parts of the Mass: from the introductory rites, through the eucharistic prayers, to the final blessing and dismissal. Those who are planning liturgies may adapt them to the community and the situation, as well as to the liturgical season.

Not all countries use the exact same eucharistic prayers. This is an acknowledgment of the need for cultural variations. The variety in the Mass from place to place helps the Church remember that the mystery of the Eucharist can never be fully expressed by one culture or rite. On the other hand, the uniformity which remains in the liturgy helps the Church to remember that the liturgy is an expression of the Truth, and not simply an expression of our mood at the moment.

Pope Pius V published a Roman Missal in 1570 intended to bring uniformity to the official order of the Mass. The Church used this missal for the next 450 years.

STUDY QUESTIONS

- ACCORDING TO THE *DIDACHE*, HOW DOES THE EUCHARIST FORM PARTICIPANTS INTO THE NEW PEOPLE OF GOD?
- WHAT WERE THREE ESSENTIAL ELEMENTS OF THE EUCHARISTIC CELEBRATION FROM THE BEGINNING?
- SUMMARIZE THE BASIC FORM OF THE EUCHARIST IN THE SECOND CENTURY.
- TRACE THE CHURCH'S UNDERSTANDING OF THE EUCHARIST AS A SACRIFICE.
- DEFINE TRANSUBSTANTIATION.
- WHY IS IT IMPORTANT FOR CATHOLICS TO UNDERSTAND WHAT THE EUCHARIST SIGNIFIES?

JOURNAL ASSIGNMENT

- INTERVIEW AN ADULT WHO REMEMBERS THE MASS BEFORE THE SECOND VATICAN COUNCIL. RECORD THE PERSON'S MEMORIES OF LITURGY DURING THOSE YEARS.

SEVEN SACRAMENTS

Though this chapter focuses on an historical survey on three of the sacraments—the Sacraments of Initiation, Baptism, and Confirmation and Eucharist— it is important to remember that Christ instituted Seven Sacraments. The others are Penance (also known as Reconciliation), the Anointing of the Sick, Holy Orders, and Matrimony. As the *Catechism of the Catholic Church* reminds us: "The seven sacraments touch all the stages and all the important moments of the Christian life: they give birth and increase, healing and mission to the Christian's life of faith. There is thus a certain resemblance between the stages of natural life and the stages of the spiritual life."[16]

IN CONCLUSION

In each period of history, the way in which the sacraments have been understood and celebrated has been shaped by the world view and dominant culture of the day. If this was not so, it would be very difficult for the sacraments to be effective signs of Christ's presence and grace. Today it is impossible to pinpoint a single worldview or dominant culture according to which we should shape our worship. Rather, we are aware of a great diversity of cultures and worldviews. Sometimes this diversity occurs right in our own community. What speaks to Catholics in one parish or one group may be almost meaningless to Catholics in a neighboring parish or group. Because of this diversity it sometimes feels as if it is impossible to maintain the unity of Catholic faith and worship which is central to our identity as a universal Church.

When we feel that our diversity is threatening to overwhelm us, a knowledge of our history can be reassuring. We are a universal Church, not only across distance, but also across time. The fact that our sacramental worship has changed significantly from one century to the next has not changed the fact that we are one Church united with all who have come before us in faith and with all who will follow us. Similarly, even if our sacramental practices seem to have significant variations from one culture to the next, or even one parish to the next, our unity will not be threatened as long as all of the variations are rooted in Catholic Tradition and are directing us to the one Truth.

There are many legitimate variations within the Catholic liturgy. Some parishes ring bells and use incense whenever possible. Others never use these things. In some parishes, the faithful kneel during the eucharistic prayer. In others, the faithful stand respectfully at this time. In some places people join hands in prayer; in other places they keep their distance. In some parishes we are filled with awe for the transcendent God. In some parishes we are constantly reminded that God is our neighbor. In some parishes we are reminded of God's overwhelming love for us. In others we are confronted with the reality of our sin. The list goes on and on. In every instance what is done may be a matter of habit or personal taste, or it may be a matter of faith. In almost all cases, the variations express a preference for the Church of one period in history rather than another. It is important to remember that all of the periods of our history are a part of our Catholic Tradition. No one period is complete in and of itself, and no one period is devoid of riches to offer us, even today.

When different communities today give expression to different elements of our Tradition, we should not fear or despair; we should rejoice. We are richly blessed by the fact that so many elements of our faith which were once distanced by time or space are now brought together to inform and challenge one another.

LEARN BY DOING

Read the following gospels that involve Jesus sharing a meal with others. What elements of Eucharist are present in each passage?

- Mark 6:34–44
- Luke 19:1–10
- Mark 2:13–17
- Luke 7:36–50
- Luke 10:38–42

PRAYER

Anima Christi

Soul of Christ, sanctify me.

Body of Christ, save me.

Blood of Christ, inebriate me.

Water from the side of Christ, wash me.

Passion of Christ, strengthen me.

O good Jesus, hear me.

Within thy wounds hide me.

Suffer me not to be separated from thee.

From the malicious enemy defend me.

In the hour of my death call me and bid me come unto thee

That with thy saints I may praise thee forever and ever.

Amen.

NOTES

1. See Aidan Kavanagh, *The Shape of Baptism: The Rite of Christian Initiation* (New York: Pueblo Publishing Co., 1978), p. 9.
2. The *Didascalia Apostolorum*, a document written slightly later in the third century, most likely in Syria, speaks of the importance of having a woman deacon to baptize and anoint females and to teach them after Baptism.
3. See *Apostolic Tradition*, pp. 16–19.
4. See *The Decree for the Armenians*, written in 1439.
5. *Catechism of the Catholic Church*, 1426.
6. #11.
7. *Lumen Gentium*, 11.
8. *Catechism of the Catholic Church*, 1325.
9. *Didache*, chapter 9.
10. *Didache*, electronic version, New Advent, Inc., New Advent Catholic Supersite, 1996. Chapter 14.
11. Justin Martyr, First Apology, quoted in R.C.D. Jasper and G. J. Cumming, *Prayers of the Eucharist*, pp. 28–29.
12. *New American Bible*.
13. See the *Didache*, chapter 14.
14. James F. White, *A Brief History of Christian Worship* (Nashville: Abingdon Press, 1993), p. 88.
15. In 1965, Pope Paul VI, in the encyclical *Mysterium Fidei*, reaffirmed the doctrine of transubstantiation. He said that following the consecration, the bread and wine do not just have a new meaning and a new purpose, they also have a new being. The way in which they impact our lives is totally different. Everything we eat changes us, but the Eucharist changes us in a way that is unlike any other food, because the nourishment which the Eucharist gives us is Christ himself.
16. *Catechism of the Catholic Church*, #1210.

THE CHURCH IS SERVANT

Catholic social justice—the subject of Unit 6—is strongly rooted in the writings of Pope Leo XIII in the nineteenth century. Even though the Church had always found a time and place to serve the poor and all of those in need in society, it was with the Industrial Revolution of the nineteenth century that new applications were needed to help people apply basic gospel principles to the changing society. Pope Leo's encyclical *Rerum Novarum* (The Condition of Labor) is the first in a large body of key documents on social issues written in the years since. These documents, which also include the 1998 document *Sharing Catholic Social Teaching: Challenges and Directions—Reflections of the United States Catholic Bishops* are summarized in chapter 6.1.

What is the meaning of Catholic social justice? Basically, it the teaching that attempts to understand how societies work and what moral principles and values ought to guide them. This body of doctrine is originally found in the Old Testament where the Hebrew prophets proclaimed God's special love for the poor. It is primarily found in the words and actions of Jesus, who came to proclaim the Good News to the poor and to teach his followers to respond first to those most in need.

Christ-like service is practiced based on three principles:

- a recognition of the dignity of every human being from conception to natural death;
- a belief in the universal destination of goods;
- a desire to promote the common good.

As the social message of the gospel must not be considered a theory, but above all else a basis and motivation for action (see *Centesimus Annus*, 57), chapter 6.2 traces the applications to the Church's service of the poor throughout her history. For example, care of families must be at the heart of any social program. Also, work has always been valued in the Church. Human work is not a matter of producing something useful, but a matter of transforming the world around us.

Primarily, the Church remains focused in her service of the poor. This is known as the "preferential option for the poor." Care for the poor is seen as a requirement of justice rather than only an expression of extraordinary love.

When you have completed Unit 6, you will be able to:

- explain how service is integral to the Catholic faith;
- tell why the Church's responsibility to care for others always takes precedence over the state's responsibility;
- name some of the key Church documents on social issues and the teachings which they promulgated;
- identify and demonstrate an understanding of three key principles of Christ-like service;
- define principles of solidarity and subsidiarity;
- understand the Church's responsibility for owning her history, the bad and the good;
- summarize this history of the Church's commitment to the poor, including its "preferential option for the poor";
- understand the Christian attitude toward work;
- recount the Church's teachings on the family at various points in history and relate these teachings to the prevailing attitude of the day;
- identify the ways in which the shifts in the Church's understanding of social issues since the late nineteenth century continue to affect the Church today;
- trace the history of the Catholic response to war;
- demonstrate an understanding of the "just war theory."

THE SOCIAL DOCTRINE of the CHURCH

" I HAVE GIVEN YOU A MODEL TO FOLLOW, SO THAT AS I HAVE DONE FOR YOU, YOU SHOULD ALSO DO."

—John 13:15

THE CHURCH ACTS

A few years ago an inner city parish on the east coast decided to keep the church doors open twenty-four hours a day. When the parish staff arrived in the morning, they found people asleep on the pews and evidence that others had been there and already left. The church took on a very pungent odor. Some parishioners complained and said the body odors detracted from their prayers. Others countered that the smell should remind them that they should never separate themselves from any of God's people, especially the poor. Gradually most parishioners have come around to regard the odors of unbathed bodies as a "holy smell."

If you met Len on the street or in a coffee shop, you would be a bit surprised to find out that he lives with a religious community of sisters. He looks like the proverbial "mountain man," with a stocky build and long scruffy beard. Len met Sister Anne at one of the low points in his life. His girlfriend had just left

him, taking their infant son. Also, he had been picked up by the police for petty theft. Part of Sister Anne's ministry involved visiting and counseling prisoners in the local jail. She invited Len to come and live in one of the cottages on her community's property. She explained that the community's mission was to help people like Len meet their basic needs for food, shelter, work, and community. Len has lived with the community for almost two years, serving as a maintenance expert and groundskeeper. Sister Anne has helped Len keep track of his estranged girlfriend and son. Now Len and his son see each other regularly.

"God's place on earth is everywhere on earth." This is the motto of the Love Your Neighbor program of a midwestern university parish that automatically deposits some of its parishioners' donations into an account meant to aid the poor. The Love Your Neighbor program operates like this: Whenever people come to the Church with a major need for example, they are about to be evicted from their apartment, their electricity or gas is being shut off, or medical assistance is needed—they are given an appointment with one of the program volunteers. The volunteer assesses the problem and directs the person to a public agency which might be able to help them. Or, if the need is pressing and all other options have been exhausted, the volunteer will give a sum of money from the Love Your Neighbor account.

All dioceses and most local Catholic parishes today have some group or some program whose purpose is to serve those who are in need. There are parishes that sponsor soup kitchens, parishes that teach basic life-skills, parishes that have monthly food or clothing drives, and parishes that support the poor in other countries. Sometimes the commitment to serve involves the entire parish while sometimes it involves a small group which acts under the auspices of the parish. One might ask: Are some of these programs are more "Catholic" than others? How integral is service to the Catholic faith? Is there a particular attitude and response to the poor which is required of all Catholics, or is it up to each individual and each community to choose the way of serving which works best for them? These are some of the questions that will be addressed in this chapter. In addition, the major Church documents on social issues from the nineteenth and twentieth centuries will be surveyed.

JOURNAL ASSIGNMENT

- NAME A LOCAL OR PARISH PROGRAM YOU ARE AWARE OF THAT IS COMMITTED TO SERVING THE POOR.

CALLED TO BE A SERVANT

At the Last Supper, Jesus wrapped a towel around his waist and began to wash the feet of his disciples. When he had finished, he instructed them to go and do the same for others (see John 13). Jesus, God's only Son, the Lord and ruler of all, chose to serve rather than to rule. All Christians must do the same. Christians cannot be the Body of Christ on earth if power is chosen over service, or if we protect our own strength rather than demonstrate a willingness to stand with others in their weakness.

The Second Vatican Council document *Gaudium et Spes* said that one of the most serious mistakes made by Catholics today is found in the difference between what they say and how they live from day to day.[1] Catholics profess to believe in the One who came as a servant and who calls us to be servants. Therefore, service is not a nice addition to our faith; it is an intrinsic part of that faith. As Pope John Paul II wrote in his letter *Veritatis Splendor*, following Christ must shape us at the very core of our being. "Being a follower of Christ means 'becoming conformed to him' who became a servant."[2] If we wish to be servants like Christ, we must offer more than charity to those in need. Charity is given from a position of power. A servant, however, must surrender power so as to empower others.

While empowering others is often seen as a praiseworthy goal, giving up power is usually seen as a bit foolish. From the beginning, many Christians have insisted on the need for power. St. Peter questioned Jesus' willingness to die (see Mark 8:31–33). We, too, tend to cling to strength and shun weakness. Not many people have the courage and the faith to imitate Christ and serve as he served by emptying themselves. Like Adam and Eve we prefer to take our security into our own hands rather than trusting in God. Whether consciously or subconsciously, we view life as a competition and we struggle to stay ahead. If we are to serve as Christ served, we need his grace to help us to overcome our tendency toward selfishness.[3]

PRACTICING OUR FAITH

British writer G. K. Chesterton once observed "The Christian ideal has not been tried and found wanting. It has been found difficult and left untried."

- What did Chesterton mean by this statement?
- Do you agree with what he said?
- Among your peer group, what evidence is there that this statement is mostly true? mostly false?

The Church's Mission to Serve

The Church is the primary instrument of God's grace on earth. The grace to serve others out of genuine love and the grace to surrender one's own power for the benefit of another belongs first to the Church. This means that the Church is called to serve, and is capable of serving, in a way that no other group or organization is. No political or social organization can ever completely imitate the Christ who preached the Good News to the poor, proclaimed release to the captives and sight for the blind, set the oppressed free, and proclaimed a year of favor from God.[4] The completion of this task belongs to the Church in which Christ is still present.

The Church has a mission to care for the downtrodden which is distinct from the mission of any political authority. No matter what the political authority does or does not do, the Church has a responsibility for making Christ known by reaching out in his name to those most in need. The Church can never simply leave the needs of the world to the state. Similarly, even as the Church allows the state to function in its own sphere, making political and socio-economic decisions, the Church retains the right and responsibility for judging political, economic, and social matters "when the fundamental rights of the person or the salvation of souls requires it."[5]

Each baptized person is called to serve the weak and bring the powerful to accountability. This means that each baptized person has an obligation to cooperate in the outreach of the Church. What is more, each baptized person must learn to see the vocation to serve as part of his or her individual identity. Service must not be seen as something that belongs to special interest groups any more than prayer or the sacraments belong only to special interest groups.[6] Further, a person's unique vocation of life must incorporate service to the Church and the world, whether as a priest, a member of a religious order or religious society, or as a committed married person. Christ committed himself to those who are in need. If a member of the Church distances himself or herself from the needy he or she is separating from the Body of Christ. When a particular parish ignores the call to serve it deprives those around and within it of a true experience of Christ.

STUDY QUESTIONS

- WHAT IS THE DIFFERENCE BETWEEN GIVING TO OTHERS FROM A POSITION OF CHARITY AND GIVING TO OTHERS AS A SERVANT?
- HOW IS THE CHURCH CAPABLE OF SERVING IN WAYS THAT NO OTHER GROUP OR ORGANIZATION CAN?
- WHO IS CALLED TO SERVE THE NEEDS OF THE POOR?

JOURNAL ASSIGNMENT

- IN WHAT WAYS HAVE YOU ALREADY BROUGHT YOUR VOCATION TO SERVE TO LIFE?

THE PERMANENT MORAL CODE OF THE CHURCH

The permanent moral code of the Church begins with the decalogue (the Ten Commandments). It is impossible to do things which the commandments prohibit without damaging one's relationship with God. The social doctrine of the Church grows out of the Church's understanding of the seventh and tenth commandments: "you shall not steal" and "you shall not covet anything that is your neighbor's." We cannot be in union with God if we fail to recognize and respect the rights and property of others. What is more, the rights and property which we must respect are first and foremost those which have been given to all people by God, and not those which have been determined by human beings.

Christ made it clear that all people deserve to be treated with respect and to have their basic needs met. Christ willingly gave of himself to meet the needs of others; we must do the same. If we fail to serve, and instead seek our own power at the expense of the poor,

the weak, and the disenfranchised, we are depriving them of that which Christ would give them. We are violating the commandments. The Church can only be true to her covenant with God if she embraces the commandments and works to see that none are deprived against their will of the things which God has given to them.

As Catholics, we claim that service to the poor is part of what makes the Church the Church. We believe that we can be recognized as the Body of Christ on earth in part because we act as Christ acted, reaching out to those whom everyone else has ignored. History records many times when the Church did not act in the best interests of the poor. Yet, our faith also teaches that even if particular parishes, particular members of the laity or the clergy, or even particular popes pursue power rather than service, the Church as a whole will never abandon the poor. Furthermore, it will be the efforts to serve the poor and not the bids for political power which will prevail in the long run.[7] Service is a key part of the Church's identity. In fact, how well we serve as Church is a key part of how we

social doctrine—The body of Church teachings which relate to our economic and political interactions within the world. The social doctrine of the Church identifies the demands of peace and justice. It grows out of the Church's understanding of the seventh and tenth commandments.

THE CHURCH IS CALLED TO SERVE

Catholic Charities USA is an association of one of the nation's largest social service networks. Catholic Charities USA serves people in need, regardless of their economic, social, or religious background. In recent times, Catholic Charities USA has been in the forefront in providing immediate and long term need for natural disasters and in the aftermath of the September 11, 2001, attacks.

Visit the Catholic Charities USA website at www.catholiccharitiesusa.org/. Read about several ways you might be an advocate for social justice on a local and national scale. Also, read about several other Catholic agencies active in working for social justice at www.shc.edu/theolibrary/jp.htm.

Write an action plan about how you can contribute to the efforts of one or more of these agencies.

understand ourselves and how we are perceived and understood by those outside of the Church. When we fail to serve, our community is weakened by sin, but our basic identity does not change.

STUDY QUESTIONS

- IF COMMITMENT TO THE POOR IS PART OF THE PERMANENT MORAL CODE OF THE CHURCH, HOW DO WE EXPLAIN SOME OF THE HORRIBLE THINGS THAT HAVE BEEN DONE TO THE POOR UNDER THE AUSPICES OF THE CHURCH?

THE DEVELOPMENT OF CATHOLIC SOCIAL DOCTRINE

When the Church's social doctrine is discussed, the discussion usually begins with Pope Leo XIII in the nineteenth century, even though the Church has cared for the poor in all ages. Why? The answer is fairly simple. Before the nineteenth century there was little perceived need for a social doctrine that was any more explicit than that found in the Gospels. It was enough to feed the hungry, tend the sick, clothe the naked, and share what one had with the poor. But, with the dawn of the Industrial Revolution, things began to change as the "Gospel encountered modern industrial society with its new structures for the production of consumer goods, its new concept of society, the state and authority, and its new forms of labor and ownership."[8] Pope Leo XIII and others understood that the Church had an important role to play in evaluating and shaping the new society. There was a need for a systematic teaching that would help people apply the principles of the Gospel to changing social situations.

Pope Leo XIII

Twentieth-century popes expanded on Pope Leo XIII's teaching. Today all Catholics are encouraged to recognize that the social doctrine of the Church is an essential element of our faith. In the encyclical *Centesimus Annus*, Pope John Paul II wrote that "to teach and to spread her social doctrine pertains to the Church's evangelizing mission and is an essential part of the Christian message, since this doctrine points out the direct consequences of that message in the life of society and situates daily work and struggles for justice in the context of bearing witness to Christ the Savior."[9]

A summary of key Church documents on social issues from the nineteenth and twentieth centuries follows:

Rerum Novarum (*The Condition of Labor*), Pope Leo XIII, 1891

- Criticizes the extremes of capitalism in which a few own all of the wealth while the majority work under conditions that are close to slavery.
- Criticizes socialism for depriving people of their right to private property and for abolishing individual freedom by making the government the final arbitrator in all decisions regarding the use of the earth's goods and the way in which wealth will be spent.
- Makes it clear that all people have basic human rights which flow from natural law. These rights include the right to suitable work and the right to receive a just wage, the right to organize labor unions, the right to private property, the right to fulfill one's religious obligations, and the right of self-determination for families. Both laborers and employers have rights and responsibilities. Workers should do what they have contracted to do and do it well. They should refrain from violence and the destruction of property. Employers should respect workers, give them what is just, and never view them as a means to an end.

Quadragesimo Anno (*Reconstruction of the Social Order*), Pope Pius XI, 1931

- Outlines the positive impact of *Rerum Novarum* on the social order.
- Highlights the problems of capitalism and communism. For example, points out that while the condition of workers in the western world has improved, the condition of workers in the rest of the world has worsened. As to communism, warns of a system which condones violence and eliminates private property. Echoes the assertion of *Rerum Novarum*, that labor and capital need each other and have responsibilities toward each other.
- Introduces the principle of **subsidiarity**, which states that communities of higher order are not to interfere in the internal life of communities of lower order; rather, they should help coordinate the activities of the lower order communities to serve the **common good**. The common good is "the sum of social conditions which allow people, either as groups or as individuals, to reach their fulfillment more fully and more easily." In other words, the state should not interfere in the internal affairs of smaller communities, such as families or work places, when those communities are functioning as they should and the rights of all are being adequately protected. Nonetheless, there are some issues and disputes which cannot be solved by lower order communities because of an inequality of power. In these instances the state can and should intervene in order to restore right relationships.

subsidiarity—The principle of Catholic social doctrine which says that no community of higher order (such as a national or state government) should do what can be done equally well or better by a community of lower order (such as a family or local community).

common good—The sum of social conditions which allow people, either as groups or as individuals, to reach their fulfillment more fully and more easily.

Mater et Magistra (Christianity and Social Progress), Pope John XXIII, 1961

- Outlines the changes which have taken place in the world since *Rerum Novarum* and *Quadragesimo Anno* and re-emphasizes the rights of workers and the rights of all to private property.
- Points to the ways in which the arms race has contributed to world poverty, and to the ways in which continued poverty contributes to the instability and violence in the world.
- Balances the principle of subsidiarity with a recognition of the need for increased socialization. For example, as modern society becomes increasingly complicated, there is an increasing need for the state to protect the rights of the weakest and to promote policies and structures which will truly serve the common good. Emphasizes the duty of the wealthy industrialized nations to help poor, less industrialized nations without undermining the unique culture of the poor nations and without trying to dominate them.
- Highlights the limits on governments: An economic system which compromises human dignity, lessens a person's sense of responsibility, or takes away the opportunity for personal initiative is unjust no matter how much wealth it produces or how equitably it is distributed.

Pacem in Terris (Peace on Earth), Pope John XXIII, 1963

- Insists that the common good, which includes peace, can only be maintained when personal rights and duties are maintained. The human dignity of all people must be respected regardless of their abilities. Society is to serve individuals, not vice versa.
- Outlines the particular rights and responsibilities which should be a part of individual relationships: the relationships between individuals and the government and the relationship between governments and between peoples of different nations.
- Calls for more rights for women, greater attention to justice, an end to the arms race, and a strengthening of the United Nations.

Gaudium et Spes (The Church in the Modern World), Second Vatican Council, 1965

- States that the Church is not bound to any political party or social system, but is nonetheless called to influence society and politics in order to improve the world.
- Points out that states have a right to defend themselves and to oblige their citizens to participate in the defense or (in the case of conscientious objectors) service of the nation. States do not have a right to indiscriminately destroy the cities of their enemies. Soldiers are morally bound to resist orders that command genocide. The arms race is immoral particularly because of its effect on the poor.
- Discusses the importance of families as the foundation of society and a concern for the increasing vulnerability of families in today's society. The right of all peoples to their own culture is underscored.
- Outlines the role of Christians in the international community and in the giving of aid.

Populorum Progressio (The Development of Peoples), Pope Paul VI, 1967

- Reaffirms the right of all people to the goods of the earth, even when that right requires stricter control over trade and ownership.
- Names poverty as the root of conflicts and ministry to the poor as a means to peace. Stresses that possession must never become the ultimate objective of either individuals or nations.
- Calls for limits to free trade in order to correct the disparity between rich and poor nations which is exacerbated by inequality in trade. For example, poor countries export raw materials cheaply yet are unable to afford manufactured goods. The right to private property is subordinate to the universal destination of goods.

Octogesima Adveniens (A Call to Action), Pope Paul VI, 1971

- Addresses the problems of urbanization, including new groups of poor and marginalized people such as the elderly, the handicapped, and those who have been displaced by urbanization.
- Condemns discrimination which still persists on the basis of race, color, culture, gender, and religion.
- Calls individuals to stand up for justice and to challenge injustice in both the social and the political realm.

Justice in the World, Synod of Bishops, 1971

- Defines justice as an essential element of the Gospel and the Church's mission.
- Calls individuals and communities to speak out on behalf of the many who suffer from injustice, especially the poor and powerless.
- Says that the Church must be a witness for justice through education, through its international relations, and through the way in which it treats its own people.

Laborem Exercens (On Human Work), Pope John Paul II, 1981

- Emphasizes the importance of work as the tangible expression of human dignity and the key to making life more humane. Work is both a right and a duty. Everyone, including the disabled, has a right to work.
- Employers should provide benefits (social security, unemployment, and disability benefits) for workers both when they are working and in the case that they might be unable to work. Workers should earn a wage sufficient to support their families. Working mothers should be given special consideration. Workers have a right to health care, leisure, and a decent working environment.
- Part of the right to work stems from the right to exercise free will. Workers should feel that they are working for themselves. People have a right to leave their native country in search of a better livelihood.

Sollicitudo Rei Socialis (On Social Concern), Pope John Paul II, 1987

- Addresses the continuing problem of global inequality and the large economic gap between the northern and the southern hemispheres and calls for a single unified world rather than a world which is divided into a "first world," "second world," "third world," etc.
- Condemns the penchant for militarism and the exaggerated concern for security in many nations.
- Speaks of the "preferential option for the poor;" that is, "a special form of primacy in the exercising of Christian charity."

Centesimus Annus (On the Hundredth Anniversary of Rerum Novarum), Pope John Paul II, 1991

- Summarizes one hundred years of Catholic social teaching.
- Calls attention to a new form of ownership—the possession of know-how, technology, and skill. Problems arise in this area because there are many who are unable to acquire the knowledge which would allow them to express their creativity and achieve their potential. In other words, "their dignity is not acknowledged in any real way." The needy must be able to acquire not only goods, but also knowledge and experience.
- Applies Catholic social doctrine to the problem of the destruction of the natural environment.

Sharing Catholic Social Teaching: Challenges and Directions, United States Catholic Bishops, 1998

- Stresses the importance of bringing together the two gifts of Catholic education and catechesis and Catholic social teaching in an effort to make more Catholics aware of the great body of Catholic social teaching.
- Highlights several key themes that are at the heart of Catholic social teaching with the intent that they will serve as starting points for those interested in exploring Catholic social tradition more fully.
- The themes highlighted in this document are: Life and Dignity of the Human Person; Call to Family, Community, and Participation; Rights and Responsibilities; Option for the Poor and Vulnerable; The Dignity of Work and the Rights of Workers; Solidarity; and Care for God's Creation.
- Presents several options for schools, adult education programs, colleges, seminaries, and the like to further the catechesis of Catholic social teaching.

BASIC PRINCIPLES OF SERVICE

In his encyclical *Veritatis Splendor*, Pope John Paul II spoke of the "simplicity" of acting morally. He said that as Christians we are called to abandon ourselves to Jesus, allowing ourselves to be "transformed by his grace."[10] Christ-like service must begin with prayer, trust, and a willingness to abandon our quest for power and control. If we wish to serve as Christ served, we must allow our efforts to be governed not by a desire to shape the world to our liking (even if it would be much better that way) but rather by a desire to be with those who are being misshaped by the world.

Several principles help to guide both individuals and communities in their efforts to become more Christ-like and to serve as Christ served. Descriptions of five of these principles follow.

Human Dignity

Respect for the dignity of every human being is foremost among the Church's social doctrine. Human beings have been created in the image and likeness of God. Because of this, human beings hold a unique place in all of creation. Humans are the only creatures on earth that God has willed for their own sake. All the rest of creation exists for human beings, but humans exist for themselves and for God. Furthermore, human beings are the only earthly creatures who are able to know and love God their Creator; humans alone have been called to share in God's own life by knowledge and love. Humans alone have been invited to enter into a covenant relationship with their Creator.[11]

Every human being has been created in God's image and every human being has been called into communion with God; therefore, every human being has dignity. No matter what a person does, and no matter what is done to a person, his or her dignity can never be lost, taken away, or destroyed. No individual or communal decision can be moral unless it honors this fundamental truth that every human being has dignity. This is the belief which underlies all of the Church's social teachings: the human person is sinful, but also righteous.[12] The sinfulness is something which people

have brought upon themselves, but the righteousness is a gift from God. Because human righteousness is from God, it must be treasured even as human sinfulness is corrected.

Every effort made to help others must respect the inalienable dignity of each and every person. Every policy advocated must do the same. On these grounds Pope John Paul II criticized both socialism and capitalism. Socialism is a flawed political system because it does not show proper respect for human dignity. Under socialism, people are seen only as elements in the social organism and are no longer autonomous subjects with free choice and a unique responsibility for choosing between good and evil.[13] Capitalism, on the other hand, is also flawed and undermines human dignity in another way. In capitalist countries, human beings often become alienated from one another. They are alienated when competition to succeed becomes so important that people are unable or unwilling to give of themselves in order to establish true communities. Societies are alienated when their forms of social organization, production, and consumption encourage unhealthy competition and make it more difficult for people to give of themselves or to establish a sense of **solidarity** with others.[14] In capitalistic societies, individuals become means to some other end rather than ends in themselves. They are seen as valuable and important because of what they can produce rather than because of who they are.

Even though a person's value is not dependent upon his or her work, human work holds a high value in Christian social doctrine. Human dignity is not an expression of work, but work is an expression of human dignity. It is through work that human dignity, which is always present, becomes tangible. Human work "proceeds from the human person, who . . . impresses his seal on the things of nature and reduces them to his will."[15] Through work, human beings are able to join with God in the shaping of the world. Through work, humans are able to obey God's command to "fill the earth and subdue it," and make it a fitting home for all people. It is through work that we develop our gifts and talents and become the people that God created us to be; and it is through work offered to God that we join in the redemptive work of Christ turning the world from death to life.

The Catholic Church teaches that the right to work is a basic human right. Serving others in a Christ-like way means helping them to find work that will allow them to express their dignity. People must work in a way that will give them an opportunity to develop their talents and their personalities even as they do the work.[16] Serving others in a Christ-like way means never valuing the work more than the worker or the product more than the one producing it.

solidarity—A genuine concern for the well-being of other people.

THE WORK OF A GREAT GRANDMOTHER

She sits in her chair staring out the window. She knows who will walk past and what times she will see them. She knows what time the neighbors go to work and what time they come home. She knows how many different friends the little girl next door has invited over to play. She knows who is included and who is excluded, and who is generous and who is selfish. She watches and she knows, but why?

Why? That is the question she has asked so many times. Why is she still alive when so many of her friends have died? Why is she still alive at age ninety-four when she can do so little? Why is she still alive when she needs help to do even the most basic things? What value does she have? What good can she do?

Her value is far beyond words. She is created in God's image and likeness. She bears witness to the God who watches and who knows, who pays attention to the little things and the big things. Her life keeps people together who would have drifted apart long ago. Because she is alive, cousins have helped cousins, nieces have remembered their aunts, nephews have not shaken the family dust from their feet. Because she is, there is a community rooted in love.

The good she offers is an unconditional love for those she only sees through the window. She cares about them, worries about them, and she prays for them—even though they don't know her. She is alive because there is work to be done. "What work?" she asks, even though she really knows. The work of love and the work of prayer.

The Universal Destination of Goods

All people have a right to use the riches of the earth to provide for themselves and their families. God gave the earth to the whole human race for its sustenance, without excluding or favoring anyone.[17] Choices made by one individual or group should not deny any other individual or group their right to the earth's goods. Private property is acceptable; indeed individuals have a right to private property to the extent that the ownership and control of certain things is necessary for the establishment of a fitting and secure home. Nonetheless, the right to private property is secondary to the universal destination of goods. No person has the right to claim as his or her own something that is necessary for another's survival or well-being. As the *Catechism of the Catholic Church* states: "The ownership of any property makes its holder a steward of Providence, with the task of making it fruitful and communicating its benefits to others. . . ."[18]

No one should take pride in their generosity or love when they give others the means to survive; in these instances they are only giving to the poor what already belongs to the poor. As St. John Chrysostom said, "Not to enable the poor to share in our goods is to steal from them and deprive them of life. The goods we possess are not ours, but theirs."[19]

Giving from one's surplus to help others survive is not a demonstration of Christ-like service; it is the fulfillment of a basic obligation. Christ-like service demands far more, including a sharing from our sustenance as we work for a world in which the wealth of the earth is distributed evenly. Following Christ means confronting all forms of cultural or social discrimination in basic

Imagine yourself in a family of four (two parents, two school-age children). The family income is $2,050 per month (after taxes). Write a monthly budget for the family that includes the following expenses: housing, utilities, phone, health insurance, food, clothing, education, recreation, and some other need that you designate. Use the classified ads from your own local newspaper to identify housing costs. Plan to share your budget with your classmates. Write about possible solutions for the poverty present in this example. Remember, if you present the option of the adults working more hours or getting education for a new job, also offer suggestions for the impending issue of childcare.

human rights on the grounds of sex, race, color, social condition, language, or religion. Any such discrimination is "incompatible with God's design."[20]

The universal destination of all goods is a reminder that human beings were not created to live in isolation or to be saved in isolation. Both our physical and our spiritual well-being are linked to the well-being of others. We cannot allow ourselves to "wallow in the luxury of a merely individualistic morality."[21] Rather, we believe in "one, catholic church." We believe in one body to which all people belong. We believe that if one member of the body suffers, all are suffering. We cannot serve as Christ served unless we are willing to look at the ways in which the things we do impact other people. We cannot serve as Christ served unless we connect to other people in their need, not in our greed. Unless we recognize our intimate connection with those we wish to serve, all of our actions will be nothing more than band-aids offered for severed limbs.

The Common Good

The third major principle governing Catholic social doctrine is that everyone should promote the common good.[22] As noted before, human beings are not created to live in isolation or to find happiness and Salvation in isolation. Interdependence is a fundamental part of human nature. It is impossible for us to attain what is truly good for ourselves at the expense of others. The duty to promote the common good goes hand in hand with a recognition of our own human dignity.

The common good depends on three things in particular. First, the common good requires respect for individuals and for individual well-being. It is found only in conditions which allow individuals and groups to exercise their rights. Second, the common good requires social well-being and the development of communities. Just as something cannot be said to promote the common good if it tramples on individual freedom, neither can it be said that something contributes to the common good which advances individual freedom to such an extent that communities are harmed or destroyed. Finally, the common good depends on peace, stability, and good order. Any action whose goal is instability cannot be said to be for the common good.[23]

As human interdependence increases and crosses national boundaries, more attention is due the universal common good. Each person has a responsibility to promote the common good to the extent that he or she is able. This responsibility begins in the individual's immediate spheres of family and work. Yet even as people pursue the common good within their immediate circles, they must not ignore the larger common good. As far as possible, every individual is called to participate in public life. The Church challenges all of us to lend our voices, energy, and talents to the pursuit of the universal common good. We all have a responsibility for renewing the larger society and for advocating those things which will increase the freedom of all people, especially the most oppressed. Even if we do not have the authority or the power to change major international policies, we do have the authority and the power to strengthen the values of those around us that will encourage policies that serve rather than dominate.

Solidarity and Subsidiarity

Two other principles in Catholic social teaching are derived from the first three. The first of these is the principle of solidarity.[24] Solidarity is genuine friendship and care between individuals both within particular economic and social groups and across economic and social groups. Solidarity means accepting the needs and hopes of another as one's own needs and hopes. The opposite of solidarity is destructive competition. Solidarity is a requirement of the natural law which is rooted in the fact that we all share a common origin and we have all been created in God's love. It is demonstrated by a willingness to share both material and spiritual goods across all boundaries. The principle of solidarity calls us to serve on a personal level, and not simply from a safe distance.

The second derivative principle is the principle of subsidiarity.[25] As human interdependence increases, the role of states in ensuring equality and justice must also increase. There is always a danger, however, that the state will intervene to such an extent that individual freedom and initiative will be lost. The principle of subsidiarity guards against this danger. It says that no community of a higher order should do what can be done by a community of a lower order. Although God is all powerful, God has not kept all power to himself. Each person has been allowed to exercise power according to his or her own abilities. We are called to follow God's example within our own interactions, respecting the freedom of other individuals and communities as much as possible.

STUDY QUESTIONS

- NAME SOME LIMITS ON THE RIGHT TO PRIVATE PROPERTY.
- WHAT DOES THE UNIVERSAL DESTINATION OF GOODS REFER TO?
- WHAT IS THE COMMON GOOD? ON WHAT THREE THINGS DOES THE COMMON GOOD DEPEND?
- DEFINE SOLIDARITY AND SUBSIDIARITY.

OBEDIENCE TO THE TRUTH

The principles which underlie Catholic social teaching represent the truth about humankind. This truth is unchanging. It is not dependent upon our desires, our feelings, or our experiences. Unless we recognize the inherent dignity of all people, the universal destination of all of the earth's goods, and the obligation to pursue the common good, we will never be truly free. We will be slaves to the destructive power of sin. The first condition of freedom is obedience to the truth.[26] This is a part of what the Church has named the "natural moral law." If the object of any action is not in harmony with this natural moral law, that action is morally wrong regardless of any good it might achieve.[27]

Each time we are confronted, individually or as a community, with a need, we must make a decision as to how we will respond. Each decision must be rooted in the natural moral law in order to be acceptable. If a decision is not only to avoid evil but to be truly Christ-like, it must go beyond the minimum requirements of the natural law and must reflect a desire to give ourselves for the sake of others. The principles of solidarity and subsidiarity help to guide us in choosing how we will do this.

STUDY QUESTION

- WHAT IS NEEDED IF WE ARE TO BE TRULY FREE?

JOURNAL ASSIGNMENT

- THE *CATECHISM OF THE CATHOLIC CHURCH* DEFINES FREEDOM AS "THE POWER, ROOTED IN REASON AND WILL, TO ACT OR NOT TO ACT, TO DO THIS OR THAT, AND SO TO PERFORM DELIBERATE ACTIONS ON ONE'S OWN RESPONSIBILITY. BY FREE WILL ONE SHAPES ONE'S OWN LIFE" (1731). HOW DOES THIS DEFINITION RELATE TO THE FIRST CONDITION OF FREEDOM, "OBEDIENCE TO THE TRUTH"?

IN CONCLUSION

As far as the Church is concerned, the social message of the Gospel must not be considered a theory, but above all else a basis and a motivation for action."[28] These words of Pope John Paul II serve as a good reminder that it is not enough to know what the Church teaches, we must bring that teaching to life in our actions.

Most Catholic parishes have groups or organizations dedicated to service. Oftentimes, the majority of people leave the work of service to a few and content themselves with being "good citizens." This is a good start. When we sincerely direct our actions so that others will benefit and when we try not to pursue our own self-interest at the expense of the community, we will be living witnesses to the truth. And such living witnesses are sorely lacking in our society. Nonetheless, for a Catholic who understands the Church as the tangible presence of Christ on earth, this can never be enough.

Catholics believe that every person, regardless of his or her faith, has an obligation rooted in natural law to respect others and to avoid doing anything which would harm the common good. Still, as members of the Body of Christ on earth, we are called to do more. We must not only avoid doing what is wrong, we must actively pursue what is good. We are called to give our energy and our talents for the sake of others. As members of Christ we have an obligation to stand with and to care for those who are in need or on the margins of society. Every Catholic is called to serve.

Some forms of service are more Catholic than others. What does this mean? First, that in order to be considered service at all, an action must respect the principles of human dignity, the universal destination of the earth's goods, and promotion of the common good. Furthermore, any action which provides for the basic needs of others out of our own surplus cannot be considered service, since it is merely the giving of what is owed. True Christ-like service must come from our own want. It must be offered from a position of solidarity with those whom we serve; it must be offered in friendship, not disdain; and it must be offered from a position of equality, or even vulnerability, and not from a position of control.

We are the Body of Christ on earth, but we are also a community of sinners. This strange duality can be seen most clearly in our efforts to serve as Christ served. Our history shines with the memories of individuals and communities who have sacrificed everything for the needy in the name of Christ. Our history is also marred by the memories of those who used the power of the Church to hurt others. Yet it is in the great works of Christian saints that the grace for service is alive in the Church.

LEARN BY DOING

Make a list of ten things you can personally do for the poor. For example,

- Babysit free of charge for a single parent who needs to work or simply needs some recreational time.
- Organize a Thanksgiving meal for the homeless at your parish.
- Do yard work for an elderly neighbor.

Share your list with three classmates. Work together to form one list of twenty-five items that you all agree are most helpful and practical to complete. Then work as a group to enact at least one of the ideas on your list. Write a report detailing the experience.

PRAYER

Grant, Lord, that I may gladly share
what I have with the needy,
humbly ask for what I need from those who have,
sincerely admit the evil I have done,
calmly bear the evil I suffer,
not envy my neighbors for their blessings,
and thank you unceasingly whenever you hear my prayer.

—St. Thomas Aquinas

NOTES

1. See *Gaudium et Spes,* #43.
2. #21.
3. See *Veritatis Splendor,* #22.
4. Luke 4:17–21.
5. *Gaudium et Spes* 76 § 5, as quoted in the *Catechism of the Catholic Church,* #2420.
6. Canon Law says that every member of the Church has an obligation both to support the Church and to promote social justice and assist the poor from their own resources (Canon 222).
7. Vatican II declared that the Church's mission is not in the political, economic, or social order (See *Gaudium et Spes,* #42). Christ has not promised the Church power according to human standards. Moreover, the Church should never be identified with a single political system and the Church should be ready to surrender even its legitimate rights and power if exercising those rights would seem to compromise the Church's witness to the truth of Christ (#76).
8. *Catechism of the Catholic Church,* #2421.
9. Ibid., #5
10. #119.
11. See *Catechism of the Catholic Church,* #355–358.
12. See *Centesimus Annus,* #53.
13. Ibid., #13.
14. Ibid., #41.
15. *Gaudium et Spes,* #67.
16. See *Gaudium et Spes,* #67.
17. See *Centesimus Annus,* #30.
18. See *Catechism of the Catholic Church,* #2404.
19. As quoted in *Catechism of the Catholic Church,* #2446.
20. *Gaudium et Spes,* #29.
21. Ibid., #30.
22. See *Catechism of the Catholic Church,* #1913.
23. Ibid., #1906–1909.
24. Ibid., #1939–1942.
25. Ibid., #1883–1885.
26. See *Centesimus Annus,* #43.
27. See *Veritatis Splendor,* #72, 77.
28. *Centesimus Annus,* #57.

RESPONDING
to THOSE in NEED

"AMEN, I SAY TO YOU, WHAT YOU DID NOT DO FOR ONE OF THESE LEAST ONES, YOU DID NOT DO FOR ME."

—Matthew 25:45

OWNING OUR OWN HISTORY

OWNING UP AND SAYING SORRY

Each person is responsible for naming his or her sins, apologizing for them to the person or group (and to God in the sacrament of Penance), and making amends through penance and reconciliation. Review the steps for examining your conscience. Write a letter apologizing to someone you have offended, address it, and seal it in an envelope. Wait forty-eight hours. Then decide whether you will mail it or discard it.

EXAMINATION OF CONSCIENCE

- Do I really love God and make faithfulness to God my top priority?
- Do I pray for guidance in all situations, big and small?
- Do I love others, including my enemies?
- Do I keep holy the Lord's Day?
- Do I follow the commandments?
- Do I care for those less fortunate?
- Do I contribute to the well-being of the rest of my family?

We believe in one . . . catholic church." We believe that we are all one people connected to one another across both time and space. We take pride and share in the good things which have been done by Catholic Christians. We know that the achievements of any member of the body are in some ways our own. We know that we are who we are in part because of those achievements. We claim and celebrate the holy people and holy actions which are part of our history. For the same reason, we sorrow for the wrongs that have been perpetrated by this body to which we belong. We know that those wrongs have also shaped us and have shaped our place in the world. We recognize that we have a responsibility to correct the wrongs that we as a body have committed, even if we as individuals are innocent. Furthermore, we recognize that the sins which tempted us once can easily tempt us again. We claim and study the low points in our history in order to know and protect ourselves from our own weaknesses. We know that we can become the Body of Christ more completely only if as part of interreligious dialogue we acknowledge, repent, and learn from our sins.

Apology to the Waldensians

For years, the Italian government designated part of its tax revenues to the Catholic Church. Then, in the early 1990s, Church tax was made voluntary. Also, taxpayers were allowed to designate the denomination they wished their funds to be directed to. The Waldensians, one of Europe's oldest Protestant groups, received surprising benefits from this change. The Waldensian Church is a small church which has been severely persecuted throughout their 800 year history. Today there are only about 20,000 Waldensians in Italy; nonetheless, close to 130,000 Italians indicated on their tax forms that the Waldensians should receive their share of the Church tax. In one year the Waldensian Church received three million dollars along with many letters explaining that people hoped this would serve as an apology for past persecutions.[1]

Apology to the Jewish Community

In October 1997, the French bishops issued a "Declaration of Repentance" to the Jewish community, acknowledging the lack of public statements by the French bishops during World War II against the internment of some 40,000 Jews in French camps or against the anti-Semitism which became a part of virtually every French national institution. "We

the Jews said in a document titled *We Remember: A Reflection on the "Shoah,"* that while the Shoah (a Hebrew word for the Holocaust) was "the work of a thoroughly modern neopagan regime" whose "anti-Semitism had its roots outside of Christianity" the question may be asked as to "whether the Nazi persecution of the Jews was not made easier by the anti-Jewish prejudices imbedded in some Christian minds and hearts." While some Jewish leaders claimed the document did not offer a strong enough apology for the Church's lack of official response to the Nazi terror, other Jews looked at its significant pieces as part of the ongoing healing between Christians and Jews. Pope John Paul II released a letter with the document on the Shoah. He wrote that he hoped the document would "help to heal the wounds of past misunderstandings and injustices."

As we examine the Church's attitudes and actions toward social responsibility, we can see our tremendous potential as "salt for the earth" and "light for the world." We can also see our susceptibility to sinfulness. This chapter examines the Church's teaching and pastoral practice with regard to some key social issues—wealth and poverty, work, family, and war—at various points in our history. Looking at these issues leads us to ask, "Where is the potential for good?" Also, "Where is the susceptibility to sin?" And, finally, "What is the lesson of this historical event today?"

are obliged to admit that the bishops of France made no public statements,[2] thereby acquiescing by their silence in the flagrant violation of human rights and leaving the way open to a death bearing chain of events." The declaration goes on to say that while Christians living today are not themselves guilty of what took place in the past, nonetheless "it is our church," and we must ask why it acted as it did.

On March 16, 1998, the Vatican Commission for Religious Relations with

JOURNAL ASSIGNMENT

- DO YOU FEEL IT IS NECESSARY TO APOLOGIZE FOR WRONGS COMMITTED BY OUR ANCESTORS? WHY OR WHY NOT?

WEALTH AND POVERTY

From its earliest beginnings, Christianity presented a challenge to the economic status quo. Jesus addressed himself in a special way to the poor and the disenfranchised in his society. He warned against the dangers of wealth and power, and he ignored the class distinctions which were so important to many in his day. The first Christians followed in his footsteps, seeking converts primarily from the lower classes. Like Jesus, the first Christians recognized no class distinctions. This was not because they were advocating a new form of society, but rather because societal distinctions faded into the background in light of what God had done in Christ.

In the Early Church

The leaders in the early Church, particularly the deacons, were expected to care for people, especially the poor, by meeting their immediate needs for food and shelter. There were no efforts by early Christians to restructure society so that poverty would be reduced or eliminated. Rather, Christians simply cared for the poor one person at a time.

In the first and second centuries, Christians believed in and spoke of the imminent return of Christ. They longed for the Kingdom where "every tear would be washed away" (see Revelation 7:17; 21:4). In this Kingdom, God would rule. Spiritual values rather than materialistic values would prevail. In the Kingdom of Heaven there would be neither Jew nor Greek, slave nor free, rich nor poor, powerful nor weak, male nor female.[3] The belief was not that these groupings would cease to exist, but that they would become irrelevant. They would be no more important than the fact that some people have straight hair and others have curly hair.

The educated and wealthy upper-class began to enter the Christian community in increasing numbers during the second century. Instead of being told to abandon their social positions, they were asked to provide financial support for the Church and her leaders. Although the early Church did not specifically confront the social ills of the day, she did work to foster genuine solidarity between people of all classes and walks of life, including women, slaves, and poor laborers.

When Jesus did not return, and the expectation of the imminent coming of the Kingdom faded into the background, the focus of the early Church shifted to immortality and life after death. The value placed on participation in society declined. Christians began to place higher and higher value on asceticism, advocating as great a distance as possible from the things of this world. When Constantine came to power a dichotomy began to appear: while many Christians were fleeing to the desert and advocating extreme asceticism, the Church was being flooded by others who were very wealthy and who viewed Christianity as a way to protect their wealth. A third group was the majority: Christians who fell somewhere in between these two extremes and who struggled to find an appropriate Christian response to money and property.

When Christian communities were small and relatively poor the question of property was fairly simple. Then it was clear that Christians were called to love and care for

One of the reasons the diaconate declined in the third and fourth centuries in the West was that the flourishing monasteries began to take on several of the deacons' charitable works of service.

one another and it was also clear that such love meant ensuring that everyone within the community had food and clothing.[4] The small number of wealthy people in the community had more than enough to do in helping to provide for these basic needs. Their wealth was not a problem.

It was not long, however, before the range of economic standards among Christians had increased dramatically, and the question of "How much personal wealth is too much?" became important. As the desert movement grew and the ascetic ideal gained popularity, there were many who began to look upon the story of the rich young man (Luke 18:18–25) as the basis for all judgments about property. Those who flocked to the desert believed that every Christian should give up everything that was unnecessary. There were others who tried to transfer the ideals of the desert to the city. They believed that each person should own no more than the minimum which he or she required. Of course the definition of what was required varied significantly. Many people also began to point out that simply giving everything to the poor accomplished very little except that the rich became poor and the poor barely noticed the difference.

Communal monasticism was developed by those who felt that

the spirit of compromise between the Christian world and the secular world was weakening the core of the Gospel message. The Church came to accept a two-fold standard for dealing with the question of property. It was understood that the "holiest" response was the path of the monastics who had given up everything. The path of compromise was also acceptable, however. People were "good Christians" as long they maintained a detachment from their wealth and as long as they shared their superfluous possessions. As the years passed, new religious orders were founded to serve the poor. These orders were welcomed and admired, but they were never viewed as the necessary path everyone must take. This dual standard gained popularity as the Church's ties with the state and with the secular world in general grew stronger.

In the Middle Ages

Over time, the Church itself began to acquire possessions in the form of land, slaves, money, and payments in kind. These gifts were accepted with the thought that they should be used for the purpose of charity. As the holdings of the Church grew,

FREE YARD SALE

With a group of classmates, collect clothing, furniture, and other household items from neighbors in your community. Then arrange to hold a "free yard sale" where the items are distributed to those in need. Arrange for a distribution place (e.g. the school parking lot) and advertise the event through agencies that help the poor. Other jobs for the day of the event include helping with transportation, providing drinks and snacks to the "customers," and making referrals to other helpful places in the community.

Cassian, an ascetic of the fifth century, wrote that asceticism was in no way an end in itself: "Our fastings, our vigils, meditation on Scripture, poverty and the privation of all things are not perfection, but the instruments for acquiring it."

bishops came to be viewed as powerful patrons who defended both the secular and the spiritual interests of the people living within their domain. At no point did the Church question the social structure which allowed some people, including Church leaders, to have wealth and power, while others were dependent on their good will for survival. Christians apparently accepted the social structure as it was and concerned themselves with caring for others within that structure.

In the Middle Ages, many people came to believe that the best way to expiate one's sins was to make a large contribution to the Church. The Church also gained property as small landowners came and placed themselves under the protection of the

Church. During these years the overall attitude was that property and possessions were meant to maintain a moderate level of comfort and nothing more. Christians were expected to give charity—not in the hopes of permanently ending poverty—but as an expression of love.

Christians no longer held one another accountable for their wealth. There was no longer any desire to equalize the distribution of wealth in the community. Monasteries were the exception to this rule. Monasticism came to be the example of the best way to live the Christian life, where property and wealth were shared equally and the needs of the poor were served.

Industrial Revolution to the Present

With the dawn of the Industrial Revolution, it became increasingly difficult to help the poor through individual or Church-sponsored charity alone. The problems facing those on the lower end of the economic scale were no longer just problems of want. The problems of exploitation of workers and inhuman work and working conditions increased. It became clear that many of the needs of the poor could only be addressed through structural changes, which would eliminate the perceived right of the rich to do whatever they pleased.

Beginning with Pope Leo XIII's 1891 encyclical, *Rerum Novarum*, the Church has used the language of rights and responsibility to talk about the relationship between the poor and the wealthy. Today's Church echoes the fifth century words of St. John Chrysostom when it says that failing to help people obtain their basic rights is stealing from them. Caring for the poor is no longer viewed as a matter of charity; it is a matter of justice.

Pope Leo XIII responded against both the dangers of unbridled capitalism and Marxism. Karl Marx (1818–1883) viewed the state as being responsible for the security of workers. Pope Leo XIII recognized Marx's brand of socialism which subordinated the individual to the state, thus destroying human dignity.

The Church no longer accepts the dual system which allows religious orders to carry the burden of genuine commitment to the poor while others only support them in that work whenever so moved. Because the Church today views care for the poor as a requirement of basic justice rather than an expression of extraordinary love, Catholics understand care for the poor as the responsibility of all people. The *Catechism of the Catholic Church* specifically states that part of the vocation of the laity is the restructuring of social life in order to obtain justice: "It is the role of the laity to animate temporal realities with Christian commitment, by which they show that they are witnesses and agents of peace and justice."[5]

Like the early Church, the Church of today has come to see that part of its task is to restore this world to the state of equality which God intended. Unlike the early Church, today's Church believes that this restoration will require structural changes as well as attitudinal changes. The equality which the Church desires is not an absolute equality. In fact, the Catholic Church teaches that a certain amount of economic inequality is healthy. What the Church is working for is equality in freedom and opportunity. The Catholic Church holds that all people should be able to meet their basic needs without undue hardship; that their lives should not be reduced to a day to day fight for survival. The Church also believes that all people should be able to participate in the economic life of their country.[6] Economic policy should not be decided only by those who have wealth, and opportunities for advancement should not go primarily to those who already have the most.

Recall again Pope John Paul II's challenge to provide a "**preferential option for the poor**."[7] This means that the poor must be given special consideration whenever any social policy is being decided. No policy which helps the rich more than it helps the poor (and thus increases the economic gap in today's already unequal economy) is acceptable. The poor have a right to special consideration from the state in defense of their rights (which include the right to participate in the economy) because they are particularly powerless to defend those rights themselves.[8] The Church insists that the state has an obligation to protect the poor against exploitation and to ensure that they receive adequate wages (enough money to support themselves and their families and to have some savings), humane working hours, and the right to express their personality at their work place.[9]

preferential option for the poor—A principle to be followed in exercising Christian charity. This principle says that God is particularly concerned with the needs of those who suffer the most and that the human community should be too.

encomiendas—A system in which a native person was "entrusted" to a settler to be "civilized" and taught the basics of Christian doctrine.

BARTOLOMÉ DE LAS CASAS

In 1511, the Dominican Antonio Montesinos preached a sermon in Santo Domingo against the exploitation of the native people. In particular, he decried the system of **encomiendas** by which a native person was "entrusted" to a settler to be "civilized" and taught the basics of Christian doctrine. In return for this teaching, the natives were expected to work for the settlers. The system of encomiendas was actually far worse than the forbidden practice of slavery. Settlers had no economic investment in those who had been entrusted to them. They had no motivation to protect their health or well-being. Abuse ran rampant.

Bartolomé de Las Casas, himself a priest, was one of the people who heard Montesinos's sermon yet remained silent because he also had an encomienda. Then, on Pentecost of 1514, de Las Casas came to the conclusion that Montesinos was right and the system of encomiendas was incompatible with Christian faith.

Bartolomé de Las Casas traveled with Montesinos to Spain to convince Spanish authorities to protect the native people with legislation. However, once back in the New World, he found that the Spanish authorities in the New World were unwilling or unable to enforce the legislation. Eventually de Las Casas was named bishop of Chiapas in Mexico. As bishop he repeatedly came into conflict with Catholics who kept encomiendas. Eventually, when he felt that he was making no progress, he resigned as bishop and returned to Spain. He spent the next thirty-nine years of his life writing about the way the Spanish were treating the native people in Mexico.

At first de Las Casas's books were widely read. Many people began to question the Spanish practices within the New World. Over time, however, those with strong interest in maintaining the economic status quo prevailed. While de Las Casas was still living his books were banned in Peru. A century later they were on the Index, a list of books Catholics were forbidden to read.

- Locate some information on the life of Bartolomé de Las Casas. Create a timeline of his life, including his birth, ordination, death, and other highlights of his life.

STUDY QUESTIONS

- HOW DID THE CHURCH'S MISSION TO THE POOR CHANGE SLIGHTLY BETWEEN THE FIRST AND SECOND CENTURIES?
- EXPLAIN THE CHURCH'S SHIFT IN FOCUS AFTER IT REALIZED JESUS MIGHT NOT IMMEDIATELY RETURN.
- WHAT WAS THE TWO-FOLD STANDARD THAT DEVELOPED IN THE CHURCH IN RESPONSE TO THE POOR?
- ACCORDING TO THE PREVALENT ATTITUDE IN THE MIDDLE AGES, WHY SHOULD CHRISTIANS PARTICIPATE IN CHARITY?
- HOW DOES THE CHURCH'S RESPONSE TO THE POOR TODAY CONCERN ALL ITS MEMBERS?
- WHAT IS THE "PREFERENTIAL OPTION FOR THE POOR"?

JOURNAL ASSIGNMENT

- WHAT DOES IT INVOLVE FOR SOMEONE YOUR AGE TO MAKE A GOOD CHRISTIAN DECISION REGARDING CARE AND COMPASSION FOR THE POOR?

WORK

Paul wrote to the Thessalonians: "When we were with you, we instructed you that if anyone was unwilling to work, neither should that one eat" (2 Thessalonians 3:10). The early Christians explicitly followed these instructions. They found work for those who had none and sent away any who were capable of working but refused. The early Christians were very careful to avoid encouraging an abuse of charity. Work was also advocated as a means to help people avoid the temptation to sin. Work was seen as a means of disciplining the body so that the spirit could be wholly directed to God.

Although everyone was expected to work if he or

she was able, not all forms of work were acceptable. Early Christians were not allowed to participate in any profession which was connected with idol-worship or worship of the emperor, or which had to do with bloodshed or capital punishment. Christians could not serve in the army. They could not be judges. Christians could not earn their living through drama, art, or rhetoric, since all of those occupations were connected to pagan worship. Christian merchants were not allowed to trade for any products which had idolatrous emblems. Nor were they allowed to serve as school teachers because of the idolatrous nature of the curriculum which was taught. The Church supported those who had to

Jesus knew the value of work. His neighbors knew him to be a craftsmen, most probably a carpenter like his foster father Joseph (Mark 6:2–3).

give up their jobs in order to be baptized.

As more and more Roman citizens from all walks of life began to join the Church, some of the restrictions began to ease. Eventually Christians were allowed to participate in most professions as long as they did not actually take part in pagan worship. Beginning with the conversion of Constantine, all occupations were deemed acceptable and part of the social order. Every profession contributed in some way to the well-being of the state and thus to the *pax terrena*, or peace on earth.

This does not mean that Christians came to view every occupation as good, but only as tolerable. Although one might participate in an occupation as a soldier, Christians did not hold that violence and war—elements of the occupation—were good. Christians were expected to maintain an inner detachment from the order of the world even as they contributed to it externally.

The strongest emphasis on the duty of work and on personal detachment from work was found in monastic communities. Every

monk was required to share in every type of work. None were to consider any task beneath them or any task as theirs alone. Work was a discipline, no more and no less. St. Francis of Assisi replaced the discipline of work with the discipline of poverty. The Franciscans were expected to beg for their money so that they might truly be one with the poor with whom they lived. Francis and others who followed him separated the importance of action from the need to produce.

Today the Church insists that all people have a right to work. It is through our work that we become partners with God in the creation of the world. It is through our work that we express the full measure of our dignity. In the eyes of the Church, human work is not a matter of producing something useful, it is a matter of transforming the world (at least a little bit) through the use of our creative gift.

STUDY QUESTIONS

- HOW DID THE EARLY CHRISTIANS FOLLOW PAUL'S INSTRUCTIONS REGARDING WORK?
- HOW DID THE LEGALIZATION OF CHRISTIANITY CONTRIBUTE A CHANGE IN ATTITUDE REGARDING CHRISTIANS AND WORK?
- SUMMARIZE THE CHURCH'S POSITION ON THE PURPOSE OF WORK.

JOURNAL ASSIGNMENT

- NAME A CAREER YOU ARE CONSIDERING. HOW MIGHT YOU USE THIS WORK TO "TRANSFORM THE WORLD"?

FAMILY

Even as the distinctions between the Church and the secular world became less defined, the Church did not compromise on her views on family life. From the beginning, the Church insisted on **monagamy** and marital fidelity, and on chastity before marriage for both men and women. The Church also rejected the idea of limiting family size by exposing (or abandoning) unwanted children, or by sterilization.

When Christianity was legalized, new laws of the state were enacted offering more protection to children and outlawing or setting limits on those things which were viewed as sins connected with marriage and sex. Extra-marital relations were outlawed. The common practice of keeping a concubine was made more difficult because all legacies given to concubines and their children were declared invalid. Divorce was limited. Prohibitions against the marriage of people of different classes were eliminated. New laws were enacted which legitimized the marriages and families of slaves and declared that the families of slaves were not to be arbitrarily separated. There were other new government laws which protected the role of the mother by allowing women to

inherit from their husbands and to be guardians of their own children if their husbands died. There were also new laws which confined women more closely to the home in order to safeguard marriages.

As with the issue of wealth, the Church took two views with respect to sexuality. Marriage was valued and even consecrated. The natural desire for sexual relations was given a proper and holy direction. Permanent marriages were seen as pleasing to God. However, virginity and celibacy were viewed as even more pleasing. The truly holy were those who would forego the pleasures of marriage for the sake of the Kingdom. Under the influence of the Church, the old Roman penalties against those who remained unmarried were removed and women were actually encouraged to enter convents.[10]

monogamy—Having only one spouse.

Pope John Paul II spoke of the value of virginity or celibacy for the sake of the kingdom of God and its relationship with marriage in *Familiaris Consortio* in 1981. "Marriage and virginity or celibacy are two ways of expressing and living the one mystery of the covenant of God with His people. When marriage is not esteemed, neither can consecrated virginity or celibacy exist; when human sexuality is not regarded as a great value given by the Creator, the renunciation of it for the sake of the Kingdom of Heaven loses its meaning." Consecrated virgins and married and single people who are Third Order members of religious communities also bear witness to God's Kingdom through their life-long commitments.

domestic church—The domestic Church is the Christian family. In the family, parents and children exercise their priesthood of the baptized by worshiping God, receiving the sacraments, and witnessing to Christ and the Church by living as faith disciples.

In recent years the Church has begun to rethink this dual status. Pope John Paul II wrote on the value of both marriage and the professed religious life, pointing out how they are two distinct ways of living out our covenant relationship with God. In order for one to be esteemed the other must also be seen as a good.[11] Recent Church statements have underscored the importance of marriage and family life for both the Church and the secular world. The family is the **domestic church** and the "original cell of social life."[12] What happens in the family shapes what happens in our society.

Catholics believe that families must be helped and defended by appropriate social measures. Furthermore, families that cannot support themselves should be assisted by the state in a way that enhances their ability to function as a family.[13] In their pastoral letter on economic justice, the bishops of the United States stated that "policies and programs at all levels should support the strength and stability of families, especially those adversely affected by the economy."[14] The United States bishops called on the state to evaluate programs and policies on the basis of their impact on families. For every program and every policy the state must ask the question: Does it help or hinder families in their efforts to support and care for one another? Unless the state finds ways to strengthen families, the state itself will be weakened.

From a Catholic perspective, care of families must be at the heart of any social program that is going to conform to God's plan for the world. This is because care for families respects both the unique dignity of each person and the social nature of each person. Within families we exercise our dignity in community, accepting basic responsibility for the development and well-being of one another.

STUDY QUESTIONS

- HOW DID THE LAWS OF THE STATE COME TO MIRROR THE CHURCH'S BELIEFS ABOUT MARRIAGE AND FAMILY LIFE?
- EXPLAIN THE DUAL SYSTEM THAT DEVELOPED WITH RESPECT TO SEXUALITY.
- WHAT DOES IT MEAN TO SAY THAT THE FAMILY IS THE "DOMESTIC CHURCH"?

WAR

Christians in the early Church were not allowed to participate in the military in any way. All forms of violence and bloodshed were considered wrong. When opponents of this principle complained that if it were to prevail the empire would perish, Origin replied, "If all Romans would accept the Faith they would conquer their enemies by prayer and supplication, or rather they would no longer have any enemies at all, for the Divine power would preserve them. There is no one who fights better for the King than we. It is true that we do not go with him into battle, even when he desires it, but we fight for him by forming an army of our own, an army of piety, through our prayers to the Godhead."

As Christianity became an accepted part of the empire, the prohibition against participation in the military was relaxed. In the fifth century, St. Augustine is attributed with developing the "**just war theory**." Augustine was concerned when various groups used violence and claimed to do so for religious reasons. He became convinced that these groups must be stopped and that the state had both a right and responsibility to stop them, using force if necessary. Augustine argued that the use of force and even war was justifiable in some

cases. He established a set of guidelines for determining whether or not a war was just. The principles laid down by Augustine have been a part of Catholic teaching ever since. Over the years the Church has made them even more specific. At the heart of the developed guidelines was the principle that, even in the midst of violence, love must be central.

just war theory—The principle outlined by Saint Augustine and accepted by the Catholic Church which says that under certain specific conditions Christians may engage in war.

St. Augustine (354–430) is a Father of the Church, and one of its greatest theologians. The Confessions is the account of his conversion to Christianity after he was inspired by his mother, St. Monica.

JUST WAR THEORY

According to the principles of the just war theory, the use of force by the state is legitimate if, and only if, the purpose of the war is just, it is not a war of aggression, and all of the following conditions are met:

1. There must be a real and certain danger; for example, if a situation threatens the life of innocent people, if basic human rights are violated, or if there is an imminent need for self-defense.
2. The right to declare a war of defense belongs to those who have the legitimate responsibility to represent the people and uphold the common good.
3. The rights and values to be gained by the conflict must justify the killing of people.
4. There must be a commitment to reconciliation among all sides after the war. Non-combatants, prisoners, and the wounded are to be treated with respect, and the indiscriminate destruction of cities or large areas of land is prohibited.
5. War must be the last resort after all other methods for achieving the peace have been tried.
6. The odds of success should be weighed against potential lives lost.
7. The damage the war will inflict and the cost it will incur must be proportionate to the good expected. There must be serious hope that the use of force will actually put an end to the aggression.

By Charlemagne's time, the Church's acceptance of war and violence was so complete that when the emperor forced his enemies to convert to Christianity at sword point the Church did not condemn his actions. In fact, many saw him as the great defender of the faith and praised him for saving so many from hell.

In 1095, the Church even proclaimed her own war. At the Council of Clermont Pope Urban II called for the First Crusade. The Crusades were a series of religious wars in the eleventh to thirteenth centuries with the primary goal of recapturing the Holy Land, most particularly, Jerusalem. Pope Urban II called upon all Christians of the west to go forth to defeat the Muslims. Besides holding the Holy Land, the Muslims threatened the Byzantine Empire. Urban's objectives for this crusade were threefold. He believed it would (1) reunite Christians in the east and west; (2) result in the reconquering of the Holy Land; and (3) bring about the Kingdom of Heaven.

The Crusades

Many Christians in the west welcomed the opportunity offered by the First Crusade. It was a time of abject misery in many parts of Europe. Crops were failing and diseases ran rampant. The Crusades offered hope and purpose to those who had none. Soon after Pope Urban issued his call a disorganized mob began to form under the loose leadership of Peter the Hermit. As they headed for Jerusalem, they practiced for their war with the Muslims by seeking out and killing Jews. They also fought many other Christians as they tried to claim food and property for their cause. Most of the group of crusaders died along the way, but Peter the Hermit and a small number of others did make it to Constantinople. They arrived at almost the same time as several other more organized groups of crusaders. The Byzantine emperor welcomed them and joined forces with them to retake Nicaea, Antioch, and finally, on July 15, 1099, Jerusalem. A horrible bloodbath followed the conquest of Jerusalem and it became evident that the region would require constant reinforcements to keep it in Christian hands.

Over the next few decades, groups of armed Christians from the west and east traveled to the Holy Land for a period of service. However, their hold was always rather tenuous. In 1187, Jerusalem was retaken by the Muslims. Another crusade was called and the crusading fervor once again swept Europe, but the further waves of crusades were relatively unsuccessful.

The Sixth Crusade was led by the emperor, Frederick II, who had been excommunicated because the pope believed he had purposely aborted the Fifth Crusade. In fact, Frederick's men had become overwhelmed by sickness and disease. Nevertheless, Frederick did achieve some success during the Sixth Crusade. Frederick and the sultan who controlled the Holy Land negotiated an agreement which gave the emperor Jerusalem, Nazareth, and Bethlehem, as well as the roads linking the three. Frederick was known as "the liberator of Jerusalem."

The warring spirit of the Crusades lived on for several centuries. The Church used much of the crusaders' rhetoric against heretics. Church leaders argued that it was justifiable to torture heretics and burn them at the stake in order to save their souls. The commonly held theology of the time was that since nothing was more important than Salvation, everything and anything was justifiable in the attempt to save souls.[15]

The Church and Modern Wars

It was only as the Church lost its control over governments that its attitude toward war and the use of force began to shift again. Even during World War II, the Church hierarchy did not speak out strongly against the war. Instead the Church remained relatively uncritical of governments involved in the hopes that she would be able to influence those governments after the war had ended. Pope Pius XII in particular remained neutral in the hopes that he would be able to negotiate a peace at some future point. In the years since the war, Pope Pius has been criticized by some for his silence.

Since World War II, the Church has taken a more active stance against the use of force or aggression by any government. Although the Church continues to maintain the position that states do have a right to legitimate self-defense, the Church is also quick to point out that in a world of modern

POPE JOHN PAUL II ON PEACE

Since January, 1979, shortly after he became pope, John Paul II used the occasion of the World Day for Peace to speak out against war and for the peaceful resolution of the world's problems. Read from at least five different statements by Pope John Paul from the website link below. Incorporate at least three quotations from these statements into your own one-page essay that speaks out for peace.

www.vatican.va/holy_father/john_paul_ii/messages/peace/index.htm

In his World Peace Day address for 2004, Pope John Paul II said that the war on terror must be multifaceted, with force being used only when absolutely necessary and even then "be accompanied by a courageous and lucid analysis of the reasons behind terrorist attacks. The fight against terrorism must be conducted also on the political and educational levels: on the one hand, by eliminating the underlying causes of situations of injustice which frequently drive people to more desperate and violent acts; and on the other hand, by insisting on an education inspired by respect for human life in every situation: the unity of the human race is a more powerful reality than any contingent divisions separating individuals and people."

warfare it is difficult to define and achieve only what is legitimate. Modern warfare does not involve soldiers only; population centers, ecosystems, and economic infrastructures are often destroyed as well. In most, if not all, cases, the potential damage of war far outweighs the potential good. The difficulties of waging a justifiable and just war are compounded by the fact that the constant preparation for war consumes our society. The Church continues to stress the point that the arms race is one of the main contributors to the problem of worldwide poverty.

STUDY QUESTIONS

- SUMMARIZE THE PREMISE BEHIND THE "JUST WAR THEORY." WHY MIGHT A "JUST WAR" NOT BE POSSIBLE TODAY?
- WHAT WERE THE MAJOR OBJECTIVES OF THE CRUSADES?
- HOW DID THE CHURCH'S ATTITUDE TOWARD WAR SHIFT AT THE TIME OF WORLD WAR II?

JOURNAL ASSIGNMENT

- WHAT DO YOU BELIEVE TO BE THE ROOT CAUSE OF WAR IN THE WORLD TODAY?

DEFENDERS OF THE POOR

Frederic Ozanam

On August 22, 1997, during the World Youth Day activities in Paris, Pope John Paul II beatified Frederic Ozanam. Beatification is one of the steps towards sainthood. Frederic Ozanam was a student, a professor, a husband, and a father who worked tirelessly for the poor. Pope John Paul called him a "precursor of the social doctrine of the Church."

In 1833, as a twenty-year-old university student, Frederic, along with a group of his friends, created the Conferences of St. Vincent de Paul. These were aimed at "helping the poor in a spirit of service." The conferences quickly spread throughout France and eventually throughout the world. From that time on, the love of those in dire need became the focal point of Frederic's life. He understood that charity alone was not sufficient to help the poor. He insisted that charity be accompanied by efforts to correct the injustices which had made charity necessary in the first place. He challenged and worked to change the political and social structures of his own day. Frederic helped others to see that every society must work to end indigence or risk losing its honor. He insisted that those who wished to help the poor must help them in their human development.

Pope John Paul also called Frederic, "a man of thought and action . . . [who] remains for today's university community . . . a model of courageous commitment." Frederic is a reminder of the power of even a single person to promote a deeper respect for human dignity.[16]

DEFENDERS OF THE POOR continued
Dorothy Day

"You love God as much as the one you love the least." In the latter part of her life Dorothy Day said that this "harsh" phrase often came to mind when she reflected upon the community life which was part of the Catholic Worker movement. From the time she joined the Catholic Church in 1927 at the age of thirty, Dorothy Day tried to live out the radical call of the Gospel. She also tried to help others understand the implications of that call in today's society.

Dorothy's parents were not church-goers, nor were they particularly concerned with the plight of the poor. In fact, when Dorothy recalled her father, it was his prejudice rather than concern for others which dominated her memories. Nonetheless, from a very early age Dorothy felt drawn to God and to spirituality, and from the time she was fifteen, she felt drawn to the poor. Long before she became a Catholic, Dorothy worked for radical (mostly Communist) newspapers, writing about the plight of the poor and the needs of workers. The majority of Dorothy's friends were Communists, anarchists who believed that religion was oppressive and that social change would only be possible if people embraced atheism. Dorothy, however, was never comfortable with atheism. She knew that God was real, and she felt drawn to prayer. In particular, she was attracted to the sacramental life of the Catholic Church. She would often wander into St. Joseph's Catholic Church on Sixth Avenue in New York because in its quiet she experienced peace and a sense of comfort. When Dorothy and her common-law husband Forster Batterham had a baby girl, Dorothy could no longer resist the pull of the Church. She was overwhelmed by love and joy at the birth of her child and she wanted to give her daughter, Tamar, the grace of faith and the companionship of the saints, so she had her baptized. In December of 1927 Dorothy broke off her relationship with Forster in order to become a Catholic herself.

Being a Catholic did not always bring Dorothy comfort. She missed Forster and she struggled with the fact that the Catholic Church was more a Church of charity than of justice. She longed for a way to bring together her faith, her social justice concerns, and her skills as a writer and reporter. On May 1, 1933, inspired and assisted by her new friend and colleague, Peter Maurin, Dorothy stood in Union Square in New York among thousands of homeless, unemployed, and frustrated people, handing out the first copy of *The Catholic Worker*, a newspaper intended to publicize Catholic social teachings and encourage the peaceful transformation of society. The paper examined the various struggles which were facing the poor and middle class in terms of gospel values.

The newspaper grew rapidly. The first printing was 2,500. Within a few months, subscriptions and bulk orders had reached 75,000. The paper quickly attracted volunteers who came to put its editorials into practice. Catholic Worker houses of hospitality were soon opened, first in New York and then in cities throughout the country. They were staffed by volunteers and provided food, shelter, and clothing for any who came. (*The Catholic Worker* is still published today at its original cover price: one cent.)

When the United States entered World War II, Dorothy Day and the newspaper maintained a Christian pacifist stand. Dorothy encouraged people to participate in acts of mercy rather than acts of war. Many of the volunteers in Catholic Worker houses of hospitality disagreed with Dorothy and left in order to join the war effort.

During the 1950s, when the Cold War was at its height, Dorothy protested the treatment of jailed Communists. She spoke of her own debt to Communists saying, "They helped me to find God in his poor, in his abandoned ones, as I had not found him in the Christian Churches. My radical associates were the ones who were in the forefront of the struggle for a better social order where there would not be so many poor."[17] She said she disagreed with the Communists's calls for violence, but then again she disagreed with many Republicans and Democrats for the same reason. In New York Dorothy was arrested several times for refusing to participate in air raids. She said she refused to be "drilled into fear" and that her refusal to seek shelter was an act of penance for a society which had created the bomb. Dorothy insisted that prayer and penance were essential parts of any effort to bring about social healing. Dorothy challenged those Catholic leaders who supported the war effort. She wondered if they had allowed their fear to blind them to Christ's presence in the enemy.

Until her death in 1980, Dorothy Day continued to defend the most disenfranchised. She called on all Christians to work for social change using non-violent means. She reminded Catholics and other Christians everywhere that all of their efforts to do good would amount to nothing if they were not undergirded by prayer. Dorothy laid much of the foundation for the Catholic social justice movement which exists in the United States today.

IN CONCLUSION

Jesus told his disciples that the world would be able to recognize them because of the love they showed for one another (see John 13:35). The first Christians expected Christ's imminent return and an ushering in of a world of love and peace. They believed that because of what Christ had done class distinctions were irrelevant and violence had been rendered powerless. Therefore they ignored the social boundaries and the struggles for power which were so important to other people in society. Christians from all walks of life shocked the rest of society because they mingled with one another as equals. They believed that the wealth which had been given to some should serve those who had none, and the needs which plagued some should be cared for by those whose needs were not so great.

The early Christians did not view this sense of communal responsibility as something which needed to be mandated. They were not interested in reforming the social structures of society. Instead, they believed that taking responsibility for one another would be a natural outgrowth of accepting the gospel. According to their way of thinking, those who had accepted Christ should not be concerned with the standards of this world and should be concerned only with the standards of the Kingdom of Heaven.

As the coming of the Kingdom was delayed, Christian hope focused less on a renewal of this world and more on the rewards of the next world. The focus of Christian social responsibility shifted from sharing among equals to giving to those who were not equal.

Today the focus of Catholic social responsibility has shifted again. Catholics are called not only to give to those in need, but also to recreate the social structures which cause extreme need in the first place. Catholics work to create a society in which the values of the Kingdom may be experienced.

The Church is the Body of Christ on earth. This means that Christ has chosen to remain on earth through the Church. Sometimes, however, that presence is partially obscured by human weakness and sinfulness. If we look closely at any period in Church history we can always see God acting through the Church, but not everything that is done in the name of the Church is desired by God. Despite the fact that everything we need to know has already been revealed by Christ, it is in the unfolding of history that the Church comes to a full understanding of that Revelation. The Church's understanding of what it means to truly follow Christ must grow and develop over time.

LEARN BY DOING

Write a report on the Catholic Worker movement in the United States. See www.catholicworker.org. Include information on the lives of co-founders Dorothy Day and Peter Maurin. In addition, write or call a Catholic Worker house listed on the website. If the house is in your immediate area, ask for ways you can help to volunteer to help their efforts. Report on what you did. If there is no Catholic Worker house near you, contact any house and ask for suggestions for ways you can serve the poor and work for justice. Report on what you found out and what you did.

PRAYER

Almighty and eternal God,
may your grace enkindle in all of us
a love for the many unfortunate people whom poverty
and misery reduce to a condition of life unworthy of
human beings.
Arouse in the hearts of those who call you Father
a hunger and thirst for justice and peace, and for fraternal
charity in deeds and truth.
Grant, O Lord, peace in our days,
peace to souls, peace to families, peace to our country,
and peace among nations.
Amen.

—Pope Pius XII (1876–1958)

NOTES

1. "Waldensians in Italy Benefit From Tax Change," *Canadian Mennonite*, vol. 1: no. 8, p. 23.
2. In fact, in August 1942, Archbishop Saliege of Toulouse did issue a pastoral letter to be read in all churches "without comment." Archbishop Saliege asked, "Why does the right of asylum no longer exist in our Church? The Jews are men; the Jews are women, they are members of the human race. They are our brothers. This no Christian can forget" (*Origens*, vol. 27: no. 18, p. 303n.).
3. See Galatians 3:28. The fact that there would no longer be distinctions between slave and free implies that wealth and power would also become irrelevant.
4. See 1 Timothy 6:8.
5. #2442.
6. See National Conference of Catholic Bishops, *Economic Justice for All*, #185.
7. See *Solicitudo Rei Socialis*, #42.
8. See *Centesimus Annus*.
9. Ibid., #14.
10. It is worth noting that the Church's attitude toward virginity gave unmarried women a status and a voice in society which they had never before had. For hundreds of years religious orders of women provided almost the only option for women who wished to live a life free from direct dependence on their fathers, husbands, or sons.
11. *Consortium Socialis*, #16.
12. *Catechism of the Catholic Church*, #2207.
13. See *Catechism of the Catholic Church*, #2209.
14. *Economic Justice for All*, #206.
15. Of course those who refused, even under torture, to say that they accepted the Catholic Church and all of her teachings believed the same thing. People on both sides believed that they represented absolute good and the other represented absolute evil. Words—confessions of faith—were the weapons which gave each side power. Catholics believed that Protestants could only be saved from eternal torment if they professed the Catholic faith. Protestants believed that they could only be saved from eternal torment if they refused to profess the "Catholic lies."
16. The quotes in this feature are taken from Pope John Paul II's homily: "Frederic Oxanam: Linking Charity with Justice," 11 (*Origins*, vol. 27: no. 12.)
17. Jim Forest, *Love Is the Measure: A Biography of Dorothy Day* (Maryknoll, NY: Orbis Books, 1994), p. 93.

UNIT SEVEN

THE CHURCH IS A COMMUNION OF SAINTS

THE CHURCH IS A COMMUNION OF SAINTS

One of the four marks of the Church named in the Creed, the Church is holy and is so because Jesus Christ, its founder, is holy. Jesus joined the Church to himself as his body and gave the Church the Holy Spirit. Together, Christ and the Church make up the "whole Christ" (*Christus totus* in Latin). As St. Gregory the Great wrote, "Our redeemer has shown himself to be one person with the holy Church whom he has taken to himself."

As members of the Church, we are all called to holiness. We are called to be saints. The communion of saints includes everyone of us to the extent that we make God's love and goodness visible and tangible in our lives. Our membership in the communion of saints brings us unity between the Church on earth and the Church in Heaven.

Mary, the Mother of God, is the "most authentic form of perfect imitation of Christ" (Pope Paul VI). Mary is the model of faith. As we follow Mary's example of faithfulness, Christ is alive in our hearts and he will act in the world through our own flesh.

Unit 7 examines the Church as the communion of saints. It is a Church with both a human and divine dimension that is clearly witnessed in the relationship between the pilgrims on earth and those Christians who have died before us. Because of Christ's Resurrection, Death has no power to divide people between Heaven and earth.

Mary, who was protected from sin from the moment of her conception, and was assumed into heaven at her death, is the model saint. Her "self-emptying" as a sign of faith is a model that we all strive to emulate. Chapter 7.1 also describes Mary as the disciple *par excellence*.

Chapter 7.2 traces the historical roots of the Catholic cult of saints. It details a history of how the Church has proclaimed saints from its earliest times and how the process of canonization became the norm in the twelfth century. In history, the Church also explains Mary's unique role in the communion of saints. Her story is detailed more completely in this chapter as well.

When you have completed Unit 7, you will be able to:

- define virtues and identify ways in which virtues have impacted your own life;
- define holiness and cite examples of holiness within the Church today;
- explain the role of the saints in the prayer life of the Catholic Church;
- articulate Mary's role in the Church;
- explain the meaning of the Immaculate Conception and the Assumption of Mary;
- outline the historical roots of the Catholic cult of the saints;
- demonstrate a familiarity with a variety of different Catholic traditions honoring Mary;
- explain Mary's unique place in the communion of saints;
- identify ways in which the Old Testament has shaped the Church's understanding of Mary;
- explain what it means to call Mary "Mediatrix."

WHO ARE the SAINTS?

"AMEN, AMEN, I SAY TO YOU, WHOEVER BELIEVES IN ME WILL DO THE WORKS THAT I DO, AND WILL DO GREATER ONES THAN THESE, BECAUSE I AM GOING TO THE FATHER."

—John 14:12

SAINTS ALIVE

The incidents described below are true. The names used are the actual names of the people involved.

It happened in Michigan. . . . A man dressed in a Confederate flag T-shirt began to heckle a group protesting the presence of the Ku Klux Klan in their town. This man became the focal point of the local people's anger. He was hit on the head with a sign and pushed to the ground. An eighteen-year-old African-American girl named Keshia Thomas was with the crowd who accosted the man. Like those around her she was angered by his shirt and his attitude. But when the man fell to the ground Keshia threw herself on top of him to protect him from those who were about to beat him with sticks. Those who were prepared to do violence looked at Keshia and stopped.

It happened in Ontario, Canada. . . . Craig Kielburger read about the assassination of a Pakistani boy, Iqbal Masih. At age ten Iqbal had escaped from slavery and begun a campaign against child labor and exploitation in his country. The big businesses in Pakistan felt threatened as Iqbal's protest gained momentum. That's when he was assassinated.

Craig was touched by the fact that Iqbal Masih was the same age as he was. He decided to find out more about child labor. When he found out that more than 100 million children around the world worked in slave-like conditions, he and some friends started writing letters, giving talks in local schools, and raising money for children who were being exploited.

It wasn't long before they had established an international organization—"Free the Children"—working to protect child laborers. Due in part to the efforts of this group, awareness of the worldwide child labor buying patterns started to change and companies were forced to reexamine their policies regarding child labor.

It happened in Philadelphia. . . . A teenager named Trevor Ferrell gave a blanket and a pillow to a homeless man. Then Trevor took it a step further. He began to collect blankets and food and distribute them to people living on the streets. His action inspired others to do the same. Eventually an abandoned hotel and another building were donated to Trevor's Campaign for the Homeless. Because of Trevor and those who joined him in his efforts, a residential living center that provided twenty-four-hour day care along with social services and educational programs was opened for women and children.

It happens in thousands of different ways, in thousands of different places—the hand of God is seen in the world through the actions of God's People. What do we call the three teens represented here? Some might call them saints. Are they? That depends on the definition of "**saint**." They have not been canonized—in fact, they are not all Catholic. They are not without faults, but then again, faults are common even to canonized saints. On the other hand, they all have been faithful to God's grace in at least one very significant way. They have all practiced a heroic virtue. They all have allowed others to see God in them and in the world, and they all have been examples and inspirations for people who wish to follow Christ.

As Catholics we believe that everything good comes to us from God. We believe that Jesus is the Truth, and every time people walk in the way of Truth they are walking with Jesus, whether they recognize it or not.[1] During the Mass we praise God, saying, "all life, all holiness, come from you." Saints act in holy ways and thus allow us to see God who is the source of all holiness. The communion of saints—another description of the Church—includes each and every one of us to the extent that we make God's love and goodness visible and tangible in our lives.

Touched by God

No one can come away unchanged from an encounter with God. In the Old Testament, to call someone "holy" was to say that he or she had been "touched by God" and set apart for a special and unique purpose. Holy people were those who recognized their own unique purpose and who accepted the particular role which God had given them. Holy people disrupted the flow of the everyday and redirected history.

The New Testament letter to the Romans addresses those who are "called to be saints." The Greek word which is translated "saints" is the same word that in other places in translated as "holy." Therefore, as someone who is holy, a saint recognizes and accepts God's unique call to him or her. Saints are people who live authentically, that is, people who are true to themselves as God has created them to be.

Society today is laced with skepticism. Perhaps it is particularly significant that Craig and Trevor were both only twelve when they began the social movements that carried beyond their teen years. They were not held back by doubts about how much real difference they could make. They saw what they could do and they acted, and God saw that their actions were enough. In calling us to be holy, Jesus tells us that we must become like children.

Keshia, too, acted because of the need of the moment and her belief that violence is never the answer. She did not begin a movement, but her action did inspire people around the country to think again about the power of love. As *Life* magazine reported, Keshia "had performed an alchemy more miraculous than turning lead into gold. She had transformed violence into peace."[2]

saint—One who has been transformed by the grace of God. In its most basic sense, the term "saint" refers to all Christians. Saint is normally used to refer to those who the Church has canonized (or acclaimed before the process of canonization came into existence), honored with the title "Saint," and declared worthy of veneration.

The *Catechism of the Catholic Church* says that the Church canonizes those who practice heroic virtue in their lives.[3] We are part of a Church that not only believes in heroes, but challenges each one of us to be one. In this chapter we will look at the way the Church understands heroism and the way she calls each of us to do the heroic.

STUDY QUESTION

- LIST THREE CHARACTERISTICS OF SAINTHOOD GLEANED FROM THE EXAMPLES ABOVE.

JOURNAL ASSIGNMENT

- WHO AND WHAT DO YOU ASSOCIATE WITH HEROISM? BE SPECIFIC.

THE COMMUNION OF SAINTS

The Church is seen as a Body of holy persons—both on earth and in heaven—who share their spiritual possessions. This is the communion of saints. By the end of the fifth century, the Church had a clearer understanding of the unity between the Church on earth and the Church in heaven. Each one was a part of the other and the gifts of the members of each served the other.

Catholics believe in a Church which cannot be divided by death. The saints are fully united with Christ, and our communion with those saints unites us more

completely to Christ. We are also in communion with those who have died and who are not yet fully united to Christ. Our prayers help those who have died and their prayers can help us.[4]

Signs of Hope

Saints help the Church understand and explain the *eschaton*, that is, the Christian understanding of the end times. Our relationship with those who have died reveals our attitude toward death and our understanding of what will happen both immediately after death and at the end of time.

Eschatology refers to the study of the end times.

Those of us living now are in the "in between time," the time between the decisive in-breaking of the kingdom of God in Jesus and the perfection of history in the **Second Coming**. Death will continue to exist until the time of Christ's return, but since the Kingdom has already begun in Christ, death no longer has the power it once had. Catholics believe that the power of death to divide people has been destroyed by Christ's Resurrection. We ask saints to pray for us because they are a part of our community. We honor and thank saints because their close unity with Christ binds the whole Church more closely to Christ. They are part of the one Body, which includes all of us; therefore, their holiness makes us all more holy, and their praise and worship of God lifts our own holiness to new heights.[5]

We believe that the Church is the eschatological community— the community of the end times. Even now she has a share in divine glory. This divine glory is most clearly seen in the actions of the saints while they were on earth and continues through their intercession in Heaven. We ask the saints to intercede for us just as we ask for the prayers of those we live with today. We believe that the prayers of the faithful do make a difference and that the faithful are most frequently used by God as channels of divine grace. It is through the saints that God "manifests his holiness and continues the work of salvation."[6]

All prayers are answered by God, but some may be answered through other members of the Church, including the saints who are in Heaven.

Jesus Works Through the Saints

Jesus is the only mediator between God the Father and humanity. Our intimate relationship with the Father is only possible because of Jesus and the Holy Spirit whom he sent. We believe that no one but Jesus can make the Father truly accessible to human beings. We also believe that since his Resurrection and Ascension Jesus has communicated with us through other people. It is the Holy Spirit speaking and acting in others, but it is the voice and the touch of those others which we perceive. We only know that it is Jesus through faith.

Saints are those who cooperate with Jesus and allow him to work through them. Saints are not themselves mediators, but they share in the mediation of Jesus. Without Jesus they can do nothing, but because of their relationship with Jesus they are able to help make God's presence visible to others. Because death no longer has the power to completely remove someone from the Christian community, saints are able to continue sharing in the mediating work of Jesus even after they die. Through the power of prayer they continue to touch other members of the Church and thus encourage the work of God.

eschatology—The study of the last things: the Second Coming of Christ, the Resurrection of the dead, the Kingdom of God, judgment, Heaven, Hell, and Purgatory.

Second Coming—Jesus' return in glory at the end of time. At the Second Coming, the Kingdom of God will be fully realized.

IN COMMUNION WITH THE DEAD

From the earliest times, the Church has taught the value of praying for the dead "that they might be loosed of their sins" (2 Mc 12:45). The *Catechism* teaches further: "Our prayer for them is capable not only of helping them, but also of making their intercession for us effective" (958). Think about someone you know who has died. Spend some time praying for this person. Consider one or more of the following ways:

- lighting a votive candle for the person;
- writing a journal entry with memories of the person;
- remembering the person at Eucharist;
- doing something the person enjoyed while on earth;
- thinking about the person while sitting before the Blessed Sacrament.

While praying for this person, ask him or her to pray for you and your intentions as well.

Our relationship with the saints in Heaven is a testimony to our belief in the power of the Resurrection and in the powerlessness of death. It is also testimony to our belief that the Church is the Body of Christ. All of the members of the Church together make up the Body of Christ; therefore, when we are in communion with the other members of the Church, we are in communion with Christ. Our communion with Christ would be incomplete if our communion with the Church did not include both the Church on earth and the Church in Heaven. We need both to experience the fullness of Christ's love.

The unity of the Church on earth is a sign of hope and seed of peace for the earth. The unity between the Church on earth and the Church in Heaven is the sign, seed, and promise of the unity of eternity. Because of this unity, we know that in the Kingdom of Heaven neither time, nor distance, nor life experience will be able to separate people from one another.

STUDY QUESTIONS

- HOW DOES SAINTHOOD EQUATE WITH HOLINESS?
- HOW DOES SAINTHOOD HELP CHRISTIANS UNDERSTAND THE ESCHATON?
- WHY DO WE THANK AND HONOR SAINTS?
- EXPLAIN THE ROLE OF SAINTS IN THE CHURCH'S PRAYER.
- WHY ARE SAINTS ABLE TO MAKE GOD'S PRESENCE VISIBLE TO OTHERS?

JOURNAL ASSIGNMENT

- DESCRIBE WHAT YOU THINK IT WOULD BE LIKE FOR THE SAINTS—INCLUDING PEOPLE YOU KNOW WHO HAVE DIED—TO COME TO MEET YOU AS YOU ENTER ETERNAL LIFE.

DOCTOR OF THE CHURCH

The Church has a designation for outstanding leaders, writers, teachers, and theologians: **doctor of the Church**. A similar title—**father of the Church**—is for people with links to the earliest centuries of Christianity. There are three basic requirements for being named as a Church doctor. The first is holiness, which can be seen as remarkable even among the saints. The second is an extensive body of writings, which the Church can recommend as free from error and faithful to the teaching of Church Tradition. And the third is significant doctrinal content in one's teaching and writings. In 1997, Thérèse of Lisieux was named as the thirty-third Doctor of the Church. She is the third woman doctor of the Church.

Shortly before Thérèse died she wrote a letter to a friend. Her friend was concerned that Thérèse would no longer love him when she reached heaven and was able to see him as he really was. Her response provides insight into the Catholic understanding of sainthood and intercession:

> I assure you, my little brother, that you don't understand heaven the way I do. To you it seems that, participating in God's justice and holiness, I will not be able to excuse your faults as I did while on earth. Are you then forgetting that I shall participate also in the infinite mercy of the Lord? I believe that those in heaven have great compassion on our wretchedness. They remember that when they were fragile and mortal like us they committed the same faults as we and went through the same struggles, and their fraternal tenderness becomes greater than it ever was on earth. That is why they never stop protecting us and praying for us. I will love you more once I am in heaven than I ever could on earth.[7]

doctor of the Church—A title officially conferred upon a saint by the pope or by a general council declaring that person to have been particularly holy, wise, and learned, and therefore a source of sound theological teaching for the Church.

father of the Church—A title for writers of the early Church who had a major impact on the development of Christian theology and doctrine. The fathers of the Church were characterized by holiness of life, orthodoxy of doctrine, approval of the Church, and antiquities. The period of the Church fathers is generally held to have ended in the seventh century.

SAINTS: THE BENEFITS OF VIRTUE

It is popular today to talk about values, but it is much rarer to hear a discussion about **virtue**. In fact, being virtuous is often looked down upon as something quaint, outdated, and not terribly useful. But without virtue, a **value** is impotent. Virtues are the habits and inclinations which lead us to be true to our values even when we find this is difficult. It is virtue which takes us from saying that we value honesty in our friends to being honest ourselves, even when it is difficult to be so.

The stories of the saints can help us to see the power and the benefits of virtue. The stories of the saints are one of the great treasures of the Church. Just as few people would spend hours practicing basketball drills if they had never experienced the excitement of a basketball game, so too, few people will cultivate virtues if they have not been inspired by the accomplishments of the virtuous. Similarly, just as few people would succeed in developing their basketball skills if they did not have an experienced coach to guide them, so, too, few people would succeed in developing their virtues without an example to follow.

The saints teach us the possibilities that open when people learn the virtues of faith, hope, love, temperance, fortitude, justice and prudence. The saints can also guide us in developing those virtues in our own lives. The actions of the saints underscore the Second Vatican Council's teaching that progress on earth is important because "it is here that the body of a new human family grows, foreshadowing in some way the age which is to come." The things which we have done on earth are the things which will be illuminated and transfigured when Christ presents the Kingdom to his Father.[8]

STUDY QUESTIONS

- NAME AND DEFINE THE VIRTUES.
- WHY ARE THE LIVES AND STORIES OF SAINTS VALUABLE TO THE CHURCH?

JOURNAL ASSIGNMENT

- WRITE ABOUT A PERSON WHO HAS MODELED CHRISTIAN VIRTUES FOR YOU.

MARY: THE MODEL SAINT

As the Church is the communion of saints,[9] Mary is the model saint. Therefore she is the model for the Church. Mary demonstrates the "most authentic form of perfect imitation of Christ."[10] Mary is the disciple *par excellence*.

As the martyrs showed their complete commitment to God in the way they died, Mary showed her complete commitment to God in the way she lived. Mary said "yes" to the angel's request that she be the mother of the Savior. Although she did not understand how it would be possible for her to have a child, and although she faced great risks because she was not married, Mary was willing to place all of her trust in God. Her total dependence on God and her complete orientation to God remind the Church of her own mission. It is not only in choosing our ultimate goals that we must be faithful; it is in each step along the way. Mary's faithfulness allows Jesus to be conceived, first in her heart and then in her flesh. If we follow her example of faithfulness, Christ will also be born in our hearts and will act in the world through our flesh.

Mary was open to the Father's will. She remained open and faithful to his will even when she did not understand some things that happened in the life of her son; for example, when she found him in the Temple (Luke 2:41–51), and later when he was surrounded by crowds of people and called those disciples his true family (Matthew 12:46–50). She accepted that her understanding of God's Revelation was imperfect, yet she continued to follow and to learn. Mary remained faithful to Jesus to his Death. Even when Mary stood and watched her own son die she did not lose faith. She allowed herself to be completely emptied even as Christ was emptied.

"Self-Emptying" and Discipleship

This "self-emptying" must be at the heart of all true faith. It is what Jesus meant when he said that whoever wishes to be a true disciple must "deny himself, take up his cross, and follow me" (Matthew 16:24). Some Christians have and will be called to follow Christ to the cross in a literal sense, giving up their lives for their faith. All Christians are called to follow Christ to the cross as Mary did. We are to stand with her and let go of ourselves so that we can completely feel the pain and emptiness which Christ experienced. We are to pour our hearts and our lives into Christ to such an extent that his suffering and death have the power to completely redefine us and our world. Mary loves Christ so much that she makes his sacrifice of love her own.

virtue—A habitual disposition to do good. Virtues are attitudes and habits which lead a person to do what God desires.

value—Something believed to be particularly important.

MARIAN PROJECTS

Do one of the following:

- Report on the history and practice of one of these popular Marian devotions:
  - ? the Angelus
  - ? Marian novena
  - ? Rosary
  - ? litany of the Blessed Mother
  - ? first Saturday devotion
- Mary's Magnificat (Lk 1:46–55) describes in her own words her willingness to give her entire being to God. Read a Scripture commentary on the Magnificat. Write an essay explaining something of its origins. Then, choose three verses that would give encouragement to the poor. Explain why you chose the verses that you did.
- Research and report on one of the following Marian apparitions:
  - ? Guadalupe, Mexico
  - ? Lourdes, France
  - ? Fatima, Portugal
- Develop a lesson for primary-age children that explains one or more of the Church's beliefs about Mary—Mother of God, Immaculate Conception, Assumption—so that they can easily understand its meaning.

If this seems too abstract, remember that Mary is Jesus' Mother. It is part of the human instinct for parents to defend their children. It can be one of the worst forms of torture to make a mother watch her child suffer. Mary watched Christ suffer without losing hope, without losing faith, and without losing love. She does not begrudge the sacrifice that he makes and that she participates in. Christ's gift of love becomes her gift of love as well. Mary joins her sacrifice of love to Christ's and thus becomes the first person to share in the work of **Redemption**. Each time we follow Mary's example and accept the suffering that comes from truly loving others we join our suffering to Christ's and, like Mary, also share in the work of Redemption.

Mary is the model of faith in her commitment to Christ, in her faithfulness, in her self-emptying, and in her love.

BELIEFS ABOUT MARY

Throughout history, the Church has formulated many beliefs about Mary. The major Marian dogmas are listed below.

Mary is Theotokos, *the Mother of God.* Mary conceived and bore the Son of God who is one with the Father. She is the Mother of that divine Son for all eternity. The Council of Ephesus (431) taught that Jesus is one divine person who has a human nature and a divine nature and that Jesus was divine from the moment of conception.

Mary was immaculately conceived. Mary was born without the stain of Original Sin. In view of the merits of the Son she would bear, Mary was redeemed from the moment of her conception. God graced Mary in this way in anticipation of her role in Jesus' Death and Resurrection.

Mary was a virgin when Jesus was born and remained a virgin throughout her life. Mary conceived Jesus without a human father; God is the unique Father of Jesus. Further, the Church has always taught that Mary was a virgin, before, in, and after the birth of Jesus.

Mary was assumed body and soul into heavenly glory. Mary is the first to share in Christ's resurrection. In 1950 Pope Pius XII officially proclaimed the doctrine of the **Assumption of Mary**.

Redemption—Christ's saving work which freed humanity from the power of sin and death and restored them to unity with God.

STUDY QUESTIONS

- WHY IS MARY THE MODEL FOR THE CHURCH?
- HOW DID MARY SHOW COMPLETE COMMITMENT TO GOD'S WILL?

MARY AS A SIGN OF GOD'S PRESENCE

The Second Vatican Council called Mary "a type of the Church in the order of faith, charity and perfect union with Christ."[11] Mary is everything that the Church strives to be and she is the sign that the Church will eventually achieve what she is striving for. Like Jesus and the Church, Mary, too, is a sacrament. She is the symbol and instrument of God's presence with humanity. It was in Mary's own body that Christ was conceived and the divine and the human were permanently joined.

Mary is nothing without Jesus. She is able to do what she does only because she is filled with God's grace. At the same time, Jesus would not be the same person without Mary. Jesus is fully human as well as fully divine. Like all human beings, he could only have been born of one particular mother. Jesus' human identity is not derived from the fact that he was born of a woman (any woman), but from the fact that he was born of a specific woman— Mary. In Mary, one of the great mysteries of our faith is revealed. In Mary, we see that God chooses to work through human beings rather than apart from us. In Mary, we must come face to face with the fact that God calls each one of us to a unique role and that each of us must say "yes" to that role if we are to achieve for ourselves and the world what God intends.

Mary is also the sign of the new covenant between God and God's people. In the Incarnation, Christ and Mary are indissolubly linked. They are united by blood; nothing can ever undo the essential nature of their relationship. In this way, Mary prefigures the Church which is indissolubly linked to Christ through the blood of the cross from which it was born. Like Mary, the Church can never be separated from Christ. The New Covenant which Christ establishes with the Church becomes part of the Church's identity, even as the covenant between God the Father and Mary became part of Mary's identity. She is forever the Mother of God. The Church is forever the Body of Christ. This is a covenant written not in mere words, but written on our hearts (see Jeremiah 31:33). This covenant of the heart is the very essence of the body of Christ, the Church.

Pope John Paul II called Mary the "unchangeable and inviolable sign of God's election."[12] That is, when Mary is chosen to be the Mother of God, God makes an irrevocable commitment to involve human beings in all that he does. In the person of Mary, all of humanity is chosen to be an eternal part of God's plan. "This election is more powerful than any experience of evil and of sin."[13] Because Mary has been elected she is freed from every stain of Original Sin. Her **Immaculate Conception** is the sign and the promise that everything which could separate us from God has become powerless. Mary's freedom from sin is the promise that one day all of God's people

Assumption of Mary—The dogma which states that the body of Mary was taken directly to heaven after her death. Mary already shares in the resurrection of the body which is promised to all the faithful.

Immaculate Conception— The dogma which states that Mary was free from the stain of Original Sin from the moment of her conception.

will be freed from the tendency toward sin and from the lasting effects of sin.

In a similar way, Mary's Assumption is the sign of the Church's eschatological hope. Mary's Assumption is the sign of all that has been accomplished through the work of Christ.[14] In her we witness the resurrection of the body and the new creation which has been promised. Mary's Assumption is the guarantee of the final resurrection of all the faithful. The Church is the community of the "now" and the "not yet." Mary makes visible the "now." In Mary, we see that the final triumph of God over evil is already accomplished, even though time has not run its full course.[15] In her assumption, Mary is oriented to the fullness of the Kingdom and every part of her has been united with God in Three Persons, Father, Son, and Holy Spirit. The Church, too, will one day be oriented to the fullness of the Kingdom and every part of the Church will be united with God. Any who look on Mary cannot help but see the glory of God which she reflects so perfectly. So too, at the end of time, every aspect of the Church will be united with God so that all who look on the Church will see the kingdom of God in its fullness.

Mary Is Also a Sign of the Church

Mary is not only the sign of the Church's hope and faith; she is also the sign of the Church's role in the world and love for the world. Mary has been called the mediatrix, which means "mediator." Christ is the sole mediator between God and humanity and has saved humanity from complete estrangement from the Father, but Mary, too, shares in the work of mediation. She has a role in making God accessible to humanity. She is the "handmaid of the Lord" and thus the model for the Church in its role as servant (see Luke 1:38). Like all the saints, Mary intercedes for the faithful and offers her assistance to them. Just as at the wedding of Cana (see John 2:1–12) she saw the need for more wine and asked Jesus to do something about it, so now she sees the needs of the faithful and makes requests to her Son on our behalf. The fact that Mary intercedes for the faithful does not distance the faithful from Christ any more than the prayers of one Christian living today and praying for another distances the person prayed for from Christ. Catholics do not approach Mary because they cannot or should not approach Christ. We bring our concerns to Mary because it is Christ's will that she and all the members of the Church share in the work of her Son. The Second Vatican Council declared:

> No creature could ever be counted along with the Incarnate Word and Redeemer; but just as the priesthood of Christ is shared in various ways both by his ministers and the faithful, and as the one goodness of God is radiated in different ways among his creatures, so also the unique mediation of the Redeemer does not exclude but rather gives rise to a

manifold cooperation which is but a sharing in this one source.

The Church does not hesitate to profess this subordinate role of Mary . . . so that encouraged by this maternal help [the faithful] may the more closely adhere to the Mediator and Redeemer.[16]

Vatican II made it very clear that all that Mary does is because of Christ. Because Christ was conceived in her, Mary was transformed into an effective image of Christ. When we cooperate with the Holy Spirit within us, we too will be transformed into effective images of Christ. Mary's role shows the power of Christ to transform and make new all of humanity.

When we, as Catholics, venerate Mary or call upon her to be our advocate, we are not distancing God from humanity. Nor, as some would claim, are we questioning the love and mercy of God or replacing it with the love and mercy of Mary. When we call upon Mary to be our advocate we are giving testimony to our belief in God's overwhelming love for humanity. We believe that God loves human beings so much that they have been allowed a share in the work of God. Mary has been given a great share in God's work because she has fully accepted the love and mercy which God has offered. We honor Mary because she has done what we are still struggling to do.

STUDY QUESTIONS

- HOW IS MARY A SIGN OF THE NEW COVENANT?
- IN WHAT WAYS IS MARY'S IMMACULATE CONCEPTION A SIGN AND PROMISE FOR THE CHURCH?
- HOW IS MARY'S ASSUMPTION A SIGN OF THE CHURCH'S ESCHATALOGICAL HOPE?
- HOW DOES MARY'S ROLE AS MEDIATOR DIFFER FROM CHRIST'S ROLE AS MEDIATOR?

JOURNAL ASSIGNMENT

- DO YOU THINK IT WOULD EVER BE POSSIBLE TO LOVE AND HONOR MARY TOO MUCH? EXPLAIN YOUR RESPONSE.

MARY IS THE MOTHER OF THE CHURCH

Mary is the Mother of Christ; therefore, she is also the Mother of the Church which Christ has established to be his own body.[17] As the Mother of the Church she has a particular role and responsibility. Just as she nurtured Jesus and helped him to grow in wisdom, so too she cooperates with Christ in caring for and guiding the Church. In a solemn profession of faith, Pope Paul VI said that Mary "carries on in heaven her maternal role with regard to the members of Christ, cooperating in the birth and development of divine life in the souls of the redeemed."

Mary's role in the Church comes indirectly from her role as the Mother of Jesus. It also

comes directly from Jesus himself. From the cross, Jesus looked on the infant Church represented by the Apostle John, (and he said to the Apostle and through him to the whole Church), "Behold your mother" (John 19:27). Mary's motherhood is a gift which Christ makes personally to the Church as a whole and to every individual.[18]

The Church is called a "Mother" because the Church follows Mary's example. The Church receives the Word of God in faith and then brings forth sons and daughters who are conceived and born of the Holy Spirit.

STUDY QUESTIONS

- HOW IS MARY THE MOTHER OF THE CHURCH?
- HOW IS THE CHURCH A MOTHER?

IN CONCLUSION

Everyone needs someone who is a good example for virtuous living. The Catholic Church offers its saints as models who can help us respond to the crises which face us and as models who can help us to live more Christian lives. A general theme of all the saints is that they were faithful in everyday things. To imitate them, we should look for God in everything we do, including mundane tasks, and in all the people we meet. We should respond to everything that life brings our way as if it were part of our ongoing dialogue with God. In this way we will develop the habit of holiness.

The communion of saints offers models for our faith and guides to help us as we reach out to the Lord. The saints in Heaven are still living members of the Church. They care deeply about us because we are a part of their community. They continue to offer help to others just as they did while they were on earth, but now the help which they offer is not determined by time, distance, the number of hours in a day, or human limitations. God gives us the grace to be holy, but accepting God's grace is difficult to do alone. The saints in Heaven offer us the support and encouragement we need to accept that grace and become truly holy.

Among the whole communion of saints Mary is preeminent. She is the perfect model of faith. Mary's faith is expressed most clearly in the words of the Magnificat:

> My soul proclaims the greatness of the Lord;
> my spirit rejoices in God my savior.
> For he has looked upon his handmaid's lowliness;
> behold, from now on will all ages call me blessed.
> The Mighty One has done great things for me,
> and holy is his name.
> His mercy is from age to age to those who fear him.
> He has shown might with his arm,
> dispersed the arrogant of mind and heart.
> He has thrown down the rulers from their thrones
> but lifted up the lowly.
> The hungry he has filled with good things;
> the rich he has sent away empty.
> He has helped Israel his servant,
> remembering his mercy,
> according to his promise to our fathers,
> to Abraham and to his descendants forever.[19]

This is the faith which Mary in turn passes on to the Church, as a mother passes on her most precious treasures to her children. Our God is a God who saves and whose Salvation begins not with the strong and the powerful, but with the poor and the humble. The Magnificat expresses the faith of the true Church, the faith which clings to God and abandons all desire to be god, the faith which uproots Original Sin.[20]

As Pope Paul VI stressed in his apostolic exhortation *Marialis Cultis*, Mary is not a timid and submissive woman, but a strong and brave woman who is willing to risk everything because she trusts and loves God.[21] Mary's role in the Church is a purely human role, in no way equal to the role of Christ. But it is a purely human role which has been transformed, as all things human will one day be transformed, by the power of Christ. Mary is the sign of a Church which will become one with Jesus and the Father, even as they are one in one another.[22] She is the sign and image of the Church which has also been called to bear God to the world. Mary is the promise that God will be born even through our humanity.

LEARN BY DOING

Read one of the following biographies of a saint or choose one of your own. Prepare an oral book report and share it with the class. Include all of the following:

- Important dates in the saint's life
- How the saint came to live a life of holiness
- Something dramatic the saint did
- Some meaningful words the saint spoke
- How the person inspired you to be a better Christian

Saint of Auschwitz: The Story of Maksymillian Kolbe, by Diana Dewar (Darton, Longman and Todd).

Story of a Soul: The Autobiography of St. Thérèse of Lisieux, by Thérèse of Lisieux (C.S. Publications).

St. Francis of Assisi, by G. K. Chesterton (Image).

Edith Stein: St. Teresa Benedicta of the Cross, by Maria Ruiz Scaperlanda (Our Sunday Visitor).

PRAYER

The Memorare

Remember, O most gracious Virgin Mary,
that never was it known
that anyone who fled to thy protection,
implored they help, or sought thy intercession,
was left unaided.
Inspired by this confidence,
I fly unto thee, O Virgin of virgins, my Mother;
to thee do I come,
before thee I stand, sinful and sorrowful.
O Mother of the Word Incarnate,
despise not my petitions,
but in thy mercy, hear and answer me.
Amen.

NOTES

1. See *Lumen Gentium*, #16.
2. "The Quality of Mercy," *Life*, July 1996, p. 10.
3. #828.
4. See *Catechism of the Catholic Church*, #958.
5. See *Lumen Gentium*, #49.
6. *Catechism of the Catholic Church*, #688.
7. Quoted by Bishop Ahern, "Thérèse, Doctor of the Church" (*Origins*: CNS documentary service, vol. 27: no. 12), p. 194.
8. See *Gaudium et Spes*, #39.
9. See *Catechism of the Catholic Church*, #946.
10. Pope Paul VI, Discourse of 21 November 1964.
11. *Lumen Gentium*, #63.
12. *Redemptoris Mater*, #11.
13. Ibid.
14. See *Redemptoris Mater*, #41.
15. Mary's Assumption and the eschatological hope of the Church go hand in hand. Mary is the sign of our hope. At the same time, the Church professes Mary's Assumption precisely because it is a fitting sign of our hope and faith in the resurrection of the body and the remaking of all creation.
16. *Lumen Gentium*, #62.
17. *Redemptoris Mater*, #5.
18. See *Redemptoris Mater*, #8.
19. Luke 1:46–55.
20. See *Redemptoris Mater*, #36.
21. See *Marialis Cultis*, 1974.
22. See John 14:20.

MARY: MODEL and MOTHER of the CHURCH

BLESSED VIRGIN MARY, WHO CAN WORTHILY REPAY YOU WITH PRAISE AND THANKS FOR HAVING RESCUED A FALLEN WORLD BY YOUR GENEROUS CONSENT

—*Saint Augustine*

TRULY OUR LADY

When we say that we believe in a Church that is "catholic" or universal, we are saying two things. First, we believe that Catholics in all parts of the world believe the same things and worship in the same way. Second, we believe in a Church which incorporates and makes room for all people and all cultures. In the celebration of the Mass, in the words of the creed, in documents like the *Catechism of the Catholic Church*, we can see the first aspect of the universal nature of the Church. In local celebrations like those that honor Mary we can often see the second.

The **veneration** of all the saints and of Mary in particular have provided Catholics from all times and places with ways of linking their own particular culture with the universal faith of the Church. In every age and in every place, Mary (and many of the other saints) has been understood to embody all that the culture considers to be ideal. Mary is often referred to as "Our Lady." Sometimes she is "Our Lady, Star of the Sea," sometimes "Our Lady of the Mountains," or "Our Lady of Fatima," or Guadalupe, or any number of other places. The emphasis is always on the fact that Mary is "one of us." In other words, she belongs here. And because she belongs here, we honor her in our own way. The May crowning, the living Rosary, and the celebration of the feast of Our Lady of Guadalupe are just a few of the ways that Catholics have found to express their faith and love for Mary in a way that is unique to their own culture. These practices also take place with respect to others saints. This chapter will trace some of the history of the Catholic practice of veneration of the saints with special attention paid to the Catholic understanding of the role of Mary.

May Queen

If you had been driving through the small Connecticut town that day and happened to pass by Holy Family High School, you would have seen quite an unusual sight: fifty-five teenagers standing solemnly in a large circle on the lawn. They were surrounded by an even larger crowd of more teenagers, teachers, and parents. At one end of the circle was a marble statue of Mary, the Blessed Mother. Someone standing near the statue was playing the flute. The circle parted at the point farthest from the statue and five more teens came forward. First, the "May Queen" dressed in a simple white gown with a tiara of flowers in her hair. She carried a gold crown resting on a silk pillow. She was followed by five attendants, each carrying a bouquet of flowers. They processed slowly until they came to the foot of the statue.

The May Queen led the Apostles' Creed. Those in attendance responded unevenly but enthusiastically. Then one of the attendants announced the first of the glorious mysteries of the Rosary—"Jesus rises from the dead"— and began to pray the Our Father. She was joined by the rest of the teenagers. As the last words of

veneration—Honor given to a person or image because that person or image mediates God (that is, makes God's presence visible and tangible). Veneration is not the same as worship or adoration. Worship and adoration belong only to God.

the prayer faded out, the girl standing to the right of the statue began the Hail Mary in a loud clear voice: "Hail Mary full of grace the Lord is with you. Blessed are you among women and blessed is the fruit of your womb Jesus." Everyone responded: "Holy Mary, Mother of God pray for us sinners now and at the hour of our death. Amen."

And so it continued around the circle until a complete decade of the Rosary was prayed, continuing on in the same way through the other glorious mysteries. At the conclusion of the fifth glorious mystery—"Mary is crowned Queen of Heaven and Earth"—the May Queen climbed the small ladder that stood behind the statue and placed the crown she had been carrying on Mary's head. After the last "Glory Be" had been proclaimed, each of the attendants placed her bouquet at the foot of the statue. Then everyone joined in singing "On This Day, O Beautiful Mother," a hymn to Mary. The May Queen and her attendants processed out. Slowly the circle dispersed. People started to laugh and talk and mingle. If you ignored the formal dress, it looked like a typical high school lunch hour on a warm spring day. The May crowning was over for another year.

Our Lady of Guadalupe

Five months earlier, if you happened to be in a small Texas border town, you would have seen another very different and yet very similar event. A large crowd gathered in the dark and cold December dawn on the grass in front of St. Matthew's Catholic Church. Some wore boots and jeans, heavy jackets, gloves, and hats. Others dressed as they would have if they were in their native Mexico: in their finest Sunday shoes and dresses or suits. They huddled close together

trying to keep warm. The door of the nearby rectory opened and out came three altar servers, one carrying a processional cross, a second carrying a large candle, and a third carrying a picture wrapped in a blue cloth. They were followed by a priest.

The priest greeted the crowd. He led prayers in Spanish and in English and lit the candle as the first server held it high. The second server raised the processional cross and the priest unveiled the painting of Our Lady of Guadalupe. The third server held the picture high. Someone began a popular Spanish song praising Mary and everyone joined in. Then the three servers and the priest led a procession into the Church.

The picture of Our Lady of Guadalupe was placed at the front of the church, with a bank of candles on the right and on the left. People came forward to place roses in a large vase in front of the picture as more songs were sung. When everyone was seated and the music had ended, the parish youth group came forward. They acted out the story of Juan Diego, the native peasant to whom the Virgin appeared near Guadalupe, Mexico, in 1531. They told how the Mother of God saw the needs of the poor and those who were discriminated against, and responded with love and compassion. The priest gave a short homily. He voiced what everyone was feeling: this was their Mother and this was the story of her love for them.

Then there were a few more songs and then everyone went over to the parish center for an impromptu concert by some Mexican mariachis. They finished in time to join in the celebration of the first Mass of the day.

ACTS OF PENANCE

The Church teaches that alongside Baptism and martyrdom, acts of penance are a way to express conversion in relation to ourselves, others, and God. The three basic forms of penance are *fasting*, *prayer*, and *almsgiving*.

Develop a penitential plan for yourself around each of these areas. For example:

Fasting

- Make a commitment to eat healthier and in appropriate quantities.
- "Give up" a certain food that you enjoy.
- Abstain each Friday from meat and meat products.
- Also: refrain from another activity that you enjoy.

Prayer

- Read and pray with an entire gospel, start to finish.
- Go to Mass during the week.
- Choose and read a complete book of spiritual reading or the life of a saint.
- Set aside at least fifteen minutes a day for solitude and prayer.

Almsgiving

- Donate extra clothing to the poor.
- Spend some time with someone who is lonely.
- Do some free yard work or babysitting for a neighbor.
- Volunteer at an community agency that serves the poor.

STUDY QUESTION

- HOW IS THE CATHOLICITY OF THE CHURCH REFLECTED IN THE WAYS THE CHURCH HONORS MARY?

JOURNAL ASSIGNMENT

- WHAT IS A UNIQUE TITLE OF "OUR LADY" THAT YOU ARE FAMILIAR WITH, PERHAPS FROM A LOCAL PARISH? WRITE A BRIEF EXPLANATION OF THE ORIGINS AND MEANING OF THIS TITLE.

GOD IS THE HOLY ONE

The early fundamental Christian understanding of holiness was the same as that of their Jewish ancestors. God is the Holy One. People or things are holy only because of their relationship with God. They are holy because God has chosen them for a special purpose, and they have been faithful to that purpose; they have been consecrated to the service of God and God has acted through them.

Jesus is the epitome of human holiness. Jesus is one with the Father—the source of all holiness. Every one of Jesus' actions on earth was both a human act and a divine act. Jesus' power is the power of holiness, the power of his divine nature, the power of God. Christians share in Jesus' power to the extent they are linked with Christ (see Matthew 19:28). For early Christians, the clearest evidence of being a **disciple** was that a person had sacrificed everything, including life, for Jesus. A **martyr** was seen as an indisputable disciple who was forevermore permanently united to Christ.

The first Christians also had strong beliefs in the power of prayer, understanding that it is the Lord who teaches, guides, consoles, and blesses them through prayer. (Recall that prayer was so central to Christianity that catechumens, who were not yet full members of the Church, were actually dismissed from the celebration of the Mass before the community began its prayers for the world.) Christians

Peter, the founder of the Church, and Paul, the Apostle to the Gentiles, were each martyred in Rome by the emperor Nero around the year 64. Peter was crucified in a public circus, hung on a cross upside down. Paul was beheaded on the outskirts of the city.

BECOMING LIKE CHRIST

Martyrdom is a process by which Christians become more like Christ. This teaching is explicit in an account of the martyrdom of Polycarp, who was burned at the stake for professing his faith in Christ. The account of his death makes connections to the Eucharist, describing how his burning corpse took on the smell of fresh bread. In part, it reports:

> The fire formed as it were an arch and, like the sail of a ship filled with wind, it surrounded the body of the martyr. And he himself in the midst appeared not like flesh being burned, but like bread in the oven, like gold and silver tried in the furnace, and we breathed the perfume of it like the smoke of incense or some other precious aromatic perfume.[1]

began to ask the martyrs—as ultimate disciples—to pray for them.

Martyrs are united to Christ in blood. Their life and death challenges and transforms the social order. As the **martyrology** (list of martyred saints) grew, the Church created a "spiritual hierarchy" which challenged the nature and the values of the established hierarchy within society. The saints provided a new set of priorities and relationships around which people could structure their lives.

Saints as Patrons

In many ways the saints in the Roman Church became the religious equivalent of a secular patron. In ancient Rome, a secular patron was a noble or wealthy person who granted favor and protection to someone in exchange for certain services. Similarly, a new Christian would choose a saint as patron and that saint would both direct and assist him or her. Christians began appealing to saints in prayers in much the same way that they would appeal to a Roman patron. Relics of saints became important tokens of a person's connection with a patron saint. It is important to note, however, that despite its similarities to the Roman practice of patronage and to some of the polytheistic cults of ancient Greece and Rome, the Christian martyrology is rooted in first century Jewish and Christian beliefs and is not simply an adaptation of pagan practices. Jews at the time of Christ venerated patriarchs, prophets, and martyrs and built monuments where they were buried. Early Christians continued this practice, honoring those whom the Jewish community honored and adding their own martyrs to the list.

The Romans were known for the practice of visiting the graves of those who had died. Christians

disciple—A follower of Christ. A disciple is someone who learns from and follows Jesus and who accepts a share of his ministry in the world.

martyr—Literally, a "witness." A martyr is someone who has been killed because of his or her faith.

martyrology—An official list of Christian saints and martyrs. The earliest martyrologies date to before the fourth century.

The *Martyrium Polycarpi* from the second century described the bones of Saint Polycarp as being like "precious stones."

PRACTICES SURROUNDING CHRISTIAN MARTYRDOM

Research and report on at least one of the following:

- how Christianity adapted and used several pagan customs involving death (e.g., relics). (See if your parish church has a saint's relic encased in its altar.)
- the martyrdom of Saint Polycarp
- Roman funeral rituals
- what is meant by martyrology (see www.newadvent.org/cathen/09741a.htm).

continued this practice, though modifying it slightly. The Romans visited a grave on the anniversary of a person's birth. The Christians visited a grave on the anniversary of the person's death, since death marked birth into Heaven. Furthermore, while in Roman practice only the immediate relatives of the deceased observed the anniversary, among Christians the entire faith community gathered at the grave.

It also became common practice to celebrate Eucharist at the tombs of the faithful, especially those who had been martyred. Christians believed that the Eucharist would join the faithful, not only to one another and to Christ, but also to their ancestors in faith. The death of the martyrs was connected with Christ's Death and thus was part of the liturgical sacrifice of the Mass. Eventually it became the custom to place the remains, or relics, of at least one of the martyrs within the altar stones in each church.

In the fourth century Augustine encouraged Christians to honor the martyrs and saints and to ask for their prayers. He also stated very explicitly that although the priest offered the sacrifice of the Mass in memory of the martyrs, and although the martyrs were named in the liturgical prayers, the sacrifice was offered to God alone. This means that martyrs are worthy of honor because they are People of God.

STUDY QUESTIONS

- ACCORDING TO A JEWISH AND CHRISTIAN UNDERSTANDING, HOW ARE PEOPLE HOLY?
- WHAT WAS THE STRONGEST EXAMPLE OF DISCIPLESHIP FOR EARLY CHRISTIANS ?
- HOW DID THE CHURCH BECOME THE EQUIVALENT OF A SECULAR PATRON?
- ACCORDING TO SAINT AUGUSTINE, TO WHOM DID THE PRIEST OFFER THE SACRIFICE OF THE MASS? WHAT DID THIS TEACH ABOUT THE MEANING OF MARTYRS?

JOURNAL ASSIGNMENT

- SHARE YOUR MEMORIES OF A FUNERAL YOU HAVE ATTENDED OR A TIME YOU VISITED THE GRAVESITE OF A DECEASED FAMILY MEMBER OR FRIEND. WHAT DID YOU DO? HOW DID YOU FEEL?

THE ROOTS OF CANONIZATION

In the early Church, martyrologies were calendars with the names of the martyrs, where the martyrdom took place, and some brief information about the martyr's life. There were local martyrologies, such as one in Rome composed in the fourth century. Martyrs on these lists were recognized by popular acclaim. Also, certain confessors who had undergone torture without wavering in their faith, and ascetics and virgins who had given up all worldly pleasures because of their faith were also honored. Between the sixth and tenth centuries the list of martyrs grew rapidly. Some of these martyrologies began to keep detailed records of the martyrs' lives.

As martyrdom diminished, more and more Christians who had died a martyr's death began to be venerated. In these cases, miracles began to be regarded as the true proof of a person's holiness. In the western Church, one of the miracles commonly attributed to saints was incorruption of the body (the body did not decay after death). The relics of the saints came to be regarded as things which not only connected a person to the saint, but as things which had healing power in and of themselves. During the Middle Ages, relics were divided and shared with many local churches. Because of this, the veneration of many saints spread beyond their own regions and countries.

As more and more saints were named and as veneration of these saints extended to larger regions, there was a growing concern with the need for regulation of who could be called "saint." Christians needed to be assured they were not honoring or asking intercession of fictional characters. It was left to the bishops of a particular area to recognize a saint as worthy of veneration. Bishops received biographies of the lives and "miracles" of those who had become known for their holiness and whose graves had become sites where numerous people visited to request intercessory prayers. If the bishop approved the biography, the body would be exhumed and moved to an altar, and a feast day for the saint would be assigned on the calendar within the diocese or province.

Over time the pope became increasingly involved in the approval of a person's sainthood. At first he was asked to give approval for a solemn transfer of the relics and the introduction of the saint for a particular area. Eventually it was reserved to the pope to formally declare that a person was raised to full honors of the altar, meaning that the person is in Heaven and worthy of veneration as a saint. This declaration is known as **canonization**. The first saint to be officially canonized was St. Ulrich of Augsburg, by Pope John XV in 933.

canonization—The process by which the Church declares that a particular member of the faithful has practiced heroic virtue in his or her life, has been faithful to God's grace, and is now fully united with God in Heaven.

A ten-person committee researched and effected the Roman Martyrology issued by Pope Gregory XIII in 1584. The current revised martyrology contains over six thousand names of saints and blesseds honored by the Church.

It was not until the twelfth century that canonization became the norm. From the thirteenth century on, a specific process of canonization has been followed. The pope appoints commissions to systematically examine and evaluate the virtuous nature of the person's life and the particular miracles being proposed. The investigations have utilized the scientific knowledge and procedures of each period of history. The person must have two attested miracles prior to his or her canonization as evidence of worthiness for sainthood.

Challenges and Clarifications

The Church's veneration of the saints was harshly criticized and severely challenged by the Protestant reformers. The reformers pointed out abuses and frauds—such as the placing of inauthentic relics at altars and the creation of inaccurate legends around the biographies of saints—which had arisen from the practice of honoring saints. They were not content with the Catholic Church's efforts to limit these abuses. However, when some reformers tried to destroy the relics in the chapel of Frederic the Wise in Wittenburg, Martin Luther demanded that they stop. Similarly, Erasmus distanced himself from the actions of his followers in Switzerland who were intent on smashing statues and other images.

The Council of Trent reacted to the Protestant condemnations by strongly supporting the doctrine of the communion of saints and by encouraging and even emphasizing the veneration of saints. Veneration of saints came to dominate many aspects of Catholic spirituality.

In 1969 the Roman Church calendar was reformed. There was a concern that the veneration of the saints had begun to clutter Catholic worship and that some of the more important seasons and celebrations were being ignored. A decision was made to select some saints for universal veneration on a particular day and others for particular local veneration. Saints were deliberately selected from every century in history, from a variety of countries, and representing a variety of different apostolates. Saints whose historicity was questionable were eliminated. The liturgical year with an identifiable cycle rather than a series of disconnected days was given new emphasis.

STUDY QUESTIONS

- EXPLAIN THE GENESIS OF MARTYROLOGIES.
- AS MARTYRDOM DIMINISHED, WHAT BECAME THE CRITERIA FOR SAINTHOOD?
- SUMMARIZE THE PROCESS OF CANONIZATION.
- WHAT WERE PROTESTANT OBJECTIONS TO THE VENERATION OF SAINTS? HOW DID THE CHURCH ANSWER THESE OBJECTIONS?

JOURNAL ASSIGNMENT

- WHAT KIND OF LIFE WOULD YOU HAVE TO LIVE IN ORDER TO BE RECOGNIZED BY THE CHURCH AS A SAINT? BE SPECIFIC.

CANONIZATION PROCESS

Canonization is the process whereby the Church officially declares that certain holy persons are saints. This process includes a detailed examination of a person's life, teachings, and works. The Church also investigates whether miracles took place through this person's intercession.

After successful scrutiny, the process proceeds to beatification, which allows the faithful to call the person "Blessed."

Finally, after the validation of further miracles, the cause of the holy person proceeds to canonization, the official enrollment in the list (canon) of saints. Today, the pope oversees the process of canonization.

- Who is the most recent saint canonized?
- When was your patron saint canonized?
- Who is a saint with a feastday on your day of birth?

MARY'S UNIQUE PLACE IN THE COMMUNION OF SAINTS

Mary's special role in the Church is based in Scripture. Elizabeth's address to Mary as "the mother of my Lord" (Luke 1:43) is the basis of Mary's title Theotokos (Mother of God). The angel's greeting to Mary in Luke 1:28 ("Hail, favored one!") is further evidence from Scripture of the importance of Mary's role. In the Vulgate (the Latin translation of the Bible), "Hail, favored one!" is translated as "Hail, full of grace!" If Mary is full of grace, then she is able to dispense grace.[2] Mary can share what she herself has been given.

Also, in the early Church Mary was understood as a necessary link between the old covenant and the New Covenant. Because of this, theologians combed the Old Testament for references or foreshadowings of Mary.[3] In the second century, St. Irenaeus paralleled the disobedience of Eve with the obedience of Mary, just as Paul had made the same comparison between Adam and Christ. Mary came to be described as the "New Eve." Whereas Eve had succumbed to the tempter, Mary triumphed over him.

THE BLACK MADONNA

A popular icon of Mary through the centuries has been the "Black Madonna." This image of Mary came from Song of Songs 1:5 in the Old Testament. Mary was understood to be the woman described in the poem: "I am as dark—but lovely." This image of Mary as a black woman has tremendous appeal to people of non-Anglo descent. It has become the symbol of the woman whom God has given to the universal Church.

By the third century, devotion to Mary was quite strong. Christian graves that were decorated with images of the saints and martyrs interceding on behalf of the deceased usually

The canonization rites for new saints take place at St. Peter's Basilica in Rome.

featured Mary in a place of honor. A prayer fragment dating from the third or fourth century underscores Mary's role as a powerful intercessor. It reads: "Mother of God [hear] my supplications: suffer us not [to be] in adversity but deliver us from danger."[4] In the fourth century, what the Arians erroneously taught about Christ (that he was the greatest of all creatures), the Church correctly taught about Mary. Also, St. Athanasisus, the bishop of Alexandria, taught that Christ became human that humans might become divine (based on 2 Peter 1:4). Mary and all the saints were understood to have modeled this teaching.

Teachings About Mary

By the beginning of the fifth century, a prayer to Mary was part of the liturgy in at least some local churches. At the Council of Ephesus (431) Mary was officially declared to be Theotokos, the one who gave birth to the one who is God. At this time, the faithful developed many other titles and images of Mary and her role in the life of the Church. One of these was the title Mediatrix. Mary was described as the "mediator of God's saving presence in history."[5] If it had not been for her "yes," Jesus would not have been born.

When the concept of Mary as mediatrix came to the West in the Middle Ages, Mary came to be seen as the one through whom humans could safely approach Christ. Because Christ's divinity and his role as judge were so strongly emphasized during that time, the faithful often lost sight of Jesus' humanity and his overwhelming love and mercy. Christ seemed unapproachable, so the faithful turned to the completely human, "sweet and gentle" Mary. St. Bernard of Clairvaux (d. 1153) gave voice to the popular theology of his day when he said that while Christ might be thought of as the floodwaters of grace, Mary was the

aqueduct which brought those waters to us in manageable amounts. Over the next several centuries, devotion to Mary continued to grow and many Catholics came to believe that the best way to approach Jesus was through Mary. The role of Mary became one of the most prominent topics in Catholic theology.

In the early part of the twentieth century through recent times, a movement developed with the goal to have Mary's role as Mediatrix declared dogma. When Vatican II was called there were many in the Church (including 382 bishops[6]) who wanted the Council to make a strong statement supporting Mary's role as mediator. There was also a petition brought from the Mariological Society of America to have Mary defined as co-redemptrix.

The discussion during Vatican II over what should and what should not be said about Mary was often heated. All agreed that Jesus is the only mediator between God and humanity and that Mary participated in the saving work of Christ. But there was a great deal of disagreement over what language was appropriate for defining Mary's participation. Finally, the Council decided that:

- its teachings about Mary would be part of its teachings about the Church;
- the title of Mediatrix would be placed alongside several other titles, such as intercessor and advocate, because it is only one expression of many which can be used to explain Mary's role;
- Christ's role as the sole mediator would be strongly emphasized. Mary's mediation is a participation in Christ's mediation and does not exist independently;
- it would be clear that Mary's role is "subordinate" to Christ and not alongside of, parallel to, or in addition to Christ.

The Council of Ephesus was convened to address Nestorianism, the false belief that there were two separate persons in Christ.

STUDY QUESTIONS

- HOW IS MARY'S SPECIAL ROLE IN THE CHURCH BASED IN SCRIPTURE?
- HOW DID MARY AND ALL THE SAINTS MODEL ST. ATHANASISUS'S TEACHING?
- WHAT DID VATICAN II DECIDE REGARDING MARY'S ROLE AS MEDIATOR?

JOURNAL ASSIGNMENT

- OF THE MANY TITLES FOR MARY, WHICH ARE YOU MOST DRAWN TO? WHY?

SCRIPTURAL ROSARY

For each of the mysteries of the Rosary—joyful, luminous, sorrowful, and glorious—read each Scripture passage. Find a photo (e.g. your own personal collection or from a magazine) or draw a sketch that represents each of the four sets of mysteries. Then go back and pray one or more mysteries of the Rosary while reading the Scripture and meditating on the photos or drawings.

First Joyful Mystery	The Annunciation	Read Luke 1:38
Second Joyful Mystery	The Visitation	Read Luke 1:42
Third Joyful Mystery	The Birth of Jesus	Read John 1:14
Fourth Joyful Mystery	Presentation of Jesus in the Temple	Read Luke 2:34
Fifth Joyful Mystery	The Finding of Jesus in the Temple	Read Luke 2:49
First Luminous Mystery	The Baptism of Christ	Read Mark 1:9–11
Second Luminous Mystery	The Wedding at Cana	Read John 2:5
Third Luminous Mystery	Proclamation of the Kingdom of God	Read Mark 1:15
Fourth Luminous Mystery	The Transfiguration	Read Matthew 17:5
Fifth Luminous Mystery	The Institution of the Eucharist	Read Matthew 26:29
First Sorrowful Mystery	The Agony in the Garden	Read Luke 22:42
Second Sorrowful Mystery	The Scourging at the Pillar	Read Isaiah 53:5
Third Sorrowful Mystery	The Crowning with Thorns	Read Matthew 27:29
Fourth Sorrowful Mystery	The Carrying of the Cross	Read Luke 9:23
Fifth Sorrowful Mystery	The Crucifixion	Read Luke 23:34
First Glorious Mystery	The Resurrection of Jesus	Read John 20:18
Second Glorious Mystery	The Ascension of Jesus into Heaven	Read Acts 1:11
Third Glorious Mystery	The Descent of the Holy Spirit	Read Acts 2:4
Fourth Glorious Mystery	The Assumption of Mary into Heaven	Read Revelation 12:1
Fifth Glorious Mystery	The Coronation of Mary as Queen	Read Psalm 136:1

THE THEOTOKOS

Gregory of Nazianzus, a Church Father, wrote the following words about Mary the Mother of God in 382 or 383:

> If anyone does not believe that holy Mary is Mother of God [the Theotokos], he is severed from the Godhead. If anyone should assert that he passed through the Virgin as through a channel, and that he was not at once divinely and humanly formed in her (divinely, because without the intervention of a man; humanly, because in accordance with the laws of gestation), he is in like manner Godless. If any assert that the manhood was formed and afterward it was clothed with the Godhead, he too is to be condemned.[7]

seen in them and praised and worshipped through them.

In the early Church, saints were recognized by popular acclaim. As more and more Christians were acclaimed saints, and as the veneration of particular saints spread to places far from the area where the saint had been known, there was a growing concern with regulation. It became important that a saint not be venerated until he or she had been officially approved. In early years this was done by the local bishops. In years since, approval is given by the pope.

Within the communion of saints Mary is given the place of highest honor. She is described as the New Eve. In the fifth century Mary was officially named the Theotokos, or Mother of God. Christians began to understand that she was a powerful advocate for the faithful and one who was able to join the faithful in their struggle against sin.

Over the years Mary has come to be known by many titles. One of these is the "Mediatrix," the mediator of God's saving presence in history. Without Mary's "yes" to the angel's request that she give birth to a Son, Jesus would not have been born. In all of her roles, Mary is able to act because she has allowed Christ to act through her. She does nothing on her own. Everything that Mary and all the saints do is because of and through their relationship with Christ, the one true mediator between God and humanity.

IN CONCLUSION

The Catholic understanding of the communion of saints in general and the role of Mary in particular has developed through history in response to the needs of the faithful. The veneration of Our Lady and all of the saints has allowed Catholics to worship God in ways that are particularly appropriate to their own culture.

The practice of honoring or venerating the saints and of asking for their prayers dates back to the first centuries of Christianity. So too does the particular honor afforded to the Virgin Mary. From the earliest days Mary and the other saints were understood to be so fully united to Christ that Christ could be

LEARN BY DOING

Research and write a report on the North American Martyrs who endured years of suffering while trying to bring the Catholic faith to the Native Americans of the northeast. The eight North American Martyrs are:

- St. René Goupil
- St. Isaac Jogues
- St. John de Lalande
- St. Anthony Daniel
- St. John de Brebeuf
- St. Gabriel Lalemant
- St. Charles Garnier
- St. Noel Chabanel

See www.catholicism.org/pages/cjjangri.htm for a synopsis of their mission in North America.

PRAYER

Lord, I freely yield all my freedom to you.
Take my memory, my intellect and my entire will.
You have given me anything I am or have;
I give it all back to you to stand under your will alone.
Your love and your grace are enough for me;
I shall ask for nothing more.

—Saint Ignatius Loyola

NOTES

1. Martyrdom of Polycarp, xiv and xv.
2. See Jaroslave Pelikan, p. 13.
3. In order to understand the development of the Church's understanding of Mary it is necessary to understand methods of biblical study which were used in the early Church. It was standard practice to read the Jewish Scripture as a foreshadowing of the Christian Scripture, and to find in them allegories and typologies which would illuminate the Christian Scripture. Thus the great Flood of Jewish Scriptures was understood as a reference to Christian Baptism. The suffering servant mentioned in Isaiah 53 was understood as Jesus. The early Church fathers used this method to deepen their understanding of Mary. They began with the New Testament statement that she was highly favored by God and then looked for Old Testament references that likewise applied.
4. Hilda Graef, *Mary: A History of Doctrine and Devotion*, Vol. 1 (New York: Sheed and Ward, 1963), p. 48.
5. Elizabeth A. Johnson, C.S.J., "Mary as Mediatrix," *The One Mediator, the Saints and Mary: Lutherans and Catholics in Dialogue VIII,* Anderson, et al. eds. (Minneapolis: Augsburg Fortress, 1992), p. 311.
6. See Johnson, p. 318.
7. "Mary as Mediatrix," *To Cledonius against Apollinaris* (Epistle 101).

UNIT EIGHT

THE CHURCH IS...

ECCLESIOLOGY

Ecclesiology means "study of the Church." The root of the word, from the Greek *ekklesia*, literally means "to call out." The Church is called out of worldly society to gather and proclaim the Gospel of Jesus Christ. The first part of this unit reviews several aspects and models of Church.

The Church Is a Necessary Part of Faith

From a Catholic perspective, Christian faith cannot be separated from a relationship with the Church, because the Church is the focal point of God's continuing presence in history. When Jesus was conceived, God became incarnate in human history. When Jesus walked the earth, God was visible and tangible. Following Jesus' Death, Resurrection, and Ascension into Heaven, God has chosen to remain visible and tangible through the Church. God has established the Church to be the Body of Christ on earth, forever joined to Christ, the head of the body, who is now with the Father in Heaven.

As previoiusly noted, the word church has its roots in the Greek word ekklesia, which means "to call out of." We are members of the Church because we have been called out of the world to be something new, to be the Body of Christ. We have been called to act together on behalf of and in the name of God. To the extent that we have answered this call and are truly united to Christ and able to act in his name, we are the Church; we are the Body of Christ on earth. Not one of us acting on our own could answer God's call and be Christ's Body. We need each other. Faith needs the Church in order to bear fruit and make God's presence accessible to the world.

It is important to remember that although the Church is the body of Christ, not everything that is done in the name of the Church is the will of Christ. Jesus has chosen to continue his work on earth through the Church. The people of the Church are his eyes, mouth, hands, and feet—but they are also still people. They still can and do sin; and when they do sin, they obscure, rather than reveal, Christ.

As Catholics we believe that there are certain things which guarantee that, despite our sins, we can never completely lose our identity as Christ's Body. We believe that the Holy Spirit is always present in the Church. We see Mary as the permanent sign of God's promise that the Spirit and the Church will never be separated. We believe that God always acts through us in the sacraments. In the celebration of the sacraments, we always act in God's name, even if we fail in other ways. We believe that God is always speaking in the dogmas which the community has accepted. In her dogmas, the Church community speaks the truth from God which the world needs to hear.

The Four Marks of the Church

"We believe in one, holy, catholic, and apostolic church." These words became an official part of the creed at the First Council of Constantinople in 381. As Catholics, we believe that the nature of the Church is not something that can be changed to suit the wishes of different people in different times. The nature of the Church is an expression of the nature of God. The Church must be one, holy, catholic, and apostolic or she cannot be the Body which reveals the nature of God.

ONE

The Church is one because the Trinity is one. The true Church cannot be divided against herself any more than the Father, Son, and Holy Spirit can be divided against one another. Unity is part of the nature of God, and the restoration of unity was part of Christ's mission on earth. Unless our life as a Church is characterized by our solidarity with one another, we have distanced ourselves from Christ and from his mission.

The formal structures of the Catholic Church underscore the importance of unity and help us to make our unity visible in our day to day lives. As Catholics, we are united by a common profession of faith, a common worship in the sacraments, and a common ethical framework. We are also united through apostolic succession. These things which unite us cross all cultural, philosophical, and political boundaries. They do not eliminate our diversity, but allow us to be one even in our diversity.

HOLY

The Church is holy because she is the body of Christ. The Church is also holy because the Holy Spirit dwells within her. To be holy means to be "set apart." All holiness has its root in God who alone is truly holy. God is the only one who is completely apart from the rest of creation, because God is the only one who is uncreated. The Church is holy—set apart from the rest of creation—because of her intimate connection with God.

God does not set things and people apart for no reason. Everything that is made holy is given a special purpose. The members of the Church have been given a purpose and a task which is different from those around them. We have been chosen by God to make his presence and his holiness visible through our lives.

Three aspects of Catholic faith and practice are particularly important in giving form to holiness. These are: the sacraments; the evangelical counsels of poverty, chastity, and obedience, and the witness of those who live by them; and the moral teachings of the Church.

CATHOLIC

The word catholic means "universal," "in totality," or "in keeping with the whole." To say that the Church is catholic is to say that the totality of the Body of Christ is present in the Church. There is nothing of God that is lacking in Christ, and there is nothing that is lacking in Christ's Body, the Church. There is nothing that is good that exists outside of the Church but not within the Church. To say that the Church is catholic is also to say that she is for all people. The Church has a role everywhere and in every situation. Finally, to say that the Church is catholic is to say that what the Church teaches is based upon the whole of Revelation: all of Scripture, the teaching of all of the Apostles, and the understanding and witness of Christians from all times and all places.

APOSTOLIC

Apostolic means "having been sent." The Church is apostolic because she has been sent into the world by Christ. Unless she remains apostolic and unless she remembers and is faithful to both her mission and the one who gave that mission, she cannot remain the Church. The Catholic Church remains faithful to her apostolic nature in three ways: 1) by recognizing that she is built upon the foundation of the Apostles; 2) by adhering to the foundation laid by the Apostles and written down in Scripture and by faithfully interpreting, living, and teaching what the

Apostles taught; 3) by accepting the continued guidance of the Apostles through their successors, particularly through Peter's successor, the pope.

The pope is the permanent and visible sign and foundation of the Church's unity. The institution of the papacy stands for a unity which supersedes national ties. Each diocese or local church is led by its own bishop. The bishop has the responsibility for adapting the Church's teachings to the particular culture and particular needs of his own diocese. Yet, when these necessary and lawful adaptations are made, it is important that the unity of the Church be maintained. The fidelity of each individual bishop, and of all the bishops together, to the pope (the bishop of Rome) helps maintain this unity. Catholics believe that without the pope, the Church would be severely threatened by competing national and cultural issues.

The Church Is Mystery

The Church is a mystery of faith that can never be fully expressed from any single viewpoint. The Church holds apparent opposites together. The Church is a joining of the human and the divine and she is essentially both. The Church is the focal point of the Kingdom's presence, but she is also the place in which we confront our own sinfulness which distances us from the Kingdom.

From the creation of the world, God has intended human beings to share in divine life. In the Church this sharing finally becomes a reality. The call to be the Church is the high point of God's invitation to us to enter into a dialogue of friendship. It is in the Church that our unity with God is complete. In the Church we are joined with God to such an extent that we are able to be God's own presence to the world. The miracle of the Church is that despite all our failings and weaknesses, God loves us so much and places so much trust in us that he is willing to act and to be known through us.

As members of the Church, God calls us to live and act as the Body of Christ in the world. We are to be Christ to the world. At the same time, we, as the Church, are to point people beyond the Church to Jesus Christ who is independent of the Church. The Church is the Body of Christ, but it is not Christ. This mystery has been explained using the analogy of marriage. According to Scripture, when two people are married they become one flesh. In their marriage covenant they do not lose their individual selves, but those individual selves become completely one in both will and action. In choosing the

Church to be his Body on earth, Christ has entered a marriage covenant with her. Christ has surrendered himself to the Church, allowing the Church to express his will to the world. The Church, in turn, must surrender herself to Christ. In order to be Christ's body on earth, the Church must make his will her own. The Church is not identical to Christ, and yet the Church is the body of Christ, because she has been joined to Christ in a true marriage covenant.

Because the Church is completely one with Christ, the Church is necessary for

Salvation. Jesus is necessary for salvation and Jesus chooses to be present on earth in the Church. Without Jesus, humanity would never have been able to overcome the barrier of sin which separated us from God. Without the Church, Jesus would not continue to be present on earth uniting humanity with God. All who recognize that the Church is the Body of Christ are called to be a part of that Church. If any reject the Church, knowing that it is the Body of Christ, they are rejecting the Salvation which Christ offers. Nevertheless, the Father can lead those who know neither Jesus nor the Church to unity with him.

Unchanging Elements Within the Church

According to a Catholic understanding of the Church, there are three things within the Church which cannot and will not change. The Church has a permanent body of dogma, a permanent ethic, and a permanent constitution.

Permanent Constitution

The "constitution" of the Church refers to her basic form and makeup. Catholics believe that the hierarchical structure of the Catholic Church is an essential part of the Church's identity. According to Catholic theology, Jesus established a permanent structure when he chose Twelve Apostles and promised to remain with them until the end of time.

The presence of the hierarchy or Magisterium maintains the continuity between the faith of today and the faith of the past. The Magisterium is the authentic interpreter of Scripture and of the doctrinal and moral teachings which have been passed from generation to generation. The Magisterium is not the Church, but it is essential to the Church. The Church is the whole Body of Christ—laity, religious, and clergy. No single group can claim to be the Church. Nonetheless, each has a particular function which it performs on behalf of the whole. The Magisterium will always be the authoritative voice concerning what is genuinely Catholic at any particular point in time.

The presence of the Magisterium in the Catholic Church has served both Catholic and non-Catholic Christians. Christians of all denominations are aware of, and find it necessary to respond to, the pronouncements of the Catholic Magisterium on many significant issues which might otherwise have gone unchallenged in the dominant culture. Furthermore, the Magisterium of the Catholic Church has ensured the preservation of certain beliefs and practices (such as the importance of ritual and an appreciation for Mary's role in Salvation History) which many Protestant churches had ignored for a time but are now reclaiming.

Permanent Ethic

Fundamental to Catholicism is the belief that God is unchanging, and therefore there are certain things that have always been and will always be opposed to God. There are certain moral teachings that the Magisterium will never have the right to change, no matter how much the world changes. This is because these moral teachings are essential corollaries of our understanding of the God who was revealed in Jesus.

Permanent Body of Dogma

Catholic theology teaches that there is a permanent body of dogma within the Church. There are certain absolute truths which must be accepted because they have been revealed to us by Jesus and will never change. Again, however, it is important to recognize that our understanding and expressions of these truths continues to develop over time.

The Church Is the People of God

God did not create human beings to live in isolation, and God does not choose to save us as disconnected individuals. God created us to be one, and God offers us Salvation as a people who are one. Salvation History is an account of God's invitation to return the world to the way it was before the sin of Adam and Eve. The Jews of the Old Testament had a command identity rooted in the fact that they were children of Abraham and Sarah and had shared the experience of the Exodus. The Law supported that common identity and held the community together, so that together they could do what none could do alone: obey the will of God and avoid the bondage of sin. The Jews believed that God had saved them as a people and formed a covenant relationship with them as a people.

The early Christians inherited this sense of a communal identity and a covenant relationship with God. The Judeo-Christian understanding of community is an integral part of Christian faith. So it is that we believe that there is no such thing as an action which affects only one person, or even only those people who are directly involved. The doctrines of Original Sin and of salvation through Christ both depend on the existence of a communal identity.

All people throughout history have shared in the communal identity of Adam and Eve, an identity which has been permanently marred by sin. Until Jesus, this was the only identity which people could share. Jesus, however, offers us a new communal identity. Whereas the communal identity shared with Adam and Eve inclines us toward division, Jesus offers an identity which inclines us toward unity. The Church is the new People of God. All who are baptized are reborn as members of this people.

Their potential is now determined by the grace of Christ rather than by the sin of Adam and Eve.

The People of God are the people in whom God's Spirit dwells; they are one because the Spirit within them is one. All people are called to be members of the People of God; none are to be excluded. The individual personalities within the People of God have not been given to us as a means of separating us, but rather as a means of uniting us more completely. Our differences are complementary.

As the People of God, the Church is a chosen race, a royal people, a kingdom of priests, and a nation of prophets.

The Church Is Teacher

Through the centuries the Church has encountered God and passed on a knowledge and understanding of the truth through Scripture, Tradition, and formal teachings called dogmas. In this way the Church fulfills its role as teacher of the faith.

Scripture

Scripture is normative for all religious truth and all Church teachings. Scripture is true in its essence. Properly understood, Scripture can never give us a false understanding of God or of the world and can never lead us to do things that God does not desire. The key words here are "properly understood." The Catholic Church teaches that Scripture must always be interpreted. Although it is the Word of God, it is the Word of God expressed in human words. It has been shaped and limited by human weaknesses and limitations. Catholic faith is not a faith "of the book." It is a living faith. Because we are different people from our ancestors, God does not speak to us in exactly the same way that he spoke to them, even though he speaks through the same Scripture. Each generation must interpret Scripture in light of its own knowledge and experience. This interpretation must take place first and foremost within the Church, which is the living Body of Christ, and it must be guided by the Magisterium, who maintain continuity with Christ and his Apostles. We cannot accept an interpretation of Scripture that would overturn or radically alter the essential elements of the faith which the Church has held through the centuries.

Tradition

The Tradition of the Church refers to all of the ways in which the Church has passed on her understanding of God's Revelation: creeds, doctrines, governmental structure, liturgies, and patterns of prayer and service. These are the things that truly make our faith apostolic. They create continuity between the Apostles' understanding of Jesus and our own.

Church fathers Irenaeus, Clement of Alexandria, Tertullian, and Origen established the framework for Catholic theology and doctrine. Irenaeus established the fact that theology and doctrine would be related to both our spiritual and our physical lives. He also outlined an understanding of history which allowed for the development of doctrine over time. Clement laid the foundations for a permanent relationship between theology and reason. Tertullian made Roman legal rhetoric a part of Christian theology. He also established the right of the Church to determine the boundaries for the legitimate interpretation of Scripture. Origen laid out rules for legitimate Christian speculation. He made it clear that there are certain things which Christians must simply accept and other things about which they are free to argue and speculate.

Dogma

Those beliefs which are essential to Christian faith are called dogmas. Dogmas are truths which we believe have been specifically revealed by God. Dogmas form the framework for a Catholic Christian world view. They shape our understanding of good and bad. They shape our attitude toward suffering and setbacks in life. They help us determine what we should try to change and what we should leave to God.

There is no list of Catholic dogmas; however, there are certain dogmas which are universally recognized as essential. These are, first and foremost, the beliefs which are stated in the Apostles' Creed and in the Nicene Creed. Catholics believe that it is not possible to remain a member of the Church and reject any of these beliefs. The act of rejecting a dogma cannot help but separate a person from the community whose very existence is a response to the Revelation expressed in the Church's dogmas.

The acceptance of Church dogma is essential to a complete faith and the deepest possible relationship with God. Not everything that the Church teaches, however, is dogma. There are many Church teachings which have not been directly revealed by God, but which reflect our best understanding of that which has been revealed. These are part of the Church's doctrine, but not her dogma. Doctrines have the official approval of the Magisterium. They establish the boundaries for preaching and catechesis within a particular place and time. They help us to understand the implications of dogma and may develop or change in response to a changing world.

Dogmas are infallible and irreformable. They cannot change in their essence. The way that they are expressed can change, however. Every statement of dogma is limited by the concerns which motivated its expression— concerns which may no longer be relevant at a later time—and by the context of human knowledge at the time the dogma was framed. As the context of human knowledge changes, the way the Church expresses dogmatic truths may change, even though the truths themselves have not changed. (The Church's response to Galileo provides an example of this.)

Each time the Magisterium declares that a particular statement or concept is part of the Deposit of Faith, Catholics are obliged to accept the assertion as true. It is a basic tenet of Catholicism that every dogmatic statement protects an essential truth which is in danger of being lost.

The Church Is Sacrament

The Church is both the sign that God is acting in the world and the means by which God does act in the world. For this reason we say that the Church is a sacrament. The unity of the Church is the sign and seed of the unity that will one day belong to the whole world. In the Church, even enemies pray the same prayers, share in the same Eucharist, and form part of the same Body. In the Church, even hatred and death are not strong enough to cause permanent division.

Catholics believe that God interacts with us through the physical world. Our God who is incomprehensible chooses to be present to us through things which we can comprehend. Our experience of God who is outside of history is mediated by people, events, and things which are rooted in history. The people, events, and things which always make God present to us are known as sacraments. Jesus is the first sacrament because, in Jesus, God is fully present to us. Every other sacrament derives its nature from the nature of Christ. Each sacrament is a sign which points beyond itself to Jesus, and through Jesus to the Trinity. Each sacrament is also an instrument through which Jesus continues his work on earth.

The Church, particularly the liturgical life of the Church, is the focal point of God's action in the world. Every element of the liturgical life of the Church directs us towards the world that God has envisioned for us. The Church is the place to which we bring the activity of the world so that it may be reshaped by the mystery of Christ and then returned to the world as something new. In the liturgy of the Church, all of the basic elements of our life together take on new meaning. The liturgy makes us participants in a world in which all that is wrong has been righted.

As Catholics, we believe that God acts through our liturgy so that when we do something ritually, we receive the grace to do that same thing in our everyday lives. The fact that we are participants in a world where wrong has been righted, gives us the grace to right the wrongs in our everyday world. We have been ritually reconciled: we are able to reconcile with one another. We have been ritually cleansed: we have the grace we need to turn away from sin. We have been ritually united: we have the grace we need to live in true unity. As we participate in the sacramental life of the Church, we are enabled to participate in the work of God in the world.

Jesus is the focal point of God's activity in history. The Church is the focal point of Jesus' continuing presence on earth, and the Eucharist is the focal point of the Church's work. All of the other sacraments of the Church are ordered to the Eucharist as their end. They help us to understand more fully what it means to be the Body of Christ and they give us the grace to live out every aspect of our lives as the Body of Christ. The sacraments ensure that the Church as the Body of Christ does the work that Christ would do in the world. The sacraments make us a community which frees the captives, strengthens the lame, feeds the hungry, heals the sick, brings forgiveness to sinners, serves the poor, and unites those who were separated.

Baptism and Confirmation

From the time of the early Church, Baptism has been linked with the descent of the Holy Spirit and the permanent marking of a person by God. In Baptism, we believe that an individual receives the free gift of God's grace and is given a new identity, an identity which allows him or her to choose the way of Christ (the way of unity) rather than the way of Adam and Eve (the path of division). Confirmation seals and completes Baptism. Baptism and Confirmation reveal the Church as a community which frees the captives and brings God's presence into the world.

Eucharist

From the time of the early Church, the Eucharist has been viewed as a sacred meal which transcends time and forms and transforms a people, and as a sacrifice which alters our relationship with God. The Eucharist is a sacrifice, but it is not a sacrifice which binds God to us. It is a sacrifice which binds us to God. The Eucharist reveals the Church as a community which feeds the hungry.

The other sacraments of the Church are Penance, the Anointing of the Sick, Holy Orders, and Matrimony.

The Church Is Servant

Catholics do not believe that service is a nice addition to our faith. Rather, service is an intrinsic part of our faith. We are called to be the body of Christ on earth. We can only be the body of Christ by doing what Christ did, by caring for the poor and the outcasts. If we fail to do that, we have failed to say "yes" to God. We are only able to serve as Christ served because, in making us members of his body—the Church—Christ himself has given us the grace to do so.

The Church is the primary instrument of God's grace on earth. The grace to serve others out of genuine love, and the grace to surrender one's own power for the benefit of another, belong first to the Church. This means that the Church is called to serve and is capable of serving in a way that is different from any other group or organization. The Church's mission to care for the downtrodden is distinct from the mission of any political or social authority. No matter what government agencies or other organizations may be doing to help people, the Church has a responsibility for making Christ known by reaching out in his name to those who are most in need.

We believe that each baptized person has an obligation to cooperate with the Church's service and to participate in that service according to his or her unique gifts and talents. Service is not something that belongs to special interest groups within the Church. It is an intrinsic part of living as a member of the Body of Christ.

Our faith teaches that even if particular churches, particular members of the laity or the clergy, or even particular popes pursue power rather than service, the Church as a whole, animated by the grace and love of Christ, never will and never could abandon the poor. There will always be those who will serve the poor because of their commitment to Christ and to his Body the Church. Both our faith and our history teach us that it is the efforts of those who serve, and not the bids for power, which will prevail and form the identity of the Church over time.

As we answer the call to serve as Christ served, there are several principles which should guide us both as individuals and as communities. The first of these is a recognition of the dignity of every human being. Every human person has been created in the image and likeness of God, and that image and likeness can never be obliterated, no matter what a person does or does not do. There are certain rights that flow from our basic human dignity and therefore belong to all people. All people have a right to be respected and seen as autonomous individuals with free choice. All people also have a right to be valued simply because they are human and not because of what they can or cannot do.

A second principle of Catholic social teaching is the universal destination of goods. The universal destination of goods asks that all necessary products are fairly distributed. God gave the earth to all people, and all people have a right to use the riches of the earth to provide for themselves and their families. The Church does recognize the right to private property, but this right is secondary to the universal destination of goods. The universal destination of all goods is a reminder that we were not created to live in isolation or to be saved in isolation. Both our physical and our spiritual well-being are linked to the well-being of others. If we wish to serve as Christ served we must commit ourselves to working for a world in which the earth's resources are distributed justly and all people are able to prosper.

A third major principle which governs Catholic social doctrine is that of the common good. The common good refers to everything which allows all people, both individually and in groups, to be fulfilled more fully and more easily. In order to promote the common good, we must respect individuals and we must also work for the good of communities. If we wish to serve as Christ served, we must consider the implications which our choices have on the common good; first on the common good of those in our immediate sphere, and then on the common good of people throughout the world. Two other principles in Catholic social teaching derive from the first three. They are solidarity and subsidarity.

Social justice in the Catholic Church today emphasizes a "preferential option for the poor." We believe that God offers special care to those in need. As the Body of Christ we must do the same. In everything we do, we must give special consideration to the poor and to the effect that our actions will have on them. In particular, we believe that the Church must work to insure that the poor receive special consideration from the state in defense of their rights. It is part of Catholic teaching that societies have an obligation to protect the poor against exploitation and to ensure that they receive adequate wages. In the eyes of the Church, not all economic systems are equal and not all political decisions are acceptable, even if they have been approved by the majority.

The Church Is a Communion of Saints

The Church canonizes those people who practiced heroic virtue throughout their lives. We hold them up as examples and guides in the life of faith. The communion of saints, however, does not just include those who have been canonized. The communion of saints is the Church, and it includes all of the members of the Church, living and dead. A saint is a person through whom and in whom God is visible. Each one of us is a saint to the extent that we make God's love visible and tangible in our lives.

Christians in the early Church believed that in the world to come, Jesus' disciples would live with him and share in his power. Martyrs were seen as indisputable disciples who had given everything for Jesus and were therefore permanently united to him. Because of their unity with Jesus, their prayers were believed to be particularly powerful. After Christ's Resurrection, death no longer had any power to break the community. Because of this the living and the dead can pray for and help each other, and it seemed logical to the early Christians to ask the martyrs for their prayers.

As time passed, the Church's sense of and belief in the unity between the Church on earth and the Church in heaven grew stronger and deeper. The Catholic Church is one which cannot be divided by death. The saints in Heaven are fully united with Christ. Because they are also still united with us, they unite us more fully to Christ.

Saints themselves are signs of hope. The fact that we maintain our connection with them even though they have died is an indication of our belief that death has been defeated in Jesus. Our belief in the value and intercession of saints is also a sign of our faith in the resurrection. Finally, our communion with the saints in heaven is a testimony to our belief that the Church is the Body of Christ. All of the members of the Church from all ages and places are part of the Body of Christ. When we are in communion with the other members of the Church, we are in communion with Christ. Our communion with Christ would be incomplete if our communion with the Church did not include both the Church on earth and the Church in Heaven.

The saints in heaven provide an example for those of us who are struggling to be saints on earth. But they are more than just distant examples; they are our friends and our companions; they share what we do. They are "of us," and what they do, they share with us.

Just as we share in the pride when our team wins, even if we ourselves have not played, so we share in the blessing of the saints even if we would not have merited that blessing on our own.

Mary: Model and Mother of the Church

Mary is known by many titles. Most rich and profound of all the titles is that Mary is Mother of God. The fact that God, who is infinite and omnipotent, chose to be dependent upon a finite and limited human being is startling. In allowing Mary to be the Mother of God, God chose to bind himself permanently to humanity. God not only became human, God relied upon a human to do so. Mary is the sign of God's willingness to accept human beings as partners for eternity. Mary is the sign of God's willingness to share his authority with humanity. Mary is the sign of all that God has given to the Church.

Mary is the model of the Church. The Church is a communion of saints and Mary is the model saint. She shows us what it means to imitate Christ in everything. Mary's total dependence on God and her complete orientation to God remind the Church of her own mission. Mary's faithfulness allowed Jesus to be conceived, first in her heart and then in her flesh. If we follow her example of faithfulness, Christ will also be born in our hearts and he will act in the world through us. If we follow Mary's example of faithfulness, we will truly be the Church.

Mary's faithfulness to God involved a self-emptying. She remained faithful to God's will for her regardless of the risks, regardless of how much or how little she understood, and regardless of how much pain it caused. Mary loved her Son so much that his sacrifice of love became her own sacrifice. She did not run from her pain, but instead joined it to the sacrifice of Christ. In this way she shared in the redeeming work of Christ.

Mary is the model of faith in her commitment to Christ, in her faithfulness, in her self-emptying and in her love. She is everything that the Church strives to be, and she is the sign that the Church will eventually achieve what it is striving for. Like Jesus and the Church, Mary is a sacrament. She is the symbol and instrument of God's presence with humanity.

Mary's immaculate conception is the sign and the promise that everything which could separate humanity from God has become powerless. Mary's freedom from sin is the promise that one day all of God's people will be freed from the tendency toward sin and from the lasting effects of sin. Mary's Assumption into heaven is also a sign of the Church's hope. Her Assumption is the guarantee of the final resurrection of all the faithful. The Church is the community of the "now" and the "not yet." In Mary, we have a glimpse of our own future.

Mary is not only the sign of the Church's hope and faith, she is also the sign of the Church's role in the world and love for the world. Christ is the sole mediator between God and humanity, but Mary shares in the work of mediation. She has a role in making God accessible to humanity. In this too she is an example for the Church. Like Mary, the Church must carry Christ into the world, and like Mary, the Church must help those who do not know Christ to bring their concerns to him.

As Catholics we believe that Mary is not only the Mother of Jesus and the model for the Church: she is also the Mother of the Church. She is the Mother of the Church because she is the Mother of Christ and the Church is Christ's body. As the Mother of the Church, Mary has a particular role and responsibility. Just as she nurtured Jesus and helped him to grow in wisdom, so too she cooperates with Christ in caring for and guiding the Church.

REVIEW QUESTIONS

Ecclesiology

1. Why can't Christian faith be separated from a relationship with the Church?
2. What is the meaning of the word "church"?
3. Why won't the Church ever lose her identity as Christ's body?
4. Why is the nature of the Church unchangeable?
5. Name the four marks of the Church.
6. How is the Church one?
7. Which aspects of Catholic faith and practice give form to the Church's holiness?
8. Give two examples of the Church's catholicity.
10. In what ways does the Church remain faithful to her apostolic nature?
11. Explain why the pope is important in the life of the Church.
12. How is the Church a mystery?
13. What is the Church's role in Salvation History?
14. Why is the Church called the "bride of Christ"?
15. What does it mean to say that the Church is necessary for salvation?
16. What are the three elements within the Church that do not change?
17. What is the constitution of the Church?
18. Explain the role of the Magisterium.
19. What is meant by the Church's permanent ethic?
20. Define dogma and explain why Catholics must accept dogma.
21. What are some characteristics of the Church's communal identity?
22. What Catholic doctrines only make sense from a perspective of communal identity?
23. How does the Church interpret Scripture?
24. What is meant by the "Tradition" of the Church?
25. Why can't dogma change?
26. How is the Church a sacrament?
27. What do Catholics believe about the power of liturgy?
28. What is the relationship of the Eucharist to the other sacraments?
29. Explain what each of the seven sacraments reveals about the nature of the Church.
30. How is the Church servant?
31. Which principles underlie Catholic social teaching?
32. Define the Church's understanding of the "preferential option for the poor."
33. How is the Church a communion of saints?
34. Define saint.
35. Why does the Church ask for the intercession of the saints?
36. How do the saints in Heaven serve the Church on earth?
37. What are some implications of the Church's belief that Mary is the Mother of God?
38. Why is Mary the model of the Church?
39. Why is Mary the Mother of the Church?
40. How did Mary's faithfulness to God involve a self-emptying?

HISTORY

The following section summarizes some of the key models and themes of the Church from the preceding section as traced through major periods in Church history.

The Biblical Church

Religious syncretism was a very real problem at the time of Christ. The Greeks, and later the Romans, made a concerted effort to convince all of the different peoples under their rule that the gods of the varying religions were really all the same. The Jewish community as a whole rejected this syncretism; however, they rejected it in a variety of different ways. The various Jewish sects—Pharisees, Sadduccees, Essenes, and Zealots—each had a different opinion regarding which aspects of Judaism were essential and unchangeable, and which could or should be altered in response to their current situation. When the Church first came into existence, the majority of Christians, Jews, and outsiders did not view it as a new religion, but rather as one more sect of Judaism that was closely related to the Pharisees.

One of the first significant questions to face the new Church was whether or not Gentiles could become Christians. As soon as that question was answered in the affirmative, the next question was which elements of Judaism were essential for Gentile Christians to observe. The Council of Jerusalem decided Gentile converts to Christianity did not have to keep the entire Jewish Law, but only those specific laws which had been given to Noah, including marriage laws.

To first century Christians, the Second Coming of Jesus was expected at any time. Christians believed that when Jesus did return a new Heaven and a new earth would be created, with the old passing away. This new Heaven and new earth would grow from the seeds of the Kingdom which were already present in the Church.

Christians were committed to serving the poor and reaching out to those in need because that was what Jesus had done. Those who served the poor were part of the new creation. Those who neglected the poor were part of what was to pass away. The first-century Christians ignored all class distinctions because they believed that in Christ these distinctions had become irrelevant.

The Church Under Roman Rule

From the very beginning, Baptism was the sign of a person's entry into the Church. Baptism was linked to the descent of the Holy Spirit and the permanent marking of the newly baptized as God's own. Baptism in the early Church was understood as a sign of one's willingness to accept death out of faithfulness to God. This was not a merely theoretical willingness, since death was frequently a real possibility.

Persecution and prejudice characterized the Roman response to the Christian Church for the first three centuries. Christianity was seen as anti-social or even barbaric, intellectually wanting, and dangerous to society. At times it was disdained but tolerated by those in power. At other times serious attempts were made to eliminate the Christian faith altogether. Yet in most instances, the prejudice and persecution strengthened rather than weakened the Christian identity and commitment, and the courage of those Christians who courageously accepted martyrdom rather than renounce their faith attracted many to the Church. St. Stephen, who was stoned to death, and the Apostle St. James, who was beheaded, were two of the first Christian martyrs.

The initial spread of Christianity occurred primarily because of the witness of the martyrs and the enthusiasm of new

Christians who shared their faith in homes and in the marketplaces. The first wave of new Christians were primarily the poor and the less educated, to whom the Christian faith offered a new sense of dignity. Only gradually did the Church attract the wealthy and better-educated members of society. Much of the early theology of the Church developed as some of these more educated Christians tried to make Christianity comprehensible and acceptable to their non-Christian peers.

It was not only the poor and the uneducated who found new hope and a new self-respect in the Christian Church. Women, too, found opportunities in the Church which had never existed for them elsewhere. Widows had an established role as leaders in the early Church. Their voluntary celibacy, poverty, and life of service in response to the Gospel were precursors to monastic life.

During the first three centuries of Christianity, several important controversies arose which were to shape the Church for all time. In the middle of the second century, Marcion and the gnostics presented a significant challenge to Christianity in denying the goodness of the created order and claiming to have a special knowledge about Jesus. In response, the Church developed the official canon of Scripture (the list of those books and writings which were to be considered divinely inspired and authoritative). The Church also developed the basic outline of the Apostles' Creed and insisted upon the necessity of apostolic succession to safeguard the true teaching of Jesus.

Another difficult issue was what to do about lapsed Christians—those who had given in to threats and renounced or pretended to renounce their Christian faith in the face of persecution. Several significant questions were raised. First, was it possible for those who had truly accepted Christ to sin? And, if it was possible, what was the appropriate response to this sin? Second, if the one who sinned was a priest or a bishop, were those sacraments which he administered following his sin still valid? The answer to both the first and second question was determined to be "yes." Christians who sinned could be readmitted to the Christian community, once following a period of public repentance. If they sinned again the community should pray for them, but the decision to forgive or not to forgive must be God's. If the one who sinned was a priest or a bishop, those sacraments which were received from him in good faith were still valid, otherwise Christians would be in constant doubt as to whether or not they had been validly baptized or had received properly consecrated bread and wine at Eucharist.

Christianity as the State Religion

In the early part of the fourth century, on the eve of his battle with Maxentius outside Rome, the Emperor Constantine ordered his soldiers to place the Chi-Rho (a symbol comprised of the first two letters in the word Christ) on their shields. When he won the battle, many saw the win as proof of the power of the Christian God. Following that battle, the Edict of Milan was issued, which prohibited the persecution of Christians. Constantine's public acceptance of the Christian faith marked a turning point in Christian history.

Suddenly the Church became a stepping stone for a person to achieve power and prestige. The appointment of Church leaders now also needed the approval of the state. Priests and bishops, who up until this point had been chosen by the people for their holiness and faithfulness, were increasingly chosen from wealthy and powerful families. Nepotism (the appointing of family members to positions) and simony (the buying and selling of Church positions) became problems that were to plague the Church for more than a thousand years.

Constantine tried to use the Church to unify the empire. This began the blending of theology and politics. In fact, the first ecumenical council (a gathering of bishops from all different areas) was actually called by Constantine because he wanted to end the Arian controversy (the argument over whether or not Jesus was truly divine) which was threatening to tear the empire apart. Constantine declared that whatever the council decided was to be the only acceptable belief and that those who took contrary positions would be deprived of the privileges and the protection which the state gave to Christian leaders. Theological arguments came to involve not only Church leaders and theologians, but also secular leaders who had the power to back one side or the other.

After Christianity was legalized, Church membership increased dramatically. The long and careful process of Christian initiation and the mentoring of new Christians which had been an important part of Church life up until this point was no longer practical. Many people became Christians without having a clear understanding of the faith, and without making any particular commitment to change their lifestyle. Furthermore, infant Baptism became the norm as the focus in the understanding of Baptism became the removal of Original Sin.

While the Church had originally refused to baptize anyone engaged in professions which were connected with idol worship, violence, or the shedding of blood, when Christianity became a state religion, all professions which contributed to the well-being of the state became acceptable. A Christianized Roman empire was seen by many as the culmination of God's plans; therefore anything that was beneficial to the empire was also considered acceptable to God. In the fourth century, St. Augustine articulated the "just-war" theory. He claimed that states had both a right and a responsibility to use force in certain circumstances and under certain conditions.

The Church structure began to resemble a secular government. A clear hierarchy, laws, and common codes of belief and behavior were established. The Church herself became a place where the power and prestige of society flourished. Concern for the poor no longer dominated Christian thought and action. Many Christians felt that it was enough for the majority of the laity to maintain a certain inner detachment from the things of this world.

Not surprisingly, there were many Christians who saw Constantine's acceptance of Christianity as a step backward. Hundreds of Christians fled to the desert to get away from the distractions of society and live a life of isolation and deprivation which would answer Jesus' charge of discipleship that one should give up everything in order to follow him.

Although those who went to the desert were seeking isolation, they were not forgotten by those who remained in the world. Many Christians knew about them and went out to the desert seeking their wisdom and guidance. These desert monastics were seen as the ideal witnesses to Christianity. Gradually a dual system of Christian holiness came to be accepted. This became even more pronounced as communal monasticism developed and more and more men and women sought the "ideal" Christian witness.

The Barbarian Invasions and the Germanization of Christianity

From the fifth to the eighth centuries, a series of invasions swept the Roman empire. The majority of the conquerors converted to Christianity because they saw it as a sign of and a means to civilization. The role of the papacy became increasingly important as an instrument of stability and authority in a crumbling society. Monasteries were also signs and sources of stability. The witness of those living in monastic communities was particularly influential in the conversion of the "barbarians."

St. Benedict is generally considered to be the father of western monasticism. His monastic rule was built around prayer and physical labor, and emphasized strict discipline without unnecessary harshness. Benedictine monasticism has strongly influenced Catholic spirituality.

St. Boniface is usually credited with the Christian conversion of much of the Germanic lands. The Germanic people were a tribal people and their conversion was generally a tribal act. When a leader embraced Christianity, so did all of his followers. Boniface moved many people to accept Christianity by his persuasive speaking and powerful personal witness. He also established a strong and stable hierarchy within the Germanic lands which helped to preserve the essentials of the faith. Within the German Church, priests and bishops were given the status of civil leaders. Bishops were seen as princes of the Church. When a priest or bishop was ordained they received certain powers and were given a certain authority. Because of this, the appointment of priests and bishops became even more political.

The Church was increasingly seen as the sign and source of stability in the midst of chaos. In fact, faith became an acceptable weapon to use against chaos. In the eighth and early ninth centuries, Charlemagne used Christianity to defeat his enemies. He offered them a choice between dying by the sword and Baptism. His act was seen as commendable, since the choice of Baptism was seen as being one that saved a person from Hell.

The Middle Ages

Gradually, the Church came to the conclusion that she had a duty and a responsibility to force all people to accept Christianity. In 1095 the First Crusade was called; it was designed to unite Christians and retake the holy land from Muslim control. Also, the Church became increasingly concerned with the errors of those who were not in the Church or not in complete agreement with the Church. There was a growing sense that membership within the Catholic Church was what entitled a person to basic human rights.

As the Church became more involved in the secular world and caught up in secular struggles for power and authority, corruption ran rampant. The Church of the latter Middle Ages was characterized both by the blatant sins of many of her leaders and by the loud cries for reform and the genuine efforts to draw people back to the message of the Gospel.

The separation of the Orthodox Church from the Roman Catholic Church (the East-West Schism) and the Great Western Schism— the period of history in which there were two and then three popes at the same time—were sources of tremendous scandal to the faithful. On the other hand, the Church was blessed by the powerful witness of many saints during this era. People like St. Francis of Assisi, St. Clare of Assisi, St. Thomas Aquinas, and St. Catherine of Siena constantly called the Church back to the teachings of Christ.

The latter Middle Ages was also a period of tremendous growth in the Church in the Americas and in Africa. Catholic missionaries had the most success when they honored and respected the culture, language, and tradition of the native peoples. Their teachings took root and lasted even after the missionaries left a particular area. The Catholic Church was only able to be truly universal when she came to understand that Christianity could be expressed in ways other than from a European mindset.

Death and sickness were a constant companion to the Middle Ages. The bubonic plague struck with great force throughout the

European continent. Arising from this situation, the Sacrament of Penance came to dominate much of a Catholic's experience. The faithful were primarily concerned with preparing themselves for death. The emphasis on penance and securing a favorable judgment made it easy for certain abuses to creep into the life of the Church: including the practice of the buying and selling of indulgences. Payment for sins came to be viewed in the same terms as payment of fines in a human court. It didn't matter who paid or why they paid as long as the proper payment was received.

The Protestant Reformation and the Council of Trent

In 1517, Martin Luther nailed his ninety-five theses to the door of the cathedral in Wittenburg, Germany, and the Protestant reformation was officially underway. The reformers wanted to correct some of the abuses in Catholicism, including the exploitation of the poor through the selling of indulgences, and the problem of uneducated clergy who had little knowledge of or interest in the faith and who used their positions to gain personal power. The reformers also challenged many significant elements of Catholic theology and practice, including the Church's insistence that only those in the hierarchy had the authority to interpret Scripture correctly; the Catholic teaching regarding sin and justification (in particular the Sacrament of Penance); the Church's understanding of the Eucharist; the authority of the hierarchy; the role of Mary and the saints in popular piety; and the Church's relationship with the state.

The Council of Trent (1545–1563) responded to the challenges of the reformers by formalizing the Catholic position on all of these issues. The Council:

- reiterated the essential nature of hierarchy and ordained ministry, rooting an understanding of all of the sacraments in the context of ordination and apostolic succession. At the same time, the council responded to the concerns about the inadequate training of clergy. The council standardized and required seminary education.

- stressed the intimate connection between Scripture and Magisterium, saying there is no such thing as uninterpreted Scripture. The Council also stated that the correct interpretation of Scripture must be in line with the interpretation which has been handed on from Jesus through the Apostles and their successors.

- agreed with the reformers that people are saved because of the grace of God and the sacrifice of Jesus; the bishops insisted, however, that personal faith is not the first step toward Salvation. Rather, the acceptance of God's grace in Baptism is the first step toward salvation. The council named Baptism as the sacrament of faith. Baptism, like the other six sacraments of the Church, is efficacious, meaning God works through it. A person's behavior does not determine the power of the sacrament, but it does determine the degree to which a sacrament is able to take root in his or her life. We are not saved by our good works; we are saved by the grace of God. Nonetheless, without our good works the grace of God will not take root in our lives, because even in offering us grace God does not take away our free will.

- insisted that it is possible for those who are united with Christ to keep the commandments. A Christian who breaks the commandments is deliberately rejecting God and loses the grace which he or she has already received in Baptism. This grace can only be regained if it is given again by

God. Therefore, the Sacrament of Penance is necessary.

- declared that the veneration of Mary and the saints was an important part of Christian piety.
- called for the standardization of Catholic worship.

The Second Vatican Council and the Church in the Modern World

The Catholic Church was not stagnant from the time of the Council of Trent until Pope John XXIII convened the Second Vatican Council in 1961. In fact, many of the obvious changes which the Vatican II enacted had been developing in the Church for many years prior. Nonetheless, Vatican II marked an enormous shift in the image which the Church presented to the world and in the average Catholic's understanding of what it meant to be a member of the Church.

The Second Vatican Council used the language of "the People of God" to talk about the Church. While other councils had focused on the role of the clergy when speaking about the Church's mission, Vatican II talked about the role of all of the members of the Church—laity, religious, and clergy. All of the members of the Church have a share in the mission of the Church. The laity and religious are called to bring the Church to the world. The clergy are called to support, guide, and coordinate the efforts of the laity and religious. Many religious and some laity work full time jobs for the Church.

The Council acknowledged the right of other Christian denominations to call themselves Christian and encouraged true ecumenical dialogue in the hope that one day all Christians might be one. The council also proclaimed the right of all people to make their own religious choices. Even if Catholics know the "truth," we have no right to force others to accept it. Furthermore, the Council said that Catholics should not be afraid to acknowledge the truth that is present in other faith traditions.

The Catholic Church has not abandoned her teachings regarding the possibility of a "just war" under certain circumstances. In the past several decades, however, the Church has increasingly questioned whether or not a "just war" is possible in the age of modern warfare. The Church has also been very critical of the modern arms race, which it views as one of the leading contributors to world poverty.

Since the late nineteenth century, the Church has increasingly turned its attention to issues of social justice. Care for the poor is now seen as both a demand of love and a requirement of justice. Over the past few centuries, Catholics have been called repeatedly to examine their own lifestyles and the structures which they are a part of, and to ask how their lives impact the poor of the world. Catholics are reminded that God has a preferential love for the poor and so should we.

Beginning with the Second Vatican Council, the Church has recommitted itself to being an effective sign of God's love and presence in the world. In order for the Church to be an effective sign in the world, the sacraments needed to be effective signs within the Church. Vatican II called for a reform and renewal of the sacramental life of the Church so that Catholics would better understand what it was that they were called to be, and would be better prepared to receive the sacramental grace which they needed in order to carry out their mission in the world.

REVIEW QUESTIONS

History

1. What is religious syncretism and how did the Jewish community respond to it?
2. Name some significant characteristics of the first-century Church.
3. Why were Christians persecuted in the first and second centuries?
4. Explain Christianity's growth, even as it was illegal.
5. How did the early Church's response to her challenges shape Christianity for all time?
6. Summarize the incident that led to the legalization of Christianity.
7. Name some ways Christianity was different after it became legal.
8. Explain the phenomenon of desert monasticism.
9. Explain the Church's role during the time of barbarian invasions.
10. How is St. Benedict a central figure in the development of monasticism?
11. Who was St. Boniface and what did he do?
12. In what ways was Christianity influenced by the Germanic tribes?
13. What tension characterized the Church of the Middle Ages?
14. Explain the causes of the East-West Schism and the Great Western Schism.
15. What aspect of faith and Christian practice dominated the Church of the Middle Ages?
16. Why did the Sacrament of Penance take on greater emphasis in the Middle Ages?
17. Summarize some of the reforms sought by Luther and other Protestant reformers.
18. Name the key elements of the Church's response as voiced by the Council of Trent.
19. How was the Second Vatican Council truly an ecumenical council?
20. What were some significant results of the Second Vatican Council for Church life?

EPILOGUE: AN OLD STORY

There was a great holy man who was revered by everyone in his village. Whenever his people were threatened by any form of disaster, he would go out to a sacred place, light a special ceremonial fire, and pray a special prayer. The calamity would always pass.

Many years later, one of the holy man's disciples had become the spiritual leader of the village. He did not know the location of the sacred place. But whenever danger threatened the people, he would go out into the wilderness, light the ceremonial fire, and pray the prayer which he had learned from his teacher, and danger would be averted.

Years later, still another disciple became the spiritual leader of the community. He did not know the sacred place, and he did not know how to light the ceremonial fire, but he did know the prayer. Whenever there was a serious problem facing his people, he would go outside of the village and say the sacred prayer. The problem would be overcome.

Eventually, a disciple of this third man became the spiritual leader. He did not know the sacred place. He did not know how to light the ceremonial fire. He did not even know the prayer. Whenever his people were in trouble, he would go into his study, close the door and say, "God, I do not know the sacred place, the sacred fire, or the sacred prayer, but I remember the story. I beg you to remember with me, and to be faithful now, just as you have always been." And the trouble would always pass.

The history of our faith is part of our faith. Our history teaches us that God has always been faithful and God will always be faithful. It is our history which allows us to see God acting through us. It is our history that allows us to understand what it means to be the Church, to be the body of Christ, to be the tangible presence of God on earth. When we know our history we can find the courage to go forward in spite of our fears and in spite of our failures, because even fears and failures have never stopped God.

A. BELIEFS

Who Is Catholic?

A summary of what it means to be a Catholic includes the following points. A Catholic . . .

★ is a Christian who belongs to a family of faith that shares Jesus' vision and responds to his presence in our midst.

★ loves each member of his or her family of faith and uses his or her unique talents to contribute to it in a positive way.

★ believes in God, who is our loving Father.

★ acknowledges the divinity of Jesus Christ, God's Son, our Lord and Savior.

★ believes in the Holy Spirit and the Spirit's powerful presence in the Church and in the world.

★ uses the many gifts of the Spirit, including the gift of faith that enables us to accept Jesus into his or her life; the gift of hope that helps us to trust the Lord and his word; and the gift of charity that empowers us to love as Christ has loved us.

★ attempts to live in harmony with Jesus' teaching by loving God above all things; by loving one's neighbor as oneself; by forgiving enemies; and by showing special care to the poor, lonely, and the outcast.

★ works for peace and justice, thus helping the Lord promote the spread of his reign on earth as it is in heaven.

★ celebrates the Paschal Mystery by living a sacramental life.

★ recognizes the need for forgiveness through the celebration of the Sacrament of Penance.

★ greatly values the Eucharist as a special sign of God's nourishing love, a way to encounter the living Lord Jesus and, therefore, fully participates in Mass every Sunday and holy day of obligation

★ prays because regular prayer deepens one's friendship with the Lord.

★ cherishes the Bible, the Word of God, and reads it regularly.

★ acknowledges the role of the Christ-appointed official teachers in the Church whose role it is to teach, to sanctify, and to govern.

★ seeks guidance from the Magisterium in forming one's conscience on moral issues.

★ serves others by imitating Jesus who washed the feet of his disciples and commanded us to do the same.

★ has a universal vision that is open to all people and to truth in Jesus Christ.

★ courageously proclaims the Gospel, thus publicly acknowledging Jesus Christ and his Church, even if this leads to ridicule and suffering.

★ has special devotion to Mary—the Mother of God and the Mother of the Church—and esteems the saints as models of how to live the Christian life.

★ is profoundly respectful of the dignity of all human beings and promotes human rights from "womb to tomb," taking special care to protect helpless unborn human life.

This list could go on. What would you add? But never forget the essentials: A Catholic belongs to Jesus Christ; to his Body, the Church; and to the world that God created and loves. A Catholic must celebrate the Good News he or she is privileged to know by proclaiming it in word and deed:

God so loved the world that he gave his only Son, so that everyone who believes in him might not perish but might have eternal life (Jn 3:16).

Apostles' Creed

....

I believe in God,
the Father almighty,
Creator of heaven and earth,
and in Jesus Christ, his only Son, our Lord,
who was conceived by the Holy Spirit,
born of the Virgin Mary,
suffered under Pontius Pilate,
was crucified, died and was buried;
he descended into hell;
on the third day he rose again from the dead;
he ascended into heaven,
and is seated at the right hand of God the
     Father almighty;
from there he will come to judge the living
     and the dead.

I believe in the Holy Spirit,
the holy catholic Church,
the communion of saints,
the forgiveness of sins,
the resurrection of the body,
and life everlasting. Amen.

Nicene Creed

....

I believe in one God,
the Father almighty,
maker of heaven and earth,
of all things visible and invisible.

I believe in one Lord Jesus Christ,
the Only Begotten Son of God,
born of the Father before all ages.
God from God, Light from Light,
true God from true God,
begotten, not made, consubstantial with the
     Father;
through him all things were made.
For us men and for our salvation
he came down from heaven,
and by the Holy Spirit was incarnate of the
     Virgin Mary,
and became man.

For our sake he was crucified under Pontius Pilate,
he suffered death and was buried,
and rose again on the third day
in accordance with the Scriptures.
He ascended into heaven
and is seated at the right hand of the Father.
He will come again in glory
to judge the living and the dead
and his kingdom will have no end.

I believe in the Holy Spirit, the Lord, the giver of life,
who proceeds from the Father and the Son,
who with the Father and the Son is adored
     and glorified,
who has spoken through the prophets.

I believe in one, holy, catholic, and apostolic
     Church.
I confess one Baptism for the forgiveness of sins
and I look forward to the resurrection of the dead
and the life of the world to come. Amen.

Gifts of the Holy Spirit

....

1. Wisdom
2. Understanding
3. Counsel
4. Fortitude
5. Knowledge
6. Piety
7. Fear of the Lord

Fruits of the Holy Spirit

....

1. Charity
2. Joy
3. Peace
4. Patience
5. Kindness
6. Goodness
7. Generosity
8. Gentleness
9. Faithfulness
10. Modesty
11. Self-control
12. Chastity

The Symbol of Chalcedon

Following therefore the holy Fathers, we unanimously teach to confess one and the same Son, our Lord Jesus Christ, the same perfect in divinity and perfect in humanity, the same truly God and truly man composed of rational soul and body, the same one in being *(homoousios)* with the Father as to the divinity and one in being with us as to the humanity, like unto us in all things but sin (cf. Heb 4:15). The same was begotten from the Father before the ages as to the divinity and in the later days for us and our salvation was born as to his humanity from Mary the Virgin Mother of God.

We confess that one and the same Lord Jesus Christ, the only-begotten Son, must be acknowledged in two natures, without confusion or change, without division or separation. The distinction between the natures was never abolished by their union but rather the character proper to each of the two natures was preserved as they came together in one person *(prosôpon)* and one hypostasis. He is not split or divided into two persons, but he is one and the same only-begotten, God the Word, the Lord Jesus Christ, as formerly the prophets and later Jesus Christ himself have taught us about him and as has been handed down to us by the Symbol of the Fathers.

From the General Council of Chalcedon (451)

B. GOD AND JESUS CHRIST

Attributes of God

St. Thomas Aquinas named nine attributes that tell us some things about God's nature. They are:

1. *God is eternal.* He has no beginning and no end. Or, to put it another way, God always was, always is, and always will be.

2. *God is unique.* God is the designer of a one and only world. Even the people he creates are one of a kind.

3. *God is infinite and omnipotent.* This reminds us of a lesson we learned early in life: God sees everything. There are no limits to God. Omnipotence is a word that refers to God's supreme power and authority over all of creation.

4. *God is omnipresent.* God is not limited to space. He is everywhere. You can never be away from God.

5. *God contains all things.* All of creation is under God's care and jurisdiction.

6. *God is immutable.* God does not evolve. God does not change. God is the same God now as he always was and always will be.

7. *God is pure spirit.* Though God has been described with human attributes, God is not a material creation. God's image cannot be made. God is a pure spirit who cannot be divided into parts. God is simple, but complex.

8. *God is alive.* We believe in a living God, a God who acts in the lives of people. Most concretely, he came to this world in the incarnate form of Jesus Christ.

9. *God is holy.* God is pure goodness. God is pure love.

The Holy Trinity

The Trinity is the mystery of one God in three persons—Father, Son, and Holy Spirit. The mystery is impossible for human minds to understand. Some of the Church dogmas, or beliefs, can help:

The Trinity is One. There are not three Gods, but one God in three persons. Each one of them—Father, Son, and Holy Spirit—is God whole and entire.

The three persons are distinct from one another. For example, the Father is not the Son, nor is the Son the Holy Spirit. Rather, the Father is Creator, the Son is begotten of the Father, and the Holy Spirit proceeds from the Father and Son.

The divine persons are related to one another. Though they are related to one another, the three persons have one nature or substance.

St. John Damascus used two analogies to describe the doctrine of the Blessed Trinity.

Think of the Father as a root,
of the Son as a branch,
and of the Spirit as a fruit,
for the substance of these is one.

The Father is a sun
with the Son as rays
and the Holy Spirit as heat.

Read the *Catechism of the Catholic Church* (232–260) on the Holy Trinity.

Faith in One God

There are several implications for those who love God and believe in him with their entire heart and soul (see *CCC* 222–227):

★ It means knowing God's greatness and majesty.

★ It means living in thanksgiving.

★ It means knowing the unity and dignity of all people.

★ It means making good use of created things.

★ It means trust God in every circumstance.

Famous Quotations about Jesus Christ

*C*hrist did submit himself unto the elements, unto cold and heat, hunger and thirst . . .concealing his power and despoiling himself thereof in the likeness of man, in order that he might teach us weak and wretched mortals with what patience we ought to bear tribulation.

Blessed Angela of Foligno

*C*hrist with me, Christ before me
Christ behind me, Christ in me,
Christ beneath me, Christ above me,
Christ on my right, Christ on my left,
Christ where I lie, Christ where I sit,
Christ where I arise,
Christ in the heart of everyone who
    thinks of me,
Christ in the mouth of everyone who
    speaks of me,
Christ in every eye that sees me,
Christ in every ear that hears me,
Salvation is of the Lord,
Salvation is of Christ,
May your salvation, Lord be ever
    with us.

from the breastplate of St. Patrick

Oh, if all were to know how beautiful Jesus is, how amiable he is! They would all die of love.

St. Gemma Galgani

About Jesus Christ and the Church, I simply know they're just one thing, and we should not complicate the matter.

St. Joan of Arc

Judaism's Belief in One God

Like Catholics, Jews are monotheistic, that is, they believe in one God. Jews believe that God reveals himself in the Torah, through the prophets, in the life of the Jewish people, and through the history of the Jews. The key event of Jewish history is the Exodus, when God freed the Jewish nation from slavery in Egypt. This pivotal event is recounted every year during the seven-day festival known as Passover, celebrated around the time of Easter.

Jews believe that the covenant God established with Abraham and the Sinai covenant require Israel to adore and serve God always, and to observe his Law. In turn, they believe God will remain faithful to them and treat the members of the Jewish nation as special.

Jews believe that God is eternal, almighty, all-knowing, present everywhere, and loving of his creation. In prayer, God is addressed as *Adonai* (Lord). Jews use God's name respectfully and avoid saying the name revealed to Moses—Yahweh—because it is so holy. Jewish faith is summed up in a prayer pious Jews recite every day, the *Shema:*

> Hear, O Israel! The LORD is our God, the LORD alone! Therefore, you shall love the LORD, your God, with all your heart, and with all your soul, and with all your strength (Dt 6:4–5).

Jews differ on how God will fulfill his covenant with them, how God's kingdom will be established, and on the nature of the final judgment. For example, some Jews believe the concept of a Messiah refers to an individual person; others think of it in terms of the community of God's People or the development of historical events; still others believe God himself will intervene directly into human history.

The Catholic Church encourages utmost respect for the Jewish faith. For example, at the Second Vatican Council, Church fathers wrote:

> This sacred Synod . . . recalls the spiritual bond linking the people of the New Covenant with Abraham's stock. . . .

> The Church, therefore, cannot forget that she received the revelation of the Old Testament through the people whom God in his inexpressible mercy deigned to establish the Ancient Covenant. . . .

> The Church recalls too that from the Jewish people sprang the apostles, her foundation stones and pillars, as well as most of the early disciples who proclaimed Christ to the world. . . .

> The Jews still remain most dear to God because of their fathers, for He does not repent of the gifts He makes nor of the calls He issues (*Declaration on the Relationship of the Church to Non-Christian Religions,* No. 4).

C. SCRIPTURE AND TRADITION

Canon of the Bible

There are seventy-three books in the canon of the Bible, that is, the official list of books the Church accepts as divinely inspired writings: forty-six Old Testament books and twenty-seven New Testament books. Protestant Bibles do not include seven Old

Testament books on its list (1 and 2 Maccabees, Judith, Tobit, Baruch, Sirach, and the Wisdom of Solomon). Why the difference? Catholics rely on the version of the Bible that the earliest Christians used, the *Septuagint*. This was the first Greek translation of the Hebrew scriptures begun in the third century BC. Protestants, on the other hand, rely on an official list of Hebrew scriptures compiled in the Holy Land by Jewish scholars at the end of the first century AD. Today, most Protestant Bibles print the disputed books in a separate section at the back of the Bible called the *Apocrypha*.

The twenty-seven books of the New Testament are divided into three categories: the gospels, the letters written to local Christian communities or individuals, and the letters intended for the entire Church. The heart of the New Testament, in fact all of Scripture, is the gospels. The New Testament is central to our knowledge of Jesus Christ. He is the focus of all Scripture.

There are forty-six books in the Old Testament canon. The Old Testament is the foundation for God's self-revelation in Christ. Christians honor the Old Testament as God's word. It contains the writings of prophets and other inspired authors who recorded God's teaching to the Chosen People and his interaction in their history. For example, the Old Testament recounts how God delivered the Jews from Egypt (the Exodus), led them to the Promised Land, formed them into a nation under his care, and taught them in knowledge and worship.

The stories, prayers, sacred histories, and other writings of the Old Testament reveal what God is like and tell much about human nature, too. In brief, the Chosen People sinned repeatedly by turning their backs on their loving God; they were weak and easily tempted away from God. Yahweh, on the other hand, *always* remained faithful. He promised to send a Messiah to humanity.

Listed are the categories and books of the Old Testament and the New Testament:

The Old Testament

The Pentateuch

Genesis	Gn
Exodus	Ex
Leviticus	Lv
Numbers	Nm
Deuteronomy	Dt

The Historical Books

Joshua	Jos
Judges	Jgs
Ruth	Ru
1 Samuel	1 Sm
2 Samuel	2 Sm
1 Kings	1 Kgs
2 Kings	2 Kgs
1 Chronicles	1 Chr
2 Chronicles	2 Chr
Ezra	Ezr
Nehemiah	Neh
Tobit	Tb
Judith	Jdt
Esther	Est
1 Maccabees	1 Mc
2 Maccabees	2 Mc

The Wisdom Books

Job	Jb
Psalms	Ps(s)
Proverbs	Prv
Ecclesiastes	Eccl
Song of Songs	Sg
Wisdom	Wis
Sirach	Sir

The Prophetic Books

Isaiah	Is
Jeremiah	Jer
Lamentations	Lam
Baruch	Bar
Ezekiel	Ez
Daniel	Dn
Hosea	Hos
Joel	Jl
Amos	Am
Obadiah	Ob
Jonah	Jon
Micah	Mi
Nahum	Na
Habakkuk	Hb

Zephaniah	Zep
Haggai	Hg
Zechariah	Zec
Malachi	Mal

The New Testament

The Gospels

Matthew	Mt
Mark	Mk
Luke	Lk
John	Jn
Acts of the Apostles	Acts

The New Testament Letters

Romans	Rom
1 Corinthians	1 Cor
2 Corinthians	2 Cor
Galatians	Gal
Ephesians	Eph
Philippians	Phil
Colossians	Col
1 Thessalonians	1 Thes
2 Thessalonians	2 Thes
1 Timothy	1 Tm
2 Timothy	2 Tm
Titus	Ti
Philemon	Phlm
Hebrews	Heb

The Catholic Letters

James	Jas
1 Peter	1 Pt
2 Peter	2 Pt
1 John	1 Jn
2 John	2 Jn
3 John	3 Jn
Jude	Jude
Revelation	Rv

How to Locate a Scripture Passage

Example: 2 Tm 3:16-17

1. *Determine the name of the book.*

   The abbreviation "2 Tm" stands for the second book of Timothy.

2. *Determine whether the book is in the Old Testament or New Testament.*

   The second book of Timothy is one of the New Testament letters.

3. *Locate the chapter where the passage occurs.*

   The first number before the colon—"3"—indicates the chapter. Chapters in the Bible are set off by the larger numbers that divide a book.

4. *Locate the verses of the passage.*

   The numbers after the colon indicate the verses referred to. In this case, verses 16 and 17 of chapter 3.

5. *Read the passage.*

   For example: "All Scripture is inspired by God and is useful for teaching, for refutation, for correction, and for training in righteousness, so that one who belongs to God may be competent, equipped for every good work."

Timeline of Church History

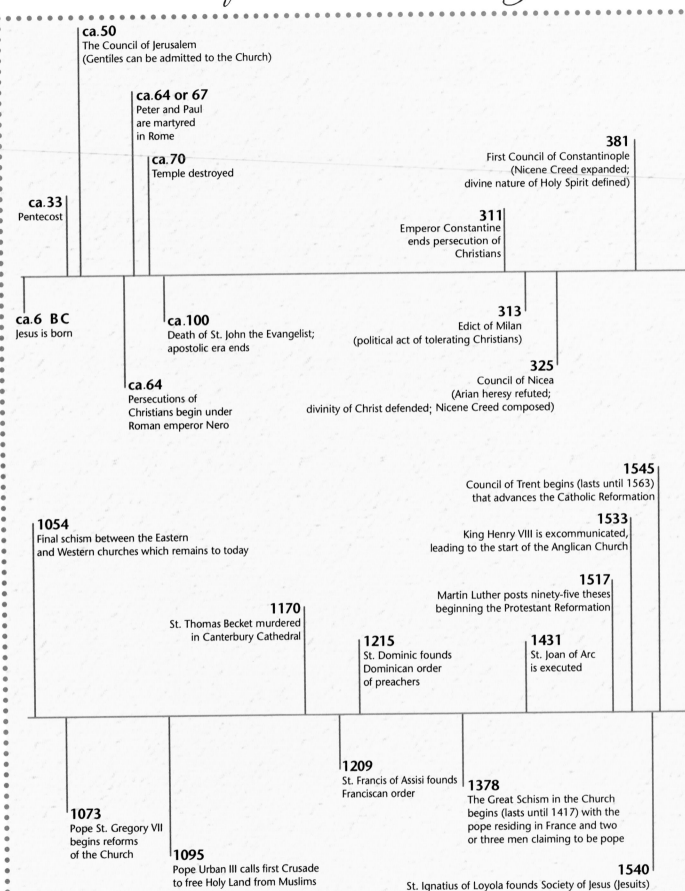

ca.50
The Council of Jerusalem
(Gentiles can be admitted to the Church)

ca.64 or 67
Peter and Paul
are martyred
in Rome

ca.70
Temple destroyed

381
First Council of Constantinople
(Nicene Creed expanded;
divine nature of Holy Spirit defined)

ca.33
Pentecost

311
Emperor Constantine
ends persecution of
Christians

ca.6 B C
Jesus is born

ca.100
Death of St. John the Evangelist;
apostolic era ends

313
Edict of Milan
(political act of tolerating Christians)

325
Council of Nicea
(Arian heresy refuted;
divinity of Christ defended; Nicene Creed composed)

ca.64
Persecutions of
Christians begin under
Roman emperor Nero

1545
Council of Trent begins (lasts until 1563)
that advances the Catholic Reformation

1533
King Henry VIII is excommunicated,
leading to the start of the Anglican Church

1054
Final schism between the Eastern
and Western churches which remains to today

1517
Martin Luther posts ninety-five theses
beginning the Protestant Reformation

1170
St. Thomas Becket murdered
in Canterbury Cathedral

1215
St. Dominic founds
Dominican order
of preachers

1431
St. Joan of Arc
is executed

1209
St. Francis of Assisi founds
Franciscan order

1378
The Great Schism in the Church
begins (lasts until 1417) with the
pope residing in France and two
or three men claiming to be pope

1073
Pope St. Gregory VII
begins reforms
of the Church

1095
Pope Urban III calls first Crusade
to free Holy Land from Muslims

1540
St. Ignatius of Loyola founds Society of Jesus (Jesuits)
to assist in reform of the Church

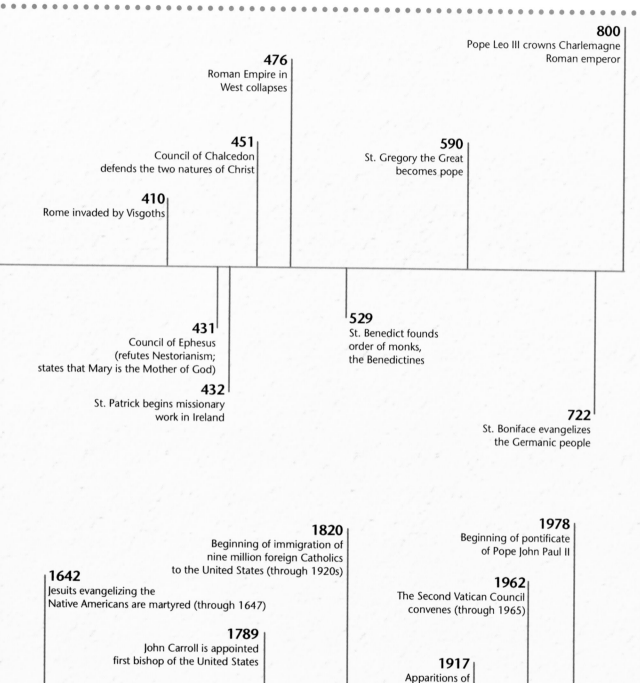

800
Pope Leo III crowns Charlemagne
Roman emperor

476
Roman Empire in
West collapses

451
Council of Chalcedon
defends the two natures of Christ

590
St. Gregory the Great
becomes pope

410
Rome invaded by Visgoths

431
Council of Ephesus
(refutes Nestorianism;
states that Mary is the Mother of God)

529
St. Benedict founds
order of monks,
the Benedictines

432
St. Patrick begins missionary
work in Ireland

722
St. Boniface evangelizes
the Germanic people

1820
Beginning of immigration of
nine million foreign Catholics
to the United States (through 1920s)

1978
Beginning of pontificate
of Pope John Paul II

1642
Jesuits evangelizing the
Native Americans are martyred (through 1647)

1962
The Second Vatican Council
convenes (through 1965)

1789
John Carroll is appointed
first bishop of the United States

1917
Apparitions of
Our Lady of Fatima

1994
Vatican and state of
Israel establish formal relations

1769
The first of twenty-one California missions
ınded (most by Franciscan Father Junipero Serra)

1869
The First Vatican Council convenes (through 1870)

1903
Beginning of pontificate of
St. Pius X (through 1914)

1891
Pope Leo XIII writes the *Rerum Novarum* encyclical,
the first of the Church's body of social doctrine

D. CHURCH

Marks of the Church

....

1. *The Church is one.* The Church remains one because of her source: the unity in the Trinity of the Father, Son, and Spirit in one God. The Church's unity can never be broken and lost because this foundation is itself unbreakable.

2. *The Church is holy.* The Church is holy because Jesus, the founder of the Church, is holy and he joined the Church to himself as his body and gave the Church the gift of the Holy Spirit. Together, Christ and the Church make up the "whole Christ" (*Christus totus* in Latin).

3. *The Church is catholic.* The Church is catholic ("universal" or "for everyone") in two ways. First, she is Catholic because Christ is present in the Church in the fullness of his body, with the fullness of the means of Salvation, the fullness of faith, sacraments, and the ordained ministry that comes from the Apostles. The Church is also catholic because it takes its message of Salvation to all people.

4. *The Church is apostolic.* The Church's apostolic mission comes from Jesus: "Go, therefore, and make disciples of all nations" (Mt 28:19). The Church remains apostolic because it still teaches the same things the Apostles taught. Also, the Church is led by leaders who are successors to the Apostles and who help to guide us until Jesus returns.

The Pope

The bishop of Rome has carried the title "pope" since the ninth century. Pope means "papa" or "father." St. Peter was the first bishop of Rome and, hence, the first pope. He was commissioned directly by Jesus:

> And so I say to you, you are Peter, and upon this rock I will build my church, and the gates of the netherworld shall not prevail against it. I will give you the keys to the kingdom of heaven. Whatever you bind on earth shall be bound in heaven; and whatever you loose on earth shall be loosed in heaven (Mt 16:18–19).

Because Peter was the first bishop of Rome, the succeeding bishops of Rome have had primacy in the Church. The entire succession of popes since St. Peter can be traced directly to the apostle.

The pope is in communion with the bishops of the world as part of the Magisterium, which is the Church's teaching authority. The pope can also define doctrine in faith or morals for the Church. When he does so, he is infallible and cannot be in error.

The pope is elected by the College of Cardinals by a two-thirds majority vote in secret balloting. If a pope is not elected after 30 votes, a new pope can be chosen by an absolute majority—that is half the votes plus one. Cardinals under the age of eighty are eligible to vote. If the necessary majority is not achieved the ballots are burned in a small stove inside the conclave chambers along with straw that makes dark smoke. The sign of dark smoke announces to the crowds waiting outside St. Peter's Basilica that a new pope has not been chosen. When a new pope has been voted in with the necessary majority, the ballots are burned without the straw, producing white smoke signifying the election of a pope.

Recent Popes

....

Since 1900 and through the pontificate of Pope Benedict XVI, there were ten Popes. Pope John Paul II was the first non-Italian pope since Dutchman Pope Adrian VI (1522-1523). The popes since the twentieth century through Pope Benedict XVI with their original names, place of origin, and years as pope:

★ Pope Leo XIII (Giocchino Pecci): Carpineto, Italy, February 20, 1878–July 20, 1903.

★ Pope St. Pius X (Giuseppe Sarto): Riese, Italy, August 4, 1903–August 20, 1914.

(continued on page 324)

The Apostles and Their Emblems

 ### St. Andrew
Tradition holds that Andrew was crucified on a bent cross, called a saltire.

 ### St. Bartholomew
Bartholomew was flayed alive before being crucified. He was then beheaded.

 ### St. James the Greater
James the Greater, the brother of John, was beheaded by Herod Agrippa. It is the only death of an apostle mentioned in Scripture (Acts 12:2). The shell indicates James' missionary work by sea in Spain. The sword is of martyrdom.

 ### St. James the Less
James the Less is traditionally known as the first bishop of Jerusalem. The saw for his emblem is connected with the tradition of his body being sawed into pieces after he was pushed from the pinnacle of the Temple.

 ### St. John the Evangelist
John was the first bishop of Ephesus. He is the only apostle believed to have died a natural death, in spite of many attempts to murder him by his enemies. One attempt included his miraculous survival of drinking a poisoned drink.

 ### St. Jude
Some traditions have Jude and St. Peter martyred together. It is thought that he traveled throughout the Roman Empire with Peter.

 ### St. Matthew
Matthew's shield depicts three purses reflecting his original occupation as tax collector.

 ### St. Matthias
Matthias was the apostle chosen by lot to replace Judas. Tradition holds that Matthias was stoned to death and then beheaded with an ax.

 ### St. Peter
Simon Peter was the brother of Andrew. The first bishop of Rome, Peter was crucified under Nero, asking to be hung upside down because he felt unworthy to die as Jesus did. The keys represent Jesus' giving to Peter the keys to the kingdom of heaven.

 ### St. Philip
Philip may have been bound to a cross and stoned to death. The two loaves of bread at the side of the cross refer to Philip's comment to Jesus about the possibility of feeding the multitudes of people (Jn 6:7).

 ### St. Simon
The book with fish depicts Simon as a "fisher of men" who preached the gospel. He was also known as Simon the Zealot.

 ### St. Thomas
Thomas is thought to have been a missionary in India, where he is thought to have built a church. Hence, the carpenter's square. He may have died by arrows and stones. It is then thought that he had a lance run through his body.

★ Pope Benedict XV (Giacomo della Chiesa): Genoa, Italy, September 3, 1914–January 22, 1922.

★ Pope Pius XI (Achille Ratti): Desio, Italy, February 6, 1922–February 10, 1939.

★ Pope Pius XII (Eugenio Pacelli): Rome, Italy, March 2, 1939–October 9, 1958.

★ Pope John XXIII (Angelo Giuseppe Roncalli), Sotto il Monte, Italy, October 28, 1958–June 3, 1963.

★ Pope Paul VI (Giovanni Battista Montini): Concessio, Italy, June 21, 1963–August 6, 1978.

★ Pope John Paul I (Albino Luciani): Forno di Canale, Italy, August 26, 1978–September 28, 1978.

★ Pope John Paul II (Karol Wojtyla): Wadowice, Poland, October 16, 1978–April 2, 2005.

★ Pope Benedict XVI (Joseph Ratzinger): Marktl am Inn, Germany, April 19, 2005–

Fathers of the Church

Church Fathers, or Fathers of the Church, is a traditional title that was given to theologians of the first eight centuries whose teachings made a lasting mark on the Church. The Church Fathers developed a significant amount of doctrine which has great authority in the Church. The Church Fathers are named as either Latin Fathers (West) or Greek Fathers (East). Among the greatest Fathers of the Church are:

Latin Fathers	Greek Fathers
St. Ambrose	St. John Chrysostom
St. Augustine	St. Basil the Great
St. Jerome	St. Gregory of Nazianzen
St. Gregory the Great	St. Athanasius

Pope Benedict XVI

Doctors of the Church

The Doctors of the Church are men and women honored by the Church for their writings, preaching, and holiness. Originally the Doctors of the Church were considered to be Church Fathers Augustine, Ambrose, Jerome, and Gregory the Great, but others were added over the centuries. St. Teresa of Avila was the first woman Doctor (1970). St. Catherine of Siena was named a Doctor of the Church the same year. The list of Doctors of the Church:

NAME	LIFE SPAN	DESIGNATION
St. Athanasius	296–373	1568 by Pius V
St. Ephraem the Syrian	306–373	1920 by Benedict XV
St. Hilary of Poitiers	315–367	1851 by Pius IX
St. Cyril of Jerusalem	315–386	1882 by Leo XIII
St. Gregory of Nazianzus	325–389	1568 by Pius V
St. Basil the Great	329–379	1568 by Pius V
St. Ambrose	339–397	1295 by Boniface VIII
St. John Chrysostom	347–407	1568 by Pius V
St. Jerome	347–419	1295 by Boniface XIII
St. Augustine	354–430	1295 by Boniface XIII
St. Cyril of Alexandria	376–444	1882 by Leo XIII
St. Peter Chrysologous	400–450	1729 by Benedict XIII
St. Leo the Great	400–461	1754 by Benedict XIV
St. Gregory the Great	540–604	1295 by Boniface XIII
St. Isidore of Seville	560–636	1722 by Innocent XIII
St. John of Damascus	645–749	1890 by Leo XIII
St. Bede the Venerable	672–735	1899 by Leo XIII
St. Peter Damian	1007–1072	1828 by Leo XII
St. Anselm	1033–1109	1720 by Clement XI
St. Bernard of Clairvaux	1090–1153	1830 by Pius VIII
St. Anthony of Padua	1195–1231	1946 by Pius XII
St. Albert the Great	1206–1280	1931 by Pius XI
St. Bonaventure	1221–1274	1588 by Sixtus V
St. Thomas Aquinas	1226–1274	1567 by Pius V
St. Catherine of Siena	1347–1380	1970 by Paul VI
St. Teresa of Avila	1515–1582	1970 by Paul VI
St. Peter Canisius	1521–1597	1925 by Pius XI
St. John of the Cross	1542–1591	1926 by Pius XI
St. Robert Bellarmine	1542–1621	1931 by Pius XI
St. Lawrence of Brindisi	1559–1619	1959 by John XXIII
St. Francis de Sales	1567–1622	1871 by Pius IX
St. Alphonsus Ligouri	1696–1787	1871 by Pius IX
St. Thérèse of Lisieux	1873–1897	1997 by John Paul II

Ecumenical Councils

An ecumenical council is a worldwide assembly of bishops under direction of the pope. There have been twenty-one ecumenical councils, the most recent being the Second Vatican Council (1962–1965). A complete list of the Church's ecumenical councils with the years each met:

Nicaea I	325
Constantinople I	381
Ephesus	431
Chalcedon	451
Constantinople II	553

Constantinople III	680
Nicaea II	787
Constantiople IV	869–870
Lateran I	1123
Lateran II	1139
Lateran III	1179
Lateran IV	1215
Lyons I	1245
Lyons II	1274
Vienne	1311–1312
Constance	1414–1418
Florence	1431–1445
Lateran V	1512–1517
Trent	1545–1563
Vatican Council I	1869–1870
Vatican Council II	1962–1965

E. MORALITY

The Ten Commandments

The Ten Commandments are a main source for Christian morality. The Ten Commandments were revealed by God to Moses. Jesus, himself, acknowledged them. He told the rich young man, "If you wish to enter into the life, keep the commandments" (Mt 19:17). Since the time of St. Augustine (fourth century) the Ten Commandments have been used as a source for teaching baptismal candidates. See chapter 9 for more information.

I.   I, the Lord am your God: you shall not have other gods besides me.

II.   You shall not take the name of the Lord, your God, in vain.

III.   Remember to keep holy the Sabbath day.

IV.   Honor your father and your mother.

V.   You shall not kill.

VI.   You shall not commit adultery.

VII.   You shall not steal.

VIII.   You shall not bear false witness against your neighbor.

IX.   You shall not covet your neighbor's wife.

X.   You shall not covet your neighbor's goods.

The Beatitudes

The word *beatitude* means "supreme happiness." Jesus preached the Beatitudes in his Sermon on the Mount. They are:

Blessed are the poor in spirit, for theirs is the kingdom of God.

Blessed are they who mourn, for they will be comforted.

Blessed are the meek, for they will inherit the land.

Blessed are they who hunger and thirst for righteousness, for they will be satisfied.

Blessed are the merciful, for they will be shown mercy.

Blessed are the clean of heart, for they will see God.

Blessed are the peacemakers, for they will be called children of God.

Blessed are they who are persecuted for the sake of righteousness, for theirs is the kingdom of heaven.

Cardinal Virtues

Virtues—habits that help in leading a moral life—that are acquired by human effort are known as moral or human virtues. Four of these are called the cardinal virtues because they form the hinge that connect all the others. They are:

★ Prudence   ★ Fortitude
★ Justice   ★ Temperance

Theological Virtues

The theological virtues are the foundation for moral life. They are related directly to God.

★ Faith   ★ Hope   ★ Love

Corporal (Bodily) Works of Mercy

★ Feed the hungry.
★ Give drink to the thirsty.
★ Clothe the naked.
★ Visit the imprisoned.
★ Shelter the homeless.
★ Visit the sick.
★ Bury the dead.

Spiritual Works of Mercy

★ Counsel the doubtful.
★ Instruct the ignorant.
★ Admonish sinners.
★ Comfort the afflicted.
★ Forgive offenses.
★ Bear wrongs patiently.
★ Pray for the living and the dead.

Precepts of the Church

1. You shall attend Mass on Sundays and on holy days of obligation and rest from servile labor.
2. You shall confess your sins once a year.
3. You shall receive the sacrament of Eucharist at least during the Easter season.
4. You shall observe the days of fasting and abstinence established by the Church.
5. You shall help to provide for the needs of the Church.

In addition, Catholics have the duty to support the Church with gifts of their time and talents and with monetary gifts.

Catholic Social Teaching: Major Themes

The 1998 document *Sharing Catholic Social Teaching: Challenges and Directions—Reflections of the U.S. Catholic Bishops* highlighted seven principles of the Church's social teaching. They are:

1. Life and dignity of the human person
2. Call to family, community, and participation
3. Rights and responsibilities
4. Option for the poor and vulnerable
5. The dignity of work and the rights of workers
6. Solidarity
7. Care for God's creation

Sin

Sin is an offense against God.

Mortal sin is the most serious kind of sin. Mortal sin destroys or kills a person's relationship with God. To be a mortal sin, three conditions must exist:

★ The moral object must be of grave or serious matter. Grave matter is specified in the Ten Commandments (e.g., do not kill, do not commit adultery, do not steal, etc.).
★ The person must have full knowledge of the gravity of the sinful action.
★ The person must completely consent to the action. It must be a personal choice.

Venial sin is less serious sin. Examples of venial sins are petty jealousy, disobedience, and "borrowing" a small amount of money from a parent without the intention of repaying it. Venial sins, when unrepented, can lead a person to commit mortal sins.

Vices are bad habits linked to sins. The seven capital vices are pride, avarice, envy, wrath, lust, gluttony, and sloth.

F. LITURGY & SACRAMENTS

Church Year

The cycle of seasons and feasts that Catholics celebrate is called the Church Year or Liturgical Year. The Church Year is divided into six main parts: Advent, Christmas, Lent, Triduum, Easter, and Ordinary Time.

Holy Days of Obligation in the United States

★ Immaculate Conception of Mary
  December 8

★ Christmas
  December 25

★ Solemnity of Mary, Mother of God
  January 1

★ Ascension of the Lord
  Forty days after Easter

★ Assumption of Mary
  August 15

★ All Saints Day

November 1

The Seven Sacraments

1. Baptism
2. Confirmation
3. Eucharist
4. Penance and Reconciliation
5. Anointing of the Sick
6. Holy Orders
7. Matrimony

How to Go to Confession

1. Spend some time examining your conscience. Consider your actions and attitudes in each area of your life (e.g., faith, family, school/work, social life, relationships). Ask yourself, "Is this area of my life pleasing to God? What needs to be reconciled with God? with others? with myself?

2. Sincerely tell God that you are sorry for your sins. Ask God for forgiveness and for the grace you will need to change what needs changing in your life. Promise God that you will try to live according to his will for you.

3. Approach the area for confession. Wait an appropriate distance until it is your turn.

4. Make the Sign of the Cross with the priest. He may say: "May God, who has enlightened every heart, help you to know your sins and trust his mercy." You reply: "Amen."

5. Confess your sins to the priest. Simply and directly talk to him about the areas of sinfulness in your life that need God's healing touch.

6. The priest will ask you to pray an act of contrition. Pray an Act of Contrition you have committed to memory. Or, saying something in your own words, like: "Dear God, I am sorry for my sins. I ask for your forgiveness and I promise to do better in the future."

7. The priest will talk to you about your life, encourage you to be more faithful to God in the future, and help you decide what to do to make up for your sins—your penance.

8. The priest will then extend his hands over your head and pray the Church's official prayer of absolution:

   God, the Father of mercies, through the death and resurrection of his Son, has reconciled the world to himself and sent the Holy Spirit among us for the forgiveness of sins; through the ministry of the Church may God give you pardon and peace, and I absolve you from your sins in the name of the Father, and of the Son, and of the Holy Spirit.

   You respond: "Amen."

9. The priest will wish you peace. Thank him and leave.

10. Go to a quiet place in church and pray your prayer of penance. Then spend some time quietly thanking God for the gift of forgiveness.

Order of Mass

There are two main parts of the Mass, the Liturgy of the Word and the Liturgy of the Eucharist. The complete order of Mass:

The Introductory Rites

The Entrance
Greeting of the Altar and of the People Gathered
The Act of Penitence
The *Kyrie Eleison*
The *Gloria*
The Collect (Opening Prayer)

The Liturgy of the Word

Silence
The Biblical Readings (the reading of the Gospel is the high point of the Liturgyof the Word)
The Responsorial Psalm
The Homily
The Profession of Faith (Creed)
The Prayer of the Faithful

The Liturgy of the Eucharist

The Preparation of the Gifts
The Prayer over the Offerings
The Eucharistic Prayer
The Communion Rite
The Lord's Prayer
The Rite of Peace
The Fraction (Breaking of the Bread)
Communion
Prayer after Communion

The Concluding Rites

Communion Regulations

To receive Holy Communion properly, a person must be in the state of grace (free from mortal sin), have the right intention (only for the purpose of pleasing God), and observe the Communion fast.

The fast means that a person may not eat anything or drink any liquid (other than water) one hour before the reception of Communion. There are exceptions made to this fast only for the sick and aged.

Three Degrees of the Sacrament of Orders

There are three degrees of the Sacrament of Holy Orders: the ministries of bishop, priest, and deacon.

The bishop receives the fullness of the sacrament of Orders. He is the successor to the apostles. When he celebrates the sacraments, the bishop is given the grace to act in the person of Christ who is the head of the body of the Church.

Priests are ordained as co-workers of the bishop. They too are configured to Christ so that they may act in his person during the

Sacraments of Eucharist, Baptism, and the Anointing of the Sick. They may bless marriages in the name of Christ and, under the authority of the bishop, share in Christ's ministry of forgiveness in the sacrament of Penance and Reconciliation.

Deacons are ordained for service and are configured to Christ the servant. Deacons are ordained to help and serve the priests and bishops in their work. While bishops and priests are configured to Christ to act as the head of Christ's body, deacons are configured to Christ in order to serve as he served. Deacons may baptize, preach the Gospel and homily, and bless marriages.

G. MARY AND THE SAINTS

Mother of God

Mary, the mother of Jesus, is the closest human to cooperate with her Son's work of redemption. For this reason, the Church holds her in a special place. Of her many titles, the most significant is that she is the Mother of God.

The Church teaches several truths about Mary.

First, she was conceived immaculately. This means from the very first moment of her existence she was without sin and "full of grace." This belief is called the Immaculate Conception. The feast of the Immaculate Conception is celebrated on December 8.

Second, Mary was ever-virgin. She was a virgin before, in, and after the birth of Jesus. As his mother, she cared for him in infancy and raised him to adulthood with the help of her husband, Joseph. She witnessed Jesus' preaching and ministry, was at the foot of his cross at his crucifixion, and present with the apostles as they awaited the coming of the Holy Spirit at Pentecost.

Third, at the time of her death, Mary was assumed body and soul into heaven. This dogma was proclaimed as a matter of faith by Pope Pius XII in 1950. The feast of the Assumption is celebrated on August 15.

The Church has always been devoted to the Blessed Virgin. This devotion is different than that given to God—Father, Son, and Holy Spirit. Rather, the Church is devoted to Mary as her first disciple, the Queen of all Saints, and her own Mother. Quoting the fathers of the Second Vatican Council:

> In the meantime the Mother of Jesus, in the glory which she possesses in body and soul in heaven, is the image and the beginning of the Church as it is to be perfected in the world to come. Likewise she shines forth on earth, until the day of the Lord shall come, a sign of certain hope and comfort to the pilgrim People of God (*Lumen Gentium*, 68).

Marian Feasts Throughout the Year

January 1	Solemnity of Mary, Mother of God
March 25	Annunciation of the Lord
May 31	Visitation
August 15	Assumption
August 22	Queenship of Mary
September 8	Birth of Mary
September 15	Our Lady of Sorrows
October 7	Our Lady of the Rosary
November 21	Presentation of Mary
December 8	Immaculate Conception
December 12	Our Lady of Guadalupe

Canonization of Saints

Saints are those who are in glory with God in heaven. *Canonization* refers to a solemn declaration by the Pope that a person who either died a martyr or who lived an exemplary Christian life is in heaven and may be honored and imitated by all Christians. The canonization process first involves a process of beatification that includes a thorough investigation of the person's life and certification of miracles that can be attributed to the candidate's intercession.

The first official canonization of the universal Church on record was St. Ulrich of Augsburg by Pope John XV in 993.

Some non-Catholics criticize Catholics for "praying to saints." Catholics *honor* saints for their holy lives but we do not pray to them as if they were God. We ask the saints to pray with us and for us as part of the Church in glory. We can ask them to do this because we know that their lives have been spent in close communion with God. We also ask the saints for their friendship so that we can follow the example they have left for us.

Patron Saints

A patron is a saint who is designated for places (nations, regions, dioceses) or organizations. Many saints have also become patrons of jobs, professional groups, and intercessors for special needs. Listed below are patron saints for several nations and some special patrons:

PATRONS OF PLACES

Americas	Our Lady of Guadalupe, St. Rose of Lima
Argentina	Our Lady of Lujan
Australia	Our Lady Help of Christians
Canada	St. Joseph, St. Anne
China	St. Joseph
England	St. George
Finland	St. Henry
France	Our Lady of the Assumption, St. Joan of Arc, St. Thérèse of Lisieux
Germany	St. Boniface
India	Our Lady of the Assumption
Ireland	St. Patrick, St. Brigid, St. Columba
Italy	St. Francis of Assisi, St. Catherine of Siena
Japan	St. Peter
Mexico	Our Lady of Guadalupe
New Zealand	Our Lady Help of Christians
Poland	St. Casmir, St. Stanislaus, Our Lady of Czestochowa
Russia	St. Andrew, St. Nicholas of Myra, St. Thérèse of Lisieux
Scotland	St. Andrew, St. Columba
Spain	St. James, St. Teresa of Avila
United States	Immaculate Conception

SPECIAL PATRONS

Accountants	St. Matthew
Actors	St. Genesius
Animals	St. Francis of Assisi
Athletes	St. Sebastian
Beggars	St. Martin of Tours
Boy Scouts	St. George
Dentists	St. Apollonia
Farmers	St. Isidore
Grocers	St. Michael
Journalists	St. Francis de Sales
Maids	St. Zita
Motorcyclists	Our Lady of Grace
Painters	St. Luke
Pawnbrokers	St. Nicholas
Police Officers	St. Michael
Priests	St. John Vianney
Scientists	St. Albert
Tailors	St. Homobonus
Teachers	St. Gregory the Great, St. John Baptist de la Salle
Wine Merchants	St. Amand

H. DEVOTIONS

The Mysteries of the Rosary

JOYFUL MYSTERIES

1. The Annunciation
2. The Visitation
3. The Nativity

4. The Presentation in the Temple
5. The Finding of Jesus in the Temple

MYSTERIES OF LIGHT

1. Jesus' Baptism in the Jordan River
2. Jesus' Self-manifestation at the Wedding of Cana
3. The Proclamation of the Kingdom of God and Jesus' Call to Conversion
4. The Transfiguration
5. The Institution of the Eucharist at the Last Supper

SORROWFUL MYSTERIES

1. The Agony in the Garden
2. The Scourging at the Pillar
3. The Crowning with Thorns
4. The Carrying of the Cross
5. The Crucifixion

GLORIOUS MYSTERIES

1. The Resurrection
2. The Ascension
3. The Descent of the Holy Spirit
4. The Assumption of Mary
5. The Crowning of Mary as the Queen of Heaven and Earth

How to Pray the Rosary

OPENING

1. Begin on the crucifix and pray the Apostles' Creed.
2. On the first bead, pray the Our Father.
3. On the next three beads, pray the Hail Mary. (Some people meditate on the virtues of faith, hope, and charity on these beads.)
4. On the fifth bead, pray the Glory Be.

THE BODY

Each decade (set of ten beads) is organized as follows:

1. On the larger bead that comes before each set of ten, announce the mystery to be prayed (see above) and pray one Our Father.

2. On each of the ten smaller beads, pray one Hail Mary while meditating on the mystery.
3. Pray one Glory Be at the end of the decade. (There is no bead for the Glory Be.)

CONCLUSION

Pray the following prayer at the end of the rosary:

Hail, Holy Queen

Hail, holy Queen, Mother of Mercy,
our life, our sweetness, and our hope.
To thee do we cry,
poor banished children of Eve.
To thee do we send up our sighs,
mourning and weeping in the valley
of tears.
Turn then, most gracious advocate,
thine eyes of mercy toward us;
and after this our exile,
show unto us the blessed fruit of thy
womb, Jesus.
O clement, O loving, O sweet Virgin
Mary.
Pray for us, O holy Mother of God,
that we may be made worthy of the
promises of Christ.
Amen.

Stations of the Cross

The stations of the cross is a devotion and also a sacramental. (A sacramental is a sacred object, blessing, or devotion.) The stations of the cross are individual pictures or symbols hung on the interior walls of most Catholic churches depicting fourteen steps along Jesus' way of the cross. Praying the stations means meditating on each of the following scenes:

1. Jesus is condemned to death.
2. Jesus takes up his cross.
3. Jesus falls the first time.
4. Jesus meets his mother.
5. Simon of Cyrene helps Jesus carry his cross.

6. Veronica wipes the face of Jesus.
7. Jesus falls the second time.
8. Jesus consoles the women of Jerusalem.
9. Jesus falls the third time.
10. Jesus is stripped of his garments.
11. Jesus is nailed to the cross.
12. Jesus dies on the cross.
13. Jesus is taken down from the cross.
14. Jesus is laid in the tomb.

Some churches also include a fifteenth station, the resurrection of the Lord.

Novenas

The novena consists of the recitation of certain prayers over a period of nine days. The symbolism of nine days refers to the time Mary and the apostles spent in prayer between Jesus' ascension into heaven and Pentecost.

Many novenas are dedicated to Mary or to a saint with the faith and hope that she or he will intercede for the one making the novena. Novenas to St. Jude, St. Anthony, Our Lady of Perpetual Help, and Our Lady of Lourdes remain popular in the Church today.

Liturgy of the Hours

The Liturgy of the Hours is part of the official, public prayer of the Church. Along with the celebration of the sacraments, the recitation of the Liturgy of the Hours, or Divine Office (office means "duty" or "obligation"), allows for constant praise and thanksgiving to God throughout the day and night.

The Liturgy of Hours consists of five major divisions:
1. An hour of readings
2. Morning praises
3. Midday prayers
4. Vespers (evening prayers)
5. Compline (a short night prayer)
Scriptural prayer, especially the psalms, is

at the heart of the liturgy of the hours. Each day follows a separate pattern of prayer with themes closely tied in with the liturgical year and feasts of the saints.

The Divine Praises

These praises are traditionally recited after the benediction of the Blessed Sacrament.

Blessed be God.
Blessed be his holy name.
Blessed be Jesus Christ, true God and true man.
Blessed be the name of Jesus.
Blessed be his most Sacred Heart.
Blessed be his most Precious Blood.
Blessed be Jesus in the most holy sacrament of the altar.
Blessed be the Holy Spirit, the Paraclete.
Blessed be the great Mother of God, Mary most holy.
Blessed be her holy and Immaculate Conception.
Blessed be her glorious Assumption.
Blessed be the name of Mary, Virgin and Mother.
Blessed be St. Joseph, her most chaste spouse.
Blessed be God in his angels and his saints.

1. PRAYERS

Sign of the Cross

In the name of the Father,
and of the Son,
and of the Holy Spirit. Amen.

Our Father

*O*ur Father
who art in heaven,
hallowed be thy name.
Thy kingdom come;
thy will be done on earth as it is in
    heaven.
Give us this day our daily bread
and forgive us our trespasses
as we forgive those who trespass
    against us.
And lead us not into temptation,
but deliver us from evil.
Amen.

Glory Be

*G*lory be to the Father
and to the Son
and to the Holy Spirit,
as it was in the beginning,
is now,
and ever shall be,
world without end. Amen.

Hail Mary

*H*ail Mary, full of grace,
the Lord is with thee.
Blessed art thou among women
and blessed is the fruit of thy womb,
    Jesus.
Holy Mary, Mother of God,
pray for us sinners now
and at the hour of our death. Amen.

Memorare

*R*emember, O most gracious Virgin
    Mary,
that never was it known
that anyone who fled to your
    protection,
implored your help,
or sought your intercession was left
    unaided.
Inspired by this confidence,
I fly unto you,
O virgin of virgins, my mother,
To you I come, before you I stand,
sinful and sorrowful.
O Mother of the word incarnate,
despise not my petitions,
but in your mercy hear and answer
    me. Amen.

Hail, Holy Queen

*H*ail, holy Queen, Mother of Mercy,
our life, our sweetness and our hope!
To you do we cry,
poor banished children of Eve;
to you do we send up our sighs,
mourning and weeping in this valley
    of tears.
Turn then, O most gracious
    advocate,
your eyes of mercy toward us,
and after this exile,
show us the blessed fruit of your
    womb, Jesus.
O clement, O loving, O sweet Virgin
    Mary.

V. Pray for us, O holy mother of God.
R. that we may be made worthy of the
    promises of Christ. Amen.

The Angelus

V. The angel spoke God's message to Mary.
R. And she conceived by the Holy Spirit.
    Hail Mary . . .
V. Behold the handmaid of the Lord.
R. May it be done unto me according to
    your word.
    Hail Mary . . .
V. And the Word was made flesh.
R. And dwelled among us.
    Hail Mary . . .
V. Pray for us, O holy mother of God.

R. That we may be made worthy of the promises of Christ.

Let us pray: We beseech you, O Lord, to pour out your grace into our hearts. By the message of an angel we have learned of the incarnation of Christ, your son; lead us by his passion and cross, to the glory of the resurrection. Through the same Christ our Lord. Amen.

Regina Caeli

Queen of heaven, rejoice, alleluia. The Son you merited to bear, alleluia, has risen as he said, alleluia. Pray to God for us, alleluia.

V. Rejoice and be glad, O Virgin Mary, alleluia.

R. For the Lord has truly risen, alleluia.

Let us pray.

God of life, you have given joy to the world by the resurrection of your son, our Lord Jesus Christ. Through the prayers of his mother, the Virgin Mary, bring us to the happiness of eternal life. We ask this through Christ our Lord. Amen.

Grace at Meals

BEFORE MEALS

Bless us, O Lord, and these your gifts, which we are about to receive from your bounty, through Christ our Lord. Amen.

AFTER MEALS

We give you thanks, almighty God, for these and all the gifts which we have received from your goodness through Christ our Lord. Amen.

Guardian Angel Prayer

Angel of God, my guardian dear, to whom God's love entrust me here, ever this day be at my side, to light and guard, to rule and guide. Amen.

Prayer for the Faithful Departed

Eternal rest grant unto them, O Lord.

R: And let perpetual light shine upon them. May their souls and the souls of all faithful departed, through the mercy of God, rest in peace.

R: Amen.

Morning Offering

O Jesus, through the immaculate heart of Mary, I offer you my prayers, works, joys, and sufferings of this day in union with the holy sacrifice of the Mass throughout the world. I offer them for all the intentions of your Sacred Heart: the salvation of souls, reparation for sin, the reunion of all Christians. I offer them for the intentions of our bishops and all members of the apostleship of prayer and in particular for those recommended by your Holy Father this month. Amen.

Act of Faith

O God, I firmly believe all the truths that you have revealed and that you teach us through your Church, for you are truth itself and can neither deceive nor be deceived. Amen.

Act of Hope

O God,
I hope with complete trust that you
   will give me,
through the merits of Jesus Christ, all
   necessary grace in this world
and everlasting life in the world to
   come,
for this is what you have promised
and you always keep your promises.
Amen.

Act of Love

O my God, I love you above all things, with
my whole heart and soul, because you are
all good and worthy of all my love. I love my
neighbor as myself for the love of you. I
forgive all who have injured me, and I ask
pardon of all whom I have injured. Amen.

Prayer for Peace
(St. Francis of Assisi)

Lord, make me an instrument of
   your peace.
Where there is hatred, let me sow
   love;
where there is injury, pardon;
where there is doubt, faith;
where there is despair, hope;
where there is darkness, light;
where there is sadness, joy.
O Divine Master,
grant that I may not seek so much to
   be consoled as to console;
to be understood, as to understand,
to be loved, as to love.
For it is in giving that we receive,
it is in pardoning that we are
   pardoned,
and it is in dying that we are born to
   eternal life.

Glossary

absolution—The release of repentant sinners from their sin in the Sacrament of Reconciliation. Even after receiving absolution sinners must still do what they can to make amends for their sin in order to recover their full spiritual health.

Apollinarianism—A false belief that claimed that although Jesus had a human body, he had no human soul.

apologists—"Defenders of the faith." Christians who worked hard to dispel the false rumors about Christianity and to make Christianity appear both reasonable and acceptable to non-Christians.

apostasy—A total denial of Christ and a disavowal of the Christian faith.

Apostle—"One who is sent." It is the name used for the twelve men whom Jesus chose and who the Church believes were given authority by Christ.

Apostles' Creed—One of two great creeds, or statements of belief, of the Church. It is considered to be a summary of the Apostle's faith. It is the ancient baptismal symbol of the Church of Rome.

apostolic—In keeping with the Apostles or "having been sent." The Church is apostolic because its faith and practice are in keeping with the faith and practice which the Apostles received from Jesus and handed on to others.

asceticism—Strict self-denial as a means of spiritual discipline. Christian ascents imitate Christ's life of self-sacrifice in order to live the gospel more faithfully.

Assumption of Mary—The dogma which states that the body of Mary was taken directly to heaven after her death. Mary already shares in the resurrection of the body which is promised to all the faithful.

baptism of desire—Seeking the truth and doing the will of God to the best of one's understanding even though the person may not understand the gospel or the necessity of the Church. The Church teaches that God allows those people who would have explicitly desired baptism if they understood its necessity to share in the benefits of the baptized.

bishop—Literally an "overseer." A bishop is a successor to the apostles and the head of a particular church (usually a diocese). All of the bishops together and united with the pope exercise leadership over the universal Church.

canon—A name for those books which have been accepted by the Church as normative for faith.

canonization—The process by which the Church declares that a particular member of the faithful has practiced heroic virtue in his or her life, has been faithful to God's grace, and is now fully united with God in Heaven.

catechumenate—The period of preparation for Baptism.

catholic—Universal, in totality, in keeping with the whole. When we refer to the Church as catholic with a small "C" we are referring to the fact that the Church is for all people in all times and in all places. Faith that is catholic is faith that is based on the entire truth as taught by all the apostles. The word Catholic with a capital "c" is used to describe the Church which accepts the leadership of the pope.

Christian—Shaped by or belonging to Christ. A Christian is someone whose life is consecrated to God the Father, through Christ, by the power of the Holy Spirit. The ordinary way of becoming a Christian is through Baptism by water.

common good—The sum of social conditions which allow people, either as groups or as individuals, to reach their fulfillment more fully and more easily.

confessors—Those Christians who refused to respond to Decius's decree to offer sacrifices to Roman gods.

Council of Trent—The sixteenth century ecumenical council held in response to the challenges of the Protestant reformation. The Council clearly outlined Catholic doctrine on such matters as authority, sin and justification, and the role of Mary and the saints.

covenant—The partnership between God and humanity which God has established out of love. The new covenant is offered through Christ. The blood which Christ shed on the cross is a sign of the new covenant.

crusades—The nine armed expeditions by Christians beginning in 1095 and ending in 1291 which were intended to drive the Muslims out of the Holy Land and in the process reunite Christians of the East and West.

deacon—One who is ordained "not unto the priesthood, but into ministry." Deacons are ordained to serve by assisting bishops and priests in sacramental celebrations and by dedicating themselves to the various ministries of charity.

denomination—A religious group defined by a specific name, structure, and set of beliefs.

desert fathers—Christians of about the fourth century who chose to live an ascetic life of prayer, fasting, and abstinence. The teachings of these men (and women) had a profound impact on the theology and spirituality of the Church and on the development of monasticism.

Didache—Also called the "Teaching of the Twelve Apostles." The Didache is a moral, disciplinary, and liturgical text written in the later first or early second century. It includes teachings on Baptism, Eucharist, fasting, and prayer.

disciple—A follower of Christ. A disciple is someone who learns from and follows Jesus and who accepts a share of his ministry in the world.

divine—Literally, "of God."

doctor of the Church—A title officially conferred upon a saint by the pope or by a general council declaring that person to have been particularly holy, wise, and learned, and therefore a source of sound theological teaching for the Church.

doctrine—An official teaching of the Church.

dogma—Those truths which the Church teaches have been specifically revealed by God. Acceptance of dogma is essential for complete faith and the deepest possible relationship with God. Denial of dogma is heresy.

domestic church—The domestic Church is the Christian family. In the family, parents and children exercise their priesthood of the baptized by worshiping God, receiving the sacraments, and witnessing to Christ and the Church by living as faith disciples.

ecumenical council—A gathering of all the Catholic bishops of the world. The word "ecumenical" pertains to a theological recognition of and willingness to learn from those of different faith traditions. Ecumenical councils determine those things which all the local churches (dioceses) will hold in common.

ecumenism—The movement and activities which seek to promote religious unity within the Christian Church and among all the people of the world.

encomiendas—A system in which a native person was "entrusted" to a settler to be "civilized" and taught the basics of Christian doctrine.

eschatology—The study of the last things: the Second Coming of Christ, the Resurrection of the dead, the Kingdom of God, judgment, Heaven, Hell, and Purgatory.

Essenes—The strictest of the four main Jewish groups of Jesus' day. The Essenes lived celibately, interpreted every law in the strictest way possible, and separated themselves from all who did not live as they did.

eucharistic prayer—The heart and summit of the celebration of the Eucharist. The eucharistic prayer follows the offering of the unconsecrated bread and wine to God. It begins with the preface in which the Church gives thanks to the Father, through Christ, in the Holy Spirit, for all his works. It includes the epiclesis (the request for the Spirit to descend), the institution narrative, the anamnesis (in which the Church remembers the passion, resurrection, and promise of Christ's return), the intercessions, communion, and a final prayer of thanksgiving.

evangelical counsels—Poverty, chastity, and obedience. The aim of the evangelical counsels is to help a person remove everything from his or her life which might hinder the ability to love as Christ loved. They are vows taken by sisters, brothers, and religious priests, but they are also recommended for all the faithful.

evangelization—Sharing the good news. Evangelization involves proclaiming the gospel in such a way that people's hearts and lives are changed. In the same spirit, Pope John Paul II first described a "new evangelization" that calls each Catholic to first deepen his or her own faith before taking on the missionary task of sharing the Gospel with others.

excommunication—The most severe penalty within the Church. A person who is excommunicated is separated from the communion of other Catholics. He or she cannot receive the sacraments or hold certain positions within the Church.

faith—Contact with the mystery of God. Faith begins as a freely given gift from God.

father of the Church—A title for writers of the early Church who had a major impact on the development of Christian theology and doctrine. The fathers of the Church were characterized by holiness of life, orthodoxy of doctrine, approval of the Church, and antiquities. The period of the Church fathers is generally held to have ended in the seventh century.

feudalism—The governing system which prevailed in Europe in the Middle Ages in which a superior or lord granted land to a vassal in return for the services (primarily military) of that vassal. The vassal did not own the land but he did receive its income as long as he remained faithful to the lord he served. Under this system all land was owned by a few powerful people. The vast majority of the population worked the land in return for food, shelter, and protection.

Gentiles—A term for non-Jews.

Gnosticism—One of the earliest Christian heresies. It stressed the importance of secret knowledge passed on to a select few. It denied the goodness of creation and the material world.

Gospel—The "Good News." Gospel refers to the good news of Jesus' life, Death, Resurrection, and Ascension. The word "gospel" is always used specifically for the first four books of the New Testament—Matthew, Mark, Luke, and John—which tell the story of Jesus and his message.

grace—The free and undeserved help that God gives us to respond to his call to become children of God and partakers of the divine nature and eternal life.

Hebrews—A term sometimes used to refer to all Jews. More specifically, Hebrews were those who insisted on maintaining the purity of Judaism, strictly adhering to all of the customs of their ancestors.

Hellenists—Those Jews who were more open to Greek and Roman influences and who were more willing to allow their faith and religious practice to be shaped to some extent by the culture around them.

heresy—The term literally means "choice." A heresy is a conscious, deliberate, and persistent or public denial by a member of the Church of one or more of the truths of faith (dogma).

hierarchy—The structural order of leaders within the Church. The term is commonly used to refer to all of the ordained ministers in the Church: the pope, bishops, priests, and deacons.

holiness—The quality of one who is living for God. To be holy is to be set apart by God—the Holy One—for a special task or purpose. A holy person is one who recognizes, accepts, and lives according to God's unique plan for him or her.

Idolatry—the practice of honoring or revering a creature instead of God, whether this be gods or demons (for example, satanism), power, pleasure, race, ancestors, the state, money, etc. (see CCC, 2113.)

Immaculate Conception—The dogma which states that Mary was free from the stain of original sin from the moment of her conception.

Incarnation—Becoming human. The event and process in which the eternal Son of God took on flesh and entered human history.

infallibility—A spiritual attribute possessed by the Church as a whole ensuring that the Church will never cease to be the body of Christ on earth. Infallibility is more commonly used to refer to the special attribute possessed by the pope and by the college of bishops in communion with the pope which ensures that when they speak on matters of faith and morals they are free of error.

Israelites—The Chosen People of God. The Israelites are the descendants of Abraham through Isaac and Jacob, also known as Israel.

just war theory—The principle outlined by St. Augustine and accepted by the Catholic Church which says that under certain specific conditions Christians may engage in war.

kingdom of God—The reign or rule of God. The kingdom of God has begun with the coming of Jesus. It will exist in its perfect form at the end of time.

liturgy of the hours—The prayer of the Church; it is also known as the divine office. The liturgy of the hours utilizes the scriptures, particularly the psalms, for specific times of the day from early morning to late evening.

liturgy of the word—The part of the Mass which includes the "writings of the prophets" (the Old Testament reading and psalm) and the "memoirs of the Apostles" (the New Testament epistle and the gospel), the homily, the profession of faith, and the intercessions for the world.

liturgy—The public worship of the Church, which includes the celebration of the Eucharist and other sacraments and the liturgy of the hours. The word "liturgy" literally means "public work." In Christian tradition, liturgy means the participation of the People of God in the work of God.

Magisterium—The bishops, acting in unison with the pope, by virtue of their ordination, constitute the magisterium. The Magisterium is the teaching authority of the Church.

marks of the Church—One, holy, catholic, and apostolic.

martyr—Literally a "witness." A martyr is someone who has been killed because of his or her faith.

martyrology—An official list of Christian saints and martyrs. The earliest martyrologies date to before the fourth century.

monasticism—A style of Christian life which stresses communal living and communal worship along with private prayer, silence, poverty, chastity, and obedience.

monogamy—Having only one spouse.

Monophysitism—A heresy of the late fifth and early sixth centuries that taught that there is only one nature in the Person of Christ, the divine nature. Following the Council of Chalcedon in 451, those who accepted the Monophysite position formed what are called the Oriental Orthodox churches.

monotheism—The belief that there is only one God.

mystagogia—Unfolding of the mystery. This is the name given to the period following the Baptism of adults. During this time, the newly baptized are to open themselves more fully to the graces received in Baptism.

natural law—The universal moral law which God has given to all people and which can be known by the power of reason alone.

Nicene Creed—A statement of the Church's beliefs issued at the first ecumenical council at Nicaea in 325 and later confirmed at the Council of Constantinople in 381. It taught that Jesus is of the same substance as God and thus divine.

Original Sin—The absence of holiness and justice given by God to the first people. Because of the sin of Adam and Eve, humans are inclined to sin and are subject to ignorance, suffering, and death.

Paschal Mystery—Christ's Passion, Resurrection, and Ascension. Christians participate in the Paschal Mystery through Baptism, Eucharist, and the other sacraments.

Penance—The name for the sacrament that allows a sinner to return to communion with Christ and the Church.

Pentecost—sometimes known as the "birthday of the Church." It was the day that the Holy Spirit descended on the Apostles and empowered them to preach the Good News to Jews gathered in Jerusalem for the harvest feast known by that name. Pentecost refers to the "fiftieth day" from Passover.

permanent constitution—Those elements in the Church's structure which were established by Jesus. It includes the presence of the hierarchy.

permanent dogma—Those absolute truths which were revealed by Christ and are so essential to Christian faith that their essence can never be changed.

permanent ethic—Those moral teachings which are essential corollaries of the Church's understanding of God revealed in Jesus.

Pharisees—One of the four main religious groups of Jews in Jesus' day. The faith of the Pharisees was based on scripture and on Jewish oral tradition. The Pharisees believed that faith should shape everyday life. They were particularly concerned with making Judaism relevant under Roman rule.

pope—The bishop of Rome. The pope is the successor of Peter, and as such, holds the highest office of teaching and governance in the Catholic Church.

preferential option for the poor—A principle to be followed in exercising Christian charity. This principle says that God is particularly concerned with the needs of those who suffer the most and that the human community should be too.

priest—Every Christian, male or female, young or old, religious, lay, or ordained, whom by virtue of their Baptism is called to consecrate the world to God in his or her daily life. This priesthood of the baptized is different than the ordained priesthood. Ordained priests consecrate the bread and wine during Eucharist and preside at the other sacraments.

prophet—Someone through whom the will of God is made known. Prophets speak and live the truth in such a way that others are able to hear and recognize God and God's will for the world.

Protestant reformation—An effort to reform the Catholic Church in the sixteenth century which led to the separation of large numbers of Christians from communion with Rome and with each other.

purgatory—The final purification of all who die in God's grace and friendship but remain imperfectly purified. Purgatory is the final cleansing away of all sin and of all the consequences of sin.

Redemption—Christ's saving work which freed humanity from the power of sin and death and restored them to unity with God.

religious indifferentism—The attitude which holds that all religions and all ways of expressing one's faith are equal or essentially the same.

religious syncretism—The attempt to reconcile or blend the beliefs and practices of various religions into one.

Rite of Christian Initiation of Adults (RCIA)—The process through which non-Catholic adults learn about and join in full communion with the Catholic Church by receiving the sacraments of Baptism (if they have not already received Christian Baptism), Confirmation, and Eucharist.

sacrament—A sign and instrument of God's presence in the world. Jesus is the first sacrament. Jesus is the sign of God's presence in history and the means or instrument through which God's presence in history is made accessible to human beings. The Church is the first sacrament of Christ. The Church is the sign and instrument of Christ's continuing presence in the world. The Church herself has Seven Sacraments through which it makes the grace of Christ's Death, Resurrection, and Ascension available and accessible to the faithful.

Sacraments of Initiation—Baptism, Confirmation, and Eucharist. It is through participation in these sacraments that one is fully initiated into the Catholic Church.

Sadducees—Another of the religious groups of Jews in Jesus' day. The Sadducees were religiously conservative. They rejected all religious teaching which was not from the Torah, including belief in the resurrection of the dead. They were willing to accept many elements of Roman culture.

saint—One who has been transformed by the grace of God. In its most basic sense the term "saint" refers to all Christians. "Saint" is normally used to refer to those whom the Church has canonized (or acclaimed before the process of canonization came into existence), honored with the title "saint," and declared worthy of veneration.

Salvation History—The story of God's action in human history. Salvation History refers to the events through which God makes humanity aware of himself and brings humanity into his Kingdom. It begins with the creation of the world and will end with the Second Coming of Christ.

Salvation—True, complete, and permanent unity with God and with one another. Salvation is the end goal of all creation. It refers to the fulfillment of the human desire for ultimate truth and goodness. Salvation is made possible by Christ's Death, Resurrection, and Ascension.

Scripture—Literally, the "writings." Scripture is used to refer to those books which have been determined by the Church to be the Word of God and to be normative for faith and morals.

Second Coming—Jesus' return in glory at the end of time. At the Second Coming, the Kingdom of God will be fully realized.

sin—An utterance, deed, or desire contrary to the eternal law. Sin is a failure to love God and neighbor. Sin harms both the sinner and the unity of the human family. Sin is an offense against God.

social doctrine—The body of Church teachings which relate to our economic and political interactions within the world. The social doctrine of the Church identifies the demands of peace and justice. It grows out of the Church's understanding of the seventh and tenth commandments.

solidarity—A genuine concern for the well-being of other people.

Son of God—A title for Jesus that refers to his relationship with the other Persons of the Trinity.

subsidiarity—The principle of Catholic social doctrine which says that no community of higher order (such as a national or state government) should do what can be done equally well or better by a community of lower order (such as a family or local community).

syncretism—The practice of blending all religions and faith traditions into one.

synod—A representative body of bishops assembled periodically by the pope to advise him on important Church concerns. It is not a legislative body.

Tradition of the Church—The faith which the Church has received from Christ through the apostles and all of the ways the faith has been passed on: in creeds, doctrines, decisions of the magisterium, liturgies, and patterns of prayer and service.

transubstantiation—The change of the essential nature of the bread and wine into the Body and Blood of Christ during the consecration.

Trinity—The central Christian mystery that one God is in three persons: Father, Son, and Holy Spirit.

value—Something believed to be particularly important.

veneration—Honor given to a person or image because that person or image mediates God (that is, makes God's presence visible and tangible). Veneration is not the same as worship or adoration. Worship and adoration belong only to God.

virtue—A habitual disposition to do good. Virtues are attitudes and habits which lead a person to do what God desires.

zealots—Jews living in Jesus' time who believed that God called them to overthrow the Roman government in Palestine.

References Cited

A Tremor of Bliss: Contemporary Writers on the Saints. Wlies, Paul, ed. 1995. New York: Riverhead Books.

African American Catholic Church in Newark, New Jersey. Knoxville: The University of Tennessee Press.

Ahern, Bishop Patrick. "Therese, Doctor of the Church." *Origins* Vol. 27, No. 12.

Anderson, H. George, et al., eds. *The One Mediator, the Saints and Mary: Lutherans and Catholics in Dialogue*, VIII. Minneapolis: Augsburg, 1992.

Bausch, William. *A New Look at the Sacraments*. Mystic, CT: Twenty-Third Publications, 1983.

Beinert, Wolfgang, and Francis Schussler Fiorenza, eds. *Handbook of Catholic Theology*. New York: Crossroad, 1995.

Bowden, Henry Warner. *American Indians and Christian Missions: Studies in Cultural Conflict*. Chicago: The University of Chicago Press, 1981.

Canadian Conference of Catholic Bishops. *Dreams, Dilemmas, Decisions: Deciding to be Church in Today's World*. Ottawa: Concacan Inc., 1994.

Chadwick, Henry. *The Early Church*. Middlesex: Penguin Books, Ltd., 1967.

Clark, Edward W.M. *Five Great Catholic Ideas*. New York: The Crossroad Publishing Company, 1998.

Clarkson, John, et al., trans. *The Church Teaches: Documents of the Church in English Translation*. St. Louis: B. Herder Book Co., 1955.

Comblin, Jose. *People of God*. Maryknoll, New York: Orbis Books, 2004.

Costello, Stephen J., ed. *The Search for Spirituality: Seven Paths within the Catholic Tradition*. Dublin: The Liffey Press, 2002.

Cullmann, Oscar. *Early Christian Worship*. London: SCM Press Ltd., 1953.

DeBerri, Edward P. and James E. Hug with Peter J. Henriot and Michael J. Schultheis. *Catholic Social Teaching: Our Best Kept Secret*. Maryknoll, New York: Orbis Books, 2003.

Dulles, Avery. *A Church to Believe In*. New York: Crossroad Publishing Company, 1982.

Elsbernd, Mary and Reimund Bieringer. *When Love is Not Enough: A Theo-Ethic of Justice*. Collegeville, Minnesota: The Liturgical Press, 2002.

Eusebius. *The History of the Church*. G.A. Williamson, trans. New York: Dorset Press, 1965.

Forest, Jim. *Love is the Measure: A Biography of Dorothy Day*. Maryknoll, NY: Orbis Books, 1986.

"French Bishops' Declaration of Repentance." *Origins* vol. 27. No. 18 (1997).

Fuellenbach, John. *Church: Community for the Kingdom*. Maryknoll, New York: Orbis Books, 2002.

Gaillardetz, Richard R. *Teaching With Authority: A Theology of the Magisterium of the Church*. Collegeville, Minnesota: The Liturgical Press, 1997.

Giussani, Luigi. *Why The Church?* Montreal: McGill-Queens University, 2001.

Gonzalez, Justo L. *A History of Christian Thought,* vol. 1. Nashville: Abingdon Press, 1970.

————.*The Story of Christianity,* vol. 1. San Francisco: Harper, 1984.

————.*The Story of Christianity,* vol. 2. San Francisco: Harper, 1985.

Graef, Hilda. *Mary: A History of Doctrine and Devotion,* vol. 1. New York: Sheed and Ward, 1963.

Hardy, Edward R., ed. *Christology of the Later Fathers.* Philadelphia: The Westminister Press, 1954.

Jasper, R.C.D., and G.J. Cuming, eds. *Prayers of the Eucharist: Early and Reformed.* New York: Pueblo Publishing Co., 1987.

Kavanagh, Aidan. *On Liturgical Theology.* New York: Pueblo Publishing Company, 1984.

————.*The Shape of Baptism: The Rite of Christian Initiation.* New York: Pueblo Publishing Company, 1974.

Kelly, John and Norman Davidson. *Early Christian Doctrines.* San Francisco: Harper and Row Publishers, 1978.

Lohse, Eduard. *The New Testament Environment.* Translated by John E. Steely. Nashville: Abigdon, 1976.

Lord, F. Townley. *Great Women in Christian History.* London: Cassell and Company, 1940.

Massaro, Thomas S.J. *Living Justice: Catholic Social Teaching in Action.* Franklin, Wisconsin: Sheed and Ward, 2000.

McBrien, Richard P. *The Remaking of the Church.* New York: Harper and Row, 1973.

McBrien, Richard P. *Catholicism.* San Francisco: HarperSanFrancisco, 1994.

McManners, John, ed. *The Oxford History of Christianity.* Oxford: Oxford University Press, 1993.

McKenna, Megan. *Rites of Justice.* Maryknoll, New York: Orbis Books, 1997.

Nash, Thomas J. *Worthy is the Lamb: The Biblical Roots of the Mass.* San Francisco: Ignatius Press, 2004.

National Conference of Catholic Bishops. *The Challenge of Peace, God's Promise and Our Response.* Washington: United States Catholic Conference, 1983.

————.*Economic Justice for All.* Washington: United States Catholic Conference, 1986.

Oden, Amy, ed. *In Her Words: Women's Writings in the History of Christian Thought.* Nashville: Abingdon, 1994.

Pelikan, Jaroslav. *Mary Through the Centuries: Her Place in the History of Culture.* New Haven: Yale University Press, 1996.

Pixner, Bargil. *With Jesus Through Galilee According to the Fifth Gospel.* Rosh Pina, Israel: Corazin Publishing, 1992.

Pope John Paul II. *Centesimus Anno.* 1991.

————. *Familaris Consortio.* 1981.

————. *Redemptoris Mater.* 1987.

————. *Solicitudo Rei Socialis.* 1987.

————. *Veritatis Splendor.* 1993.

Pope Paul VI. *Marialis Cultis.* 1974.

————. *Mysterium Fidei.* 1965.

"The Quality of Mercy." *Life* (July 1996).

Rahner, Karl. *Theological Investigations.* Vol. 14, "Ecclesiology, Questions in the Church, The Church in the World." Translated by David Bourke. New York: The Seabury Press, 1976.

Russakoff, Dale. "Young 'Hero' of Homeless Ready to Trade in His Halo." *Washington Post* (December 25, 1991), A3.

Rybolt, John E. and Frances Ryan, eds. *Vincent de Paul and Louise de Marillac: Rules, Conferences and Writings.* New York: Paulist Press, 1995.

Schmidlin, Joseph. *Catholic Mission History.* Techny, IL: Mission Press, S.V.D., 1933.

Segundo, Juan Luis, S.J. *The Sacraments Today.* Maryknoll, NY: Orbis Books, 1974.

The One Mediator, the Saints and Mary: Lutherans and Catholics in Dialogue, VIII. Anderson, George H. et. al. editors. Minneapolis: Augsburg, 1992.

Troeltsch, Ernst. *The Social Teaching of the Christian Churches.* Vol. 1. Translated by Olive Wyon. Chicago: The University of Chicago Press, 1981.

Vinje, Patricia Mary. *Praying with Catherine of Siena.* Winona, MN: St. Mary's Press, 1990.

Ward, Mary A. *A Mission for Justice: The History of the First,* 2002.

"Waldensians in Italy Benefit from Tax Change." *Canadian Mennonite* vol. 1. no. 8.

White, James, F. *A Brief History of Christian Worship.* Nashville: Abingdon Press, 1993.

White, James F. *Roman Catholic Worship: Trent to Today.* Collegeville, Minnesota: The Liturgical Press, 2003.

Name and Subject Index

Abraham, 94
Absolution, 74, 116; and penance, 204
Act of Faith, 335
Act of Hope, 336
Act of Love, 336
Adam and Eve, 41, 43, 92-93, 95, 96, 298
Africa, 83
Albert the Great, St., 163
Albigensians, 163
Alexander VI, St., Pope, 164
Alexander VII, Pope, 210
Alexander the Great, 63
Alexandria, 137
Almsgiving. *See* Generosity
Ambrose, St., 115
Angela of Foligno, 316
Angelus, 334-335
Anima Christi, 213
Anointing the Sick, 190
Anthony the Great, St., 73, 156-157
Apollinarianism, 139
Apologists, 68, 136
Apostasy, 73, 146
Apostles, 48, 323
Apostles' Creed, 18, 19, 29, 134, 139, 299, 314
Apostolic succession, 20, 28-31, 66, 296
Apostolic Tradition of Hippolytus, 200
Apostolicity of the Church, 27-31, 295-296
Aquinas, Thomas. *See* Thomas Aquinas, St.
Argentina, 164
Arianism, 32, 139, 143, 160, 286, 307
Armenian rite, 20
Asceticism, 160, 240
Asia, 83
Asia Minor, 69
Assisted Suicide, 140
Assumption of Mary, 269-270
Athanasian Creed, 19
Athanasius, St., 286
Attila the Hun, 73-74
Augustine, St., 15, 67, 154, 201-202, 249-250, 277, 282, 307
Avignon, 79
Aztecs, 165

Baltimore, 169, 171
Baptism, 42, 73, 115, 117-118, 198-203, 300; effects of, 190; of infants, 201-202; necessary for salvation, 97; and sin, 96, 199
Barbarians, conversion of, 159-160, 161, 307-308
Barry, John, 168
Bartolomé de las Casas, 244
Basil the Great, St., 158
Beatitudes, 326

Benedict of Nursia, St., 160-161, 308
Benedictine rule, 75, 160, 161
Bernard of Clairvaux, St., 73, 77, 286
Bernardone, Peter, 162
Bible. *See* Scripture
Bishop of Rome. *See* Pope
Bishops, 19, 49; college of, 30, 145
Black Madonna, 285
Blessings, of the Catechumens, 33; of God, 99
Body of Christ, 15-16, 18, 44, 61
Boniface VIII, Pope, 115
Brébeuf, Jean de, 167
Bride of Christ, 23, 46-47, 61
Bubonic plague, 75
Byzantine rite, 20

Caecilian, 114-115
Calcutta, 22
Call of God. *See* God, call of
Callinicum, 115
Campaign for the Homeless, 260
Cardinal virtues, 326
Carroll, Charles, 168-169
Carroll, John, 168-169, 171
Carthage, 113
Cassian, 241
Catechism of the Catholic Church, 243, 262, 316
Catechumenate, 200
Catherine of Siena, St., 79, 91, 308
Catholic church, and worship life, 99
Catholic doctrines, 95-96; and communal identity, 95
Catholic Moral Teachings. *See* Moral teachings
Catholic Worker Movement, 253, 254
Catholicism, formal structures of, 16-17
Catholicity of the Church, 25, 295
Catholics, definition of, 92; distinctives of, 26; identity of, 313-315
Celibacy, 77, 247, 305
Centesimus Annus, 222, 226
Central America, 164-165
Chalcedon, symbol of, 315
Chaldean rite. *See* East Syrian rite
Charitable giving, 242
Charlemagne, 75, 76, 115, 208, 308
Charles V, 165
Chesterton, G. K., 219
Chi-Rho symbol, 71
Chrysostom, John, St. *See* John Chrysostom, St.
Christ-likeness, 281
Christianity, 69-70, 139; legalization of, 71-73; objections to, 67-68; rise and spread of, 65-66, 159, 164-170

Church, 18-24, 47-55, 294; authority of, 115; calendar of, 284, 328; as dwelling place of God, 67-68; as eschatological community, 263; and kingdom of God, 23, 41; and Mary, 270-271; precepts of, 327; and salvation, 25, 43-44, 45-46, 119, 294; and Scripture, 132-133; symbolic significance of, 19, 23, 179-180; and tax, 238; as teacher, 145-146, 298-299. *See also specific topics*

Church history, 60-62, 305-310; timeline of, 320-321

Church membership, 112-113; and sinners, 23; and salvation, 119

Cistercian movement, 77

City of God, Church as, 71-74

Clare of Assisi, St., 163, 308

Clement of Alexandria, 136, 137-138, 154

Clovis, 159

Cluniacs, 76-77

Cluny, monastery of, 76

Common good, 223, 230-231

Communion of saints, Church as, 262-264, 302-303; and Mary, 285-286

Community, necessity of, 15-16

Confession, 328-329

Confessions, The, 249

Confessors, 112

Confirmation, 198, 202-203, 300; effects of, 190

Conscience, 50-51, 52-54

Constantine, 71-74, 114-115, 143, 240, 246, 306-307

Constantinople, 72, 74, 141, 250. *See also* Council of Constantinople

Constitution of the Church, 48-49, 297

Constitution on the Sacred Liturgy, 210

Coptic rite, 20

Cortez, Hernando, 165

Council of Clermont, 250

Council of Constantinople (first), 18, 19

Council of Ephesus, 142, 286

Council of Florence, 119, 141, 204

Council of Jerusalem, 111, 112, 305

Council of Nicea, 18, 72, 143

Council of Trent, 79-82, 117-118, 119, 284, 309-310; catechism of, 202; and Eucharist, 210

Covenant, 43

Creation, 92

Crusades, 60, 77-78, 250-251, 308

Cultivated field, Church as, 76-78

Cyprian, 113

D

Das, Subashini, 22

Day, Dorothy, 15, 253, 254

Deacon, 207, 240

Death, 183, 262-263

Decius, 69, 112-113

Declaration of Independence, 168

Declaration on the Relationship of the Church to Non-Christian Religions, 84, 317

Declaration on Religious Freedom, 84, 119

Decree on Ecumenism, 84

Dei Verbum, 135

Deposit of faith, 144-145

Desert fathers, 156-157

Devotions, 331-333

Diaconate. *See* Deacon

Didache, 155, 199, 205-206

Diego, Juan, 279

Dionysius of Alexandria, St., 148

Discipleship, 53, 280

Dispensation, 108

Diversity, of the Church, 20-21; of gifts, 20

Docetism, 139

Doctors of the Church, 265, 324-325, list of, 325

Doctrine, 133, 136; and dogma, 144-145; and social issues, 221-226; teachers of, 136-138

Dogma of the Church, 54-55, 128-129, 138-140, 297, 299; and doctrine, 144-145; infallibility of, 144, 145; and philosophy, 137-138

Dogmatic Constitution on the Church, 83-84

Dogmatic Constitution on Divine Revelation. See Dei Verbum

Dominic, St., 163-164

Dominicans, 163-164

Domitian, 136

Donatism, 32, 114

DuBourg, Louis, 171

Dulles, Avery Cardinal, 6

E

East Syrian rite, 20

Easter, 201

Eastern Catholic Churches, 20

Ecumenical councils, 145; list of, 325-326. *See also particular councils*

Ecumenism, 17, 84

Edict of Milan, 71

Education in America, 169-170

Egypt, 94

Ekklésia. See Church

Encomiendas, 244

End times, 262-263

Environment, 143

Erasmus, 284

Eschatology. *See* End times

Eschaton. See End times

Essenes, 64-65

Ethics. *See* Moral teachings

Ethiopian rite, 20

Eucharist, 41, 80, 114, 182, 186-187, 205-210, 301; and Christ's Presence, 185; dishonoring of, 100; effects of, 190

Eusebius, 72

Euthanasia, 140
Evangelical counsels, 23-24
Evangelization, 152-155, 171-172
Excommunication, 146
Exodus, of the Israelites, 94

F
Faith, 13-14, 16-17, 294; and community, 15-16,
    95; gift of, 15; and mystery, 40; and works,
    116-118, 219
Familiaris consortio, 247
Family, 247-248
Fasting, 280
Ferrell, Trevor, 260
Fathers of the Church, 265, 324
Feudalism, 76-77
Florence, 79
Forgiveness, 41
Formal structures of Catholicism, 16-17
Fourth Lateran Council, 78, 204
Francis of Assisi, St., 162-163, 308; prayer of,
    173, 336
Franciscans, 162-163, 165
Franks, 75, 159
Frederick, II, 251
Frederick the Wise, 284
Free the Children, 260
Freedom, 102, 130

G
Galerius, 71
Galileo, 143, 144
*Gaudium et Spes, See Pastoral Constitution on
    the Church in the Modern World*
Gemma Galgani, St., 317
Generosity, 229-230; as penance, 280
Gentiles, 65, 110, 154
Glory Be, 334
Gnosticism, 26-29, 32, 133-134, 136, 139
God, 60; attributes of, 315; call of, 14, 18, 41;
    gifts of, 20; holiness of, 22, 280; love of, 25, 99,
    147; presence of in Church, 13, 19, 180-181;
    and sacraments, 183
Gonzalez, Roque, 164
Good news. *See* Gospel
Good works, 116-118; of mercy, 327. *See also*
    Servanthood
Gospel, 130-131, 152-154
Grace, 118, 180; and sacraments, 183, 184
Grace at Meals, 335
Greeks, 63
Gregory XIII, Pope, 283
Gregory the Great, St., 73, 74
Guadalupe, 279
Guardian Angel Prayer, 335

H
Hail, Holy Queen, 334
Hail Mary, 279, 334

Hebrews, definition of, 110
Hellenists, definition of, 110
Heresy, 138, 139-140, 146, 163
Hierarchy of the Church, 48, 53. *See also*
    Magisterium
Holiness, of the Church, 22-24, 295; of God, 22,
    280; of the individual, 22, 263; and love, 23
Holocaust, 239
Holy Land, 78
Holy Orders, 20, 188, 329-330; effects of, 190
Holy See, 30
Holy Spirit, 23, 41, 101, 130; and communion of
    saints, 19; fruits of, 314; gift of, 13, 44, 199-200,
    314; and inspiration of Scripture, 131; and
    sacraments, 197
Hopi, 19
Hugh of Saint Victor, 189
Humanity, dignity of, 52, 227-228, 242, 301;
    rights of, 115; sinfulness of, 52; unity of, 92
Huns, 159

I
Idolatry, 23
Ignatius of Antioch, St., 18, 19
Ignatius Loyola, St., 289
Images of the Church, 61, 85-86. *See also
    particular images*
Immaculate Conception of Mary, 269-270
indefectibility, 145
Indulgences, 116
Industrial Revolution, 242
Inquisition, 60, 78
Interpretation of Scripture. *See* Scripture,
    interpretation of
Iowa, 12
Irenaeus of Lyon, St., 18, 19, 136-137, 285
Isaiah, 66
Islam. *See* Moslems
Israelites, 43, 62-63, 94; and communal identity,
    95; faith of, 16. *See also* Jews
Italy, 73, 79

J
James, St., 305
Jerome, St., 15, 73
Jerusalem, 110, 250-251
Jesuits, 165-170
Jesus Christ, 44, 133, 139; baptism of, 198; as
    founder of the Church, 19; incarnation of, 13,
    23, 41, 138, 139-140; and Mary, 267; mystery
    of, 20-21; necessity of for salvation, 45; passion
    of, 185; and restoration of human nature, 95;
    second coming of, 41, 263; as servant, 219; as
    Son of God, 138; works of, 263-264
Jewish-Christian relations, 238-239
Jewish sects, 64-65, 305
Jews, 94, 110; faith of, 139
Joan of Arc, St., 317

John, St., 110
John XV, Pope, 283
John XXIII, Pope, 40, 61, 83, 224
John the Baptist, 198
John Chrysostom, St., 155, 229, 242
John Damascus, St., 316
John Paul II, Pope, 14, 129, 177, 219, 222, 239, 243; and family 247, 248; social teachings of, 225-228, 250-251
Judaism, 63, 64-65, 305, 317
Juliana of Monte-Cornillon, 209
Julius II, Pope, 160
Just war theory, 249-250, 307
Justice in the World, 225
Justification, 80, 117
Justin Martyr, 154, 206-207

Kennedy, John F. 169-170
Kielburger, 260
Kingdom of God, 23, 41-42
Knowledge, 130
Ku Klux Klan, 260

Laborem Exercens, 225
Lactantius, 71
Laity, 53
Lalemant, Gabriel, 167
Latin America, 83
Laud, William, 105
Law, 112, 117; as gift from God, 94
Leo III, Pope, 75
Leo, IX, Pope, 77
Leo X, Pope, 52
Leo XIII, Pope, 119, 122, 222-223, 242
Leo the Great, Pope, 73-74
Leo Martyr, St., 186
Licinius, 71
Life Teen, 103
Litany of the Saints. *See* Saints, litany of
Liturgy, 20-21, 83, 99, 182-185, 210; and imperial protocol, 72; of the hours, 161, 333; and Roman rite, 208; and sacraments, 328-330; of the word, 206-207
Lombard, Peter, 189
Lombards, 74, 159
Loretto, 22
Love feast, 67
Lumen Gentium, 62, 119, 186
Luther, Martin, 80, 116-117, 284, 309

Magisterium, 17, 29-30, 39, 49-50, 297, 299; disagreement with, 50-51; and Dogma, 54-55, 144-146; and interpretation of Scripture, 29, 50, 137
Magnificat, 273
Marcion, 133-134, 136, 139
Marialis Cultis, 273
Mariological Society of America, 286

Marks of the Church, 18-24, 295-296, 322. *See also particular marks*
Maronite rite, 20
Marriage, 46-47, 247-248; effects of, 190; interfaith, 108-109, 120; and sex, 111
Martyrdom, 68-69, 113, 154, 167, 280-281
Martyrium Polycarpi, 281
Mary, 139, 303, 330, 331; assumption of, 269-270; beliefs about, 268, 286-287; devotions to, 268; dogma of, 141-142; immaculate conception of, 269-270; as mediatrix, 270-271; as model saint, 267-268; as mother of the Church, 272; as Mother of God, 285, 288; as a sacrament, 269-271; veneration of, 278-279
Maryland, 168-169, 171
Marx, Karl, 242
Mass, 185, 206-208, 210; order of, 329; sacrifice of, 282; for those in purgatory, 74-75
Mater et Magistra, 224
Maurin, Peter, 253
Maxentius, 71
Maximus Daia, 71
Mediatrix. *See* Mary, as mediatrix
Memorare, The, 274, 334
Mendicant orders, 162. *See also particular orders*
Merton, Thomas, 15
Mexico, 164-165, 244
Michigan, 260
Milan, 115
Military service, 249
Missionaries of Charity, 22
Missionary mandate, 25, and servanthood, 220
Monasticism, 73, 75, 246, 307; communal, 241, 242; of the desert, 156-158; western, 160-161
Monica, St., 249
Monophysitism, 32, 139
Monotheism, 139, 143, 317
Monte Cassino, 160
Moral teachings, 24, 51-54, 221-226, 297, 301-302, 326-327
Morning Offering, 335
Moses, 94
Moslems, 78, 120, 250-251, 308; faith of, 143; rule of, 74
Mother of God. *See* Mary
Mother Teresa. *See* Teresa, Mother
Mystagogia, 42. *See also* Baptism
Mystery of the Church, 40-42, 296-297

Native Americans, 19, 166-168
Natural law, 163-164, 232
Nero, 68
Nestorianism, 32, 141-142
New Evangelization, 152
New Testament. *See* Scripture
Nicea. *See* Council of Nicea
Nicene Creed, 18, 139, 143, 299, 314

Nicomedia, 143
Noah, 43
North America, 166-168
Novatianism, 32
Novenas, 333

Obedience, 232
Occupations, 245-246
Octogesima Adveniens, 225
Old Testament. *See* Scripture
Ordination, 81; power of, 101; of priests, 188
Origen, 136, 137-138, 154, 155, 249
Original sin, 96, 147; definition of, 95; and Mary, 269
O'Rourke, Sara, 38
Ostrogoths, 159, 160
Our Father, 334
Our Lady of Guadelupe. *See* Mary, veneration of
Our Mother, Church as, 79-82
Ozanam, Frederic, 252

Pacem in Terris, 224
Pachomius, 157
Papacy. *See* Pope
Paraguay, 164
Paschal Mystery. *See* Jesus Christ, passion of
Passover, 94, 205
Pastoral Constitution on the Church in the Modern World, 37, 84, 153, 219, 224
Patrick, St., 159, 316
Paul, St., 18, 19, 20, 47, 84; as Apostle to the Gentiles, 154; and Barnabas, 110-111; letters of, 134; and sacraments, 186; teachings of, 92, 198-199, 245, 266
Paul III, Pope, 79, 83
Paul VI, Pope, 171, 225, 272, 273
Peace of the Church, 19-20
Pelagianism, 32
Pelagius II, Pope, 74
Penance, 114, 116-118, 204; acts of, 280; effects of, 190
Pentecost, 44
People of God, Church as 96-104, 109, 297-298
Persecution, 67, 68-69, 113, 305-306
Peter, the Hermit, 250
Peter, St., 19, 110, 111, 219; as first pope, 30
Pharisees, 64, 66
Philadelphia, 260
Pius V, Pope, 210
Pius IX, Pope, 119
Pius X, Pope, 202
Pius XI, Pope, 223
Pius, XII, Pope, 251, 255
Polycarp, St., 281-282
Pope, 19, 26, 30-31, 49; and canonization of saints, 283-284; corruption of, 76; increasing power of, 73-74; infallibility of, 83; list of, 322-324

Populorum Progressio, 225
Portugal, 164-165
Poverty, 229-230, 240-244; preferential treatment for, 243
Prayer, 335-336; and the Eucharist, 206-207; and penance, 280; power of, 263-264; and the Psalms, 162
Prayer for the Faithful Departed, 335
Prayer for Peace, 336
Prescription against Heretics, 137
Priesthood, 81; necessity of, 188; and ordination, 101
Private property, 229
Prophet, 102
Protestant Reformation, 79-80, 116-117, 284, 309-310
Protestants, 26, 80, 117, 137
Purgatory, 74-75

Quadragesimo Anno, 223
Reconciliation, effects of, 190
Red Sea, 94
Redemptoris Mater, 14
Reform of the Church, 76-77, 80-81
Regina Caeli, 335
Relics, of saints, 281-282
Religious indifferentism, 120
Religious rites, 20
Renewing the Earth, 143
Rerum Novarum, 223, 242
Resurrection of Jesus, 41; power of, 264
Revelation, 25-27, 48, 130-131
Rite of Christian Initiation of Adults, 33, 42, 203
Roman Empire, 64-74 passim, 305-307
Romans, 63
Rome, city of, 68, 71, 73-74
Rosary, 278-279, 287, 331-332
Rule of Benedict, 75
Rwanda, 178

Sacrament of Salvation, 44. *See also* Church, and salvation
Sacraments, 18-19, 20, 80-81, 178-179, 192-193, 212; Christ as, 180-181; and the Church, 181, 186-187, 300-301; effects of, 189, 190-191; and grace, 184, 185, 197; and holiness, 24; of initiation, 26-27, 197; list of, 328; and liturgy, 328-330; power of, 186, 189-190; and redemption, 182, 189; as transformative moments, 196-197. *See also particular sacraments*
Sacrifice of the Eucharist, 209-210
Sadducees, 64
Saints, 261-262, 330-331; canonization of, 283-285; communion of, 262-264; intercession of, 283; litany of, 26; as patrons, 281-282;

veneration of, 278, 283-284
Salvation, 25, 45-46, 119, 121, 147-148, 296-297; doctrine of, 95; for Gentiles as well as Jews, 110; history of, 43-44, 94; and unity with God, 97
Sao Paulo, 165
Sarum Primer, 193
Schismatics, 143
Scholastica, 160
Science, 130
Scripture, 61-62, 110, 131-134, 298-299; authority of, 80; canon of, 29, 133-134, 317-319; interpretation of, 29, 132, 135, 137
Second Vatican Council, 40, 62, 83-85, 119-120, 135, 161, 310; and evangelization, 153; and Mary, 269-271, 286-288; and Protestants, 137; and sacraments, 186, 204, 210; and servanthood, 219
Serra, Junipero, 165
Servanthood, 219-220, 301; principles of, 227-231
Seton, Mother Elizabeth, 169, 171
Sexuality, 52, 111, 247
Sharing Catholic Social Teaching: Challenges and Directions, 226
Sheepfold, Church as, 74-75
Shoah. *See* Holocaust
Sign of the Cross, 333
Sin, 16-17, 41, 74, 147-148, 327; and baptism, 199; confession of, 182, 238; and destruction of unity, 93; and truth, 130. *See also* Original sin
Sinners, 52; and Church membership, 23
Sisters of Charity, 169, 171
Social doctrine of the Church, 221-226, 301-302, 327. *See also* Moral teaching
Solidarity, 228, 231
Sollicitudo Rei Socialis, 226
Son of God. *See* Jesus Christ
South America, 164-165
Spain, 164-165
Stations of the Cross, 332-333
Stephen, St., 110, 111, 305
Stephen VI, Pope, 76
Sublimus Dei, 83
Subsidiarity, 223, 231
Suffering, 140
Sweeney, Mike, 103
Syllabus of Errors, 119
Syncretism, 28, 63, 305
Synod, 113

Temptation, and evangelical counsels, 24
Ten Commandments, 221, 326
Teresa of Avila, St., 44
Teresa, Mother, 22
Tertullian, 136, 137, 155
Theological virtues, 326
Theology. *See* Dogma of the Church

Theotokos. *See* Mary
Thomas Aquinas, St., 163-164, 234, 308, 315
Thomas, Keshia, 260
Tiber River, 76
Tradition of the Church, 135-138, 299
Transubstantiation, 209
Trinity, 96, 128, 315-316; dogma of, 141; and unity of the Church, 19
Truth, 54, 130; obedience to, 232; and Scripture, 131-134; and tradition, 135

Ulrich of Augsburg, St., 283
Unam Sanctum, 115
Uncircumcised. *See* Gentiles
Uniformity and the Church, 20-21
United States, 165, 166-170
Unity of the Church, 19-21, 295; and diversity, 20-21; and ecumenism, 84 and papacy, 30; and sacraments, 185
Universal destination of goods, 229-230
Universality of the Church. *See* Catholicity of the Church
Urban II, Pope, 77-78, 250
Urban VIII, Pope, 165
Uruguay, 164

Values, 267
Vandals, 73-74
Vatican II. *See* Second Vatican Council
Vatican Commission for Religious Relations with the Jews, 239
Veritatis Splendor, 219, 227
Vineyard, Church as, 62-63
Virginity, 247
Virtue, 326; benefits of, 266; heroic, 260, 261
Visigoths, 159
Vulgate, 81, 285

Waldensians, 238
War, 77-78, 249-252
Wealth, 240-244
West Syrian rite, 20
Widows, 155
Witness of the Church, 28
Word of God. *See* Scripture
Work, 245-246
Works. *See* Good works
World War II, 238, 251
Worldview. *See* Dogma of the Church
Worship. *See* Liturgy

Yahweh. *See* God

Zealots, 65

Scripture Index

GENESIS

1:28 43
2 92
2:18 92
2:20 93
2:23 93

DEUTERONOMY

6:4-5 317
14:2 94
26:16-19 94

PSALMS

136:1 287

ISAIAH

5-11 66
53:5 287
55:10-11 187

MALACHI

1:11 207

MATTHEW

5:23-24 205
5:48 46
7:24-25 11
10:1-43 53
12:46-50 267
13:52 59
16:18-19 322
16:24 267
17:5 287
18:15-20 46
18:20 . . . . . .15, 48
19:28 280
25:41 119
25:45 237
26:29 287
27:29 287
28:19 . . . . . .109, 199, 322
28:19-20 . . . .25, 151
28:20 195

MARK

1:9-11 287
1:10-11 198
1:15 287
6:2-3 245
8:31-33 219
10:38 198

LUKE

1:28 285
1:38 287
1:42 287
1:43 285
2:34 287
2:41-51 267
2:49 287
4:18 131
9:23 287
12:50 198
18:18—25 . .241
22:42 287
23:34 287
24:13-35 206

JOHN

1:14 287
2:5 287
3:16 314
3:29 46
6:7 323
8:32 130
10:2-4 75
10:16 107
13 219
13:15 217
13:34 45
13:35 254
14:6 102
14:12 260
15:1ff 66
19:27 272
20:18 287

ACTS

1:11 287
2:4 287
4:1-21 110
6:8-7:60 110
7:58 111
8:14-17 200
8:16 199
9:17-18 200
10-11 110
10:44-48 200
12:2 323
15:1 111

ROMANS

6:3-4 199

1 CORINTHIANS

12:12-26 84
12:19-20 20
13:12 16

EPHESIANS

1:18-21 56
4:3 20
5:21 97
5:29-32 46

2 THESSALONIANS

3:10 245

2 TIMOTHY

3:16-17 319

2 PETER

1:4 286

REVELATION

7:17 240
12:1 287
21:4 240

Photo Credits

ASSOCIATED PRESS
Page 77, 157, 178, 230, 239, 242, 243, 249, © Associated Press

CLEO PHOTOGRAPY
Page 25, 187, 206, 260, 296 © CLEO Freelance Photo

THE CROSIERS
Page 18, 47, 71, 75, 136, 156, 163, 165, 166, 188, 192, 241, 262, 268, 270, 277, 298 © The Crosiers

CORBIS IMAGES
Page 22, 30, 50, 63, 83, 103, 113, 144 © Corbis

CATHOLIC NEWS SERVICE
Page 44, 49, 79, 80, 84, 111, 159, 160, 171, 202, 222, 252, 253, 265, 279, 285 © CNS

SKJOLD PHOTOGRAPHS
Page 92, 128, 132, 182, 218, 227, 229, 247, 272 © Skjold Photographs

SUPERSTOCK
Page 19, 43, 60, 62, 64, 68, 92, 95, 115, 141, 169, 198, 208, 267 © Superstock

W.P. WITTMAN
Page 183, 215, 217, 237, 257 © W.P. Wittman Photography Limited

PICTUREQUEST
Page 97 © Picturequest